VOICES
OF THE
ANGELS

VOICES
OF THE
ANGELS
THE NEW THOUGHT MOVEMENT
WAS A WOMEN'S MOVEMENT

SANNA ROSE, M.A., RScP

outskirtspress
DENVER, COLORADO

Outskirts Press, Inc.
http://www.outskirtspress.com

ISBN: 978-1-4327-8549-9

Outskirts Press and the "OP" logo are trademarks belonging to Outskirts Press, Inc.

PRINTED IN THE UNITED STATES OF AMERICA

In *Voices of the Angels* I am reminded of the reasons why I was first attracted to the New Thought Movement: the passionate conviction of its early writers. I discovered in this book new voices expressing ideas that are inspiring and stimulating, even though they were penned so long ago in a time when different social stressors prevailed. *Voices of the Angels* will be of interest to any person who has a fondness for the metaphysical movement known as New Thought as a source of both inspiration and history.

Dr. Edward Viljoen
Senior Minister, Center for Spiritual Living, Santa Rosa
Santa Rosa, California

With a good ear and a fine hand, Sanna Rose has done an excellent job of bringing the voices of these women into the present. As a New Thought minister and a feminist, I am touched by their power, their vision, and their tenderness. You may never have heard of some of them, yet they have affected all of our lives and will surely continue to do so. These writings are generations old, yet, as Mrs. Fannie James said, "New things shall be revealed and must be while the Spirit continues to lead us into all Truth." There are revelations in these passages.

Reverend Robin Gail
Windsor, California

Kudos to Sanna Rose for creating a work that features the women of New Thought! Mary Baker Eddy, Emma Curtis Hopkins, and their lesser known students, have brought us a wealth of metaphysical ideas. It is time to acknowledge them!

Margaret Stortz, D. RSc
El Cerrito, California

Dedication

I lovingly dedicate this book to my mentor and friend Rev. Marilyn Mooney who made her transition in July 2010. She encouraged me to get my book published. She was passionate about the history of New Thought and very excited about the title and subject matter of this work. She imparted to me how important it is to publish more works about New Thought, especially in regards to the role of women in its development. Thank you for your love and support, Marilyn. You are a part of this legacy known as New Thought.

Preface

The texts, lectures, and books of these New Thought writers were taken and edited from the public domain. I have listed links and resources at the end of each section. The dates of these publications range from the late 1800s to the early 1900s. I have left the language of the era intact as much as possible to preserve the flavor of the culture at the turn of the century.

The photos and images that I include in this work are meant to impart the same images and photos that were in circulation during the years these women were writing, and active in their social and political work. They could have easily been included in the newspapers and journals that were widely read in the late nineteenth and early twentieth centuries. I also want to impart the images of the women of the times, give a face to the population that was reading, listening, and learning about New Thought for the first time.

I used the World Wide Web as a resource for the brief biographies of these writers. Several of them have web sites devoted to their history and their writings. Much of this information is readily available through the computer network on an individual basis. My goal was to create a literary home that represented this collective group of women who appeared on the scene heralding a new way of living and thinking, thus the New Thought Reader format was born. There are more New Thought women writers of the period that are not represented here. I was simply unable to include them all, and chose as best I could. Please refer to the web sites listed for more information.

The Resources page at the end of the book contains a list of books of interest for further reading as well as a list of the resources quoted and used in the Introductory Chapters.

In an effort to keep this volume to a reasonable size, and to feature the women writers themselves, I have been brief in the introduction and presentation of my postulate that the New Thought Movement played an important, if not vital, role in the Women's Movement, was indeed a Women's movement in and of itself. It was definitely instrumental in sustaining the social changes taking place at the time.

I wish to thank and acknowledge my Religious Science community at the Center for Spiritual Living, Santa Rosa, California where I am licensed as a spiritual counselor (RScP). My thanks to our senior minister, Rev. Dr. Edward Viljoen for his referrals, support, patience, and willingness to loan me one of his books. Thank you to our Dean of Education, Rev. Dr. Kim Kaiser, for his insights and practical suggestions, to Rev. Robin Gail, for her friendship and support, for Brenda Kobrin, RScP, and Suzanne Sackett who willingly took a peek as first viewers of the manuscript. Thanks goes to Rev. Dr. Chris Michaels, senior minister at Center for Spiritual Living in Kansas City, for his encouraging words. For editing support I wish to acknowledge Diana Badger of Sebastopol; thanks for her professional eye. Randall Friesen deserves a special thank you for sharing his valuable expertise and working with me on the ebook edition. A loving thanks goes to my daughter, Amber Dawn-Sutter, and her husband Julian Sutter, and to my son Joseph Gray, whose technical expertise, support, and words of encouragement were life savers for this project.

Sanna Rose, M.A., RScP
Practitioner in Religious Science

Ford Model T 1908

Table of Contents

Mrs. Abby Scott Baker, Suffragette, Washington D.C.

"Angels are Divine Thoughts:
whisperings of Truth and Love in the soul."
Fannie James, *Studies in the Science of Divine Healing*

Begin the Day
by Ella Wheeler Wilcox

Begin each morning with a talk to God,
And ask for your divine inheritance
Of usefulness, contentment and success.
Resign all fear, all doubt, and all despair.
The stars doubt not, and they are undismayed,
Though whirled through space for countless centuries,
And told not why or wherefore: and the sea
With everlasting ebb and flow obeys,
And leaves the purpose with the unseen Cause.
The star sheds radiance on a million worlds,
The sea is prodigal with waves, and yet
No luster from the star is lost, and not
One drop is missing from the ocean tides.
Oh, brother to the star and sea, know all
God's opulence is held in trust for those
Who wait serenely and who work in faith.

Poems of Power, Chicago: W. B. Conkey, 1902

Introduction

This book brings together and honors several early New Thought women writers at the beginning of the New Thought Movement. Other writers have done a very good job in presenting a scholarly, analytical, fact based history of the New Thought Movement, whereas I am presenting this book inspired by, and based in, my experience in New Thought as a Religious Scientist for the past 11 years. I am very excited to consider the possibility that the philosophy and practice of New Thought principles and teachings were instrumental in creating and supporting the social changes that were so desperately sought by women, children, and African Americans at the turn of the century in America.

These changes were poised to unfold in women's civil rights, the abolition of slavery, radical changes in the child labor laws, and in spiritual healing alternatives to the prevalent allopathic medical practices that were often less than successful in diagnosing and treating illness and disease. The educated, middle class of women of the time period between 1848 and 1920 were very active in the social, political, and spiritual issues of the times. Whether it was championing changes in voter rights for women, abolishing slavery, or engaging in alternative approaches to healing, these women in positions of power were writing, teaching, speaking, and healing their women comrades through their work. They were inspired and passionate about revealing the Truth as they were learning it, experiencing it, and receiving it through Divine Guidance and meditation.

The writings and Truth teachings of these women contributed to the creation of what is known in the New Thought philosophy as a *mental equivalent* necessary for social and personal changes to take place. That is, one must have the inner capacity to first envision and then embody changes within oneself before they will manifest in the world. "As we bring ourselves to a greater vision than the range of our present concepts, we can then induce a greater concept and thereby demonstrate (manifest) more in our experience." (Science of Mind, Ernest Holmes, 1938, pg 610) As such, the outward changes that took place socially, and politically in the early 1900s also required changes within each person individually, as well as within each home, and at each work place. In other words, these changes took place on all levels.

As a Religious Scientist who practices the spiritual principle that there is only One Presence, One Divine Intelligence at work everywhere, all the time, I believe that what was operating through these women writers, teachers, and ministers was a power greater than any one of them. This power was at work bringing more humanity and Truth into how people lived together and related to one another in the trenches of an antiquated, exploitative, patriarchal, paradigm. It is quite believable to one who understands, practices, and knows the power and effect of New Thought principles that the power of the Divine Feminine was moving through New Thought women teachers, healers, writers and publishers. It was as if these women were the voices of the angels heralding a major shift in social consciousness. They could very well have been the midwives of the 20th century.

Pansy Hawk Wing, a Lakota Sioux elder, beautifully describes the way of the Divine Feminine in the book *The Unknown She*, by Hilary Hart:

"Feminine power", Pansy explains, "is the power of the inner space. 'Women were given an extra charge by the Great Spirit, the added responsibility of procreation.' Women carry the power to create, the instinctual wisdom of inner space, how what is needed can come into the world. Women bring this power and wisdom wherever they go...."
(pg 89)

"Our way of leading is a combination of very direct and indirect at the same time," Pansy goes on to say. "This is the story of the spider and the spider web. If you look at the spider web it is a very light and fine material. And the spider is very heavy. There's a lot of weight there, but the web holds. The Lakota style of leading is similar in that what seems is not what is. It might not look like you're leading. We don't lead by moving people around, telling them what to do. A leader is present in the background. The leading is hidden, like the spider's web, but the job gets done, like the spider being held." (*The Unknown She,* pg. 90)

The Truth teachings and writings of these turn of the century women provided a "web" of New Thought ideas that functioned as a mental, emotional, and spiritual stronghold during that time's social and political shifts into a new paradigm. As women emerged out of the social oppression of the 19th century these women writers and forerunners of the New Thought Movement functioned as the hidden leaders of women's march into freedom and emancipation. Their writings provided beacons of encouragement, self-worth, and strength.

These New Thought women were active in the philosophy and the practice of New Thought primarily due to the effects of these practices that facilitated their own physical healings of health challenges that the medical establishment of the times could not cure. They were thus personally inspired and passionate about sharing the practice of these Truths. There didn't seem to be any intention on their part to lead or act as the heralds of any particular social movement per se. Yet, their influence could not help but contribute, in a hidden way, to the larger, national collective movement toward more freedom for all of its citizens, and for the civil rights of several social groups including women's civil rights, the abolition of slavery, and changes in the child labor laws of the era.

Most of the women who became writers, speakers, teachers, and founders of churches in New Thought were inspired by the healings they experienced through their work with the New Thought teacher, Emma Curtis Hopkins. Ms. Hopkins was a primary influence in the

New Thought Movement and began her education with Mary Baker Eddy in Christian Science. A brief biography is presented later in this book.

It is important to emphasize that the New Thought Movement was characteristically a women's movement. In *Each Mind a Kingdom*, by Beryl Satter, Associate Professor of History at Rutgers University in Newark, New Jersey, the author states: "While women were overrepresented in all Protestant denominations at this period (1848-1900s), many New Thought followers understood themselves to be part of a woman's religious movement that would herald a new woman's era". (pg. 8) Ms. Satter continues to state: "Most interesting about New Thought, however, are the interconnections between New Thought, and the turn-of-the-century women's movement leaders, early progressives, and proto—and pioneering psychologists. New Thought will be analyzed, therefore, as a popular intellectual discourse that both drew upon and deeply influenced the ideas of women movement leaders, early progressive reformers, and turn-of-the-century neurologists and physicians." (pg 9) "These early progressives... believed that New Thought meditations would help to bring about a new era in the development of the race." (pg 8)

"The promise of economic independence or even wealth, the excitement of travel; freedom from domestic life; the joy of healing; new circles of friends and comrades; a sense of self-respect and a newly won respect from others; and the conviction that one was helping to inaugurate a spiritual era of woman's power—these were the sparkling lures that drew women and some men into the world of mental healing in the 1880s and 1890s." (*Each Mind a Kingdom*, pg 94)

A number of women in the New Thought Movement were the founders of New Thought Churches of the Movement, i.e., Divine Science, Home of Truth, Society of Pragmatic Mysticism, Church of Christ Scientist, and United Divine Science Ministries. This New Thought philosophy is rooted in the Divine Feminine of the 1900s which stems from the history of American women as pioneers, frontier women who in breaking new ground were creating a new way for equality, social justice, religious understanding, and healing to permeate their lives. Their prolific writings were widely published and read; their classes were well attended and flourished, they were sought-after speakers and healers. "Small but growing numbers of women believed that in the hands of today's high-minded woman, Christian or Spiritual Science could be a tool that would speed the millennium and inaugurate a new "woman's" era. As Helen Wilmans, who had once been a reform journalist and who had become a mental healer, declared, "'It is a noticeable fact that the Mental or Christian Science movement, (out of which the New Thought Movement was born), is a women's movement…In this movement woman's *real* voice has been heard for the first time in the history of the race.'"(*Each Mind a Kingdom,* pg 97)

"Elizabeth Boynton Harbert (a leader in the women's suffrage movement) explained the full implications of the new mental-healing techniques: 'when woman recognizes that she is free…she will give to the world a new race, and the golden age will dawn. It is dawning even now… *Woman is at last free, because she…has discovered the spiritual laws through which her work is to be accomplished.'* (*Each Mind a Kingdom,* pg 25) The women involved in this exciting movement were relieved to understand themselves now as children of God, with a "'rightful inheritance'" of health, rather than simply as children of women, inflicted with the curse of hereditary illness. (pg 97)

Herein is a presentation of the ideas of nine women who were very influential in the beginnings of the New Thought Movement in early 20th century America. Some of their writings presented here are books in their entirety; other presentations are major excerpts from their body of work.

One of the joys in the writings of these early New Thought women is in how concise and simple their styles were in presenting the theory of New Thought. The special language they used, no doubt reflective of the fact that they were women, I find refreshing and tailored to the female psyche. The healing experiences of these women became the basis for their passion and commitment to write, teach, and reach out to other women, resulting in the formation of different branches for the practice of New Thought. For example: the Brook sisters, Nona Brooks, and Fannie Brooks James, along with Malinda Cramer were the co-founders of Divine Science. They and their family members experienced major physical healing from working with this philosophy and they committed a good deal of their time and lives to sharing and teaching the Truth for the benefit of others.

Nona Brooks and Malinda Cramer both had severe health problems, and they made it their quest to discover answers that would take them beyond what the world and mainstream medicine had to offer. It was in their time of meditation and study that their answers came. Theirs was a study of Truth, and their teaching was established on the message as revealed to them. They sought to establish avenues for sharing this message of Truth with others by forming study groups, churches, and printed materials. Essentially, their teaching was that we are in this world but not of it.

"I dare say that the suffrage movement may have benefitted from observing so many women in places of power or position". (Janet Friedline, Divine Science Minister, Washington, D.C.) Cramer acknowledged the preponderance of women in her organization writing in one article, "The question has been frequently asked: 'Why are women active in new religions?'" She explained that because women are "wondrously intuitive and susceptible to Truth," they could "take the lead in awakening the starving world to its greatest need....The women of the present time...are sowing the seed that will...enrich the world and purify humanity of all the false and selfish elements that exist upon the earth." (*Each Mind a Kingdom*, pg 98)

Dr. Emilie Cady was a successful physician during the turn of the century which was very unusual for a woman, and the exception. Her contemporaries were Emmet Fox and Ernest Holmes. She worked with Myrtle and Charles Fillmore in founding the Unity branch of New Thought, and received many testimonies of healings and profound change as a result of reading the Unity text book *Lessons In Truth*, of which she was the author. "Healing of the body is beautiful and good. Power to heal is a divine gift, and as such you are fully justified in seeking. But God wants to give you infinitely more." (*Lessons in Truth*, Emilie Cady)

Emma Curtis Hopkins, the "teacher of teachers", was the recognized founder of the New Thought Movement, and Ursula Gestefeld experienced a direct healing in her work and studies with her. (See brief biography of Emma Curtis Hopkins.)

Elizabeth Towne uses some delightful domestic metaphors to describe the human condition, like the yeast rising in a loaf of bread, or the story of the Jellyfish. Her femininity enriches her teachings and welcomes the female reader right into the arena of New Thought with very accessible examples of the uses of the principles in the philosophy. She wrote directly to the women of the times.

Annie Rix Militz was involved with the Unity branch of New Thought; was a popular teacher, and in this reader writes about the power of Concentration and how best to be in control of self. Annie Rix Militz disseminated the teachings of the Hindu teacher Swami Vivekananda, stating adherence to "the principle that Truth is Truth wherever it is found and whoever is sharing it." (1)

Florence Scovel Shinn in *Your Word Is Your Wand* offers us a plethora of affirmations to use in a wide variety of circumstances. These served as valuable spiritual tools in the New Thought teachings.

My intention in compiling this reader is to present these early women writers and lecturers of New Thought so that their teachings, and the flavor of this cultural era undergoing tremendous change can be experienced and revealed, linking us in companionship with our women ancestors whose shoulders we all stand upon. There are many similarities amongst these women and their teachings, and yet they are each unique in emphasis and style. Their passion in and of itself was an important contribution as well; they were working in a social environment where women had no civil rights, and where ill health was a threat to their quality of life. At a time when the Suffrage movement was in its beginnings, with women in the United States not being granted the right to vote until 1920, the influence of these women simply cannot be underestimated.

As you read these women's writings, keep in mind the social context in which they were written. These stories and teachings were delivered to an audience of an oppressed class of women. The writers were imparting their passion and encouragement to those who were not being treated well by their male counterparts. Some of them share stories of men who responded to their writings and teachings with oppressive and condescending behaviors and comments. They lived amidst a battleground between the sexes, and it is inspiring to witness the dignity and perseverance with which they faced male hostility, and a social structure tenaciously clinging to the status quo. Much of their language reflects the dominant patriarchal mindset that was alive within the women themselves; there was no practice of a gender neutral concept. Elizabeth Cady Stanton, a co-leader of the suffrage movement with Susan B. Anthony wrote "The Woman's Bible". (See Appendix C) Perhaps this was the first attempt at gender equality in the classics of literature.

It is hard not to admire these women who were opening the doors of social change with New Thought as a cornerstone for their movement. This is our "her-story", and as women, and men, we must honor and share these stories and pair them with the "his-story" of the men of the times. Only then will the Wholeness of our inheritance be revealed. We owe a great debt to these forebears, who committed themselves to the social and political changes that we enjoy living in today. We are their vision of the future, we are their intention made manifest, we are the fruit born from the seed they planted, and I honor them. They forged the stream carrying the ideal of what could, and in some instances, would be a higher ground for us all to stand upon.

Links & Acknowledgement:
1. http://thehomeoftruth.org/

What Is New Thought?

Between the 1870s and the 1910s, New Thought could most accurately be defined as a religious healing movement that claimed that "spirit", "mind", or human thought had the power to shape matter, overcome heredity, and mold desire. (*Each Mind a Kingdom*, Beryl Satter, pg 9) The New Thought movement has roots in American Christianity as well as the metaphysical and romantic climate of the 19th century that came as a reaction against the religious skepticism of the previous century. This fruitful period saw the birth of New Thought, Christian Science, Transcendental Meditation, theosophy, and other related movements. (1)

The term New Thought comes from the mystical teaching most perfectly embodied by Christ, that as we renew our thoughts we transform ourselves. "As thou hast believed, so be it done unto thee." (Matthew 8:13, *The American Standard Bible,* 1901) New Thought is a practical spirituality rooted in the timeless mystical traditions universally found throughout the world. It is an inclusive tradition united in the understanding that there is only one power, this power being God. God is all Good, and the manifestation of evil comes from the acts and choices of individuals and groups of people who have gone astray from the truth of our unity with God and each other. Christ taught there are two commandments "Thou shalt love the Lord thy God with all thy heart, and with all thy soul, and with all thy strength, and with all thy mind; and thy neighbour as thyself." (Luke 10:27) This statement reflects the understanding that we are all one and that what we do to another we ultimately do to ourselves.

This basic premise of New Thought, that God is Good and omnipresent, is based upon principles of Universal Law as demonstrated and taught by historical figures such as Buddha, Danika, Lao Tzu, and embodied most perfectly in the person and teachings of Jesus the Christ and Wayshower. As mentioned above, New Thought is inclusive and draws on the wisdom of all traditions that teach the truth of our Unity with God/Good and the omnipresence of God/Good.

In New Thought, the appearance of disharmony is considered to be demonstrative of the manifestation of an inner belief of separation from God or a distraction from focusing on the presence of God. When we maintain a focus on God and Good then disharmony dissipates and wholeness is restored.

New Thought offers all spiritual seekers the means to achieve inner peace and transform outer circumstances through the understanding that "our mental states are carried forward into manifestation and become our experience in daily living." (2)

New Thought teachings date back some 150 years to the Transcendentalists such as Ralph Waldo Emerson and Walt Whitman. William James, the father of American psychology, in his landmark book, *Varieties of Religious Experience*, speaks of New Thought: "The leaders in this faith have had an intuitive belief in the all-saving power of healthy-minded attitudes, in the conquering efficacy of courage, hope, and trust, and a correlative contempt for doubt, fear, worry, and all nervously precautionary states of mind. (pg 69) The popular concept of "positive thinking," launched by Norman Vincent Peale in his book *The Power of Positive Thinking*, came from New Thought teachings. Wayne Dyer, Deepak Chopra, Eckhart Tolle, and Oprah Winfrey are among today's more prominent advocates of New Thought ideas.

The earliest identifiable proponent of what came to be known as New Thought was Phineas Parkhurst Quimby (1802–1866), an American philosopher, mesmerist, healer, and inventor. Quimby developed a belief system that included the tenet that illness originated in the mind as a consequence of erroneous beliefs and that a mind open to God's wisdom could overcome any illness. (4)

Phineas Quimbey

During the late 19th century the metaphysical healing practices of Quimby mingled with the "Mental Science" of Warren Felt Evans, a Swedenborgian. Notable pioneers in the movement also included Charles Fillmore (Unity Church), William Walker Atkinson, and much later, Ernest Holmes (Religious Science). (5)

Phineas Parkhurst Quimby, who was known as Park, could also be considered the founder of not only the New Thought Movement but perhaps the whole Metaphysical Movement in America. Quimby was born in Lebanon, New Hampshire, Feb. 16, 1802, as one of seven children of the village blacksmith. When he was two the family moved to Belfast, Maine where he spent the greater part of his life. This is where he lived when he died there on January 16, 1866. (*Spirits In Rebellion*, Charles S. Braden, 1963, pg 47)

Quimby used mesmerism in his early healing work, but discrepancies in his observations led him to believe that there was a greater power that required neither trance nor medium.

Quimby's basic premise was "The trouble is in the mind, for the body is only the house for the mind to dwell in…Therefore, if your mind had been deceived by some invisible enemy into a belief, you have put into it the form of a disease, with or without your knowledge. By my theory or truth, I come in contact with your enemy, and restore you to health and happiness. This I do partly mentally, and partly by talking till I correct the wrong impression and establish the Truth, and the Truth is the cure."(8)

The spread of Quimby's ideas came largely from four of his patients. They were Annetta G. Seabury, Julius A. Dresser, Mary Baker Glover Patterson (later Mary Baker Eddy), and Warren Felt Evans.

Mary Baker Eddy, healed by Quimby, was the first to organize a healing ministry and eventually organized the movement known as Christian Science. In 1875 she published *Science and Health* in which she set forth a philosophy of healing of which she claimed to be the discoverer.

A small group of which she was the minister had been organized in Lynn, Massachusetts, and in 1881 they moved to Boston where the foundations of Christian Science were laid. (*Spirits In Rebellion*, by Charles S. Braden, 1963, pg 132)

There was a great deal of controversy regarding Mrs. Eddy's claims of being the discoverer of mental science. However, it is generally believed that if not for Mrs. Eddy's work at organizing the movement, there may not have been a New Thought Movement, for many of her students broke from the organization to begin new works. (*Spirits In Rebellion*, pg 132)

Emma Curtis Hopkins influenced New Thought more than any other single teacher. She first took classes with Mrs. Eddy in 1883. By September, 1884, she was the editor of the Christian Science Journal, and by November, 1885, her name was not to be found in the Journal. It is not clear why she was dismissed, but it is said that she began reading other metaphysical books besides Mrs. Eddy's writings. She was an independent thinker with a clear understanding and an ability to effectively communicate to others.

She opened her own headquarters in Chicago, although it is not clear when, probably in 1886.

In 1888, she placed an ad that said she would receive patients for mental cure at her residence. It was also announced she would speak at Kimball Hall. Mrs. Eddy denounced her again, and bracketed her with Julius Dresser, A.J. Swartz and Mary Plunkett, saying they had stolen her teachings. Mrs. Eddy called them Mind Quacks. (*Spirits In Rebellion*, pg 142)

Emma Curtis Hopkins was known as the teacher of teachers. The list of persons who sat under her teachings in Chicago at the Christian Science Theological Seminary and other classes she taught includes: Frances Lord; Annie Rix Militz (Home of Truth) and Harriet Rix; Malinda E. Cramer, co-founder of Divine Science; Mrs. Bingham, teacher of Nona L. Brooks, co-founder of Divine Science; Helen Wilmans, writer and teacher; Charles and Myrtle Fillmore, founders of Unity School of Christianity; Charles and Josephine Barton; Dr. Emilie Cady, writer of the Unity textbook "*Lessons in Truth*"; Ella Wheeler Wilcox, New thought writer and poet; Elizabeth Towne; and considerably later, Ernest Holmes, founder of the Church of Religious Science. She lived until 1925. (*Spirits In Rebellion*, by Charles S. Braden, 1963, pg 143)

Hopkins was also decidedly feminist, interested in social-action causes, intimate—especially in her later years—with a literary and artistic community, and considerably tolerant of views other than her own. (*A Republic of Mind & Spirit*, Catherine Albanese, pg 316)

More About New Thought

The New Thought Movement can by all rights be considered the child of Emma Curtis Hopkins as mentioned earlier. She served as its most vocal writer, coiner of the phrase, and acted as a hub for its early and rapid growth. She was a powerful woman, who taught that in a benevolent world based on original goodness, the rights of women's equality were of paramount importance and must take a backseat to nothing.

During the mid to late 1800s while Hopkins was fighting for women's equality and becoming one of the feminist movement's most vocal proponents, President Abraham Lincoln was carrying these same principles to new heights through his Emancipation Proclamation ensuring freedom for all regardless of race.

Abraham Lincoln seated 1864

At the turn of the century New Thought Churches such as Christian Science, New Thought Christianity, The Church of Divine Science, The Unity Society of Practical Christianity, Unity Church, Unity School of Christianity, and the Church of Religious Science all sprang to life and within just a handful of years grew to embrace millions of followers and students, each branch adding their own special something to those same core teachings.

The principles underlying the New Thought Movement focused on getting tangible results in the real world. They maintained that at their core all people are born into original goodness, and that doing the most possible good for the most people possible always results in the most possible good for each individual.

The New Thought Movement is behind such monumental accomplishments as American Independence, the Emancipation of Slaves, and Women's Right to Vote in the United States. The movement itself is about empowering all people on a global level, and elevating humanity to a place where inequality of race, gender, or creed is nothing more than a long forgotten memory.

Another aspect of New Thought is that it embraces a minimalist creed, leaving the individual free to relate directly to God. It's a do-it-yourself religion, and in this way continues its ties to its mystical origins. While New Thought originally was applied to problems of sickness, it rapidly expanded to include other life challenges such as lack of money or difficulties in relationships with others. It synthesizes the seeming opposites of practicality and spirituality.

American philosopher and psychologist William James referred to New Thought as the American people's "only decidedly original contribution to the systematic philosophy of life." James emphasized the New Thought side of Mind-cure. He characterized the movement as "a deliberately optimistic scheme of life, with both a speculative and a practical side" and the basic purpose of "the systematic cultivation of healthy-mindedness". (7)

New Thought is expressed in Romans 12:2 (*The American Standard Version of the Holy Bible,* 1901), "Be ye transformed by the renewing of your mind." It is interesting to note that all the early leaders of New Thought came from Christian backgrounds, yet most had found organized religion restrictive or repressive and turned away from it.

The New Thought movement is active today through its branches of Unity churches, Divine Science Centers, and the United Centers of Religious Science, currently known as United Centers for Spiritual Living. The Association for Global New Thought is a nondenominational organization with an active membership. (See Appendix A) New Thought tolerates great latitude in beliefs and practices. Its followers seek total life transformation and empowerment through changing their thought processes and forming permanent new thinking patterns. Thoughts held in mind produce after their kind. Another way of saying this is: like attracts like. As above so below. This encompasses the belief that the world is made up of thoughts, or subconscious thought patterns. Materialism would be its opposite.

If indeed this is a universe of thought, then changing one's thought changes the universe. (6)

Links and Acknowledgements
1. newthoughthistory.orgNew_Thought_HistoryNarrative_History.html

2. newthought.infobeliefsbeliefs.htm

3. en.wikipedia.orgwikiNew_Thought

4. en.wikipedia.orgwikiNew_Thought: referenced "Phineas Parkhurst Quimby". *MSN Encarta*. Archived from the original on 2009-11-01. Retrieved Nov. 16, 2007

5. en.wikipedia.orgwikiNew_Thought

6. *New Thought: A Practical American Spirituality*, by C. Alan Anderson & Deborah G. Whitehouse, 2003, Authorhouse Publisher, Pgs. 4-6

7. websyte.comalanhealism.htm1885. Referenced *The Primitive Mind-Cure* H. H. Carter & Co. James, William. 1902. *The Varieties of Religious Experience*, Mentor edition.

8. http:websyte.comalanquimby.htm . Referenced as: (3:208; references of this type are to volume and page of Quimby's *Complete Writings*

History of New Thought Chart

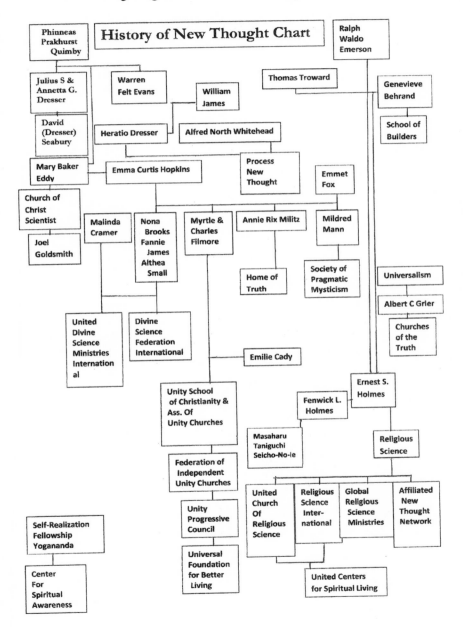

History of New Thought Chart

Phinneas Prakhurst Quimby

Ralph Waldo Emerson

Julius S & Annetta G. Dresser

Warren Felt Evans

William James

Thomas Troward

Genevieve Behrand

David (Dresser) Seabury

Heratio Dresser

Alfred North Whitehead

School of Builders

Mary Baker Eddy

Emma Curtis Hopkins

Process New Thought

Emmet Fox

Church of Christ Scientist

Malinda Cramer

Nona Brooks Fannie James Althea Small

Myrtle & Charles Filmore

Annie Rix Militz

Mildred Mann

Joel Goldsmith

Home of Truth

Society of Pragmatic Mysticism

Universalism

Albert C Grier

United Divine Science Ministries International

Divine Science Federation International

Emilie Cady

Churches of the Truth

Ernest S. Holmes

Unity School of Christianity & Ass. Of Unity Churches

Fenwick L. Holmes

Masaharu Taniguchi Seicho-No-Ie

Religious Science

Federation of Independent Unity Churches

Self-Realization Fellowship Yogananda

Unity Progressive Council

United Church Of Religious Science

Religious Science Inter-national

Global Religious Science Ministries

Affiliated New Thought Network

Center For Spiritual Awareness

Universal Foundation for Better Living

United Centers for Spiritual Living

Timeline of *New Thought Leaders*

Phineas P. Quimby	1802 – 1866
Elizabeth Cady Stanton	1815 – 1902
Susan B Anthony	1820 – 1906
Mary Baker Eddy	1821 – 1910
Malinda Cramer	**1844 – 1906**
Ursula Gestefeld	**1845 – 1921**
Dr. Emilie Cady	**1848 – 1948**
Ella Wheeler Wilcox	**1850 – 1919**
Emma Curtis Hopkins	1853 – 1925
Fannie Brooks James	**1854 – 1914**
Annie Rix Militz	**1856 – 1924**
Nona Brooks	**1861 – 1945**
Elizabeth Towne	**1865 – 1960**
Florence Scovel Shinn	**1871 – 1940**
Emmet Fox	1886 – 1951
Ernest Holmes	1887 – 1960

Historical Events

1801	Thomas Jefferson elected President of the United States
1808	Beethoven performs his Fifth Symphony
1812 – 15	War of 1812 between the United States and the United Kingdom
1821	Missouri becomes a state
1825	John Quincy Adams elected president
1830s	Oregon Trail to pacific northwest
1836	Arkansas becomes a state
1837	Michigan becomes a state
1845	Florida and Texas become states
1846	The U.S.-Mexican War begins
1848 – 55	Gold Rush
1848 – 1920	Suffrage Movement
1850	California becomes a state
1861 – 65	Civil War
1861	Lincoln President
1862	Emancipation Proclamation
1865 – 77	Reconstruction
1865	13th Amendment freeing slaves passed
1865	Assassination of Lincoln
1866	Ku Klux Klan
1868	Typewriter invented
1876	Battle of Little Bighorn
1876	Telephone Invented
1879	Light Bulb invented
1881	Clara Barton creates Red Cross
1908	Ford Model T
1912	Titanic sinks
1914	WWI; & Mother's Day created
1918	Red Scare & the Depression
1920	19th Amendment Women's Rights
1945	WWII
1941	Attack on Pearl Harbor
1945	Atomic Bomb on Hiroshima
1946	Benjamin Spock's Child Care Book
1955	Rosa Parks
1960 – 1980	2nd Wave of Women's Liberation & Birth Control

Who Was Emma Curtis Hopkins?

Emma Curtis Hopkins
(1853-1925)

Emma Curtis Hopkins is aptly known as the "teacher of teachers". Although her main strength was in lectures and classes, she produced a body of work that is considered seminal for New Thought today. Her works include:

High Mysticism
Scientific Christian Mental Practice
Resume – Practice Book for High Mysticism
Esoteric Philosophy in Spiritual Science
Judgment Series in Spiritual Science
Bible Interpretations
Self Treatment

Class Lessons 1888
Bible Interpretation: From the Book of Job
Drops of Gold

Emma Hopkins came across Mary Baker Eddy, founder of Christian Science, through a friend and had a healing session with her. She then took a class with Eddy and to pay for this class she worked on the *Christian Science* magazine. Hopkins' intensity and intellect were helpful to the success of the magazine during these early years.

When she had finished paying for the class, she got fed up with Mary Baker Eddy and the restriction she imposed of having to only read the bible and Eddy's books, and parted ways. Being a loving person, she respected all persons and therefore never condemned Eddy or other people.

Aided by her access to the Dartmouth College Library, Emma started her own school, which some state was the foundation of the New Thought movement.

Mrs. Hopkins' gift for teaching revealed itself early in her life. Before she was fifteen years old, she had entered Woodstock Academy as a student and because of her recognized genius, was given a place on the faculty. Thus, after leaving the *Christian Science Journal*, she found her purpose emerging through her role as an independent leader and teacher.

As an independent teacher, Mrs. Hopkins taught in many cities (among them New York, Chicago, Kansas, San Francisco) having large classes wherever she went. Later she founded a seminary in Chicago. It was a regularly incorporated school and the graduates, mostly women, were ordained ministers and so recognized by the State of Illinois. Students came from all parts of the country to study with her and go out and carry the message of healing and comforting to the people. Authors, preachers, homemakers—came to her for instruction and she touched them with the quickening power of her illumined soul.

Among her students were many who later became prominent teachers and leaders within the New Thought movement. "During her Chicago years, Hopkins taught Charles and Myrtle Fillmore, who founded Unity, and during her New York years, she taught Ernest Holmes, who founded Religious Science. Nona Brooks, who studied with Hopkins, co-founded Divine Science with Malinda Cramer; still another student, Annie Rix Militz, founded the Homes of Truth…A series of other Hopkins students, well known in movement circles, spread out across the nation, bringing Hopkins' brand of metaphysics to numerous communities." (*A Republic of Mind & Spirit,* pg 317) Other students included H. Emilie Cady, author of the Unity textbook "*Lessons in Truth*", and the New Thought poet Ella Wheeler Wilcox.

Mrs. Hopkins was way ahead of her times in the freedom offered students in a group activity that the faculty of the seminary became. Her natural instinct for leadership quickened that capacity in her students, many of whom themselves established independent movements and went on to minister to mankind. "Hopkins described the coming of a Mother God who would help 'usher the dawn of a new time', wherein the poor may be taught and befriended, women walk fearless and glad, and childhood be safe and free." (*Each Mind a Kingdom,* pg 92)

"Hopkins proclaimed a coming third age of the Holy Ghost. This Holy Ghost, however, was distinctly feminine—identified with the Shekinah of the Hebrew Bible as well as with the New Testament Spirit—and was also a sign of a feminist future to be. The coming age would be a better era than before, and Hopkins—far more than Eddy—avidly supported social reform causes…. Her pamphlet essay *The Ministry of the Holy Mother* appeared during her Chicago years. In it the divine Mother was conjoined to both the Spirit and ministry of God in a mystical statement that was also a declaration about service and about Hopkins conviction that any adequate idea of God required the feminine… The divine Mother received her due in Hopkins thinking more than the divine feminine ever would later in New Thought.

After the leadership of women in the initiating years of the movement, by the early decades of the twentieth century, a new generation of men would rise to prominence as leaders, and the divine Mother would recede." (*A Republic of Mind & Spirit,* Catherine Albanese, pg 319-320, referenced Harley, *Emma Curtis Hopkins,* pg 82-83)

Here's what Charles Fillmore had to say about Emma Curtis Hopkins: "She is undoubtedly the most successful teacher in the world... in many instances those who enter her classes confirmed invalids come out at the end of the course perfectly well. She dwells so continually in the spirit that her very presence heals and those who listen are filled with new life. He doubts "'if ever before on this planet have such words of burning Truth been so eloquently spoken through a woman.'" (*Spirits In Rebellion,* pg 144)

The following tribute was paid to her in Unity Magazine (1925): "'Her brilliance of mind and spirit was so marked that very few could follow in her metaphysical flights, yet she had marked power in quickening spirituality in her students.'"(1)

"Specifically, in the first graduation ceremony of the Emma Hopkins College of Metaphysical Science in 1889, Hopkins graduated a total of 22 individuals of which 20 were women. Her school encouraged an interpretation of the Trinity based on ideas initiated by Joachim of Fiore, which stated that there were three eras in the history of this traditional trio. The first was the patriarchal idea of 'God the Father', the second was a time of freedom for the general population which was signified by the birth of Jesus, and the third, 'the Spirit, the Truth-Principle, or the Mother-Principle,' focused on the power of women. The latter element of this interpretation of the Trinity was embodied by the pioneering roles which each of these New Thought women had in helping to even the playing field of the genders." (1)

Mrs. Hopkins lived until 1925. After her death her sister Estelle Carpenter took over her work, aided by teacher, Eleanor Mel. Further, Ethelred Folsom, who had studied with Mrs. Hopkins and apparently had accompanied her on a trip to Europe, set up an organization to perpetuate Mrs. Hopkins' influence. The public was invited to attend classes on Mrs. Hopkins' teachings, and her works were published and distributed under the name "*The Ministry of the High Watch.*"

Scientific Christian Mental Practice is Emma Curtis Hopkins' masterpiece, and is one of the greatest of all works based on mysticism. In it she says, "When the Lord is your confidence you will never find yourself at all deceived by the ways and speech of men and women, though they be very brilliant, if they speak outside of the Principle that demonstrates healing and goodness and life." (*Scientific Christian Mental Practices,* pg 86)

This reader features several female students of Ms. Hopkins, and for further reading one can refer to her works listed previously. Ms. Hopkins' book *Scientific Christian Mental Practice* is featured in classes taught throughout New Thought Churches and Centers today, and her work is considered to be a major influence in the movement.

Links & Acknowledgements
1. This quote is taken from this web site: *emmacurtishopkins.wwwhubs.com CornerstoneBooks: http:cornerstonebooks.net*

Suffragettes on their way to Boston
Library of Congress Prints and Photographs Division
Washington, D.C. 20540

Battle Hymn of the Women
by Ella Wheeler Wilcox

They are waking, they are waking,
In the east, and in the west;
They are throwing wide their windows to the sun;
And they see the dawn is breaking,
And they quiver with unrest,
For they know their work is waiting to be done.
They are waking in the city,
They are waking on the farm;
They are waking in the boudoir, and the mill;
And their hearts are full of pity
As they sound the loud alarm,
For the sleepers, who in darkness, slumber, still.
In the guarded harem prison,
Where they smother under veils,
And all echoes of the world are walled away;
Though the sun has not yet risen,
Yet the ancient darkness pales,
And the sleepers, in their slumber, dream of day.
And their dream shall grow in splendour
Till each sleeper wakes, and stirs;
Till she breaks from old traditions, and is free;
And the world shall rise, and render
Unto woman what is hers,
As it welcomes in the race that is to be.
Unto woman, God the Maker
Gave the secret of His plan;
It is written out in cipher, on her soul;
From the darkness, you must take her,
To the light of day, O man!
Would you know the mighty meaning of the scroll.

Poems of Experience. By Ella Wheeler Wilcox.
London : Gay and Hancock, Ltd. 1910.

Elizabeth Towne

(1865-1960)

President of New Thought Alliance (1924), &
Editor of "Nautilus" magazine.

You are a jewel!
In exactly the right setting
for the present.

But the setting
may be made over!
By believing and working.
You are the jewel that
polishes itself and
secretes its own setting
by wanting to, trying to,
and keeping at it.

Lessons in Living —1910

In her work presented here, Mrs. Towne speaks directly to the feminine psyche of the time which was basically entrenched in the Victorian culture of the oppression of women, and was duty bound in service to men. She presents the principles of New Thought in metaphors of the domestic life, making these new ideas accessible to women through *their* language and through the daily activities of home life with which they were all familiar. Mrs. Towne was truly a pioneer and advocate for women during the Suffrage movement in the early 1900s as she reached out to change their thinking, suggesting a new mental equivalent, and identity of self, that would facilitate the social changes on the horizon.

A strong local voice in the women's suffrage movement, Towne also distinguished herself by becoming Holyoke's first female alderman, first female candidate for mayor, and a radical thinker who set forth her ideas for ending poverty in pamphlets and articles in which, among other things, she proposed a universal wage of $5 a week for every man, woman, and child. (1)

Born in 1865, Elizabeth Towne was the daughter of one of Oregon's earliest pioneers. In 1900, at age 35, she reversed her father's footsteps and headed east to Holyoke, Massachusetts, where she became a pioneer in her own right.

Though never an official publication of the New Thought Movement, *Nautilus* was probably the most widely read of the many that have appeared over the years, and was very influential. It was a private enterprise of Elizabeth Towne, who, originally a Methodist had taken up New Thought, and then became a teacher.

She married at quite an early age, but the marriage proved to be an unhappy one and ended in divorce. She had to support herself and her children. At one point, while still living in Portland, Oregon, she felt the need for added income. Her schooling had been interrupted by her early marriage and she had no background in business experience; but one day, as she tells it herself, it suddenly came to her that she should undertake to publish a small periodical. She had no capital with which to begin, but secured some help from her father in the amount of $30 per month for a six-month period, and so launched the magazine which by a kind of inspiration she chose to call *Nautilus*.

In May, 1900, Elizabeth brought the *Nautilus* to Holyoke, Massachusetts, and there married William E. Towne, a book and magazine publisher and distributor, and together they eventually built up a substantial and even profitable business in the publishing and distribution of the magazine, and of New Thought books. The first issue of *Nautilus* made in Holyoke, June 1900, was 4,500 copies, and the printer's bill was just $36.93, including the wrapping. Within a short time this little four-page paper had grown to be a handsome illustrated magazine. Besides the big subscription book business done by the firm almost 50,000 copies of *Nautilus* were mailed out of Holyoke each month. It was far and away the largest customer of the Holyoke post office. It took four girls a whole week to wrap up a single issue of *Nautilus*. All this had grown from the most modest beginnings.

On Sunday morning of December 9, 1910, Holyoke woke up to find that a fire had broken out and gotten enough headway during the night to destroy the home of Mr. and Mrs. William E. Towne, and of *Nautilus*. An unusual building then rose up from the ashes of the old home of *Nautilus*. Strangers usually decided that it was a school house—and that was not a bad guess either. For years the *Nautilus* office had been known as the high school annex because its editor, Mrs. Elizabeth Towne, insisted that all of her employees shall have been trained in some high school. (2)

Home of the Nautilus

"Elizabeth Towne was very proud of the office girls. She selected them with great care and they looked like a sewing club or a lot of college girls, more than anything else. 'Our office supplies schooling as well as work,' says Mrs. Towne. 'We teach the best methods we know for doing all kinds of work believing that responsibilities honestly discharged and all work efficiently and good-willingly done make for character, and character makes for success and happiness and health. Honest work for the worker's sake is the first principle of our business. We 'graduate' our workers just as a school does—when a helper reaches the place where she no longer grows by doing our work, we are glad to present her with our little 'Well done,' as a sort of diploma, and pass her on to new opportunities. In the ten years of our experience with Holyoke girls, we have had over seventy in our employ, for periods ranging from six weeks to more than seven years. Many of the finest positions in the city and elsewhere are now filled by girls who are glad of what they learned with us. Several are applying efficiency methods in their own happy homes. We are proud of our girls.'"(3)

"It is quite evident that Mrs. Towne was very much the editor of *Nautilus,* and she wrote constantly for the magazine and published numerous books and pamphlets of her own and others' on New Thought lines. Her husband was the associate editor and wrote most of the *Nautilus* advertising, in addition to publishing his own quarterly, *American New Life*, and carrying on his regular work of selling books by mail. Mrs. Towne's son, Chester, who carried the first issue of *Nautilus* down to the post office on his shoulder, was associated with the magazine also as Chester Holt Struble, managing editor and advertising manager. These three formed the trinity that evolved the bigger, better, brighter *Nautilus,* exponent of New Thought, self-help, and human efficiency through self-knowledge."(3)

"Many famous New Thought writers contributed to *Nautilus* at one time or another, Ella Wheeler Wilcox, Edwin Markham, Anne Warner, Edward B. Warman, Horatio W. Dresser and Orison Swett Marden are among the well-known helpers who contributed some of their best work to *Nautilus.* William Walker Atkinson, one of the leading New Thought writers of the time, also joined the staff of writers."(3)

"The *Nautilus* business was incorporated as the Elizabeth Towne Company, a close corporation. The Elizabeth Towne Company owned the magazine and carried on all the subscription business connected with the publishing of *Nautilus,* as well as the publishing and distribution of books by Mrs. Towne and other New Thought authors."(3)

"While *Nautilus* had been thus growing and expanding, its editor's books were selling by the hundreds of thousands. Mrs. Towne was the author of thirteen books of various sizes, and the publisher of many more. One of her own books reached a sale of a hundred thousand copies, and *Experiences in Self-Healing,* which contains the life story of the author, covering a period of twenty years, also had a tremendous sale." (3)

Besides her editorial, book making and home making life, Mrs. Towne was a lecturer of note, having crossed the continent on lecture tours. She has a generous paragraph in "Who's Who?", the standard American Hall of Fame. She was a member of the International Lyceum Club. In Holyoke she was deeply interested in local philanthropic work, with a special fondness for the Holyoke Boys' Club.

Her twelve years' residence had made her an ardent Holyoker, and a lover of all New England. People who met Mrs. Towne were at once impressed with the qualities that created her success. She had a message and the brains to present it well. She had high courage, rare judgment, a most attractive personality and with all these an immense capacity for hard work. These qualities mean success in any path in life. They have led to the practical application of the motto of *Nautilus* that appeared on the title page of every issue.

The Chambered Nautilus

Build thee more stately mansions, O my soul,
As the swift seasons roll!
Leave thy low-vaulted past!
Let each new temple, nobler than the last,
Shut thee from heaven with a dome more vast,
Till thou at length art free,
Leaving thine outgrown shell by life's unresting sea!

Oliver Wendell Holmes

In 1924 Elizabeth Towne was elected president of the International New Thought Alliance and assumed editorship of the INTA periodical *Bulletin* also. The size of *Bulletin* doubled in a short period from around sixteen pages per issue to as many as thirty-two, and once even fifty-six, under Mrs. Towne's editorship. Nor was this the only change effected by Mrs. Towne. The *Bulletin* assumed a sprightliness of manner reminiscent of the *Nautilus*. Nothing Mrs. Towne had anything to do with could fail to register something of the enthusiasm and energy which was her natural character.

Begun in 1898, *Nautilus* continued for more than fifty years until in August, 1953, Mrs. Towne announced that the advancing years of the editor and the increasing costs of production made it seem wise to discontinue publication with that issue.

A letter from a former president of INTA recalls his seeing Elizabeth Towne walking arm in arm down the street one day with poets Edwin Markham and Ella Wheeler Wilcox, an impressive sight as he recalled it. Elizabeth Towne was without doubt one of the more colorful characters in the history of the New Thought Movement. The following books are by Elizabeth Towne:

Joy Philosophy
How to Grow Success
Happiness and Marriage
Lessons in Living
Lessons in New Thought
Just How to Wake the Solar Plexus
Practical Methods for Self-Development
The Life Power and How To Use It
How to Use New Thought in Home Life
Health Through New Thought and Fasting (with Wallace Wattles)

The title page of Towne's book *The Life Power and How to Use It* is shown in the opening sequence of the 2006 movie *The Secret*, and the film presents many of the ideas that she promoted.

For this publication I have included her work *Joy Philosophy.*

Links & Acknowledgment
1. Remarkable Women of the Pioneer Valley Project by the Pioneer Valley History Network, referenced from a Pamphlet dated 1934-1935 in the collection of the Holyoke Public Library, Holyoke History Room: pvhn2.wordpress.com1900-2elizabeth-towne-2
2. http:elizabethtowne.wwwhubs.com
3. holyokemass.comtranscriptpeoplenautilus.html, *"The Story of the Nautilus"* noted from the publication *Holyoke Daily Transcript Thirtieth Anniversary* edition published in 1912.
4. elizabethtowne.wwwhubs.com

Suffragettes Marching 1900s
Library of Congress Prints and Photographs Division
Washington, D.C. 20540

Joy Philosophy
(1911)

Introduction

I know that there is, if not a "higher intelligence," at least a fuller intelligence than this personal one I call my own. Many a time in my life I have been absolutely certain that some particular thing was the only right thing—that if it did not come to pass just that particular way the loss would be infinite and the harm deep as hell itself, and utterly irreparable.

Well, it did not come to pass as I thought it must in order to keep the earth from wobbling on its axis.

And do you know it wasn't very long before I was fervently glad it did not come around as I thought it must and ought to. The way I thought utterly wrong was absolutely right and beneficent.

Many a time I have had such experiences, in little things and big. I know there is a fuller intelligence than mine; and I know that when my intelligence goes awry from lack of far-seeing, that this fuller intelligence overrules mine. I am glad to believe this—glad to know that when I get in a quandary there is Something to bring things out right in spite of me.

And do you know—I believe this fuller intelligence is after all my own intelligence. It is I who am doing it all the time. Intelligence is not confined in bodies or brains,—no. It fills the universe. All this space between you and me is pure intelligence in which we live and move, and through which we think. But we are conscious only of that small portion of our intelligence represented by our bodies. This great sea of intelligence is infinitely the larger part of us, but it acts sub-consciously, or super-consciously. But it does act, and for my individual good, as well as for the good of all others. I am glad to be overruled by it. It makes me feel safe to know that if I make a mistake in judgment I shall be over-ruled by this fuller intelligence which is over us all.

This book is written to help awake your faith in the fuller intelligence which works sub-consciously in us all; and to help arouse within you the joy of living in consciousness with your Limitless Self, which is my Self, too. Health, happiness and success to you, my readers.

ELIZABETH TOWNE
Holyoke, Mass.

A Good Morning in Two Worlds

Good morning! Isn't it a glorious sunrise? Just see!—not alone one sun is showing its golden rim above the world's edge, but ten million suns are rising upon ten million waiting hearts, and shadows flee to find a place of rest. Truly, a good morning to you of the NEW THOUGHT, whose hearts have turned to smile straight at the sun of life.

I AM the sun of God. Just as this dear, old green earth is turning its face to the sun so you and I are turning our attention to the I AM sun.

"The worlds in which we live are two—The world I AM and the world I DO."

Too long have we faced the world *I DO*. Too long have we judged ourselves and others by the dim light of what hath already appeared. We have been discouraged with comparing the already accomplished with itself. We said, "I can do no more than has been done; there can be nothing new under the sun." So we have journeyed, and gazed, and regretted that it was all done. Everywhere we looked it was all done. "Every art and science and business is overdone," we said, "there is no chance to Do anything except what Tom, Dick and Harry have already done to death. There is no chance here for me."

I AM the ideal world. Ah, that is where the sun shines and youth plays eternal and almighty. In the world of ideals I AM omnipotent, omniscient, all-pervading. In the world of *Doing* I AM lost among the many and the already-accomplished.

I have just read a letter from one who has been for *22* years a book-keeper for one firm. For *22* years he plodded mechanically up one column of figures and down another, and drew his little salary. Now the firm has passed out with its head, and this man is left at 45 without a salary. He is "worn out" and nobody wants the remnants—I had almost said the remains.

This man is a sucked orange and is meeting the natural fate of such. But unlike the orange, he was a free-will offering to the world *I DO*. His young ideals were choked off and crushed out. He said, "A salary in the hand now is worth two fortunes I *might* develop if I followed my ideals. I think I *might* in time work into something great if I worked along another line for myself, but I *know* I can draw a salary if I work for this man. I fear to trust 'the world I AM.' And anyway, life is short and what's the use of trying so hard? So I'll add up columns, draw my salary and eat, drink and be merry." So his ideals for lack of expression went into winter quarters, and are still hibernating—awaiting a new incarnation in the world *I DO*.

But it is never too late to turn to the sun I AM. One's muscles may be weak and his joints stiff; his brain cells may cry out for a little more slumber, a few more columns and then a long sleep; but still one *can* turn over if he will. It is never too late to begin putting what I AM into what *I DO.* Even if one is 45 and a sucked orange, with no time to accomplish much in this incarnation, he can at least get ready for a better start in the next. So it is never too late to consider and express what I AM—the ideal.

Do you know that your ideals and desires are really YOU?—the I AM of you? Your body and your doings and even your education are but white caps on the surface of YOU. They are but an infinitely small and evanescent portion of your resources. They are what you have already realized of your infinite resources.

The giraffe used to have a short neck. That was all he had expressed of himself. But his pasturage ran short and he began to reach up after the palm leaves. He reached and looked and reached again. This unwonted exercise stretched his neck until it is now long enough to easily reach the palm tops. So it has ceased to grow longer. As long as he kept *reaching out* his neck kept growing.

What are *you* reaching out after? Do you see in the world I AM something that is worthwhile? Will you reach after it in the world *I DO?* Do you keep on reaching, and looking, and reaching again?

Between reachings do you retire into the world I AM for inspiration and power for further reaching?

This alternation from Being to Doing—from I AM to *I DO* —is the secret of power and progress and success. It is the *soul's breathing.* You inhale in the world I AM; you exhale in the world *I DO.* The more easily and regularly you vibrate between these two the more complete is your realization of health and success.

When you have that tired and unsuccessful feeling due to too much exhaling in the world *I DO,* just rise into the realm I AM and by imagination and affirmation pump yourself full of—I AM power.

I AM wisdom.

I AM love.

I AM what I desire to be.

ALL Things work together for the manifestation of what l AM.

Then rise again and express your regenerated self in Doing. There was one man who talked back at me for that "Good Morning" article. I received from him an unsigned note which began by acquainting me with his opinion that he is "a very old man" and therefore entitled to assume authority and correct pert, little, young and conceited things like me, for the good of their souls; and it closed with calling my attention to a small attached card bearing in a little black frame this admonition: *"Trust in the Lord with all thine heart; and lean not unto thine own understanding. In all thy ways acknowledge him, and he shall direct thy paths."*

In my Bible, which is well thumbed by the way, and copiously underlined and annotated, these lines are underscored with red ink. If the sender of that card had dug the verses out of his own Bible instead of finding them where somebody else had put them, his eyes might have traveled down another line where they would have rested upon this: *"Be not wise in thine own eyes."* And he would *not* have found after that any clause to the effect that he is entitled to become wise in his own eyes when he shall have become "a very old man." The "aged" do not necessarily "understand judgment."

But there! I am reminding myself of old Dr. Driver, "the only man who ever downed Ingersoll." But when a man fires Bible verses at me I enjoy dodging 'em and firing the whole Bible back at him. And when a man fails to sign his name to his communication it takes some effort to think of him as anything but an impersonal sort of target that sets itself up and dares you to hit it. Now if there is anything I do enjoy it is hitting the bull's-eye. But if I thought the bull's-eye had any tender feelings to be hurt I'd fire the other way.

But seriously, I do not mean to lay myself liable to be hit with that particular saying of David's. I have lived with it, and tried to let it live with me, for at least 15 years. And I thought everybody knew that I AM is what the Bible calls God, or the Lord.

When I say, I AM power, I lean to *God,* the only power. When I say, I AM wisdom, I call *God.* When I say, I AM love, I reckon myself nothing and God ALL, for God is love. When I say, I AM what I desire to be, I count myself as *God's* manifestation, with *his* desires written on my heart. The desires of my heart are *God's* desires. He worketh in me both to desire and to think, as well as to will and to do *his* good pleasure.

'When I tell you to rise into the ideal and pump yourself full of I AM consciousness I bid you identify yourself with God, the one soul of all people and things; I bid you realize your oneness with *all* power, wisdom, love; I bid you in ALL your ways and thoughts and desires and deeds acknowledge HIM, the One-Power, One-Wisdom, One-Love, as the director of your every way.

When you are disturbed, unhappy, unsuccessful, agitated, you are breaking the connection between God and yourself, by *not taking him into* your thoughts and desires. You are counting him OUT. So I say, stop and pump yourself full of I AM *God.* Power and Wisdom and Love are only names of God. Whenever you reckon yourself Power or Wisdom or Love you *take in God.* When you say, I am weak, or ignorant, or unloving and unloved, you *deny* God and force him out of your thought. Or at least you try to. Then let him in. In all thy ways acknowledge him. In all thy desires acknowledge him.

And verily he shall direct thy paths, and they shall be paths of peace and pleasantness and plenty.

The Present Tense

To think or not to think—that is the question raised by different exponents of the New Thought. Most of our teachers have been telling us that by thought we are created and by thought we are saved from death. But Sydney Flower says thought is killing us all. We are clogging up with Brain-Ash. And now I come to think of it, Jesus of Nazareth said, "Take NO thought."

Evidently thought and its results are decidedly important to us who mean to Live and let who will do the dying.

But I fancy the thought advocates are not so far off as might appear. Truth is ever paradoxical.

And it is her paradoxes which MAKE us think, and do it in spite of ourselves. Truly, it were vain to say, Stop thinking.

It is useless to say, Forget.

The child thinks, and I suspect him of thinking harder and more nearly true than does the grown-up. But a child thinks *new* thoughts; or rather he thinks the same old thoughts *with variations*. And all his thoughts are made light and bright by vivid and *hope-full* imagination. It is as if his thoughts by some divine alchemy of imagination are transmuted into gas or electricity before his brain is stoked with them. There is no Brain-Ash in a child; there is only glow and the white light of electricity.

But we grown-ups are stingy with our fuel. We put out the alchemic fires of imagination and burn our Facts direct.

Our consciousness is like a little bird in a wooden hogshead. It flies around and around, and bruises its poor little wings against the sides; it soars three feet and bumps its head; it falls three feet and—thinks. "Life is only a wooden hogshead of a treadmill," it says, and willingly gives up its little ghost.

In a child's mind even stone is endowed with life; to the grown-up everything is dead. So the child's thoughts are alive and the grown-ups' are dead. The child's thoughts being alive have power to *move* him—truly, "he is full of life." But the grown-up is full of death and Brain-Ash.

Because the child's thoughts are alive he is so interested in the Now that it is easy to forget the past and ignore the future. The grown-ups' thoughts being dead, he takes refuge from the stench—he seeks again the *live* thoughts of his youth.

The cure of Age is interest, enthusiasm and their consequent activity of mind and body. "Assume a virtue if you have it not," and thus *re-call* it. *Play* with your work. Wipe out the past, forget the future, and *play*. Live *now*. Be a child *now*. Endow with life all things you touch. Permit nothing to remain cut and dried. Cut it by another pattern, *your own* brand new one. Talk to it, smile at it, *imagine* things to it, and of it. Quit being serious. "Dignity is a peculiar carriage invented to cover up the defects of the mind." Quit covering up *anything.* Be a child, smiling.

Oh, but you can't feel so? Nobody asked you to feel it. Just Do it, DO it, DO IT!—and never mind feeling. Practice makes perfect and *feeling follows.* Go in to win and keep at it, until you are the happiest kid in the bunch.

Mr. Flower says you cannot have youth and wisdom. He intimates that wisdom goes with Age. Dearie, don't you believe it.

The wisdom which goes with Age is a dirty little wooden hogshead counterfeit. Only in proportion as one stays young is he wise. *Real* wisdom is in The Limitless. It is in the electric atmosphere which is breathed by children and fools. In the hogshead it is deadened by the heavy effluvia of dead *things.* All true wisdom, all poetry, all art, all invention, comes to the child-brain in The Limitless. Only as poets, artists, inventors get out of the hogshead do they find that which lives, and stirs the dead things within.

A Mush or a Man—Which?

Man in the natural and unregenerate state is an unprincipled being. He is moved by every shadow of feeling. These shadows being cast by people, things and events without, his mental and physical activities represent but a conglomerate of other people. He is a jelly-fish, receiving for the moment the impression of any finger which pokes him. Whether he wants to be or not, he is nothing but a "mush of concession" to every passing person or circumstance. *He is constantly affected from without.* He lives and changes his being according to what is thrust upon him by other things. He has no principle for individual living, except that of stinging the hand which touches him.

The fate of the unprincipled jelly-fish is ever the same. His own power of initiative is so primitive that he is propelled by every current of wind or wave. Everything stands aside for even the sucker, who knows where he is going. But the jelly-fish has no destination. His one object in life is to *keep from being hurt,* and to this end he floats with any current. He effaces himself as much as possible to keep from being seen and eaten. And I suspect he is often indignant and tries to sting because he has succeeded in his attempt not to be noticed. But when he happens to be noticed by *too* large a fish he is gobbled up in a jiffy. If he escapes being eaten he is cast on the beach to lament away his feeble life in a too-ardent day.

Poor little unprincipled jelly-fish! But occasionally a jellyfish gets tired of being a more or less unwilling mush with a red pepper sting. He grows a shell to protect himself, and becomes a clam. He shuts himself up with his own opinion of the selfish world outside. He loses his red pepper sting, but if you get *too* close to him he nips your impertinent fingers, and shuts the door in your face. He has his opinion of you and he wants to be let alone.

But after a time he gets tired of himself and his opinions—deadly tired. He begins to think even the jelly-fish stage of life is preferable to the clam's. At least the former had a change once in a while, and he saw something of life. He wishes he were a child again—he means a jelly-fish.

But even a clam cannot grow backward. So he becomes a crawfish and goes sidewise. He evolves some ugly legs, shoulders his shell, and his opinions, and goes sidling forth to see the world again. Really, he is growing a glimmer of a principle to live by. He has built himself a shell which makes him impervious to most outside forces; he has grown tired of trying to enjoy himself; and he has actually made a start at *doing* something on his own account, uninfluenced by the without.

Good little crawfish! He is on a fair road to growing quite a backbone of his own. By and by, as exercise hardens his muscles and stiffens his backbone and limbers his little legs he will discard his ugly shell and walk out straight ahead, instead of craw fishing. He is growing a Principle to live by—the principle of self-expression. He is growing Wits as well as a backbone and well muscled legs, to take him out of harm's way and to enable him to gratify his own individual desires.

A man in the jelly-fish stage is sensitive on the outside. And he is so absorbed in these outer sensations that he is conscious of nothing *within* himself. His soul-center is as insensitive as his circumference is sensitive. He *has shrunk into* himself so persistently that he has deadened and dammed the power which is meant to *flow outward* from his soul-center. He is therefore utterly unconscious of the law or principle of his own being.

His solar plexus is a hard knot and he is so used to it that he does not know it. He has cringed and cowered and shrunk into himself until his solar center, his soul-center, is in danger of petrification. Life is a dull ache, and the harder the ache the tighter he shrinks inward.

Poor little man, he would better brace up and be a clam; or a crawfish; or better still, a *man* with a backbone that holds him up straight and leaves his solar center free to expand and fill him with vim and gumption to stand other men's buffets, and carve a path of his own out into the Free Country where he can do as he pleases. He would better consult his soul-center than his "feelings." He would better grow sensitive on the inside and give his thin skin a rest.

The principle of all being is to EXPRESS, to *press outward.* The jelly-fish, the clam and the crawfish of the human race press *inward* instead of outward. If one of them by any chance does happen to unbend and make a move to ex-press himself he is turned backward again by the first little show of an obstacle, or the adverse opinion of some other clam or crawfish. There is no *principle* in him—he is worked from without. He is attracted by this thing, and repelled by that, moved back and forth and in and out, galvanized or paralyzed, all from *outside.* And he throws out innumerable little antenna for sensing these outside influences. He is so absorbed in them that he has no consciousness left for the soul-center within himself, where his principle of being is trying to manifest. His *soul's* influence is the last influence he looks for or responds to.

Such a being is unhappy, unhealthy, unsuccessful; and he grows more so until he gets desperate and quits. Then he begins to withdraw consciousness from the outside and wake up on the inside. He begins to consult *himself* and *do* as *he desires.* Hitherto he has been so absorbed in *outside* things that he was unaware he *had* any desires on his own account. Now he begins to explore himself. He expands and grows sensitive on the inside. When he senses a little desire there he pushes out and *acts* upon it—even if he *does* run against a snag or two, or a dozen. He has got hold of one end of the principle of his own being and is acting upon it. Henceforth, his way is *straight ahead,* instead of crawfishy or clammy.

Now a strange thing begins to manifest. In the old days the man was always getting into somebody's way and getting hurt. He spent his time tacking and backing and scudding to keep from being hurt. But now that he has turned himself right side out and started *ahead,* he discovers everybody else hurrying to get out of *his* way, and even to *help him along.* Things seem to loom as obstacles, but lo, as he keeps *straight ahead* they melt away, and he goes onward.

In every man's soul is a course mapped out, a chart and compass for his guidance. If he consults *his own chart* and follows it he finds there are no collisions. His course is a true orbit, where all intruding matter is dissipated before it reaches him. His *atmosphere* burns it up, and renders it harmless. It is the crawfish who in his attempt to keep out of one orbit sidles into another and meets the comet's fate—disintegration and absorption.

This is a wonderful universe—a one-verse. There is an orbit for every being and a being for every orbit. *Every orbit is written on a heart,* a soul, and may be found only by consulting *that* soul.

Look up at the stars—just a conglomerate of bright spots. Surely if they moved a little there would be collisions. But look closer. They do move, at infinite pace, and there are no catastrophes. There is an order among them so perfect that it takes long study to appreciate it.

Now look at people—a conglomeration of wriggling worms of the dust. But look more closely, dear. It will repay you, for human orbits are no less true than starry ones. The closer you get to human *hearts* the better you will understand their orbits. The closer you get to *your own* heart the nearer you will approach the hearts of others.

The more faithfully you *follow* the orbit written on *your* heart the surer you are to escape disaster.

Grow sensitive on the soul-side, and know that your course is sure.

In *Harper's* for November there is an interesting and significant article by Carl Snyder, upon "The Newest Conceptions of Life." He says: "Physiology's present answer to the old riddle is, very simply: Life is a series of fermentations."

He also says there is a destructive ferment, and, likewise, a constructive ferment, conditions alone governing, "When starch, or dextrin, is submitted to fermentation by the malt enzyme, it is hydrolyzed—that is to say, split—by taking up water into one of the simpler sugars, glucose. *But if the resulting product is not removed,* the action soon comes to a standstill. Add more starch, it will begin again; but add to the quantity of sugar, and the reverse process is begun; the glucose is converted into starch. The enzyme, then, is able to rebuild the molecule it has pulled apart.

"For every vital function, a ferment."

"Naturally, the very first question is what are these ferments, these enzymes? *That is the biochemical problem of the hour.* Their activity seems bound up rather with the peculiarities of their atomic structure, of their chemical architecture, so to speak, than with any mystery of ingredients. They are compounded of the simple elements of water, air and carbon. *It is how these are put together that is so puzzling.*"

Then he goes on to say: "But this close pressing of the most intimate secrets of life has another implication of far more interest to men and women of today. It is, in brief, that perhaps all the processes of life are reversible—growth even; that under given conditions the oak might become an acorn, *the grown man a child,* the adult organism, led back through the successive stages of its development to the primitive germ from whence it sprang." And he gives a real illustration of the process of growing young again: "A plant-like little affair, Campanularia, living and developing normally in the water, undergoes an amazing transformation simply upon being brought into contact with some solid substance." Then he describes the process by which it returns again to its original state.

Life is a series of ferments which *may* be reversed. When we stir up a sponge for bread we put in a little yeast and a little flour for it to work upon. All night long the yeast particles are busy separating the solid wheat particles and filling them with yeast-life. In the morning the entire mass is beautifully "light."

Everywhere in creation life and light are synonymous terms. Even the "lightness" of bread sponge is its aliveness.

Now, what do you do with a light sponge? You use it to leaven a loaf. You stir it down, and stir in more flour, and knead and knead it until there is a big, solid loaf—within which is the germ of life. Again the yeast-life works, until the whole mass is "light" again—until all that wheat flour you *worked in* has been separated and made light or alive. Perhaps you repeat the process several times, before you finally *kill* your bread by baking it.

If you let your dough rise too long, you know what happens—it gets "too light"; the yeasty principle has nothing more to work upon; the loaf is now *all* yeast; it begins to get sour, and then bitter; it grows porous, gaseous; its surface becomes wrinkled and its once round, smooth cheek falls in; it shrivels; and in due time, if let alone, it will dry up and blow away.

Good, live dough is not the result of *a* fermentation, but of a *series* of fermentations, each arrested at the proper moment, and more flour added.

Human life is like unto it. The human being who works and works on one line becomes sour and wrinkled. In order to make good human beings they should be allowed to work on one line until they are full of *lightness,* of the joy of life. Then there should be kneading down and a new beginning.

Now, this is all in your mind. Fermentation is a *mental process.* The "ferments or enzymes" are the life or mind principles drawn, not from air or water or carbon, but *through* them. They are "spirit," love, *life.* The "wheat flour" consists in the *facts* which are worked into your mind, and *upon* which your soul-stuff works, digesting, assimilating it. The same identical process takes place in a loaf of bread that takes place in your mind. *All is life.* ALL IS MIND.

A little leaven leaveneth the whole lump, but the moment the whole lump is "light" there must be another working down.

If we do not know enough to work down our own minds Mother Nature does it for us. As soon as we get comfortably past the light point; as soon as we begin to *settle* and wrinkle and die; as soon as life grows monotonous; there is a jolting and a working over. We "lose" our property and our ease. We are detached from the sides of our environment and friends. We are buffeted and soundly thumped, and we find ourselves *set down* in new conditions to begin all over again. Good old Mother Nature has set us to *rise again.*

If we are really wise and willing we go at the task with a will and quickly rise. Having risen once we ought to know we can do it again, and do it *more quickly* than before. You know that is the way with our dough—every time we knead it down it comes up more easily.

Unless we are careless and put it in a *cold place,* it is a cold day when the bread won't rise. But it would be a cold day, indeed, when a human being *couldn't* rise. No matter how much he has been detached from, nor how much he has been worked down, he *can* rise if he will. That is the only difference between the loaf of bread and the man. The loaf of bread has to be raised in spite of itself—it has to be kept at just the right temperature *from the outside.* But a man has in himself the power to *make his own temperature.* He can *work himself* up to the rising point.

He can shut the door of his heart against the immanent Love and Will of the universe—shut in and *stay* down in the dark. He can *open* the door of his heart to Love, the "enzyme" of all life, which *creates its own warmth.*

The only reason a man does not open his heart to Love and Will, and begin straightway to rise again, is because he does not yet understand that the buffetings of "fate" are no more "against" him than are the kneadings of the housewife against the success of her bread.

Life must be a *series* of beginnings and workings-up. Eternal life must be an eternal series of workings-down and risings up. *A single day's* life must be a series of "fermentations."

Notice a child. See how readily he *enters into* every change. He is worked down and even sat on, many times a day, and yet he rises quickly and with joy. He never passes that *just-right* point of lightness where his cheek is round and his flesh moist—where he can be *readily* detached from his surroundings. He never shrivels and falls in and *cakes to the pan,* like his elders. He forgets, quickly, the working-down, and enters heart and soul into the business of rising NOW. He is so absorbed in *his* work, the *work of growing light,* that he heeds little the workings-down which are but for a moment.

Out of sight is out of mind. He *forgets* what others do to him. He LIVES Now—he rises.

The Center of Light

In ancient days the priests of the Hebrews wore upon their breast-plates over their hearts certain jewels called "Urim and Thummim," meaning "Lights and Perfection," by which they received answers from God. When their people were beset on every hand by enemies, and at their wits' end to know which way to turn, the priests turned to God. After purifying themselves and praying they asked God, "Shall we do thus?" and they watched the Urim and Thummim jewels for the answer; if the jewels appeared dark and opaque the answer was, No. But if they lighted up, as a human face lights when it hears good news, then the answer was, yes. And the people grew lighter too, and went and did as God had indicated.

Now, right along beside this story of ancient people I will tell you another—tell it just as 'twas told to me, by a woman of to-day, whose name you have doubtless heard. She writes: "I was washing my breakfast dishes one morning and the thought came to me that I would go and see a friend who lived several miles away. I finished my work and started to dress for my journey, when there came over me such a feeling of depression, or despondency, or gloom, that I was startled. I kept on getting ready, at the same time trying to reason away the feeling. But it would not go. Finally, having donned my hat and one glove I started for the door, when such a wave of heaviness came over me that

I went back into my room and sat down, and I said 'God, I want to know the meaning of all this.' And the answer came loud, strong, firm, *'Stay at home.'* I staid, and as I took off my coat and hat such a feeling of *lightness* and relief came over me that I seemed to walk on air. At the time I supposed the voice (I call it a voice for want of a more definite term) had told me to stay at home because someone was coming who needed my help. But no one came that day or night, and several times the thought flitted through my mind that perhaps it was all nonsense after all, and that I might as well have gone. Well, the outcome was that the train I would have taken, had I gone, met with a fearful accident wherein many were killed or badly wounded. This is only one of many such experiences I have had." And I could tell you still others on my own account.

The One Great Intelligence has built in *every human heart* a "Urim and Thummim," which, as a guide, transcends any human brain that ever existed, or ever will.

In fact, every *great* brain is the result of enlightenment from this very center. At one's wits' end there is infinite light, only waiting to be used. And if only one's inward eye is single toward this light *his whole wits* shall be full of light.

In olden times people were too dull and material to consult the Light until they had groped into all sorts of trouble in the dark. They supposed it necessary for man to get to his utmost extremity before the Light would shine upon his way. They nosed in the dust and darkness, believing that their natural source and habitat. Then in their hours of extreme need they washed off the dust and went in bare-footed to consult the center of Light upon the breastplate of rightness, over the heart of one consecrated to God.

And they never knew that *every* man in the multitude carried a center of light in his own breast—a center which only needed *washing off the dirt* and letting out the kinks in their nerves and muscles to reveal a center of Light in every breast in that multitude—centers so light and so true that the jewels on the High Priest's breastplate *cast only their composite shadow.*

"There is a light that lighteneth every man that cometh into the world." *And it is not the light* of *reason,* but the light that lighteneth reason.

It is not located at the center of anybody's breastplate, to be seen of every Tom, Dick and Harry who runs and reads. It is located *under* the center of his breastplate, at the solar center of his being. Here his center of Light shines out bright and clear when he is doing the right thing; and when he is doing the wrong, or unwise thing, the clouds of dull feeling roll over and darken his center of Light, and say *No* to him.

And if he goes heedlessly on acting against the admonitions of his center of Light, the clouds keep piling up, and his heart sinks down and down under the leaden weight and he rarely ever catches even a glimpse of his center of Light. He is "gloomy," we say. And he grows reckless and defiant and rushes on blindly to "a bad end."

He never understood himself. He never knew that the center of Light within him is his most precious possession, the star alone which could guide him into all good. So he hid it with clouds of doubt, and fear, and distrust—with clouds of *ignorance,* of NON-RECOGNITION. He "paid no attention" to it.

And so used was he to living in clouds of distrust that he never realized that there could *be a lighter heart* than his. He laughed loudly, and tossed off sparkling wine, and thought he was having a "good time."

Until the crash came, having obscured his center of Light, there was nothing but his brain to guide his actions. He made mistakes. Then came the crash and a standstill; and he found himself and his heavy heart and the dark clouds, and the bottom dropped out of everything.

But in the midst of despair he found the priceless jewel—the Urim and Thummim—his own center of Light. And behold, the crash was a Good Thing—the best business investment he ever made. He has through it realized the Way, the Truth, the Light of his own soul. Now, he will walk softly in the Light and there will come no more crashes.

I wonder if you think this is a fanciful bit of symbology. It is not. It is plain fact described in the plainest language I have at command.

You have a light at your center, in the region called the solar (or light) plexus. When you feel depressed you feel the effects of *literal* clouds, caused by doubt, distrust, fear, anger, resentment, grief, etc.

Back of those clouds shines the eternal Light, at your *center*— the light meant to guide *you and no other,* on *your* way.

Shall I tell you what to do? *Get still.* Quit running around after somebody to tell you what to do. Quit thinking around and around in an endless circle. Quit thinking at all. *Be still.* Keep whispering *"Peace"* to the troubled elements of your atmosphere.

After a bit the winds and waves of emotion will obey you and subside. The clouds will roll away and your center of Light will shine out in all its glory. *Then* you will know what to do.

When you are *still* then you can ask, "Shall I do thus?" and the lighting or the darkening of your heart will give you the correct answer.

The Law of Being

"God is Love."

God, or love, is the law of every being. By love every being was created; by love he is held together; by love he grows.

Through lack of love man is weak; through lack of love he is ignorant; through the waning of love he dies.

Love is the e-motive power of every being; the power which proceeds forth from the central sun of himself, giving life to his body and environment; just as the sun-power proceeds forth and gives life to the planets. As the sun is the source of life, light, power, in the planets, so is the soul-center the source of life, light, power, to the members of the human body.

Love is soul-radiance, the only power for accomplishment.

Love makes worlds go round; it keeps hearts throbbing and children growing.

Love is wisdom.

Love is will.

Wisdom and will are twined, like two strands in a cable,

Wisdom and will, twined in One, issue forth from the soul-center as rays from the sun.

The soul-center of being manifests as the "solar plexus" a great ganglion back of the stomach; from which nerves radiate to even the backwoods neighborhoods of the body. The solar plexus is the power house of the individuals. *God, or love, is the power.*

The brain is the central station where the individual sits and *controls* the power. He rings it off, or on, little or much, *with a single thought.* The individual at the brain controls the power house and all its workings, *in a general way,* just as Uncle Sam at Washington controls in a general way the power of the United States.

But the individual's brain is not the only brain he has, any more than Washington is the only directing center Uncle Sam has. Every city, little or big, is a directing center; it draws its own appropriation of power and uses it as it pleases—within *its limits*—*which* are set by the intelligence at Washington.

Every ganglion in the body is a little brain which governs in a measure the use of its own appropriation of power from the soul-center, the solar-plexus; *but always with the consent of the central intelligence,* the brain—the Washington, D. C., of the body.

Money represents power, the will-strand of love. Whenever a city needs more money than it can draw by its own wisdom, it calls on Washington to send a special appropriation. Washington may pass a law enabling the needy city, or state, to draw more money; or it may appropriate the amount direct from the government source; or, when these processes are too red-tapey, it might make a general call to all hands to dispense with routine and send the money anyhow. This was what happened when Roosevelt called for help for the Mt. Pele refugees. Money was poured in from all directions, instead of being sent through regular channels.

Whenever one of the lesser brains of the body, one of the ganglia, records a condition of *want* among its cells it tries to draw power to overcome the difficulty. If it cannot do this on its own account it sets up a cry that is heard at the central station of consciousness and government—the brain. When that cry comes we say we feel *pain* in the region of that particular ganglion. If we give our stomach more than it can do we hear a loud call for *power*—*we* feel a dull or painful sensation there.

When that call comes it draws *special attention* from the seat of general government—the brain.

Now, if the individual whose seat of government is in that brain happens to be wise enough and "strenuous" enough, he will do just what Roosevelt did; he will call for POWER from any and all directions, to relieve the want of power in the stomach. And he will call in perfect faith that the demands will be met with an overflowing abundance.

This is the method of self-healing.

Of course, if the individual whose seat of government is in that brain happens to be a weakling fraidie-cat, he will do nothing but groan over the conditions in his stomach; he will lament and ache with it, instead of bracing up and demanding power to change those conditions.

Wherever the individual's ATTENTION goes his *power* goes too. All the individual needs to do is to say the word for his power to pitch in and make things straight. Until he does that his power stands around and *waits,* just as all the pocketbooks in the United States just waited until Roosevelt pulled himself together and called resolutely for *money.* That call set up an electric *thrill* which ran through all the little pocketbooks and set them to pouring out the help called for.

When the individual takes that same positive, resolute, commanding and *full-of-faith* attitude, he may ask what he will and it shall be done unto him. He may say the word which will send through his body an electric thrill of health, with a concentration of power in any desired spot.

He may open up every one of those ganglionic centers of power and send their surplus of energy to any given point, for any given purpose. In his own domain he may arise greater than Roosevelt.

Every ganglion in the body is a storage battery of *both wisdom and will,* drawn originally through the central battery of the solar plexus.

The solar plexus draws its power from the Great Unseen. The intangible becomes tangible at the solar center; the hitherto undirected power of space and eternity here *begins* to be directed; the uncontrolled here comes under control; the unexpressed begins here to ex-press.

You can readily see that great power depends primarily upon a free solar plexus. *Great* power can never be expressed under a tight corset, which binds and packs the solar plexus.

Great power, of mind or body, can never be expressed under either a binding corset or binding *thoughts.*

Fear thoughts are the only binding thoughts there are. Every little fear gives a pucker to the solar plexus, and shuts out just that much power. A starved and distressed body is the direct result of shutting off the solar radiance by fear thoughts—or cinches.

Get rid of fear as fast as you can, and your expanding solar plexus will burst every band, mental or physical.

The first step toward getting rid of fear is to know that your source of power and wisdom is the same great and limitless source from which all men must draw; and that your point of contact with this boundless supply is *within* you, not on the *outside* of you. When you remember this you are not scared by the *outside* appearance of anything or any-body. You do not look to money or a "pull" for power to accomplish; you are not afraid the money or "pull" of another will be stronger than *your* pull on the infinite source of all things. You know that *his* money and pull came by way of his own private *pull on the universal,* and instead of growing scared and kicking and threshing around in a des-perate attempt to grab some of the results of *his* pull, you just quietly get down to business and your *own* pull on the universal.

When you look at the *results* of other people's pulls on the infinite source, comparing them with your own, you are sure to grow discour-aged, or desperate and fearful. One reason is that you belittle your own results; another is that you *cannot see what the other man* FAILED *to get.* You see the results of his *successful* pulls on the infinite, but you compare them with your own *unsuccessful* attempts, instead of compar-ing with your successes. You are unfair to yourself, and you exaggerate what he has accomplished.

Desire governs what one draws from the uncreated. Your desire and his were not alike; so his outward appearances will not stand judgment from *your* standpoint.

Let him alone and find yourself. You are unique. You cannot be compared with anything under heaven. Your pull on the infinite is infinite. But *it's different.* Tend to it strictly, and see what the results are. Quit looking at the other fellow and generating fear thoughts—fear that he will get ahead of you. Look at your own ideals and desires, and rejoice in your own pull on the universal.

When you remember your source, and your different-ness, you are not afraid. When you go about *your own* work in your own way you rejoice in it all, and your solar plexus expands and power flows in and radiates to every corner of your body and on out to the outermost edge of your atmosphere; and away beyond-who knows how far beyond? Ah, then you *enjoy* what you do; you enjoy *yourself;* you LOVE; you are radiating love; and love, you know, is *God,* the only power and the only wisdom. And the chief end *of you is to enjoy God, or love, forever.*

How It Works

Quit looking at *things* and being afraid.

Look to your ideals and desires, and remember your source and infinite supply. Keep dwelling mentally on your infinite supply; keep *using* that supply according to your ideals. Fears will drop away from you and power and wisdom, Love, *God,* will flow into you and through you.

Never admit a fear. Bid it get behind you. Never admit a "can't.' Pull yourself together and declare "I can—I WILL."

Fear makes you *feel* paralyzed. *Ignore it.* Rise up and ACT, and you will see how little power the fear really had. Fear is but a paltry stage-trick hypnotist. *You* cannot be hypnotized if you *refuse to look at fear.* ACT and fear flees into the bottomless pit whence it came—into nothingness.

Keep on acting as if you felt no fear. In due time the feeling of fear, the hypnotized sense, will disappear for good. You will smile, and your solar center will expand and let in more *God-feeling*, more power and wisdom, than you have ever had before.

Sometimes you may be too badly paralyzed to act as if you had no fear. Well, then, just *breathe*. You are never too paralyzed to go out of doors, or to an open window, and *breathe*.

Right breathing will dissipate fear. By using the chest and abdominal muscles properly you can shake the kinks out of that paralyzed solar plexus and *let in power*. An influx of power from the Infinite will enable you to turn your back on fear and act as you *desire* to act.

When you are anxious and afraid your breath comes in short shallow gasps and you can literally *feel* fear clutching your—"heart," you call it. You feel fear clutch your solar plexus. Now, take a slow, full breath, clear down to the bottom of your lungs, and clear *out* as far as the walls of your chest will go; hold the breath as long as you can without straining; and then see how very slowly you can exhale. Keep your lips firmly closed all the time, but do not press the teeth together; and see you stand *straight*, chest *out*, hips *back*, head up, with crown high and chin in.

Ah, now—after even *one* such breath you feel decidedly less paralyzed. Your solar plexus is not in quite so hard a knot, and there is a brighter look in your face. A good beginning. Now take another such breath, and yet another. Take a dozen of them. *Now*, you will find yourself decidedly less paralyzed. You can go out and ACT now, as if you never had a fear. Of course, your teeth may chatter a bit, and you may feel a trifle weak in the knees, but the hypnotic spell is broken, *power is* pouring into you from the Infinite, and you can ACT. Go right along and *do* it. Keep on breathing deeply and telling yourself that you *can* and you WILL.

And you will succeed. And next time it will be much easier to do.

After practice it will grow so easy that you will forget you ever had that paralyzed, hypnotized feeling, of being *afraid* to do what you desire to do. You will have taught your solar plexus to *stay open* and *let in* power, instead of collapsing just at the critical moment when you needed extra power.

Then there are other ways of taking the kinks out of your solar plexus and letting in the power. Any sort of physical shaking accompanied by "I *can* and I WILL" statements will help; especially if the shakings are repeated rhythmically a few times.

Take a good, full breath and stamp your foot and say "I *can.*" Then take another full breath, stamp your foot again and say "I WILL." Repeat several times.

Many a time I have freed the kinks this way after everything else seemed not to no avail. When I used to suffer horribly from blues and discouragement I used to go away up in the big garret, where none could hear me, and rage up and down its length a time or two, and stamp my foot sharply and declare aloud to myself, "I'm *not* blue— I'm NOT—I am HAPPY; I AM happy—I AM; everything is just as it *ought* to be, and I LIKE it so—I *do*—I DO—I'm HAPPY, I tell you—I AM !" And I'd stamp it down hard. And this little exercise never failed to help relieve me from that horrible burden at my "heart"—at the solar plexus. I have "concentrated" and "affirmed" by the hour, all to no effect apparently; but five minutes of this sort of shaking up always freed me, and I went about my work feeling as if I had thrown off a nightmare and found the sunshine. Try it.

Then, there is another way, suggested to me by Dr. Paul Edwards. He said whenever he is in need of refreshing, as after a long day's work, he goes away and shakes himself up for ten minutes or so. He stands up and gets as loose and limp as possible, all over; and then shakes himself just as a big dog does when it comes out of the water. He calls it taking physical exercise with relaxed muscles.

Prolonged effort reduces the power faster than it can, under ordinary conditions, flow through the solar plexus. All the nerves get into a partly collapsed condition, as if the energy had been *sucked* out of them, leaving them dry and *flabby.* All the little muscles which encase the nerves are contracted. This keeps the Infinite from flowing in again. So Dr. Edwards' idea is scientific. He relaxes from head to foot and literally shakes the kinks out; and immediately he is filled again with power from the Infinite reservoir.

All sorts of depressed feelings come from this depleted condition of nerves; and anything which will loosen up the muscular contraction will remedy the condition. Sometimes a single thought will be *dynamic* enough to do it. Sometimes a single hour or so of right thinking will do it. If one can be perfectly still, body and *mind*, for even five minutes, the desired end will be accomplished. But it takes an adept, made adept by years of practice, to attain *quickly* the state of mental and physical stillness necessary to quick recuperation from states of depression. It takes a real master to speak peace to himself in such a way that he is *quickly* obeyed.

And the master attains mastery by a long series of just such little exercises as those I have just given you. All these little "physical" drills get your body into the habit of minding your mental commands. After you have used them long enough your body will obey the mental commands alone.

"I can" and "I will" are words of power. Say them softly to yourself—say "I will" and note the *freedom* with which the sound leaves your lips and throat, *which are never closed on the word.* The sound pours freely forth to vibrate the ethers. Now say "can't" and note the effect; the *t* sound can only be made by inhibiting the vowel sound—by *cutting off* the flow of sound. The use of these words *has the same effect on the solar plexus*—the will-words allow a free flow of soul-power; whilst the can't words *shut off* your soul-power. Will-words *open the solar plexus* to radiate power to all your being; whilst can't-words check the flow of power—just as your tongue checks the a-sound with the tight *t.*

Say "will" with a *will,* and you can actually *feel* power radiate through your entire body; that is, if you say it *freely;* but if you say it *behind gritted teeth* it has nearly the same effect as the t-sound. The clenched teeth *mean a clenched solar plexus, and an inhibition of soul-power.* Muscular tension of any sort inhibits for the time being the free flow of soul-power; whether the tension come from clenched teeth or from a tongue clenched in the t-sound.

Speak to yourself the words which open up your soul-flow; the *can* and *will* and *love* and *joy* words.

Use these words with all sorts of bodily exercises for shaking out the muscular kinks. These are the words and exercises which make for life, health, happiness and success.

All desirable things are the result of *letting out* the soul power which eternally presses *for expression through you.*

Good Circulation

Do you know that a plant will not grow without leaves? And it will not bear fruit, and will die early, if it has too many leaves? The plant suckles moisture from the earth and *the sun* draws that moisture away again, through the tiny and innumerable pores of its leaves. So the healthy existence of a plant depends upon the *living stream* of moisture which must continually flow *through* the plant. Simply to flow *into* it is not enough; and when the stem is severed we quickly see the results of too much flowing *out,* with nothing flowing in. Death is the inevitable result of any continued disturbance of that steady *flow* of sap up from the earth, *through* the plant, and on out again into the atmosphere.

Of course, a sterile earth can give little sap to the plant and it soon dies; and the more fervently the sun kisses it and draws upon it the more quickly the plant expires. On the other hand, if the leaves are plucked, so that there are not pores enough for the sun to suck the sap through, the plant must die.

But plants are wonderfully intelligent little things, and full of ingenious contrivances for *regulating* supply and demand in such a way as to maintain the equilibrium which means health. The little wild things are wiser than we tame beings, in looking out well for number one. The cactus grows thick, fleshy leaves where it stores up moisture for use in the long, hot seasons when supply is small and demand great. And it glazes its leaves so that the sun cannot draw from it all the moisture it would. Many plants and trees glaze the entire upper sides of their leaves, so that the sun may draw from the shaded side only, where he cannot kiss so fervently. Some trees turn only the edges of their leaves toward the sun. And a great many refuse to grow wide leaves, and the drier the soil the narrower the leaves, even in trees of the same family. All plants show this intelligence.

We human beings are built by the same Intelligence and after the same manner as plants. Our healthy and continued existence depends upon the same law. We, too, draw our sustenance from the earth and give it all off again through our pores and lungs. To glaze our skin pores would kill us. To shut off our breath would kill us. In either case our *giving off* would be curtailed beyond our limit of endurance. And, of course, to cut ourselves entirely loose from earth (at present)—to cut off our supply of food and water, would end our existence. So we try to maintain a *poise* of receiving and giving, to the end that we keep on living. Eternal life depends upon eternal poise of receiving and giving. It depends upon our ability to LET *life flow through us,* unimpeded and freely. This is the law of being.

Law is omnipresent. Not a crack nor cranny in all the universe, in all time and space, which is not *filled* with Law. No place so tiny that the Law is crowded out. No place so large that the Law is dissipated into nothingness. Law is the all-pervading "fourth dimension" of matter, as well as of spirit.

Two and two make four. This is Law. It works just the same whether it expresses through worlds or atoms or through ideas only. Two worlds and two worlds are four worlds; two ideas and two ideas are four ideas.

The law of *perpetual flow* is the law of continued existence of any form, whether it be "physical," "mental" or "spiritual."

A physical body which refuses to give off as much as it receives quickly dies; if it persists in giving off *more* than it receives it quickly dissipates itself. A mind which refuses to receive as much as it gives soon grows weak; if it refuses to give it stagnates and decays.

Do you see that the law of life is *a good circulation?* And that it works in body, mind, *and money?* A plant draws its stream of life from the earth. Man has loosed himself from the earth and is learning to depend less and less upon it as his source of supply. He is learning to live not by bread alone, but *by the word.* He is drawing his supply more and more fully and consciously from the *unseen.*

But this does not free him from the law of good circulation. Plants receive carbon dioxide and give off oxygen. Man receives oxygen and gives off carbon dioxide. Plants receive from the coarser and more tangible forms of 'matter" and give it out again in finer essence. Man does the same.

But man has likewise thrown out roots in the Great Unseen, through which he receives an ever increasing portion of his sustenance, which is brought down and given out in coarser form to earth and plant. Man's veins and arteries carry the transmutations of earth matter, which he invisibly gives out; while his nerves *reverse* the order, and throb with wisdom and love, which come down from "spirit" into "matter" and are given off in coarse and concrete form.

Just as man must receive food and give out to the atmosphere, so he must receive from the spiritual atmosphere and give downward to earth. He must *express* wisdom and love, inspired from above earth; express it in terms of earth. Thus it is true that

"The worlds in which we live are two,
The world I AM and the world I do."

Human and divine life are One, and the individual continues to exist as long as there is *good circulation between the ideal and the real.*

Some time in past ages man's feet were simple roots, fast to earth. He learned by centuries of effort to pick his roots out of the ground and walk off on them—in search of more food. This is a great advantage to him. But if he should now go up in a balloon and stay there for some days, breaking *all* connections with earth, he would melt into thin air.

In childhood the imagination is firmly rooted in the ideal world, and his feet are at the same time firmly set upon the earth. So he grows fast, mentally and physically, and increases in wisdom, love and power.

But by and by he begins to detach himself from the *ideal.* He detaches one rootlet after another and all the other earth folks pat him on the back and congratulate him because he is "growing up" and becoming "sensible." So he goes on detaching himself from the world of spirit, whilst he plants himself more firmly in earth. By and by he is altogether detached from heaven. He scoffs at such silly, childish visions of glory. He has got both feet loose from the ideal.

About this time he reminds me of Pat's horse, which up and died just as Pat had got him well trained to live on sawdust.

Man dies for no reason except that he educates himself to live on earth instead of in heaven, with babes and idealistic fools.

Of course, every man has a right to make his choice of associates and places. But by and by, we are all going to be wise enough to choose childhood and a good circulation.

Low Living

Just as blood circulates in the arteries and veins, carrying material food to every portion of body and brain, so *thought force* circulates in the nerves, carrying *spiritual fire* for the transmutation of matter into *higher forms*.

All disease is due to the clogging either of nerves or veins, or both. The eating of rich food in greater quantities than can be assimilated and eliminated produces thick, sluggish blood, which tends to deposit sediment at every twist and turn of veins and arteries, thus choking the flow. When a stream gets into this condition navigation has to be abandoned until the stream is dredged out again. When the human body is so choked and clogged with stagnant matter inflammation, fermentation, sets in, a "sick spell" occurs and the doctor administers a cathartic to excite the secretions and dredge out the festering debris. Then the patient "feels better" and free circulation is once more established.

Of course it is not easy to know just how to regulate the supply of rich food so that the circulation shall not become clogged; at least it is not easy whilst we cling to the habit of eating three or four square meals a day, whether we feel hungry or not; and whilst we tempt appetite with all manner of highly seasoned dishes.

Wild animals have to hunt for their food, which consists of but one thing at a meal. They work for all they get. Unless hungry they do not hunt. No one calls a catamount or an eagle to highly seasoned feasts at regular intervals. Catamount or eagle eats *when he is hungry.* And before eating he has to wake up and work for his dinner. This induces full breathing and sets his blood to racing at such a rate that it clears the track and leaves room and power enough to take care of the new meal. No sluggish circulation in wild animals and no disease.

Here is a hint for man. Of course if you are never sick or depressed; if you are strong and well, and growing stronger, you may need no hints. But if you are not all that you desire to be just try a little judicious starving, along with plenty of exercise and fresh air. Live on plain foods, principally fruits and nuts, and skip a meal now and then, or even half a dozen meals, until you get down through that veneer of cultivated appetite—down to real *hunger,* of the sort that impels a catamount to travel for miles and wait patiently for hours to find that for which he hungers.

Hunger is an infallible guide as to *what* to eat, and how often. It is the real voice which comes up from arteries cleansed and *ready* to carry fresh supply to waiting body.

But appetite is the whining call of an *unrested* stomach and unready arteries, which have been *taught* to cry at stated intervals.

Most of us are the slaves of spoiled appetite; but we have never once in our stuffed lives since childhood been really hungry and known the real joy of eating.

Clogging of the arteries and veins results in clogging of the brain and nerves. It is impossible for a man with a clogged and diseased body to think his best. The clogging presses against nerves as well as arteries and prevents free circulation of thought.

And only *free* thought is high thought.

A man with a clogged system will think cramped, negative thoughts. He can't help it. His nerves are cramped. His doctor may say he is "nervous," but "nervousness" and "weak nerves" are simply cramped nerves—cramped in a clogged system.

Now I know that it is quite possible to take the kinks out of one's nerves by mind power alone—provided one is not too badly clogged and cramped. *But high living will eventually choke off high thinking,* and

NO human being can reach his highest thinking along with high living. Reason and *all human experience* proves this.

And I leave it to you if it is not vastly more sensible to reduce your living and thus free your cramped nerves to the free flow of high thought than to attempt to live high and *force* high thought through "weak nerves." The only bit of you which may refuse to agree with this statement of the case is *your spoiled appetite.* Are you going to pamper that and starve your high thought? It is for you to decide.

But now let us suppose that with your whole being you *will* serve the God of High Thinking. You are going to practice low living that you may more fully serve the God of High Thinking. You are fasting your body into an unclogged state. You are feeding it upon simple foods, such as nuts and fruits, which are not thickening to the blood, as are meat, condiments and pastries. You are exercising freely and taking deep, full, outdoor breathing exercises to promote good circulation of blood and free the nerves. You are doing all this, and you are rejoicing in the glorious feeling of health and courage and freedom which comes to you. You are bright, alert, ready, with "a heart for any fate."

But you want yet higher thinking. Good! Your nerves are free now, and *ready to receive higher thought than any they have ever carried.*

Now fill them with *"incessant affirmatives"* of your HIGHEST IDEALS. "Go into the silence" and see how *still* you can be, mentally and physically. Simply *rest* until Spirit can *form within you the mental picture of what you are to work for.* Keep being still, and waiting expectantly, until "it comes to you" just what to do.

To that clean body and brain of yours it will come quickly and with joy.

Keep free in body, and keep looking mentally for new things to "come to you," and the way will grow brighter and brighter. *You* will grow brighter and brighter and brighter. And whatsoever things you desire you shall have.

Say "I *can* and I *will.*" It will fill you with power.

Above all things, say *"I AM what I desire to be."* It is true. You have made conscious connection with The Infinite.

The Limitless Self

"Who are you?"

"Who? Me? *Who am I?* Why, I am the man who was five times elected the mayor of Podunk. That's who I am."

"And who are you?" I asked a rather ragged looking woman.

"Oh, I am the wash-lady," she answers.

"I am a sales-girl in the big department store across the street," says another.

I asked a little child, "Who are you?" and it answered, "Who am *I?* Why, why, I'm just *me.* "

"Well, but what *is* me?" And he looks puzzled, and up and down, and gives it up. But he is sure he is *me* and nobody else.

The five-times elected man has crystallized into a mayor; the woman who does washing has crystallized as a washing machine; the sales-girl has settled into a mere part of the great selling-machine across the street.

Only the child knows that *me* is *undefined,* undefinable, unconfined, limitless. But he doesn't *know* that he knows it. Consequently as he grows up he becomes so interested in what he *has done* that he thinks it is *himself.* He has grown legs and arms, a teacupful of brains, a little knowledge and a reputation, and when you ask him who he is, he thinks of himself as a mixture of legs, arms, brains, doings and reputation. He is *limited* in his own estimation by what he has done. He remembers it all. Every time he says "I" he sees a panorama of things he has done, or has failed to do. He is little or great, a failure or a success, according to his depreciation or appreciation of what he has done.

The child has forgotten his past. When he says "I" he defines nothing. He sees simply a rosy nebulous mist 'out of which worlds and other wonders may be formed. There is to him nothing formed and fixed. He is a glorious and untrammeled Reality and all things are possible. He is full of the joy of power and prospect.

"Of such is the kingdom of heaven," and "except you become as a little child" you shall remain forever imprisoned by *what you have done and left undone.* This kind of prison is hell, where one grows *not* "in wisdom and in knowledge," but in *hate*—hate for himself and his "life." And his prison walls keep pressing in and in, and by and by they are simply the walls of a coffin.

And it is all so needless. One only needs to *forget,* to be again a child in the rosy mist of glorious possibilities.

Forgetting is so easy, too. It is only a matter of displacing one picture with another, just as one paints a new picture right over the old one on a canvas. As the new one appears the old one vanishes.

Ah, it is *easier* than that. Memory is just the original stereopticon show, where the old picture fades as the new appears. Change the slide and presto the old has vanished from view. Keep on slipping in new slides and by and by the old one will find its way into the ash barrel and the ash barrel will be dumped into the bottomless pit of oblivion. Oh, it is *easy* to forget by *putting in new slides.*

It is our memories which limit us. If we didn't die once in a while and forget, we would surely curl up into something too insignificant to mention. As long as we persist in piling up our doings and misdoings in a great burden of memories we shall continue to be borne down by them to earth and the grave.

As long as we clutter up "memory's walls" with back-number pictures of ourselves and our powers we shall need to call in Death, the Junk Man, to renovate for us.

But we are learning—by and by we will get waked up to the desirability of keeping "memory's walls" *freshly* decorated with *new* and tip-to-date conceptions. This thing of hanging on to old things simply because they are old is not only silly but it is death-dealing.

Our mental pictures are the source of our inspiration and power, or of our *lack* of inspiration and power, all according to the style of pictures we entertain. There is no power or inspiration or wisdom to be got out of things that are past. He who dwells upon fleeting *things* runs on with the water after it has passed the mill-wheel—on and on down the stream and out into the ocean, accomplishing nothing. The wise man stays by the mill and *looks for more water* to turn his wheel.

If water fails he conjures steam or electricity—always something new. Always he looks *ahead,* not behind, for his power.

Why don't we do that? When all things are failing us why do we think of the time when we *used* to have water to turn our wheel? Why do we look down stream at the water that is past? What *good* will that water do us *now?* And does not the thinking of it simply fill us with despair and paralyze effort and common sense? Of course.

There is plenty more power where that flying water came from. Look up stream, not down; and be ready.

Your mental pictures are your ONLY source of power and wisdom. Your continued growth in wisdom and power depends upon your development as a mental artist. And *that* depends wholly upon quiet, wide-awake *persistence.*

Have you held beautiful mental pictures and worked faithfully to put them on life's canvas? And did you fail? Well, what of it? There is *more* canvas ready. You have learned by your mistakes. Now *wipe off everything* and take a NEW mental picture. Get away from the old one. Begin as if this were your very *first* attempt in all the world.

Relax your physical efforts for a time. Get limp all over and *let* a new mental picture form. It will be a better work of art than *the last* one—it will be nearer true to principle. We learn to make true mental pictures by making them. We learn by everyone we make, even though the picture itself is smashed.

And by and by we learn to make such mental pictures as can be worked out without a mistake.

Success lies all in *keeping at it.* Faith and work will accomplish *anything you can picture mentally.*

When you cannot work a thing out just as you picture it, it is because you have not *looked carefully enough at your picture.*

If an artist keeps his eyes too steadily fixed upon the canvas where he is working out his picture he never makes a good picture. *He looks at his model,* looks long and with joy. As he looks he sees something new. Then quickly, lightly, with as few motions as possible he reproduces what he saw *in the model.* If he is not satisfied with his reproduction he *looks at his model again*, and keeps looking until it comes to him, just how to get the effect he is after. Then a few more quick, light strokes and success is his. This is what the *wise* artist does. The foolish one *keeps looking at the canvas*, to see where the mistake lies; his eye is filled by his imperfect work. The wise artist fills his eye with the *perfect model*. The unwise artist, seeing only mistakes, is discouraged and incapacitated; while the wise artist *feasts upon the perfections of his model*, and is inspired to try, try again until he hits it *just* right.

Ideals

You and I are artists. But we are prone to look too long and often at our canvas—the results of our efforts; and too little at our Ideals, which are the sources of all effort and power of accomplishment.

Let us take special times every day for gazing upon our models—our Ideals. The first thing in the morning and the last thing at night should be daily given to special gazing upon *what* we *desire*. Then many times a day we should pause in *our efforts,* for a few moments' study of the Ideal.

Choose for these sittings the same hour, the same place, and even the same chair facing the same way. Let the chair be an easy one, but with a straight back.

Keep your appointments with your Ideal to the minute as nearly as possible. But if at any time you are unavoidably hindered take the earliest moment possible.

And remember always that the matter of *first* importance is to *keep sweet.* To let a change upset you simply necessitates extra time and effort to get settled again.

Sit bolt upright, resting against the back of your chair and in an easy position. Keep absolutely still, with eyes *resting* (not *fixed)* always on the same spot, straight ahead and slightly above the level. Do not get into a *rigid* state, but see that you *are still.* Aim not to move once during the entire sitting, which should be about half an hour long. Perhaps less to begin with.

Now having disposed of your body rise mentally to the highest heights you can picture. For instance, take your highest business ideals; picture it in rosy colors and *definite* outline. *Stretch* it. Make your ideal just as large and fine as possible.

Picture out the details as plainly as possible. Make it definite. *Decide* just what you mean to work for and to realize. Let us suppose that you are a married man with a family of small children whom you wish to educate. You don't want just barely enough to send them to college on, leaving yourself a broken down and poverty stricken slave in the end. Neither do you want to remain a hack worker in a mean position and have somebody die and *give* you money to school your children with—whilst you keep on doing hack work. You want to be a MAN, so valuable to the world that you can *command* plenty of money as your RIGHT. You want to GROW in wisdom and knowledge until a more remunerative work will call you and be *glad* to pay for you. You want, say $5,000 a year, to come *easily* to you as a result of your own good and *enjoyed* effort. Then you can hold your head up and enjoy looking any man in the *eyes—kindly,* as a brother and equal. Then you will enjoy *sitting straight* and being still and happy.

Keep filling in the details of your Ideal and get just as *enthused* over it as you possibly can. But keep your muscles relaxed. Rise above the body and revel in your Ideal.

There is a reason for this;—when muscles are relaxed they are in condition to be filled with power *from the Ideal held.* Tensed muscles keep out the mental energy. Mind is positive to muscle, and *relaxed* muscles are receptive to mental power. So loose the body and get enthused over the Ideal. Let your mental picture wake as much emotion as possible; for emotion is real creative force, and *creates after the pattern held in mind.* If you hold a fearful picture in mind *emotion* creates it. Job said "I feared a great fear and it came upon me." If you hold a beautiful picture emotion creates that. Fear and joy, and all intermediate shades of feeling, are *the same force—the* soul-force out of which all creation is made.

So I tell you to do your best to get enthused and exalted over your

Ideal. Keep telling yourself that your Ideal is *you*, and that in due time you will prove it in terms of matter. If it is not *you* what is it? Your Ideal exists *within* you, does it not? And therefore it *must* be you. And your poverty, or your work, or your "conditions," exist *outside* of you, do they not? Then they are *not* you. What exists within is *you*.

Of course your "conditions" have their mental pictures within you too—*pictures which preceded the conditions themselves.* In past years, perhaps in past ages, you have held with emotion the mental pictures of these very conditions, hence their creation. But these pictures have grown old, as people grow old, and are ready to be laid away and dissolved in ashes. Every single day and hour you are dwelling with emotion upon more mental pictures which are to take their place, both inside of you and out. So, I bid you take special hours for holding with enthusiasm the sort of pictures you *want* to create; instead of letting your mind perpetuate the same old things over again. And I bid you put into this Ideal picturing all the emotion you can summon, to the end that you the more quickly and vitally, create what you want.

Of course this is not at first easy to do. Conditions will come in between you and your Ideal—conditions which arouse fear; which is emotion, remember—your creative energy. Your emotion has habitually gone out to conditions, recreating them. And when you picture your Ideal it seems cold, dead and unreal.

But here is another place where practice makes perfect. Repeated efforts will soon switch emotion into new channels, permitting the old mental pictures to shrivel. And conditions will follow.

And the more regular the efforts the more quickly will energy acquire the *habit* of flowing in the new directions. There is enormous power in rhythm of effort. One soon gets into the swing of a new thought and it fairly does itself. By rhythmic effort one soon creates through the Ideal a heart-throb. The Ideal passes the period of gestation and comes forth into the actual.

Make light of the actual. Do not permit it to play upon your emotions. But exalt the Ideal. Glorify it. Accord it all power. Rejoice in it and give it your most loving thought. Return to it at regular intervals, and always enthuse over it—to yourself.

As to other people, keep mum. Many a man's Ideal is still born because he wastes his energy in talk; and because he draws to himself the opposition or contempt of others. *Be still;* make no noise, except when there is something to be gained by it. Noises of all sorts use up your mental energy. In stillness power is generated. Be still.

After a few days of faithful practice at gazing upon your Ideal you will find your whole life changing. You will find yourself with more heart for your work, and things will seem easier to do. Depressions will grow less frequent and less profound, and in time they will entirely cease, and you will find new ideas coming to you about *how* to do your work. Then your interest in it will increase and you will begin to know the joy of the successful artist.

When you arrive at this stage you will wake some morning to find yourself making more money and you will find yourself with a little real faith, or conviction, that in due time your Ideal will become real. After that all is easy—our Ideal will *live you,* instead of having to be carefully nurtured at stated intervals.

Between the times when you gaze specially upon your Ideal it is well to forget it as fully as possible Put your best thought into your work. But never neglect your stated seasons with your Ideal.

All life is growth, and a live Ideal is no exception. *Let* it grow. Stretch your imagination to take in all you can. When you find yourself approaching the $5,000-a-year mark you have set for yourself you will find yourself wanting $10,000. Now don't accuse yourself of never being satisfied. Just rejoice in this evidence of spiritual growth, enlarge your operations and go in to win on a larger scale.

When you have got your children well educated don't stagnate. Look within and find another Ideal to work for.

Your Ideals are God-given for use. Look eagerly upon them and know that they are Life.

You do not make your Ideals; they make you—if you keep mentally in touch with them.

ELIZABETH TOWNE

"I Can and I Will"

The effectiveness of "I can and I will", as a statement to live by depends upon the manner in which you say it.

To say "I can and I will" through gritted teeth and with clenched fists is to defeat the very object you aim for. To assume a prize-fighter attitude toward life is to invite a licking. And yet it will not do to say "I can and I will" in a limp, half-hearted fashion.

The right manner, which means the effective manner, of uttering this potent phrase depends upon a correct knowledge of the meaning of "I." "I can and I will" may be the truth or a lie, just according as you define "I."

For instance, a foolish man who happened to be mayor of Minneapolis said to himself, "I can and I will make a lot of money for myself out of the criminals of this city." There were others who said the same thing. That mayor reckoned the "I" simply as so much personal cuteness pitted against the city. He gritted his teeth and pulled in all the money in sight. He pitted himself *against* the city, which rose up and placed him behind prison bars. He may still be gritting his teeth and saying, "I can and I will get out of here." He may be able to get out of those particular prison walls, but all the world will be to him a prison. He will have to skulk and hide—he is not *free*. The money he took was never his and he knew it. And he could not keep it, though he said mightily "I *can* and I WILL."

You see, "I" to that mayor meant a small something bounded by a skin, a suit of clothes, a hat and a pair of shoes. The rest of the city, and the world, and the universe at large, seen and unseen, had no part in the "I" he placed before "can and will."

The undefeatable "I" has no such puny boundaries. It fills all space and expresses through all personalities. It is ONE and never goes back on itself. Sooner or later—generally sooner—it punishes fully every puny rebel who rises against it.

In other words, a man must consider *all creation and uncreation* when he says "I." If he fails to do this his success is but a transitory imitation and his down-fall sure, as in the case of Minneapolis boodlers (19th c., one displaying unsportsmanlike behavior).

It is a foolish and short-sighted business policy which ignores the Golden Rule. To do unto others that which you would not like done unto yourself is to bite off your nose in order to leave more blood for the rest of your face.

All life is One, and the good of all is the good of each one; the hurt of one is the injury of all.

When a man realizes this his personal "I" has expanded and merged in the "I" of omnipresence, omniscience and omnipotence which really *"can* and WILL" do things. He has found the Sublime Self which cannot be denied. Instead of gritting his teeth and driving ahead *against* the will of the Whole he identifies himself *with* the Whole. He works with All, and All with him the entire universe backs him.

Clench your hands and say "I can and I *will"* several times in succession through closed teeth. Note how you force all the breath out of your lungs as you repeat it, and how exhausted you feel by the effort. Why? Because you shut yourself off from the source of breath and will-power. You tried to act and will from the little skin-bounded "I". The result is that your skin-bounded self is quickly exhausted of the power it had—had from where? From the All.

Now straighten up and stand like a young god. Look upward and imagine yourself possessed of all power in heaven and on earth. Imagine that all the world and the starry hosts are waiting, alert and with shining eyes, to do your bidding. Imagine that you are to touch the button now and instantly they will spring to do the rest. The instant you say "I can and I will" the entire powers of the universe are to be set in motion. Ah, your eyes shine and your whole form expands with gladness, you unconsciously take a full breath and "I can and I will" rings forth in its full harmony. You are filled with joy and a sense of full power. You feel that you "can and will," and that it will take no clenched muscles, gritted teeth and brute will to accomplish, *for all creation will back you.*

Will is not a matter of straining muscles and set jaw, but of quiet, firm RECOGNITION of your oneness with all creation, and of creation's *readiness* to further your cause.

The most effective practice for the cultivation of will is that of dwelling mentally upon the Sublime Self. Go away by yourself for a half hour or more and simply *remember,* and try to *feel,* this unity of the personal self with the Sublime Self. Do not try to *argue* yourself into believing and understanding how it can be so; simply relax your muscles, lift up your soul and try to *feel* as if it were so.

At first you will see little result, except that you feel more *quiet* than has been usual with you. You will be less easily and frequently upset, and recover more quickly. Rejoice in this and keep at the recognition exercises.

Very soon you will find this peace deepening in you, and you will find it growing, *easy* to do many things you had considered hard. You will find yourself remembering without effort that ALL things are working *with* you, and that you are free to do as you will.

Keep on with the practice and you will find all the deepest desires of your heart, growing easy of accomplishment. You see, you are making sure your *connection* with the All-Self. Instead of having to do things all by yourself as you used to, you have opened the sluice for the Sublime Will to flow into and work through you for the accomplishment of what you desire.

Desire the Creator

Hunger has built the universe.

Hunger is desire.

Desire is love.

Love is God.

Of course we agree that God built the universe.

But it was not a God on a great throne outside the universe— *one* at whose behest angels and devils picked up handfuls of world-stuff and fashioned things, which were then set running.

It was God, or desire, *in* the universe, which has grown it up to its present state, and which will keep on growing it through all eternity.

Find desire in your own self—good or bad desire, it is all of one piece—find desire in yourself and you find God. Study the motions and results of desire in yourself and you will understand how God works to create worlds and peoples.

Note how a desire for food affects you. Does it cause you to sit still and sigh? Not until you have *first* tried every ingenuity you can think of to gratify your hunger. Desire impels you *first* to effort.

You go first to all the places where you have been accustomed to find food. We will suppose that you find nothing in the pantry, and of course that discovery whets your hunger. You again go over all the shelves, hoping to run across something. Nothing there. Now note that up to this point your hunger has impelled you to do just what you have been in the *habit* of doing. Of course this effort has done nothing further than *fix a habit* of looking in certain places for food.

But now: You have failed to find the food and hunger urges you a bit farther. You begin to think. You keep moaning inwardly, "Where can I find food?" Your wits grow a little keener as hunger sharpens. You begin to think. Mentally you recall all the places you have ever heard others speak of as abounding in food. Your sharpening hunger impels you to an entirely new kind of effort—for you. You go prowling about in search of places you have heard others speak of. Your hunger is now impelling you to follow *race* habits of thought. But you still fail to find food. Your hunger grows sharper and sharper and your wits follow suit. YOU try everything you ever heard of and still no food. There is famine in the land. You have exhausted your personal resources and the race resources, and still hunger grows and urges you.

Then at last you begin really to *think*. Your wits go feeling out beyond all the realms you ever heard of before, or they go roaming with a new intelligence and questioning over the same old ground. Sticks and stones and all sorts of things nobody ever dreamed of eating are now with new eyes examined and tested, and by and by you discover food and satisfaction where nobody ever before dreamed of finding it.

At last hunger has made you *think*—*it* has made you *in this particular thing* wiser than the whole race. It has differentiated you from the rest of your kind. It has impelled you to a little higher mark of intelligence than has even before been reached.

Now the rest of your race gazes at you and calls you "so original, you know." And it straightway adopts your new food and is differentiated as you are.

This is the way desire has created the world as it is, and this is the way desire is every moment changing it.

We evolve by the acquisition of knowledge and wisdom.

Desire impels us to the acquisition of knowledge and wisdom.

Can you see why a too prosperous nation or individual begins immediately to degenerate? All his hungers being readily gratified his wits are dulled and he ceases to gain intelligence. Soon the sameness of that in which he lives grows irksome and he loses his desire to live. Disintegration sets in. He is tired of the same old thing, even though that thing is beautiful and comfortable.

When a nation or a man gets into this state of satisfied stupor it takes the Goths and Vandals to keep him from dying completely.

It takes necessity to keep evolution going. Or else it takes an overwhelming ambition, which is after all the same thing.

And underneath and in it all is Desire, the great God, creating after his own image and likeness.

The more desire a man has the greater god is he, and the faster he evolves consciousness of his god-ship.

For thousands of years the race has been trying to crush out its desire and the result was a paralyzed and half-dead race, with only here and there a live spot.

The "new thought" is really the thought that desire is God and should be *encouraged* to express. This new encouraging of desire has already resulted in wonderful growth and lengthening of individual life.

"Oh," exclaims the Orthodox One, "how can all desire be good—how can desire be God and yet impel people to such terrible misdeeds—surely there are devil desires as well as God desires" And yet this same Orthodox One has read many times how "God hardened the heart of Pharaoh" to resist God's own commandments about letting "his children go." Now harken: When you found no food in the pantry, and none in all the land, and still hunger grew, you went out without chart or compass into strange places, and you tried many queer things. Some of these things proved bitter and unprofitable and you left them and went on and on. And at last you found the New and Good thing. But it was the *very same* old desire that made you try the bitter and unprofitable things, and the New and Good thing. You did not try the bitter things because you *desired* bitter things did you? Of course not. All the time you hungered, hungered for the Good thing; and kept seeking it; and as soon as you knew the bitterness of the bitter thing you left it and went on, still seeking.

You see, you were in a Strange Land. You had never been that way before. How could you know what was bitter and what Good, except by trying them? Of course there were people who told you of the bitterness, but there were still others who scoffed at the warning—who told you they had tried it and knew better. And they pointed out to you many personages who used the bitter things and yet looked sleek and prosperous. And you were hungry, hungry. So you tried the bitter things, and found them unsatisfying. And hunger kept urging you until you found the New and Good.

Now was hunger any more "evil" when you tasted the bitter things than when you ate of the Good? Of course not. It was simply blind, and *had to abide by your wisdom.*

It impelled you to try bitter and Good alike, and *each trial increased your wisdom.*

So is it with the good and evil of this world. The one good Desire is the life-urge of us all. Whether it urges us to heaven or hell it is still good—and *it still urges.* When in answer to its impulse we taste the bitter we learn the lesson and go on. When we find the good we return to it again and again.

But whatever we taste *we are taught something;* and that is what all Desire urges us to do—to *learn.*

In answer to the impulse of desire we grow in wisdom and knowledge—the *only growth there is.*

This Desire-God which works in us to will and to do of its good pleasure is a good God. It must be as good in me as in you; as good in the worst sinner as in the sweetest saint. The only difference between saint and sinner is a difference in *wisdom,* not in *desire.*

Since desire urges us to grow in wisdom and knowledge it is evidently only a question of time when we shall *all* know enough to turn from the bitter and find the New and Good. Is not the One Desire urging us irresistibly on *for its own satisfaction?* God in us is not only the hope of glory, but the absolute certainty of success.

Desire and Duty

Desire has urged us so long and so hard. We have persistently cuffed it into the corner and gone after new gods.

But despised Desire, deprived of its surface expression, has sunk deeper and deeper into our souls and refused to be comforted. After trying everywhere else for satisfaction, for a god to guide us, we have come back again to poor neglected Desire. In our extremity we see Desire with new eyes: we begin to *think,* and to understand. We try to coax Desire out of the corner and make peace with it. "The stone that the builders rejected" has become "the chief of the corner."

The only way to find peace is to follow desire. Desire is the only guide to heaven, and the road lies through hell. Worse yet, it trails a labyrinthine way over the dead-levels of indifference, where Duty lies in wait to nip its every expression.

Sometime you will grow to hate the dead-levels where Duty stalks. You will wake to the duty of being undutiful; to the desirability of following desire to the mountain-tops. You will look at desire with new respect and ask it to lead you up and out of hell and the dead-levels.

Hell comes before the dead-levels, you know, and all on the road to Transfiguration Mount. And when you begin to want desire to guide you, you will have been a long time on the dead-levels.

Then desire will whisper to you that she is God and you want to follow her. And when you agree she will begin *by leading you straight away from Duty.*

Many, many times your faith will not stand the test—you will turn back again from following desire. You will turn to duty because you are *afraid* to leave her.

Well, never mind; caution and conscience are good things and easily taught. Follow Duty when you must.

But keep your eye on desire and follow her every time you dare. "Lay for" desire and make haste to follow her every time you can. Keep in mind that desire *is God.* Keep watching and she will *prove* it. When you just *must* follow Duty, do it; but tell yourself it is *desire* you are following—not Duty. *You are doing your duty, not because you must, but because you* DESIRE *to.* Always remember this. Never humor Duty to the extent of letting her think she is *making* you do things for her sake.

Let me whisper something to you: *Duty is a sham.* She is a hollow mockery. She wears a dignified demeanor to cover her real nature. Duty is DESIRE *in a goggle-eyed domino which* scares you stiff. Just you follow desire and never, *never* give Duty the satisfaction of thinking you'd follow *her,* and by and by she will get tired of masquerading. She will take off her mask and you will smile to see that she really *was* desire all the time, and you knew her not.

You see, you and other folks had such a habit of cuffing desire into the corner every time she tried to lead you that she *had* to go and cover herself up in order to get you to follow her at all. So all along on those horrid dead-levels where you thought Duty was leading you such a stupid and righteous chase, you were *really* following desire all the time.

Now, if you will keep telling Duty to her face that you *know* she is only desire—that *you* are following desire and *not* Duty; if you will keep resolutely sticking to it Duty will soon give it up and take off her mask, and you will really *see* the smiling face of desire where you thought there was only stern-eyed Duty.

I write Duty with a capital D because that is the way we have always thought of her. But desire has always been just plain desire to us—something naturally and loveably wicked and familiar; so familiar that we bred contempt for her. But our eyes are opening.

Do you remember that when you say "must" to the children they straightway are "willful"? Children are true to God, to desire— "of such is the kingdom of heaven." When you dress desire up as a googly-eyed scarecrow Duty, the child will have none of it. He might have been just on the point of following desire into the very thing *you* desire him to do, but one sight of Duty is enough—he won't go a step.

And you call him stubborn, contrary, bad. You are mistaken. He is only *true to God.* And until you become like unto him you cannot enter the kingdom of eternal youth and joy and godliness.

Practice doing as you desire, to the end that you may desire to do as you will. You cannot go far astray, for in your real essence you are the *Good God,* who cannot go back on himself.

Duty is a fetish of the conscious or objective mind, whose processes comprise only about *five per cent of all your thinking.* The other 95 per cent mind is subconscious and *is true to desire.*

Desire is the drawing power of 95 per cent of you; will is the drawing power of only 5 per cent of you. Then do you wonder that desire often governs you *in spite* of your little *will* to follow Duty?

Your little per cent thinker has conjured up Duty as a guide, whilst your 95 per cent mind sticks to desire. You are two-minded, at war with yourself.

Unmask Duty and you will find yourself ONE and invincible. The 5-per-cent tail will lose his job of wagging the 95-per-cent dog, and you will reach Transfiguration Mount.

God and the Devil

"You seem to think God put all our desires in our hearts. What if we have desires to do things we know are not right, and the doing of which will hurt someone's feelings? I do not believe ignorance is the only cause of sinning. We do things we *know* are wrong." C.B.

If "God is All," where can a desire come from if not from God? There is *no* thinker but the One Great Thinker you call "God." All creation is made up of God's trains of thought. The real, informing, thinking self of *all* beings is that same One Thinker. He (or It) is working through all ages to *think* out the justice, love, wisdom that is in Him. He weighs one side of a thing through me, and another through you; and He waits patiently until He can figure it all out and arrive at the meeting place of truth.

Just as in your individual mind you seem to weigh and reason first one side and then another, so the One Thinker weighs and reasons *all* sides of The Truth through all people. Sometimes you are inclined to think one thing is right, and then you change your mind and go over to the other side. So the One Thinker seems to change His mind and go from one side to another.

He first decides that the Israelites shall go; then He thinks through Pharaoh and says they shall not. Then He thinks still louder through Moses and they start. Then He sees Pharaoh's side again and "hardens Pharaoh's heart" (that is just what the Bible record says), and tries again to hold them. Then inch by inch He fights over the two sides in His mind (there isn't any place but God's mind, and we are all in it) until he finds the point of perfect justice, or equity.

The same One Thinker, or God, has debated within Himself as to whether the Filipinos shall go free or belong to the United States. You thought the people of the United States and the legislators in particular were doing all that thinking and talking for and against. Why, bless your heart, the people and the legislators are dummies in God's mind—they are little thoughts moving around in the mind of the One Thinker—thought through which He weighs and balances and decides the equities. He thinks out and *proves* His intuitions in this way.

Now don't all of you anti-expansionists jump up and screech at me that it is not equity that we should own the Philippines. You are only one side of the debate. And don't all you expansionists come smiling around to pat me on the back. You are only the other side of the question.

I AM on the fence and I can see you both. All keep still now and

I will whisper to you a secret *God hasn't thought it all out yet.* He is still thinking alternately on one side and then on the other. It is nip and tuck with him whether to hold the Filipinos or to let 'em go. But He *thinks* He'll let 'em go—*when he finds a way.* He's thinking it out through you and me and Governor Taft and President Roosevelt and the rest.

There is just One Mind, which fills space full. All minds are inlets of the One Mind. All thoughts are thoughts of the One Mind.

Desire is the *will* of the One Mind. All desires are inlets of the one desire or will. *All desires are of God.* They are God's desires, fitting in with that particular train of thought. As the thought changes so will the desires. God's thoughts and desires change through all eternity. His desires fit the particular train of thought He is working out—one thing in you, another in me; changing in each of us from day to day; but *always God.*

God is proving through you and me what is right and what is wrong; what is just and what is unjust.

Wrong ALWAYS brings unhappiness; right ALWAYS brings happiness.

It is not enough that you have been *told* that it is "wrong" to tell lies. God hardens your heart to tell lies and suffer for it until you have so thoroughly proved the wrong and unhappiness of lying that NOTHING could tempt you to lie. So it is with all other wrongdoings.

But lots of times we think things are wrong when they are not really so. We have been told things are wrong—we do not know for ourselves. God "tempts" us to prove things. The gaining of wisdom is all we are here for—here in God's mind. We learn, and God proves, as much by our wrong deeds as by our right ones. By lying and suffering for it we learn first to wish for truth, then to work to gain it; then finally we love it and live it.

But not all in one little span of life perhaps. That is the trouble with people who are so greatly worried over right and wrong—their noses are always to earth and a death makes them lose the trail. They see a *single* being in one short span of life; instead of looking up and taking all life and *all* lives as a Whole. But they, too, are learning.

Let Us Play

Except you become as a little child you shall in no wise be able to "concentrate." Concentration is the natural mental attitude of a child. A child is one-minded. When its attention turns to any given object its whole being is polarized to that object. To all intents and purposes there is nothing in existence beyond the one thing to which the child's attention is turned.

Did you ever notice a fine horse when its attention is turned toward something? He "pricks up his ears" and they point directly at the thing that has attracted his attention. Every cell in a child's body, and every atom in his soul, "pricks up its ears" at the thing his attention is attracted to. Every cell and atom receives clear impress of the thing attended to. This is "polarization," or concentration. This is the secret of the child's marvelous aptitude for learning. It is likewise the secret of good memory and the joy of living.

But the child forgets the art of polarized attention as he grows up. The main cause for losing the art is lack of gumption in parents and teachers. The child is charged with "musts" and "don'ts" to which he is *compelled* to pay attention. Every little cell is made to carry such burdens that it simply has not the *heart* to "prick up its ears" and take in a new impression. Only here and there is found anything *vital* enough to polarize attention.

Burden-bearing is the great cause of lack of concentration, cause of lack in learning, lack of memory and of joy of living.

If we were a bit wiser life would be a continual playground, where we'd simply *grow* in wisdom and knowledge and self-use by having a good time at our games.

When we *must* play there is no joy in it. We *must* play the business game and support our families. We *must* "keep up appearances." We *must* do as others do. We *must*—*we* MUST. Nonsense! The only *must* there is about it all is the cue we took from our PARENTS and teachers and the traditions of men. We are hypnotized to think we *must*.

And it's all a lie, too. Suppose you try it once and see. Suppose you sit down and say you will not. Who is to compel you? *Nobody.* You have heard of women who took to their beds and stayed there—out of pure lack of anything else to attract the attention they wanted. They could have walked if they would—as circumstances proved—but they wouldn't. They went to bed. And somebody or other always met the compulsion and took care of them. They refused to even take care of themselves; they slid the *"must"* off themselves. *And there was always somebody else ready to assume the "must."*

That is it—we *assume our own burdens.* The less vigorous and determined and wise we are the more of these burdens we assume—burdens dropped by others.

And what good does it do to bear burdens? None—worse than none. The woman who dropped hers and went to bed simply stagnates and atrophies for lack of activity; and the woman who assumes the burden of walking and thinking for her wears herself out for nothing at all. If she had walked out and left the woman in bed that woman would have got up again and walked and thought for herself.

All our burden-bearings are as utterly foolish and unavailing as that. I have before me letters from two women who are still toting their sons around, although the sons are past the thirty mile-stone, and do not even take the trouble to let their mothers know their whereabouts. If those mothers had dropped those boys years ago and made the most of life for themselves they would be now such bright, handsome attractive women that they couldn't keep their sons away from them.

The burden-bearing woman (or man) tires herself so with *useless* efforts of mind and body that she has not energy enough left to keep herself in even decent trim. She gets bedraggled and falls away back to the tail end of the world's never-pausing procession.

Women as a class do not think and command themselves to best advantage. They are content to shoulder any old burden they see slipping from the shoulders of another, and to spend days and energy in feeling. Any kind of a feeling will keep the generality of women from thinking. Women shoulder indiscriminate and useless burdens and feel themselves into innocuous desuetude.

It is a hardship when one does not learn in childhood to read and write. But it is not an irremediable evil. One can learn when he is 20 or 40 or 60. A great authority on the Greek language learned the language after he was 80. He couldn't have done it though if he had fagged himself with burdens other people had dropped.

It is never too late to drop burdens and use energy to some purpose. All one has to do is to declare "I have no burdens—life is a play-ground!—and stick to it.

You *have* no burdens—they are all an hallucination. Life is a play-ground. This is the TRUTH. Just tell it to yourself until it works its way into your semi-paralyzed mind and makes itself felt. Relax physically and mentally. Lie idly under the apple tree and look up to the blue sky and let fancy play with the world. You will find new and happy TRUTH in common things, as Newton did.

Lie there and let truth regenerate you. By and by you will think of something you want to go play at. Perhaps the pervading humor of the world will suggest that you want to make mud pies again. Perhaps it will suggest a blackberry pie instead. It is a *lot* more fun to make blackberry pies than mud ones; and it's such pleasure to watch the other children's shining eyes whilst you all eat.

Perhaps you will prefer to go play the game of business. Well, play that. This whole great play-ground is before you. Go *play*. Make your own choice of games and have a good time.

Somebody says, "Life is real, life is earnest." But I say unto you that "Life is really what you *think* it." It is a great game, a tragedy, or a sentence at hard labor, just as you will. If you don't like what it has been use your ingenuity to make it different.

Above all things *drop the burdens*. Refuse to make bricks without straw. If the world won't let you go just go anyhow.

There is always a Red Sea to cut off pursuers and obliterate your tracks—unless perchance you dig up your old tracks and lug them along through the wilderness. If you do, I give you fair warning, you'll never get across the border into the land flowing with milk and honey.

This is a new, glorious day—different from any other day—a clean, beautiful day. The Red Sea has wiped out all the old days; the new days are not yet born. *This* is the *only* day there is. *Go play in it.*

"Whatsoever thy hand findeth to do, do it with thy might." One thing at a time, and that thing done with all thy heart— this is concentration, the secret of Life and Creation itself. And it is a simple little thing—so simple that a child does it without effort, and any man or woman can acquire it again by practice.

Remember, that every time you say to yourself, "I *must,*" you tell a lie, and you commit a crime against yourself. You lay upon yourself a burden and rob yourself of the joy of doing.

Every time you catch yourself saying, *"I must,"* DENY it *hard.* Sit down in a chair, relax all over and ask yourself solemnly *who* says you "must." *You* said it. *You* are doing all the compelling. Why? Simply because you choose to do this particular thing. There is *no* compulsion about it. You CHOOSE to do it—you *want* to do it. You are exercising your divine FREE WILL to do it. Oh, of course you can say, "If it wasn't for this, that or the other I wouldn't do it." But that does not alter the fact that you *can* fold your hands and leave it undone if you choose. But you desire to *do* it. You *choose* to. You *want* to.

Keep at this practice of logic until you realize that you have thought yourself completely out of the old "must" feelings. As you emerge from the "must" feelings you will find the joy of life filling you, and you will find memory and other faculties regaining the vigor of youth.

Everything but a mushroom or a toadstool takes *time* to manifest. You have been growing into the "must" habit since childhood. It may take time to outgrow it. But perseverance will accomplish it. And the more *faithful* you are in practice the more quickly will you realize the freedom, joy, youth you desire.

The joy of life is HERE and NOW. Joy of life is the power of accomplishment. All things are easily possible to him that believes—and *practices.* "The proof of the pudding is in the eating."

The Old Clothes Man

"Some months ago you wrote in a short letter to me, stating that when a person leaves this earth, death is only a door to another state of life, and that we don't enter it unless it is best for us at that time and place. Do you consider death in all its different forms, in a young person as well as old, best for them, no matter whether they die from accident or natural causes? Mr. Towne writes in his article on reincarnation in October that what we learn during one life is carried forward into the next. Now how much knowledge can a child have learned when death comes, compared to an older person? If death is the door by which we enter another state, and that is spiritual, what comes from that? Do we inhabit this earth again? Won't you and Mr. Towne give us a little more light on the subject?"

When we are children and go to school we work problems on a slate—or used to. If we made a little mistake and quickly discovered it we wet our forefinger on the tip of our tongue and wiped out the mistake, and then we filled its place with the correct figure, or figures. But sometimes we made a mistake away up near the top of a long problem of long division, and that mistake was carried on down until there were more mistaken figures than correct ones. Then we wet our little sponge and wiped the whole thing out of existence, and did it all over again. Sometimes we did this several times over before we learned how to do the "sum" correctly.

We are still doing that sort of thing. Life is really a "problem," which must be done by mathematical rule. Our bodies are simply the figures on the slate. Everyday we work away like more or less sensible and happy children; every day we find ourselves making and correcting mistakes, wiping off a little here and adding a bit there. Our bodies record all this, mind you.

But sometimes we fail to see our mistakes in time to correct them a little at a time, and sometimes we have not the patience to correct them. The mistakes are carried all through our bodies, just as through our problems on a real slate. Then we discover what a lot of blunders there are to correct, and we grow discouraged and quit trying. This re-laxation of effort and will and interest is the wiping off of the slate. We do it ourselves—do it *sub-consciously,* from the habit of ages of wiping off the slate. That which goes out of a body at death is the *real* person and he it was who wiped off the slate, who withdrew himself from the body.

No man dies unless he is ready to die—unless his mistakes of thinking (his body is built of his thoughts, you know,) are so in pre-ponderance that he cannot hold himself longer as an organization.

A body is an organization of thought things which must fit in and work together. When a man's mind is filled with warring, opposing thoughts, he is disorganizing himself. It is as if he turned wolves and li-ons and dogs all into the same corral, to oppose and rend each other, as well as to tear down whatever else was therein organized. Lions, wolves and dogs are warring organizations.

A man's body in order to endure must be *one* organization—every part must work *with* every other part. But as long as a man thinks into his body, one day good things, kind things; and another day ugly, re-vengeful, death-dealing things, he is turning lions and lambs together. And it is only a question of time and the kind of thought when he will cease to be an organization—he will fall to pieces, a victim to opposing forces.

And a man need not even be ugly himself in order to die. He needs only recognize ugliness in others. The Pharisee who has spent his life in ferreting out meanness and obscurity in others is as full of meanness as the nastiest sinner that walks. Man becomes what he thinks upon.

But such a one may be strong and healthy a long time because nearly his whole body is organized of the one kind of thought. So full is he of "evil" that he is an organized evil—a one-mind of evil.

It is the "good" and the goody-good people who fill themselves up on the warring factions of good and evil, whose bodies are choked with the warring and who suffer most and die youngest.

The same thing is true of people at all ages. Wisdom does not nec-essarily come with years, though no soul ever lived five minutes that did not in that time discover and eliminate mistakes by waking up to more or less truth. All experience enlightens—even that of being born to die in a day or a week.

Don't imagine babies are such ignorant little lumps. They are not. They are wise enough to choose their environment—just the one best calculated to teach them what they most need to know NOW. To be sure they do not choose parents as you and I would go out and look over a stable full of horses and choose one. They do better than that. As the birds obey the desire to fly south when winter comes down with frosty breath, so the infant soul obeys its sub-conscious desire for a particular parentage. In other words, parent and child are attracted; and each furnishes to the other the particular sort of experience necessary to its next further growth.

Just as we sometimes wiped off our problem before we had half a dozen figures down, because we had found our mistake and wished to correct our work, so the infant soul may find a big mistake and wipe out its body—only to begin again somewhere else.

Oh, don't be skeptical because you can't remember doing such things. You cannot remember many things that happened just a few years ago. How then, shall you remember back to the time you chose your parents? Or still further back to the infinitely greater number of parents you may have chosen in succession, since the beginning of eternity. You cannot even remember those problems you put on and wiped off your slate at school. Is it, then, wonderful that you forget some other things?

But you can do other problems like those you learned on, and do them almost unconsciously, so easy has it become. You learned much on those old forgotten "sums"—you remember the "how," but you forget where you learned how. So, no wonder you forget your old bodies and experiences. But the wisdom gained with them is still with you.

And every hour you are learning new truth—and forgetting *how* you learned it. The babe is conscious, and the babe learns—fast, *fast*. But it forgets *how* it learned. And if it is not *pleased* with its experience and learning it lets go its body and passes on—to other experiences.

Those who die do so because they are ready. And they "are taken away from the evil to come."

"Accidents" are results of "natural causes." An "accidental" death is a "natural" death—and sometimes much easier, and preferable to a so-called "natural" death. Who would not, if left to a decision, unbiased by public opinion—who would not prefer instant death in the electric chair to a slow rotting by cancer or tuberculosis? One death is as "natural" as another.

No man dies unless it is best for him to do so.

Has anyone supposed it lucky to be born? I hasten to tell him it is just as lucky to die, and I know it.

There is nothing about death to be afraid of. It is but a wiping off of the mistakes which have handicapped you. YOU go on forever.

Death is as natural and as good as life.

Only the fear of death can harm you, by tearing down your body before you want it wiped out.

It is said the first mark of insanity is that the patient fears and hates his best friend. The fear and hatred of death is insanity. To fear death for yourself is foolish. It but hypnotizes you, and death charms you as a snake charms a bird. You die before you would need to if you had not feared death.

It is still more foolish to fret over the death of another. In this case you not only add the death-dealing forces to your own body, hastening death for yourself; but your heavy thought handicaps in the outset of his new state of existence the friend for whom you grieve.

Spiritualists who claim to see and converse with departed souls often tell their friends that the "spirit forms" are "so weak and worn" that they are not able as yet to communicate with their old friends. The medium says the new made "spirit" is "heavy" over the unhappy state of its earth friends.

Why should not this be so? If our heavy thoughts ever affect each other (and we know they do) then death does not change it. *Our thoughts carry help or hindrance to those of whom we think, be they dead or alive.*

We think we must eat right and live right and think right for the sake of our unborn or new-born babes, that they may have the best possible start in their new existence. We need just as much to eat right and live right, and especially to think right, in order to give our "departed friends" the best possible start in the new life upon which they are just entering. We need to lay aside every small personal consideration, and bid them a hearty good-speed with every thought of them. We need to cultivate peace, and quiet joy, and willingness to have them go, for their sakes.

We can easily do this if we remember to be glad with them, instead of selfishly fussing around our own little personal "loss." They have wiped off the slate and gone on, with added wisdom, to better things. Why not be glad with them, *and for them!*

Whether we are spiritualists and believe in departed spirits; or evolutionists, who believe in an immediate reincarnation; or theosophists, who believe in a rest before reincarnation; or Catholics whose friends may be in purgatory; or Protestants who hope they are in heaven— whatever we are, the fact remains that our friends can no more fly beyond the reach of our help or hindrance than they can fly beyond our thoughts.

Let us *help* those who have "passed out." Let us treat them for power and love and joy and progress. Let us make them glad by being glad ourselves.

Death is good.

But it will cease to be necessary as we cease to make and perpetuate mistakes.

Being afraid of death and mistakes is the greatest mistake of all.

Get rid of it. Face death in your mind, until it loses all terrors for you. Call it *good.* Tell it if ever the day comes when you want to die you will do so with a good grace. Call death *friend,* and not foe. Tell it you may need it someday to wipe off your body, but remember that YOU couldn't die if you would. Death is only your old-clothes man—you may need him, and you may not.

For my part, I don't care whether I ever die again or not. If I keep on building better and better, (and I see no reason why I shouldn't), I shall live right along indefinitely, maybe forever.

But if ever I get myself into such a tangle as some folks do, and as I have got into in times past, I shall do what Jesus did— give up my body.

Ida C. Craddock, sweet, earnest, clean soul, chose, for the sake of forcing her teachings upon an unready world, to butt her head repeatedly against the stone wall of Law, until she was so bruised and discouraged that she—wiped off her slate by conscious will. She made the martyr's choice and mistake, which means always death.

If ever I got tangled up as Ida Craddock did I might end the matter as she did—as Socrates ended his troubles.

But I hope to avoid the paths that lead to death. I love to live, and I mean to keep on living more and more fully and positively. I am seeking FIRST the law of Life and to live it. Ida Craddock sought FIRST to convert and reform the world. The world, which did not want to be reformed, nor even to be taught too fast to reform itself, made things so warm for Ida Craddock that she couldn't stand it.

It seems a great pity. But it isn't. Ida chose her own course, knowing the result; she has learned her lessons, wiped off her mistakes and gone on to do still better work for herself and the world.

Jesus of Nazareth did much as Ida did. He spoke out in meetings, and out of it, until he stirred people up to crucify Him. *He wanted* to be crucified, in order that He might prove that He could live again.

But I want to live all the time, and I don't care whether or not I prove anything to anybody but myself.

Jesus and Ida Craddock deliberately trod the road to death. According to their faith and work, it was unto them.

I am treading my own individual path *where no death is.*

Death lies waiting for him who works against the established order—who makes crosses and carries them.

Life lies within and without for him who, resisting nothing, grows out of the established order—as a branch from the tree.

I believe I have found eternal life. Time alone will prove it. To live is to love and *work with* all things, knowing that all is good and all is life.

To resist *anything* is to cut off so much of life.

To fear death is to bring it upon you.

Get busy with LIFE.

Fannie James Brooks

(1854-1914)

New Thought Teacher Co-founder of Divine Science

Fannie James reaches out to the public with the Bible in tow. She uses scripture, which is well read by the culture of the times, and the teachings of Jesus the Christ, to drive home the teachings of New Thought, and the freedom this teaching imparts. She points her intellectual pen at the familiar religious interpretations of the Bible and offers women, and men, a fresh, more life-enhancing, self-empowering view of how to live a fulfilling and religious life according to the High Thought perspective as written about right there in their familiar scriptures. She is another New Thought woman pioneer working to break the social roles and chains of oppression internalized from religion, and habitual, unconscious social practices. She was a voice that was heard, and was influential during the Women's Movement at the turn of the century.

Fannie Brooks James was born in Louisville Kentucky on February 26, 1854 and she died in New York City on December 4, 1914. Fannie Brooks, sister to Nona Brooks, became Mrs. Ben James. Fannie James studied New Thought under Mabel MacCoy, a former Mrs. Hopkins' student in Chicago.

Fannie James had begun teaching classes. At first she held the classes in her own house in Denver, though her husband refused to allow her to go out and give treatments. She had corresponded enthusiastically with a woman in San Francisco, Malinda E. Cramer (See Malinda Cramer), who through a personal healing had come to the same ideas regarding healing that the Brooks sisters had, and who used essentially the same methods. She had given the name Divine Science to the system of teaching which she utilized, and had been ordained a minister. Mrs. Cramer held a class in Denver, and it was this Denver visit which brought her into contact personally with Nona Brooks and Fannie James, the co-founders of the Divine Science movement.

Fannie James, influenced by Mrs. Cramer, suggested to her class that they too call their teaching Divine Science. The teachings are scientific, she declared, "because they are proved in our experience," and as to the term Divine, "the subject concerns the understanding of God as Omnipotent." Thus Divine Science came to Denver, and has ever since been thought of as associated with that city. It was New Thought, though not so recognized by name. (1)

Link & Acknowledgement
1. http:nonabrooks.wwwhubs.com

Telegraphone with Operator 1898

Studies in the Science of Divine Healing Divine Science

1896
New Light Upon Old Truths
By Mrs. Fannie James

TO ALL WHO SEEK MORE LIGHT.
"SEEK AND YE SHALL FIND"

Some Final Words
Realization for Health
How to Realize Illumination, or Understanding

Important to All Readers

AS the lessons in this book are designed to be studies upon the Science, or right knowledge of Divinity, the subject is taken from its starting point in the Divine, and step by step it is developed from the Source and Cause of all things. Therefore each study makes that which follows it plain, and it is decidedly important that the lessons be read, or studied rather, in their order. To one who has never had the opportunity to study this truly Divine Science, we would suggest that they may find, by careful thought, a complete understanding of the principle and practice of the Science of Life, in these lessons. So we advise such, to lay aside questions at first; read each lesson to gain clearly the point considered in it; let all else alone. Read one lesson each day, or even on alternate days; reread often, until the subject of it is understood, before studying the next. By so doing, without a teacher, the knowledge of the Science may be gained, and its practice understood.

Introductory Thoughts
The Kingdom of Heaven

THE words of Jesus the Christ are growing in significance or, are coming to us with deeper meaning today than in any age before this. One minister has said, "The Bible means more to us than it did to our parents; it will mean more to our children than it does to us." Another said, "The Sunday school children of to-day are better able to understand Jesus' teachings than were the disciples of old."

Jesus said to his disciples, "I have many things to say unto you, but ye cannot bear them now"; which plainly shows us that Jesus was limited in his speaking of the Truth, by the dullness of his hearers. He could give to the disciples only what they were able to "bear", or to receive. He sometimes rebuked their lack of understanding. (Matt 15:16; Mark 8:21).

From His words quoted, and those which followed "Howbeit, when He, the Spirit of Truth, is come, he will guide you into all Truth", we may conclude that Jesus had a reserve of Truth, which he would gladly have expressed, but that it could not be understood even by the disciples; and that he knew and foretold in these words how the revelation of fuller Truth would continue from the Spirit throughout the ages to come, until "all Truth" had been received and understood. This certainly contradicts our past ignorant belief, that all revelation ceased with the "good old times"; and that the "voice from heaven" has long been silent; it can speak to us no more! Is revelation finished? The Truth will never cease to speak within our souls, while there is anything of God not comprehended. "Take heed how ye hear." (Luke 8:18).

"There is nothing covered that shall not be revealed." (Matt. 10:26). Revelation cannot be finished until every mystery is made plain: revelation is not therefore limited to any time or place; and whenever or wherever there is the spirit to receive and be taught, fuller and higher Truth is being made known.

One says, "Revelation is unveiling"; but the veil is on the face of man and not on the face of God. "The veil is a fitting symbol of our own ignorance; with every new revelation of Truth the 'veil' grows thinner. "Which veil is done away in Christ?" (Cor 3:14-16)

Christ is "The way, the truth and the life." As fast as we are able to be led in the "Way," and to "bear," or carry in our hearts the "Truth," and to "hear," or understand the so called "mysteries" of "Life," just so surely is the "veil," or lack of understanding, being "done away."

"Clouds and darkness are round about Him," is David's conception of God, and with Jeremiah we have been willing to say, "Thou hast covered thyself with a cloud, that our prayer should not pass through." (Lam 3:44). But we may rejoice in the increasing light, which now reveals that around God are no impenetrable clouds!

As well might we say on a cloudy day, "The sun has wrapped himself in clouds and darkness." The clouds that hide the sun from us, and shut out the warmth and brightness of its presence, are around our earth, and arise from the earth. These intercept the light of the sun, so that it does not reach us, but the sun shines on and on unaltered by the clouds around us.

So the clouds of darkness, fear, sorrow or doubt that seem to come into our lives, are around us, and not near the source of Light and Love. Neither do they come from the source of Love, but arise from our own incompleteness, or incomplete understanding.

As long as we see "clouds" about us, there is need of further revelation, or unveiling. As long as we have the Spirit of God, the Spirit of Wisdom, Truth and Love with us, we shall still be taught of God, and shall go on hearing Truth more and more clearly.

New things shall be revealed and must be while the Spirit continues to lead us into all Truth. Revelation never ceases unless we close our eyes and ears to it. Shall we then shrink from the "new," or shall we "Prove all things, holding fast that which is good"? (Thess 5:21)

Jesus said, "Ye shall know the truth, and the truth shall make you free." (John 8:32) These words express a truth for all times, as long as man anywhere is not free. The promise is given today, to every yearning one, who feels the depression of bondage to the flesh, or to "the ills that flesh is heir to."

From these words we may gather three suggestions: First, that ignorance, or not knowing the truth, is the cause of our bondage; second, that the relief from all bondage shall come through knowledge of truth; and third that we shall come into this knowledge and be made free. In this last is the promise of progression and hint of continued revelation. How could we otherwise come to know all truth?

Also in this is the blessed assurance that when we have understanding of the truth as it is, we shall have perfect freedom. "Where the Spirit of the Lord is, there is liberty." (2 Cor 3:17) "My people are destroyed for lack of knowledge." (Hos 4:6)

What is this Truth that shall make us free, and where is it to be found? Jesus declared, concerning his mission to earth, "To this end was I born, and for this cause came I into the world, that I should bear witness unto the truth". (John 18:37) Certainly this Divine One understood that the need of man was to know the Truth, and announced himself as the teacher and living witness of Truth.

From Him then we may expect to catch the clearest idea of what and where Truth is. We would not still be asking these questions if man could have understood his answer to them at that time. He said, "The kingdom of heaven is at hand. The kingdom of God is within you." (Matt 10:7, Luke 7:21)

If we are able now to "bear" these words, we shall find in them no uncertain sound. The kingdom of God—all that heaven is —the kingdom of Truth, of Love and of Peace, is not afar off, but at hand, within us!

We have heeded these words so little, that our heaven, our good, and our peace "at hand," has been literally overlooked, as we have tried to stretch our gaze into the beyond. We have been taught to place our happiness in the future, at some other time and place. We have sung, "I'm but a pilgrim here, heaven is my home." We have put off everything good to a future heaven. How can we see and enter into "heaven" right here and now, if we do not know the truth about it being at hand, and within us?

Like the patriarchs of old, we have "Died in the faith, not having received the promises, but having seen them afar off; and truly, if they had been mindful of that from whence they came out, they might have had opportunity to have returned." (Heb II, 13-15)

When shall we become "mindful?" When shall we accept our heaven? Not until we know the truth of it. "Now is the accepted time." Now is the time to accept and there can never be any better opportunity than now, for it is all right here. "At hand.", "Within you."

"How far from here to heaven? Not very far, my friend;
A single hearty step will' all thy journey end.
Hold, there! where runnest thou? Know heaven is in thee.
Seekest thou for God elsewhere, His face thou'lt never see."

Is not our question answered? Where is the Truth? Everywhere! Heaven is the kingdom of Truth. Heaven is wherever God is. God is everywhere. Truth's "kingdom" is within us, is all around us. Our only need is to know the Truth, to have our eyes opened and our faces un-veiled to see the ever present goodness and Truth.

We remember the story of one who sought the temple of fame. He had been told—by those who had never been there to see—that it stood on the summit of a distant mountain. The youth left the plane of his everyday life, forsook all else and spent the years of his life in toil-ing up the steep mountain in order to reach the temple. At last, aged and weary, he attained the height and looked eagerly for his treasure; he saw no temple, and, wandering on, he met an old man, who looked sadly at him, appreciating his earnest and worthy effort, but pitying his mistake, and said: "My friend, the temple you seek stands in the midst of the place you have left."

May we not expect something like this to greet us as we finish life's journey here, thinking to find our heaven at the end of our faithful toiling to attain it? Shall we have to learn then instead of now, that our heaven is within us? If we listen to the voice of the one who knows, we will have no reason for any delusion. Heaven is now and always "within you at hand."

Heaven is God's presence, and God's presence is the Truth which we may know and accept at this moment as now and here; and know-ing this Truth, shall make us free.

Truth never changes; it is "The same yesterday, today and forever."

It fills the universe of God, hence all Truth is here and now, and all that is true is eternal.

There is no new Truth. Man may gain new ideas of the Truth, and revelation of God must bring new ideas to us, but this does not alter one iota of the Eternal Truth.

Truth must contain many things new to us, and these new things must be among the "many things" that Jesus could not tell to his dis-ciples, but promised that the Spirit should reveal them as soon as they could be received.

Why then be afraid of a new idea of Truth? Why hesitate to accept something that has not been "seen" or "heard" before by us? It is written, "Eye hath not seen, ear hath not heard, neither hath it entered into the heart of man, what God hath prepared." (Cor 2:9) We have not yet conceived of the things that Truth hath in store for us; we never shall know if we refuse to accept a new idea.

This idea of progress in spiritual understanding is clearly taught in the Bible. "Greater works shall he do" ("that believeth on me," which makes these words apply to believers of every age.) Paul speaks of "milk" for "babes," and "strong meat" for "full age." Simple spiritual thoughts for us in immature consciousness, but strong sustenance for fuller developed thought. "That we may grow up into Him in all things." "Till we all come…to the measure of the fullness of the stature of Christ." (Eph 4:13) "Therefore leaving the principles (or first teachings) of the doctrine of Christ, let us go on to perfection." (Heb 6:1-2)

Truth is never afraid to declare new things. It says, (Isaiah 42:9), "New things do I declare"; (43:19) "Behold I will do a new thing"; (62:2), "Thou shalt be called by a new name" ; (65:17) "Behold I create a new heaven and a new earth"; (Ezek 11:19) "I will put a new spirit within you", (Matt 26:28) "This is my blood of the new testament"; (Mark 16:17) "They (that believe on Me) shall speak with new tongues", (John 13:34) "A new commandment give I unto you", (Cor 5:77) "If any man be in Christ (the Truth) he is a new creature, all things have become new", (Col 3:10) "Put on the new man", (Rev 2:17) "To him that overcometh will I give. . . a new name", (3:12) "I will write upon him my new name", (5:9) "They sung a new song", (27:5) "Behold I make all things new."

Why, we cannot enter into Truth until we are ready to accept all these "new" things. Truth is not changing. "New things" are only the eternal things seen by a new light even by Divine illumination called the Spirit. The church has always feared to entertain the idea of progress in religion. The Jewish church is the first example of this. One says: "If Jesus had taught no higher truth than the Jews had received from their forefathers, they would have heard him gladly, but they could not accept His "new doctrine."

We cannot blame the Jews. We find the same mistaken zeal today, the same rejection of a higher truth not understood by our religious leaders. We remember it is recorded by Matthew, "All the chief priests and elders took counsel against Jesus to put him to death"; and again, "The chief priests and elders persuaded the multitude that they should destroy Jesus." Isaiah's words seem to be fulfilled: "The leaders of this people cause them to err." (Isa. 9:16)

Then, as now, the church of God refused to hear any doctrine new to it; it said: "We have Moses; we know that God spake unto Moses; as for this fellow, we know not whence he is."

Judge them not, Oh Minister of God, for "Wherein thou judgest another, thou condemneth thyself." It was no easier then to accept a "new doctrine" than it is now. It was just as hard to give up the old and sacred conceptions then as it is now.

"The common people heard him gladly." Those that were humblest in their opinions had little to lay aside, could come as a "little child" and receive. (Matt 11:25; 1 Cor 1:19, 27) But "The first shall be last." It is hard when we feel that we have so much of Truth, to humble ourselves to listen to "new doctrine; to give up what has seemed so sacred, for a new idea.

Truth calls upon us to "Leave all and follow Me," even "Mother" and "Father"—our dearest past conceptions—for Truth's sake. "When that which is perfect is come, that which was in part shall be done away."

The world has been crying for "more light," and then shrinks in alarm at the "new things," that "more light" reveals. If we stand in a dark room, we see little that the room contains, we scarcely can tell where we are. If we stand in the kingdom of heaven, with our souls darkened, we cannot "see" what heaven is holding for us, nor know even where we are! Bring a light into the dark room, and how different everything appears; the light does not bring in anything, but it enables us to see what was already there, and to realize where we stand.

So the soul illumined sees everything in a new light, and begins to know where it is. This is the "new heaven and the new earth", promised heaven and earth seen by a diviner light, revealing what was not seen by us before, *new to us.*

Jesus came as a light to the world, not to bring anything that was not always here, but to throw light upon the world. As it is written of him, "He came to bring life and immortality to light." Men were suffering and dying not for any lack of good in the world, but because they did not know the truth, could not see the presence of Good.

He brought to light, or to man's consciousness, the immortality he had not known, and led man's thought out of darkness into light; out of ignorance into knowledge of truth; out of bondage into freedom.

"That is the light that lighteth every man that cometh into the world." (John 1:9) But "If the light that is in thee be darkness, how great is that darkness." Every man has the light of the Divine within him, but if he becomes unconscious of this truth, he is in deep darkness to himself. Jesus' mission was to show the Truth to man, and thus rekindle the light of that Divine in man, by which he should see his way to the Father, and understand the tie that eternally unites him with his Divine Source. That "tie" is the Divine Nature in man, which Paul speaks of as the "Christ in you, your hope of glory." This unites man with God, and is the at-one-ment which Jesus revealed, or brought to light. Only now is this being truly understood by man.

"The path of the just is as a shining light, which shineth more and more, until the perfect day." Our "light" within must increase until it blends with the Eternal, or enters the "Perfect day". At first "We see through a glass darkly"; this is when understanding is feeble. "But then face to face." When our consciousness is clear, we see without any veil.

Truth is not changing, our light upon it is growing. Our forefathers lighted their rooms with a tallow candle. Electricity with all its possibilities was right with them, but they understood not its use. It was better to have a candle than no light, but would that satisfy them now? Would they not now accept the brighter light, and shall not we? Do we show disrespect to their memory when we use electricity instead of candles?

Do not let us put the new religious "light" out of our lives, because our fathers had it not. May we not imagine that they too have gone on into better light? We need not worry about leaving their light, they have left it too.

We pray for spiritual understanding, but are ready to refuse it, if it comes through a channel unknown to us. A simple story is told of a nest full of birds which were deserted by the mother-bird. Hunger beset them and an attempt was made to give them food for which they were crying, but as the strange hand approached them, their open mouths were quickly shut in a flutter of fear, making it impossible to give them that for which they cried. The food was then laid on the edge of the nest and they were left for the night. In the morning all were dead. Too afraid to take their food from a new source, and too blind to see it "at hand," they suffered and died for their own ignorance.

"May we not," says the writer, "for the same reason, lose the good sent to us in answer to our cries"? The cry of these birds may be heard all around us. "Give us our spiritual bread, and our water of life, but give it to us in the old familiar way which we know so well."

One says: "It takes two to make a gift, one to give, the other to receive." God, the Giver of every good gift, has never withheld anything from us. David sings: "The earth is full of the goodness of the Lord. (Psl. 33:5)

If we lack any good, it is because we have not known how to accept and appropriate the good that is everywhere. God has given all; we have not received.

"Our citizenship is in heaven." (Phil 3:20) Not is going to be, but is now. The world needs a Savior today just as much as it did 1,800 years ago. The same Divine Power, the same pure Life, the same Truth, the same Love, and the same spiritual Presence is with us. "Lo, I am with you always."

Let us admit this Presence and Power, and then shall we hear in each new voice that speaks the assuring words, "It is I, be not afraid."

If we follow the inner call of Truth, we shall have the outer evidence. The disciples, without a question, followed a voice strange to them, which bade them "come." They left all, and followed without any evidence. After this willingness and obedience, they received abundant proof; so will every disciple of Truth. Let us "Be careful to entertain strangers" even strange or new thoughts, "for thereby some have entertained angels unawares." "With all thy getting, get understanding for understanding is a wellspring of Life." (Proverbs).

God

OUR responsibility is twofold; first, to obey the truth as far as we understand it; and we read, "God gives his spirit to them that obey," which is to say, that more light comes to them that obey what light they have. The spirit of understanding comes in greater fullness to them that are obeying the Truth they already see.

But unless they are looking for, and ready to listen to higher understanding, they cannot receive the reward of their obedience! Hence, our second responsibility is to be ever on the alert for higher revelation, ever ready and willing to catch a hint of something beyond what we have yet thought of.

It is not a new Truth we seek but a new consciousness of Truth. What shall bring this new consciousness to us? Jesus said to the disciples, "It is expedient for you that I go away; for if I go not away the Comforter will not come unto you." The "Comforter" is the Spirit of Truth, the inner guide. While Jesus is with the disciples, they look to Him personally, and lean upon His power and understanding. But His desire was to teach them how to be led by the spirit, which must be heard within them. Thus would their individuality be strengthened, and they learn, as each soul must sooner or later, to hear the guiding voice within them, and to come in direct touch with the Infinite.

This is true for every disciple. There is but one True Teacher. Jesus himself was learning from this One, and was showing to man, not what he personally could do, but what Divine Presence and Power, Divine Love and Truth, can do in humanity.

So he said to one who called him "Good Master," "Why callest thou me good, there is none good but one." As if to say, "I am not here to glorify myself, but God, the Father of All; if you see good in me trace it back of my personality, to the One Source of good which is Universal, therefore is for all alike. As I manifest this good, so may you. Greater works shall ye be able to do, but all by the One Power."

This inner guide, is that which shall lead us into new consciousness, it is called in Scripture, the "Still Small Voice," and of this leading it is written; "They shall be all taught of God." (John 6:45) This inner voice is the "Light that lighteth every man," (Prov 20:27) which God has placed in each soul, to guide it into all Truth.

We cannot see by the light that lighteth another. We may get the spark that shall set our lamp to burning, from another's light, but that is all! It is written, "The spirit of man is the candle of the Lord." (Prov 20:27) Whatever consciousness, or inner light any soul receives, it is set aflame by Infinite Love and Truth.

The voice of Truth keeps speaking in the soul, for it is always there, "Behold I stand at the door and knock." Once in a while some soul hears, and this is revelation! If it has ever been, it must be now, for Truth never changes.

The Whole Truth, includes all the fragments of Truth ever known. So that as we advance into better knowledge of Truth, we shall not lose any Truth we ever possessed. But one may ask in what relation does a new Truth stand to the old?

We may find illustration for this in our schools. Where there are many grades and a pupil passes from one to a higher, just as fast as he can accomplish the work required in each grade.

It is a pupil's pride to push on into new work, and learn new things; and it is a teacher's purpose to assist the child in his progression. Each grade belongs to the one school, and has equal honor in its place. The last grade does not hold the first in contempt, but in high esteem, as having been a stepping stone in the way of advance.

One must learn his A B C's before he can become an author, and though he shape the world's thought by his writings, he never ceases to use his A B C's learned in the first grade.

No Truth gained is ever lost; the higher contains all the Truth of the lower.

Truth has been compared to a cone which has its base in a circle, and its summit in a point.

The circle well represents the eternal nature of Truth, and its omnipresence, encircling the universe.

But as the cone rises to its summit it terminates in a point, so as man's consciousness of Truth is lifted up, he begins to see the unity of all Truth. As it is written: "That in the fullness of times he might gather together in one all things in Christ." (Eph 1:10) Christ is the final Truth into which all things shall be drawn. "If I be lifted up, I will draw all men unto me."

"Seek ye first the kingdom of God, and all these things shall be added unto you." (Mat 6:33)

For centuries we have been pleading. "Thy kingdom come". If the kingdom is "at hand," and "within us," whence is it to "come"? It has already come. The Divine promise is, "Before they call I will answer." (Isa 65; 24)

Before we asked for the Kingdom to come, it was with us! We must come to a knowledge of it, and the result of our "seeking" has been to find it "at hand." And finding the kingdom, we find within it all good Things—ours, here and now.

Are we ready then, to hear a new doctrine, and to let the light within us be our guide? We desire better conditions, we long for satisfaction, but if we are unwilling to receive new ideas upon life, we shall have to continue to submit to old conditions, in the old ideas.

If the "Spirit of Truth" is leading us, we must expect to be led into more spiritual ideas of all things. Our conception of God, of Christ, of man and of life, will become more spiritual.

As our spiritual sense of things is quickened, we shall be glad to find our material sense being "done away." Jesus said, "The flesh profiteth nothing, it is the spirit that quickeneth," and we read that many of his disciples hearing this, "Went back, and walked no more with him," (John 6: 60-66), for they said, "This is a hard saying." They were not able to "bear" it, but shall not we search deeper into the words, and seek for their highest meaning?

May we not say with Paul: "Henceforth, know we *no man* after the flesh; yea though we have known *Christ* after the flesh, yet henceforth know we *him so* no more?"(Cor 5:16) For are we not going to search for the *spiritual* idea of God, of Christ, and of man?

Divine Science encourages this search, made by the light of Spirit. The name has a significance.

Science is "knowledge, Truth ascertained; knowledge duly arranged." Having for its foundation, or starting point, a Truth that never changes, all its knowledge is derived from, and agrees with this changeless Truth.

And this Science we are now to study is Divine, because the Truth with which it begins and from which it judges of all things, is Divinity. God is the basis and foundation of all its knowledge.

For where shall we look for the changeless, but to God, the Eternal, "In whom is no variableness, nor shadow of turning." Where shall we seek for a beginning, and Source, Itself without beginning, but in the Infinite Mind of Wisdom and Spirit of Truth! Now this is our foundation, for in this Great Eternal Being, we shall find a Cause or Source, therefore a *reason*, for everything that is.

Let us then search in Spirit and in Truth for a clearer, and above all, a more *spiritual* understanding of this Great Being we call "God."

We read, "Other foundation can no man lay, than is laid, which is Jesus Christ." Here we learn that the foundation for Truth's building is already laid: like all Truth it is eternal!

"Order is heaven's first law," and the order in every building is, that the foundation shall be laid first. The strength and safety of the building depends upon the perfection of its foundation.

What is the foundation of Divine Science?

The foundation for all Truth is "Jesus Christ;" not a personality, but the "Word" which was "In the beginning with God, and was God." "All things were made by him," (John 1:3) by the Eternal Word of God! With us always.

This Foundation and Cause of all things is in our midst today, and ever has been in the earth.

Of it Jesus said: "Before Abraham was, I am;" and again, "Lo! I am with you always."

How easy then to find and lay our foundation. It is God with us, and through us, above and below us, God everywhere present. "All in all."

Then, to know certainly the changeless Truth or real nature of all things, we must find the Truth of God.

First we will think of God as Source and Cause of all things; not making things of nothing, but of His own Life and Being, this Great Mother-Father God, brings forth all the forms of Life. "One God and Father of all, who is *above all*, and *through all*, and *in you all*." (Eph 4:6) "For *of* Him, and *through* Him and *to* Him are all things." (Rom 11:36)

God the Source and the Cause, the Beginning and the end of everything; as Spirit saith: "I am the Beginning and the end" "The first and the last." "I am *all* in the beginning, and *all* in the end. I am the *all* of *everything!*"

This is just what we mean by speaking of God as Principle, which is thus defined by Webster: "The source and origin; that from which anything proceeds; the beginning; the first."

Principle is changeless Truth, Foundation and Cause, out of which visible things are brought forth.

God *is* the beginning of all things. Think of this! Everything that lives and moves, begins its life in God – Life. "With Thee is the fountain of Life." Everything true has its origin in God. All that is, is in and of God! We cannot emphasize this too much.

In the Word we read, 'The same fountain cannot bring forth sweet and bitter water." From the same source cannot come sweet and bitter. Nothing can come from God that is not *in* God. If the "fountain" or source of Life is sweet and good, it can send forth only that which is pleasant and good.

What then is the nature of this Fountain that supplies all Life? What do we know of it?

We know that God *is good*, hence must say everything begins and ends in Good. God never changes if good, then always good, and sends forth only good to His creation. "Oh, taste and see that the Lord is good." (Psl 34:8) "For Thou, Lord, art good."(86:5) This teaches us then that the Source of life is good, and when I say with the Psalmist (87.7) "*All* my springs are in Thee," I understand that everything that comes into my life has origin in this Great Fountain of Good.

Moreover, not only is God good, but all the good there is as—Jesus said: "There is none good but One." I cannot look anywhere else for my good, but to God. I cannot find good in anything else. I must look to God only for my good health.

I must know then where God is, and what God is, to know where and what my good is.

God is the Source of good. God is the *only* source of good. God is the source of *good* only, nothing else but good can come from God.

We know God not only as *a* Source and Cause, but as the *only* Source and Cause. There is but *One Source*. "I am the Lord, and there is none else; there is none beside me."(Is 45:5-6) "One God and Father of all", And Jesus answered: "The first of all commandments is, Hear, O Israel, the Lord, our God, is One Lord."

We have thought it easy to believe in *One* God; but now that we find it means to believe in One Good; One Cause only, is it so easy?

We know God as Life; therefore as the only Life, and the Only Source of Life; so it is written, "Whoso findeth me, findeth Life." (Prov 8:35).

We know God as Love; as Paul says: "For God *is* love." Not Loving, but is love itself, and changes never! Love is God. "Everyone that loveth is born of God." (John 4:7) The source of everything is Love!

"God is Light." (John 1:5) God is Truth. "I am the light of the world; I am the Truth," Jesus said. There is just One Light, One Understanding, One Intelligence, One Truth.

God is the Infinite Mind—All Wisdom.

"God is Spirit." God is Substance (*Sub*, under, and *stare*, to stand,)—"that which underlies all the outward."—Webster. Spirit is the one only Substance.

The *Substance* of all things is not the visible but the Invisible; is not matter, but Spirit. "The things that are not seen are eternal." We should rejoice in this. "Things are not what they seem," but altogether better! So Jesus said: "Judge not by *appearances,* but judge righteous judgment."

Science teaches us to judge of things by their Source. If all things proceed from One Source, they are contained *in that* Source, before they are visible, and they can be only what that Source is.

We have seen that the Origin of all things is Light, is Love, is Good, is Spirit, or Intelligent Mind; is Truth, and, like a Great Fountain, this Light and Love, Truth and Life, is pouring forth its perfect Substance into all the forms of Life. In countless ways it is making itself visible to us.

But where shall we find this Great Source which is our Life, Substance and Intelligence? Do we say, like Job, "Oh, that I knew where I might find him, that I might come even to his seat"? (Job 23:3)

We long for God, because we long for Truth, for Peace, for Love, for Understanding, for Life. Jesus said that to know God aright is Life, eternal. Our desire for life, Peace and Good, is really our *cry for God.* Where shall we find Him? *Everywhere.* "In Him I live." (Ads 17:28) Think of this! I live in Life eternal, in Intelligence, in Spirit, in Truth and Love, in All Good. Of course I do if the kingdom of God is within me—at hand.

Do we believe that God is *Omnipresent?* We say yes; but think, do we believe God is *All-*Presence? "God omnipotent means good everywhere present," and this admits of no other presence but Good. Do we believe that God's Presence fills every spot and space, and do we refuse to see anything that is not the presence of Good? Yet this is just what *Omni*-presence means.

The Bible supports this idea: (Jer 23:24) "Do I not fill heaven and earth? saith the Lord." (Psl 139:7) "Whither shall I go from thy spirit, or whither shall I flee from thy presence? If I ascend into heaven Thou art there. If I make my bed in hell, behold Thou art there." God's presence, remember, means the presence of Changeless Love, Truth and Life, fills heaven and earth, and behold is to be found even in hell!

What is the difference between "heaven" and "hell"? Heaven is where God's presence is *recognized* as "all in all." Hell is where God's presence is not recognized. Both are "within" us.

But as if these words were not enough to convince us, we hear still further, in Eph. 1:23, about "The fullness of Him that *filleth all in all*"; and again, Col 3:11, we read, "Christ is all and in all." This is what God omnipresent means.

Omnipotent All-Power admits no other Power. God's Power is the Only Presence. Can we accept this? Paul says this very thing, in Rom. 13:1, "There is no power but of God." Can we now admit an evil power or an evil presence? Can we claim any longer a Source for evil?

Non-recognition of God as Omnipresence, Omnipotence, as All in All, is the only cause, presence or power of evil. Hence to recognize God as All-Presence, All-Power, All-Intelligence, Omniscience, shall be the destruction of every claim of evil, error, or fear.

Condensed Statements

"In the beginning was the word."
Divine Understanding begins with the word.
In imitation thereof we begin by speaking the word.
"The kingdom of God is within you."
"The kingdom of heaven is at hand."
God is Everywhere. God is here.
God is Light. Light is here. God is Truth. Truth is here.
God is Good. Good is here. God is Peace. Peace is here.
God is Freedom. Freedom is here.
Now am I in All Good Presence.
Now am I in Perfect Freedom.
Now am I in Changeless Love and Truth.
Now am I in Eternal Life.
Now am I in Full Light, for "I live, move and have my being in God.
In Light, Truth, Love, Freedom, Goodness and Peace."
"God is All and in all."

"The Truth shall make you free."
"Whenever the Christmas season
Lends lustre and peace to the year,
And the Ling-long-ling of the bells,
Tells only of joy and cheer,
I hear in the sweet wild music,
These words, and I hold them true:
The Christ who was born on Christmas morn,
Did only what you can do.
Each soul that hath breath and being
Is touched with heaven's own fire;
Each living man is part of the plan,
To lift the world up higher.
No matter how narrow your limits,
Go forth and make them broad,
You are, every one, the daughter or son,
Crown Prince, or Princess of God."

Christ, The Divine Man

ALTHOUGH Truth may be Omnipotent, and perfect Love be Omnipresent; though we may "live move, and have our being" in God, the All-Good; though we dwell in the kingdom of heaven, if we are not conscious of these truths, and do not know the wonderful meaning to us, we may go our way, in lack of all things, losing the blessedness that is ours.

"Heirs of God, joint heirs with Christ," we may, through ignorance of this, be slaves of misery and poverty. As Paul declares: "Now the heir, so long as he is a child, (without understanding), differeth nothing from a servant, though he *be lord of all.*" (Gal 4:1)

Truth must be recognized in order to be realized by us, and to become a power in and through our lives.

It is said that seeds have been found in the hands of mummies, which being planted, have burst forth into growth, after having been dormant for centuries. The seed had within it all the Life-principle, waiting development, but *the hand that held it was dead.*

The Divine Life and Truth begins in the soul as a seed. It may be held in a dead consciousness, but the Truth-seed never dies. It is waiting its opportunity. It is implanted by Divine Hand in *every soul.* One says, "When Jesus said he had finished the work, he had sown the entire field with seed; the seeds were small, the harvest is universal".

"We think that heaven will not shut forevermore,
    Without a knocker left outside the door:
    Lest some belated wanderer should come
    Heart-broken, asking just to be at home.
    So that the Father will at last forgive,
    And looking on His face, that soul shall live.
We think there will be watchmen through the night,
    Lest any far off turn them to the light.
    That He who loved us into Life, must be
    A Father, Infinitely Fatherly.
    And groping for Him, all shall find their way
From outer darkness, through twilight, into perfect day."
    "His mercy endureth forever."
    "Every knee shall bow, every tongue confess."

What is this knowledge that we need to make us free?

The knowledge of God, and of man's relation to God; the right understanding of these will break the bonds of our captivity and give us consciousness of Eternal Life.

Jesus said, knowing the Truth makes free, also knowing God is Eternal Life—two most precious boons, Freedom and Life, *are* ours for the knowing. Knowing what? That they are ours! "All things are yours," Paul affirms. Life and freedom are mine now. The Truth makes me *know* I am free. Understanding God and my relation to God, convinces me that I am Eternal Life, for I am *made* of Eternal Life; I am Peace, because I am made of everlasting Peace. I am changeless Love and Truth; for I am made of Love and Truth that changes never.

"I am, because God is." God is the reason or cause of my being at all; the Source and Substance of my existence.

All that I am must be found in God my Source, and most truly I cannot be anything that God is not, for I have no other Source. God is all. I cannot be something else.

To know what I am, I must know what God is, for in God I have my beginning and in God I shall have my end. God is "All and in all."

What is God? Goethe says, "The Most High cannot be spoken in words." Then words, either written or spoken, can only hint of the highest conception of Truth, and each soul must go for itself to the Infinite Fount, to receive within its own consciousness.

To form a practical idea of God, take paper and pencil and write the word "God"; then write with this word every term that expresses God to you. Do not forget the Infinitude of God, and when you write beside the word God "One" write with it, "*All.*" The One God is all there is.

If you write "Mind," let the One Mind be *All* Mind; declare that the One Mind is all Mind; then cast out belief of something beside God, by *saying,* There is no other Mind, no mortal mind.

If you write the word "Love," let it be to you *All.* "Love fills all, I live in perfect Love. There is no fear or hate."

Whatever you write with God—"Life," "Strength," "Spirit," "Light," "Good"—declare it *All.* Deny the claim of any opposite. Make this a common practice if you would see God everywhere.

So we love to think of God as changeless Good, filling all: the Only Power, controlling all, Principle, or Source of Life, pressed out into all. Perfect Truth and Love pervading all. Eternal Mind and Substance sustaining all. Ever present Fullness, supplying all, The Only Intelligence enlightening all. "Since God is all, there is no room for any opposite."

Can any limited personality be attached to such an exalted idea of Infinite Being? Can we for a moment think that such a Universal idea of Deity can be compatible with the cramped notion of God, as dwelling in any one time or place in greater fullness than in another?

"The fullness of Him that filleth all in all, without shadow of turning," must teach of Limitless Presence and Power, "That God may be all and in all," in every time and every place the same.

One says, "We are as much in the presence of God now, as we shall ever be." The only possibility is to become more and more conscious of God's presence. Our heaven is growing nearer, as our knowledge of God's presence expands.

To understand my relation to God, I must study Jesus Christ, for I am nothing to God except by and in the Christ.

"No man cometh to the Father but by me." Jesus Christ, we have been told, is the *foundation* of every created thing. All the universe of Spirit, (and there is no other universe), is built upon Christ. What is the meaning of Christ? "Now know I am no man after the flesh. Yea, though I have known Christ after the flesh, yet henceforth know I Him no more." If we will find the spiritual idea of Christ Jesus, we can then understand how every man is founded upon Christ, and how "Christ is all in all."

Many sayings of Jesus, which cannot refer to personality, will also be made clear to us, as "Before Abraham was, I am." "Lo, I am with you always." This "I am" that has been and shall always be in the world, cannot possibly be the personal Jesus, it must be something more. There is plainly reference to an impersonal presence. Also, when Jesus said of his disciples, "That they may be one in us, I in them and Thou in me," he must have referred to a spiritual or soul relation, and not to any personality.

"In the beginning was the Word, and the Word was with God, and the Word was God." (John 1:1) Christ is here called the "Word" of God, which signifies the expression of God, or the expression of Life, Truth and Love. This eliminates all idea of personality.

A minister called the attention of his listeners to the fact that in the Gospels the name Christ applied to the Divine Nature of the Son of God, and the name Jesus to his human nature.

Let us try to understand Jesus' relation to God, for it is the type of every living soul. "I am the way," shows us that there is no other way.

Jesus himself claimed no personal advantage over any one. He said, "I am the light of the world," also, "Ye are the light of the world." "As the Father hath sent me even so have I sent you." "The works that I do, shall ye do." "That the world may know that Thou hast loved them as Thou hast loved me."

He showed what God could do in man, and that the Divine Power that governed him is universal, hence is for all alike.

One says, "Jesus solved the human riddle; he has shown us in himself, that God and man are one inseparable life; God in Jesus, is God in our humanity."

Another declares, "Christ comes not merely to show Divinity to us, but to evolve the latent Divinity that is implanted in every one of us." Man was ignorant of the Divine in himself. The Truth, always there, lay dormant in his soul. Jesus was the first to rise out of this deadness of consciousness. He was the first of heaven's children, to know who and what he is, the Son of God. Paul speaks of this when he speaks of Jesus as "The *first-born* from the dead." (Col1:18) "The first-born of *every* creature." (Col 1:15) Into his consciousness shall every soul follow as fast as it awakens from its dream of ignorance.

By what Power did Jesus know and manifest the Divine Life and Truth? There is but One Power, One Presence, One Mind or Intelligence. Jesus recognized the One as All. He said, "Of myself I can do nothing". He claimed no individual power, no power but that which is universal, therefore is for all.

One says, "We must not try to imitate Jesus in his self-confidence." But was Jesus' reliance upon himself, or was it upon the One Divine Power and Presence, and shall we not imitate him in this?

Jesus' sole dependence was upon the Divine Nature which he was manifesting, the Christ or Expression of God, his own spiritual Being and Life. The same must be the strength and moving power of every living soul. Each one may say as truly as could Jesus: "I can do *all things* through Christ which strengthened me." (Phil 4:13)

This Christ is the Whole Divine Nature, always with us, of which each soul is a partaker.

"Christ is all in all." (Col 1:11) We need to accept this in its fullest sense, for then shall we come to see *Christ Only*; Begotten of God: Divine Self-hood; Divine Man, as all Self-hood, as the Only Man. Not seen "After the flesh," but in the understanding of God's Divine Idea of Man. All personality is lost sight of.

This is the Foundation and Substance of every living soul. Christ is God's complete Idea for all men. We are to come *into* Christ, by letting the old self "go", die to our consciousness, and know Christ to be *all*. All therefore of me.

Jesus knew perfectly that he was nothing apart from the Divine, but recognizing his Divinity, declared all power, life, perfection and truth to be his, because of his relation to the Infinite. No other has yet comprehended this as Jesus did, but "All shall know Him."

"Beloved, now are we the sons of God, . . .but we know that when He shall appear, we shall be like Him." When we are *like Him*, he shall appear to us again. Then we shall be able to see Him.

"Christ *in you*, your hope of glory." (Col 1:27) The Divine in you is your claim upon God, and through It and in It shall you be glorified. "In His Son the Father sees us, And as Sons He gives us place."

How shall I truly accept Christ as my *substitute*? By putting myself as I have thought myself to be, *entirely* out of mind, and where I have looked upon self, see Christ as the *Only* Self. I can then say with Paul, "I *no longer live*, but *Christ liveth* in me," or in place of the old me. This is true *self*-sacrifice, to be made "Once for all." We have been trying to patch up and make better the old self. We have repented of a sin here, and a shortcoming there, and where the sin has rent the soul, we have tried to put in a new piece, a better condition. Shall we recall Jesus' words: "No man putteth a piece of new cloth into an old garment for the rent is made worse." (Matt 9:16) This is just what we have endeavored to do, to patch up our old lives with new Christ-life. What has been the result? Is sin destroyed and its effects banished?

If not, let us listen to the "new" way. Entirely *discard* the old self; do not try to improve the mortal, but accept the Divine Self in its stead.

If the Divine is exalted and the mortal denied a place, soon it will "No longer live," but the Divine will be all life.

"Likewise, *reckon ye* yourselves also to be *dead unto sin*, but *alive* unto *God* through Jesus Christ our Lord." This is to "Put on Christ." (Rom 13:14) Put out of thought the self that sins, and looking at Christ, or man's Divine Nature as *all* of man in God's image, declare: "Christ is *my* Divine Nature; Christ is my Life and Being; Christ is my Self-hood, when I find myself in God. I accept Christ as the All-Truth of me, for "Christ *is all and* in all."

Of such, the Divine saith: "Their sins and their iniquities will I *remember no more*." Having once truly accepted Christ, we can have no more memory of sin, but will say with Paul, "If I do that which I would not, it is *no more I* that do it." The Divine of me cannot sin, suffer, or be sick. Continual sacrifice for sin is not Divine method, and is therefore not acceptable to Deity. (Heb 10:1-3, 5, 6, 8, 11-14)

Accepting the Divine of us—Child of God—instead of the child of evil, we make a sacrifice "once for all," or rather accept the eternal sacrifice in Christ.

One says, "True humility is not to think meanly of oneself, but not to think of self at all." Accepting Christ instead of self is not to think of self at all; therefore not to think of the sinner. It is to be so filled with the Divine Idea of Perfection, Love, Goodness and Truth, as to have no room for any other idea.

Jesus taught the Divine Nature of man when he bade him say "Our Father." This declares man to have a Divine origin. We say this is man's only nature, for there is no other origin.

Jesus emphasizes this when he bids us "Call no man on the earth your father, for One is your Father even God." The command is acknowledge no Life-giver, no Source, or Cause but Spirit.

We have always recognized the "spark" of Divinity in man; why is it but a spark? Is the Divine so feeble that it must yield the right of possession to another power? No, for there is no other power! It simply means that we have acknowledged the Divine so little that it has seemed but a spark to us.

Now, if we will exalt the Divine in man, lift it up, in all our ways acknowledge him, we shall soon realize the spiritual sense of Jesus' words: "If I be lifted up, I will draw all men unto me." Truth will fan the "spark" into a great "flame" when we lift up Divinity in all.

Condensed Statements

God is manifest to me through Christ within, "Because that which may be known of God, is *manifest in them*." (Rom 1;19)

I am heir of all good through the Divine in me. God only is my Father, Source, Origin; hence my only inheritance is good.

In the Divine of me, I am the child of God. I am the child of Good. Child of Light. I am born of Love. "I am free-born." I am child of Truth. I inherit all Good, all Love, all Light, or Knowledge, all Peace, all Wholeness.

I have no lack. I do not lack good. I have no lack of Love or Knowledge. I have no lack of Peace or Health, for "I" am Divine.

By the Christ, or the Truth, I am made free.

"If the Son shall make you free, then are ye free indeed." (John 8: 36)

The Holy Ghost
Divine Consciousness

THAT which is born of spirit is spirit. The child has the nature of the Father. If God is our "Father" we may rightfully claim to be of Divine Nature. Having been blind to this, all kinds of conceptions have gathered around ourselves but "The Truth shall make you free."

We have heard of the artist, who looking upon a rough stone said, "There's an angel in that stone." There was no *visible* evidence of it, yet he began his work of chipping away, with patience and skill, bit after bit of the stone that hid the angel, until at last there stood before all eyes the visible representation. The artist mind saw the invisible angel, hidden beneath the rough exterior so Divine Mind sees Divine nature buried out of sight perhaps in humanity, and with patience and skill destroys mortality's claims, one after another, until the perfect being is revealed. What further endorsement do we find in the word of God, for the Divine in man?

In its first chapter we read: "God created man in *His own image*; in the image of God created He him;" and again in the same first chapter are these words; "And God saw everything that He had made, and behold it was *very good.*"

Is there anything that God did not make? "*All things* were made by Him; and without Him was not anything made that was made." (John 1:3) God made *everything*, and pronounces *all* He made "very good"; then there is no reality in evil.

Whatever there is, God is responsible for it, and more than that is the Source of it: there is "none else." "Whosoever is born of God doth not commit sin, he cannot sin; because he is born of God." (John 1:9). "We know that we are of God." That which is born of God and cannot sin, is the Divine Man, the "Image and likeness" of God; for that which comes forth from God is like God.

As we have been admonished to call none other "Father," we must acknowledge ourselves born of God, and must know further that all that is born of God is pure and perfect. "Be ye therefore perfect even as your Father in heaven is perfect." (Matt 5: 48)

"Be ye holy for I am holy." (Pet 1:16)

My only claim of perfection and holiness must be, because God my only source is Perfect and Holy. That which comes from God and is of God must be holy; the image of God cannot sin. Christ, Son of God, is the Divine Nature of all, and in the Christ, or *Truth* of myself, I am Divine. Jesus said, "I am the Vine, ye are the branches," and it is written in the same book: "If the root be holy, so are the branches." (Rom 11:16)

Paul says, "That we may present every man perfect in Christ Jesus," which means spiritually, and in no other sense can anyone be in Christ Jesus, that we may present every man perfect in the Divine of himself.

Man has never yet been bettered by condemnation; would it not be wise to try the opposite course? See the "angel" or the Divine Nature, the Christ presence in every soul, no matter how hidden; deny the truth of all seeming error; it is not born of God, and all that is real is of God. Break away the false ideas that obscure the angel and watch the result.

"The worst way to improve the world is to condemn it. Men might be better if we better desire of them." "Man is the image and glory of God." (Cor II: 7). "Men, which are made after the similitude of God." (James 3:9)

It is certain that man in his spiritual nature is Godlike, and when we see or understand but *One* Source, One Life, One Mind, and One Substance, Spirit we shall know that man's true and only nature is Spiritual. "God hath *made man* upright, but they have *sought out* many *inventions.*" (Ecc 7:29) Man has invented many false ideas about himself, and these false claims have gathered so densely about him, as to cover his "eyes" with a thick "cloud", so that the inner glory of God is not recognized.

This "cloud", or veil, is "done away" when we see Christ, the Holy One of God as "All in all." We "die" to the old idea of self which was false, and become alive to the Divine idea, the Eternal, though "new" to us.

Paul beseeches us to put on this new idea of man when he says:

"That ye *put off* concerning *former conversation* the *old man* (do not any longer talk about the man of sin; the man of God never sins), which is corrupt according to the deceitful lusts. And be *renewed* in the *spirit* of your minds. And that ye *put on* the *new man* (the new idea of man) which *after God*, is created in *righteousness* and *true holiness.*" (Eph 4:22-24)

The Bible gives full encouragement to look at God's perfect work, and to put away the old idea of unrighteousness.

If we once realize God as "All and in all"—*All that is in all*—we can never again admit the truth of something beside God. The source and cause of error and evil, is the belief in *something beside God.* A belief in two Minds, two Substances, two Powers, and two Truths, opposite to each other, is all the evil there is, and this belief is false.

"I am the Lord, and beside me there is none else." Let us get from this statement all the practical interpretation that we can.

The Lord is Life—All Life—then it may read: "I am All Life and beside Life there is none else, no opposite to Life." According to which we safely conclude there is no death. Life is All Power, All Presence.

What a joyful message if we can receive it!

The Lord is Good, All Good; then it may read: "I am All Good and beside Good there is none else," which plainly states, there is no evil. Good is All Power and Presence.

The Lord is Spirit, then it may read: "I am spirit, and beside Spirit there is none else." This teaches us that all is Spirit, there is no other substance, no other Presence.

The Lord is Love, and so it may read: "I am Love, and beside Love there is none else." There is no hate or fear. "Perfect love casteth out all fear." (John 4:18)

All is Love. The only Presence is Love.

If Spirit is *All*, then I am Spirit.

Spirit has no clouds and darkness. Spirit is Light; then I am Light.

Spirit has no sin, sickness, or death in it. Spirit is Holiness, Wholeness, and Life eternal. I am Holiness, Wholeness, and Life eternal. I am Understanding for I am Spirit.

"There is a Spirit in man and the inspiration of the Almighty giveth them understanding." (Job 34:8)

This "inspiration" of the Almighty is what we have known as the Holy Spirit, and here it is declared that this Spirit "giveth understanding."

The Holy Spirit of God is Divine Consciousness or Understanding, which illumines the soul, revealing to it the truth of the Infinite Love, Life, and Peace; by the Light of the Spirit each individual may know the unlimited Presence and Power of all Good, and may claim this Presence and Power as its own.

God is manifest to us visibly in Jesus.

"He that hath seen me hath seen the Father." (John 14:9)

God is manifest to us in the Invisible in Christ, the Divine Nature in each.

"For that which may be known of God is manifest in them." (Rom 1:19)

Christ is God's Divine Idea; in Christ we see what the Divine Idea is for *all*. The Light *by which* we see this Divine Idea, is Divine Consciousness, or the Holy Ghost. By this inner light are we led into all Truth, it is God-Consciousness within us.

The unpardonable sin is to refuse to see this Light, and to be led by it for as long as we refuse its guidance we must remain in darkness, or lack of knowledge; by no other power can we be enlightened concerning our Source and our Divine Nature. The sin of ignoring the Light Divine must be given up, it can never be excused: by no other leading can we find the Father. This Holy Spirit guides us *from within*; it is the consciousness of God in the soul.

God is known as a Trinity in Unity called Father, Son and Holy Ghost. Our three lessons thus far have presented the spiritual idea of this Trinity.

God, the Infinite Mind of the Universe and man. Christ, the Divine Idea of the Infinite Mind. Holy Spirit, the Divine Consciousness of the Infinite Mind. There is no perplexity in this understanding, to see how the Three are One.

Mind to be complete and perfect must have within it a Perfect Idea, and Perfect Consciousness. Also, Idea and Consciousness cannot exist without Mind to contain and include them.

If we expect to accomplish anything, the very first fact is that we have an idea in mind of what we want to do, and how we want to do it. All we do is based upon, and begins in that idea. So Christ is the Idea in the Supreme Mind from which all created things begin.

That which enables a mind to carry out, or manifest its idea, is its consciousness by understanding that it can do a thing our mind acts. So the Holy Spirit is the *Acting* Power of Supreme Mind, by which the Perfect Idea it contains is carried into expression.

Christ is the Whole Truth of creation which is in the Infinite Mind *before* creation. Christ is the *Universal* Man, the Divine Idea and Divine Nature of every individual. This is what Jesus meant by saying,

"I am the Vine"—there is just One Divine Man, "Only Begotten Son of God," "For whom the whole family in heaven and earth are named." The "whole family" are the many "branches" of the one vine. All individuals branch out from the One Divine Nature.

Study the parable of the vine and branches to understand how all individuals are related to the One Universal Man of God.

Christ is the "Vine," the root and beginning of all living souls, which are the branches. Note the process when the vine begins to put forth its life in the spring; here and there are seen buds pushing their way out *from within* the *parent stem*; we know these buds are the first appearance of the great branches into which they shall grow; but all the life and substance of the branch still and always is drawn *from within* the vine. There is one vine, but many branches. Like to this is the relation of each and all individuals to the One Divine Soul. Divine Man is the Holy Root, there is but One Divine Man—individual souls are the many branches, pressed out from within the One Divine Soul, having life of its Life and substance of its Substance.

"If the root be holy so are the branches." When we see all in the Christ, and of the Christ, know the Christ or Divine Nature as the "root," we see also the purity and perfection of all.

But the vine with its branches which it has put forth is not yet complete. A third necessity exists; from the branches must proceed fruit: if the branch adheres properly to the vine it bears much fruit, if it becomes severed from the vine, both branch and fruit wither and die. "Abide in me," says the "Vine," "and ye shall bring forth much fruit, for *apart from me ye can do* nothing."

The individual can be and do nothing of itself. Jesus represents the most perfect branch of this great Christ-Vine, and yet he said, "Of *myself* I can do nothing." He knew that apart from the great Principle of Life and Being, he individually could accomplish nothing. If *He* said it, we surely must.

The "Vine" is of the Universal, Omnipotent, Divine Life, Substance and Intelligence, that is the only Source of individual life. It is Man, as Spirit. "*I am* Spirit." "I am the Vine."

The "branches" are of individual life, substance and intelligence, *expression* of the Universal. "Man is the expression of God."(*Science and Health*) This is the living, active soul; Image of God.

The "fruit" is of the visible universe, the earth, the spoken word; the true "body." The "fruit" is the inner Life and Substance, made visible; it is the third and last step in the Divine process. It has come from within Spirit; it is the "likeness" of God.

Hence the soul which is Man's individuality is the Image of God, and the body is the likeness of God. There is but one life, and one substance for vine, branch and fruit; so there is but One Life and One Substance for Spirit, soul and body.

As the Vine, branch and fruit make one perfect and complete vine, so do spirit, soul and body make one perfect and complete Spirit.

Spirit is creator of the living soul, and soul is maker of the body, not of its own power, but by the Power back of the soul—even Divine Spirit.

One says, "Our natural bodies begin to form as soon as our souls exist, and because they exist. The soul's life is the power that forms the body." "For of the soul, the body form doth take, For soul is form, and doth the body make."

"The mind of man is God," (*Science and Health*), for *All Mind* is God, there is but One Mind. Man, as Divine Being, is eternally in and of that Mind; as an individual, man *expresses* that Mind; thinks its thoughts, and then speaks these Divine thoughts into words, so the thought and word unfold from within Divine Mind; are contained within Divine Mind before they are thought or spoken.

We can learn from this the method or law by which Infinite Mind expresses Itself, viz: Mind, forms its thoughts and speaks its words.

Let us compare these various statements:

1st. Being	2nd. Acting	3rd. Result
1. Mind	Vine	Spirit
2. Forms Its Thoughts.	Forms Its Branches.	Forms Its Soul.
3. Speaks out Its Word.	Puts forth Its Fruit.	Makes Its Body.

Back of you and me and all of us, is the Great Infinite One. As Jesus said, "My Father is the husbandman." Everything begins in this One known when manifest to us, as Christ—still One—for it is simply the Spiritual Truth and Life of the Father, expressed in all. "All are one in Christ."

The consciousness of Truth, Life and Love, or Divine Understanding is the Holy Spirit of God, the Light of the World, lighting each soul to see its Divine Nature, and to know that *all that is*, is Spirit, and its manifestation in soul and body; is Mind, and its expression in thought and word.

One God All

One Mind is All Power.
One Life is All Presence.
One Substance is All Reality.
One Spirit is All Intelligence.
One Law is All Love.
One Good is All Truth.
All is Spirit. All is God. All is Mind. All is Good.
If God is *Omni*presence, there is nothing *anywhere* but God.
There is no *presence* of evil.
If God is *Omni*potence, there is no opposition to God.
There is no *power* of evil.
If God is *Omni*science, there is no knowledge
but of God.
There is no *knowledge* of evil.
There is no mind of evil.
There is no cause of evil. "God is all and in all."

The Work of Thought

THERE is no power against, or contrary to God. God is the Infinite or All Mind of the universe. The whole Idea of creation is within this Infinite Mind, which also contains all consciousness.

Every idea in the world comes forth from the One Perfect Idea of God, for It is all. All Understanding in the world comes forth from the One Perfect Consciousness, for It is all.

So God, as All Mind, Idea, and Consciousness, pervades all living souls, and acts within them. This action of Infinite Mind is called Divine Thought. Paul declares, "Not that we are sufficient of ourselves to think anything as of ourselves; but our sufficiency is of God." (2 Cor 3:5)

We are entirely dependent upon our Divinity for our ideas, our consciousness, and even our thoughts! When we receive the consciousness of this Divine Idea within us, Christ is born to us; and

"Though Christ a thousand times in Bethlehem be born,
If he's not born in thee, thy soul is all forlorn.
Could but thy soul, oh man, become a silent night,
God would be born in thee, and set all things aright."

I cannot claim to be anything in and of myself, or apart from the Infinite. What I am, individually, is wholly according to what the Great "I am" is.

The name "I am" is full of new meaning to us now. It is not *originally* my individual name. It is eternally the name of Divine Being.

The real "I" or self belongs in this Divine Being, whose name is "I am."

There is but One I am. "I am that I am" is received by Moses as the Divine Name. It is becoming to us a sacred name. We have used the name "I am" as if it belonged to us wholly, to handle as we chose; but now we are learning to say "Hallowed be Thy Name."

We say "I am" in this understanding of it, with reverence; for it is God's Name, it is God's Nature; it is God's Presence, "descending upon us like a dove."

"I am" is always Life, Spirit, Love and Truth, filling us to fullness, so that there is no lack, in that which I am.

"I am" is Wholeness, Perfection and Health, the Mind of Good that is All in all. There are not many I ams, but One, even God. So I understand that to say "I am afraid, I am sick, I am weary, I am weak," is to speak falsely; the *I am* is none of these things.

"I am," as I now speak it, is my "new name," because it appeals to me with such new meaning. "I will write upon him my new name." (Rev 3:12). I will give him a new consciousness of my name.

Only my *Divine Nature can say I am.* I have no being apart from God, "In Him I live, move, and have my being."

To know *what I am*, I must know what the *All I am* is. Hence, when I say "I am," I speak not of myself but of God. It is enough to know what the Great I am is; since It is *All,* It includes me. To speak truthfully then, I silence all opinions and beliefs, in order to *listen.* "Be still, and know, (for then shall we know), that I am God."

Let us conceive of the individual as being perfectly still. In this silence of the soul, he hears the testimony of the Spirit within him. "I am Spirit . . . the beauty of holiness, the perfection of Being, imperishable glory, all are mine, for I am God. I give immortality to man, for I am Truth. I include and impart all bliss, for I am Love. I give Life without beginning and without end, for I am Life. I am Supreme and give all, for I am Mind. I am the Substance of all because I *am that* I am." (*Science and Health*)

When the individual soul thus hears from within, it has "become a silent night," and Truth is forming *itself* in soul and body. Our thoughts are being put out, that the Divine may do its own thinking in us, and speak its own words.

"For it is not ye that speak, but the Spirit of your Father which speaketh in you."

Many mistake the intention of these high declarations, supposing the individual is speaking of himself, but instead of this he has put self *out of the way*, and is letting the spirit of God speak through him.

This spirit spoke through Jesus, (as he said, "The words which I speak, I speak not of myself"). What did it say?

"I am the light of the world." "I am with you always." "I am the Truth. I am the Life." "I am the resurrection and the life." "I and my

Father are one." "Abide in me." "He that liveth and believeth in me shall never die." "Come unto me." "In me ye shall have peace," etc.

This "I am" and "me" is the Divine Nature of which we have been speaking, it says the same words within each, for Jesus spoke not these words of himself individually, but of the Father, or Spirit of Truth.

When we learn to speak the I am rightly, we have found a refuge from every ill! Into it we may run and escape every claim or belief of mortality.

When we go into the "I am" we enter God's World, Spirit's realm.

It is in *our own* little world, which means our belief of separation from God that sin and evil exist.

There is no sin in God's World; no evil in God's universe, no darkness in God's presence, and God's world is the only world. God's universe fills all; God's presence is all in all! Hence a world of sin, evil and darkness, is a false belief. There is no world of our own, apart from God.

My belief in a world of sin is my mistake, resulting from my idea of separation.

Jesus came into *our* world, came to us in our *belief* of separation from God, to show us the truth of our oneness with God.

"I have overcome the world", not God's world, but the false idea of the world, the world and the self apart from God that we have believed in. The truth shall make you free.

The world of separation has no true existence, for God is all in all. It is therefore a belief which Truth destroys; in this belief of separation is all the claim of sin and suffering.

To destroy or overcome this world of suffering, man must come into consciousness of oneness with God; this ends our belief of separation, and is the end of *our* world of sin and death.

Then we see the "new earth," or God's World filled with Divine Nature.

Oneness with God is the at-one-ment.

In this conscious oneness, self is surrendered. God is all; then we say, I am what God is, for I cannot be something beside God. Therefore I let

God, or "The Spirit of My Father," say within, "I am Life Eternal and Changeless. I am Spirit and Power. I am Light and Truth. I am Fullness and Freedom. I am Health, Goodness, Perfection, and all Love."

This is what I am, for there is no other "I am." I think this that I am, and my soul is radiant with Light. Then I speak what I think, and my body is full of Light, full of Strength, full of Good, full of Health, because I see what I am.

There is no "I am," no Being anywhere, that is not *in* Peace and Health.

In thus thinking, "We have the mind of Christ." (Cor 2:16) And are willing to "Let the word of Christ dwell in us richly in all wisdom." (Col 3:16, 17)

"And whatever ye do in word or deed do all in the name of the Lord Jesus, giving thanks to God and the Father by him."

The "name of the Lord Jesus" is this very "I am" that we are to believe in and to abide in, for it is the Great Christ presence which includes all, "I in them and they in me." "That they may be one in us."

As soon as I see the One that I am, I can also see what I am not!

I begin to think of the true I am; I know that I live in Mind and not in body.

I am spirit, and am manifest in soul and body.

I am Mind, and am expressed in thought and word.

We have studied Mind, and have found the meaning of Its three-fold aspect. We have seen the Son to be in the Father. This is the place *Divine Man* holds, he is co-eternal with God, therefore is Eternal Life, Changeless Truth, and Perfect Substance. The many living souls are but branches out of the One Man and therein have they all Life, Being, Intelligence, and Substance. The fruit of these branches is the body, perfect and complete in all good when the branch abides in the vine. Thought is the busy worker; gathering material from within, from Source and Cause Invisible, from the I am that is always Wholeness and Perfection, it conveys what it has gathered into the visible, or fruit.

Thought is building the visible universe, and it turns only to spirit for its knowledge, the outer will be in the very likeness of Spirit.

If we see in our visible "world" things contrary to good or God, then thought has turned away from Spirit to gather its material for building, and brings forth other than Spirit's fruit, "For the fruit of the spirit is in all goodness and righteousness and truth." (Eph 5:9).

Misery, error, and evil, are not fruits of Spirit. Has thought power to bring forth these?

It is written, (Jer 6:19), "Behold I will bring evil upon this people, even the *fruit of their* thoughts," and again "As a man thinketh in his heart so is he."

The soul of man is the power God has given him to think divinely, and thus image all Good. If thought has been wedded to something beside Spirit, it has failed to image God in the earth. Among the wonders shown to Christian in the Interpreter's home, was a man raking in the dust, and so intently was his attention fixed upon this, that he did not see held just above him a crown, waiting for the upward look of his eye, and the lifting of his head.

"Thou hast crowned him (man) with honor and glory. Thou hast put *all things* under his feet," but thought has been so busy looking into the "dust" of its own stirring up, so intent upon seeing man as a "worm of the dust, that it has not seen the crowning of man by Divinity, nor lifted its head to receive the God given glory!

Now by Divine Consciousness, are we able to see man by a Diviner light. We are beginning to believe in the Divine Idea of Man and to accept it as all of man.

When thought sees truly what is in Being or Source, all things will *appear* right and good, for "Thoughts expand into expression." (*Science and Health*)

Body is the thought made visible.

We must therefore carefully guard our thinking. Let Truth and Divine Consciousness, which speaks only of good, control it.

"Stand porter, at the door of thought." Guard the very entrance of thought, decide whether God's Idea alone shall enter your thought. You can decide, for you are the thinker.

"If we are wise," says one, "We will not permit anything to enter our thoughts that we are not willing to have expressed in our bodies." "Think the thoughts of Infinite Mind. Watch your thinking, control it with Truth. There is a channel, so to speak, through which the Light (of Divinity, the Life, the Perfection, Wholeness, etc.) is conveyed to its destination, and this channel is man's capacity to think."

Perfect Life, Divine Peace, all Goodness and Health, Intelligence and Freedom, are all ours, for "We are Christ's and Christ is God's" (Cor 3:23). Thought is the "channel" by which these Divine qualities are conveyed to their destination. Their *destination is the body*. Thought should continually pour into word and body, all perfect qualities contained in Divine Source. Thought and conditions of body are as Cause to effect; change the thought, and conditions of the body will change.

I must be the Mind of Good, before I can think good, or act good.

Good thinking comes from Good Being, and good doing results from good thinking.

I cannot make myself good by *acting* good. I must begin where all things begin, in Being. See the truth of my Being. I am Good, is first; I think good follows; I act and speak good is the result.

I am perfect in Mind, for Mind is God.
I am perfect in Thought.
I am perfect in body.

Silence Self, and Listen

"*Be still*, and know that I am God."

I am. Mind, Idea, Consciousness.

"In him dwelleth the fullness of the God head bodily; and of *his fullness*, have all *we* received, and grace for grace."(Col 2:9; John 1:16)

I am the fullness of the God head bodily.

In Source I am Life, Strength, Intelligence, Love, Wholeness, Freedom, Fullness, Goodness, and Truth. In Source I have power to *express* Life, Strength, Wholeness, Goodness, etc. In Source I am *conscious* of having power to express my Wholeness, Strength, Life, etc. I know the Truth of Being Whole. "In him ye are complete."

I think of my freedom and peace. I declare now my strength and completeness.

By the Law Divine, as I recognize and declare my Peace, Plenty, and Satisfaction, the Truth of Peace, Plenty and Satisfaction resounds through all my existence. The One Only Voice that speaks "I am Peace," is God. My soul and body echo that voice and say, "I am Peace."

The True I Am

Light. Love. Peace. Strength.
Health. Goodness. Perfection, etc.
I think what I am.
I speak what I *think* I am.
Result of thought: The body full of Life, strength, health, etc.

The False I Am

Life *and* death. Love *and* fear.
Peace *and* discord. Strength *and* Weakness.
Health *and* sickness. Goodness *and* evil.
Perfection *and* imperfection.
I *think* what I am. I speak what I *think* I am.
Body the result of what I *think* I am.

Which "I am" have we been thinking, the true or the false? The body answers our question; well and sick; strong and weak; living and dying.

Our Judgment Day

EVERYTHING begins in mind, is expressed in thought, and manifest, or spoken forth in word.

Mind is the Actor, or Thinker. Thought is the action, and word is the fruit or result. Every action must have an actor before it, and a result following it.

Every thought must have a thinker preceding it, and a spoken word following it.

Mind is the *spirit* of Man; his Divine Being and Life, his Intelligence and Substance.

Thought is the *soul* of Man. Image of Eternal Mind, Life, Being, Intelligence, and Substance.

Word is the *body* of Man, that which results from thought, which shows forth thought, likeness of Eternal Mind, Life, and Substance.

Thought is the *invisible form* of Mind, Life, etc.

Body is the *visible form* of Mind, Life, etc. "By one spirit are we all baptized into one body."

When all have One Mind, One Intelligence, and that the Mind of Christ or Truth, we shall see but one kind of body, perfect and pure.

When we see no Cause but Infinite Mind, we shall see no result but a perfect body.

Mind works through thought into word. Spirit works through soul into body.

Mind is the Only Power, and Cause of everything. All things begin to form in Mind.

Thought is the action that forms things. The work of the soul is to form the Image of the Divine within itself, and to bring Its likeness into the visible.

Body is the thing formed by this action. The body of this perfect method is the likeness of God the fruit of Spirit.

Stillness is the Universal Man, the "I am"; enter therefore into the silence, if thou, my soul, wouldst learn what I am.

Action is the individual man, expression of God, manifestation of Divinity.

Mind is the Universal Man, Fullness and Freedom.

Thinking is the individual man; the Divine Acting, declaring itself.

Spirit is the Universal Man, Changeless Self-hood.

FANNIE JAMES BROOKS

Living soul is individual man, "Thought of God," as Phillips Brooks has said; Image of God, action of God.

Thought stands between the Invisible and visible. By the action of thought is the Invisible made visible; this is the law of expression.

Divine Thoughts are the angels of God; Love Messages straight from the heart of the Infinite Soul, to the living soul the spiritual "ear" of man. "Angels are pure thoughts winged with Truth and Love. Angels are not messengers, but messages of the true idea of Divinity flowing into humanity. These upward soaring thoughts, never lead mortals to self, or sin, but guide them to the principle of all-good." (*Science and Health*).

"When the angels look into the soul of man, they see only the good and true."

> "And it seems to me that the more we grow,
> Like the angels in love and duty,
> The less we shall see of evil in all,
> And the more of good and beauty.
> And so the good shall increase, increase,
> And evil shall vanish away,
> Until the Truth in each heart shall glow,
> Like the light of a perfect day."

When "The Lord is in the midst of thee," (in the midst of thy thoughts), "Thine eye shall not see evil anymore." (Zeph 1:15)

In our ignorance of God, and belief of separation, we have conceived of two selves, a spiritual nature, and a carnal nature. The latter is the sinner, the former the saint. One the child of the evil one; the other child of God.

Both of these natures, our belief declares, inhabit our tenement of clay, though they are opposed one to the other. Conceive of deadly enemies living together in one house! Would we expect very much peace or harmony in that house? Yet under just such circumstances, as we have supposed, we have been trying to find health and peace of mind!

133

One speaks to us of peace; the other holds us in bondage. "Nevertheless what saith the scriptures? *Cast out* the bond woman and her son; for the son of bond woman shall not inherit with the son of the free woman." (Gal 4:30)

We are to cast out of our mental household the thought, or belief of bondage to "the world, the flesh, and the devil," and the fruit of such thought will also go, for "We are not children of the bond woman but the free. Stand fast therefore in the liberty wherewith Christ (the Truth) hath made us free, and be not entangled again with the yoke of bondage." (Gal 57)

We "*put off* the old man," the self apart from God, the "sinner" that must die, when we see Christ, Divinity, "I am," as *all*. It is simply growing out of self into Christ, after we receive the revelation that came to Paul, of which he said, "It pleased God to *reveal* His Son *in me*" (Gal 11:5).

When self is dead, Christ is all. The growth out of self is strongly pictured in these words:

> First, "All of self and none of Thee.
> Second, Some of self and some of Thee.
> Third, Less of self and more of Thee.
> Fourth, *None* of self and *all* of Thee."

There is therefore now no condemnation to them that are in Christ Jesus. For the law of the spirit of life, in Christ Jesus, (perfect idea of man), hath made me free from the law of sin and death." (Rom 8:1-2)

"If ye be led of the Spirit, ye are not under the law." (Gal 5:18)

"Reckon ye yourselves therefore, to be *dead unto sin*, but alive unto God." (Rom 6:11)

We have not seen the impossibility of accepting Christ, and still holding on to the sinner! But we must receive Christ as *all*. See no more condemnation, no law of sin, no bondage to the ills of the flesh, no self but Divine Nature, the all that I am. This means perfect freedom to us, and wholeness in spirit, soul and body.

"In the spiritual philosophy of Jesus, religion and health are viewed as one. Health of body was external holiness, and holiness was internal health."

"How shall we take hold of this new realization? By using the new thoughts and speaking the new words faithfully.

See what I am, think and declare it. See what I am not, cast it away by denying it. "Know ye not, that to whom ye *yield yourselves* servants to obey, his servants are ye, whether of sin unto death, or of obedience unto righteousness." (Rom 6:16)

"Be ye transformed by the *renewing* of your minds." "Finally, whatsoever things are pure, are true, are lovely, are of good report think on these things." (Phil 4:8)

The more steadfastly we think upon good, the less of evil shall we see; the more earnestly we think upon Peace, the less of discord shall we see, the more we think upon righteousness, the less of sin shall we see; the more we think upon Health, the less of sickness shall we see.

Not that thought has this power in and of itself, but good thought, health thought, life thought, *expresses God*, and fulfills the law of all Being, of all Mind, therefore the law is *completed* in good results of health, peace, and rightness. It is the law of God.

If we will listen to the general conversation around us, what shall we hear? Constant acknowledgement of God, the Good? Do we talk of good health, and perfect love, or is our talk of ill-health, and much fear? Our speech shows what our thoughts are. If thoughts mold our conditions, is it any wonder that in every direction there are signs of sin, sickness and death? The outer is but an expression of the inner.

The light of Truth shining more clearly within us, shows us our mistakes, uncovers error and destroys it for us.

In this light we now discover many opinions and beliefs, not based upon changeless Love. We believe so many things that could not come from changeless Love, which are to be separated from our thought and cast out. We cannot talk as we once did, for we do not think the same. "From the abundance of the heart the mouth speaketh."

We are trying to "Let love become a habit of the soul," as Drummond says: to let good become a habit of thought. In order to do this, we are led to deny a place to evil in our thoughts, somewhat as Paul says. (Eph 4:27)

"Neither *give place* to the devil." When we see God everywhere, we cannot consent to allow evil a place. There is no place for it. When we see Truth clearly, we cannot give error a place. When we recognize Love as Infinite, we can find no place for fear. If Life is all, death has no place. Seeing Perfection fill all, we can grant no place to imperfection.

Truth revealed, shows us the One All, without any opposite, and says to claims of evil: "Depart from me, I never knew you"; which is to say, you are not of Truth.

Jesus said of the devil, the personification of all error, "He was a murderer from the beginning, and abode not in the truth, for there is *no truth* in him." "For he is a *liar*, and the Father of it." The origin of all evil is a lie. It says, There are two minds, two wills, two powers, etc., and all sorrow and trouble come from this falsehood.

Now we are beginning to separate and to cast away from the self all that the I am is not, and to maintain firmly that which I am.

This process, into which I find myself drawn, began in the first dawn of spiritual consciousness. When man awakened from the "dust," or from the wholly material conception of himself, and "Became a living soul," (Gen 2:7), he became alive to, or conscious of the fact of his spiritual being. He heard Truth saying then, even though he heard in feeble consciousness, "Thou shalt not partake of the knowledge of good and evil." (Gen 2:11) This is the interpretation we may find beneath the letter of those words.

Later on, man receives the same instruction under another figure. "Thou shalt not sow thy field with mingled seed."(Lev 19:19) "For what a man soweth that shall he also reap." Another way of saying, Thou shalt not believe in good and evil, for if thou dost, thou shalt reap good and evil.

Jesus represented this condition of thought by a parable (Matt 13:24-30). He illustrated the good seed by "wheat," and the evil seed by "tares." He saw thought as a field sown with mingled seed. The kingdom of heaven, which is "within you," was planted with good seed only; but *men fell asleep*, and *in their sleep* saw "an enemy" planting tares! *Asleep* to Truth, we see an opposite to Truth. This is the "origin" of evil.

So good and evil are held side by side, until thought awakens to the fact of good as all; then it questions, "Whence the tares"? It did not know before, that the tares had no right to be there. Something is arousing thought, and it at once desires to separate the wheat from the tares.

This shall be done, Truth replies, "In the time of harvest." Then "I will say to the reapers: Gather ye together first the tares and bind them in bundles to burn them, but gather the wheat into my barn."

Our first question has been, since Light revealed the true nature of all things as good, "Whence then is evil"? Truth answers: *You have been asleep!* The harvest is the awakening time of thought. It is called in other places, the Judgment day.

To judge is to discern, or distinguish between; and our "Day of Judgment" is when by Divine Light within, our thoughts are able to distinguish, and thus separate, between the true and the false claim.

The "Reapers" are Divine Thoughts, directed by Truth, in this sifting and separating. We understand the process when we have entered into it.

What is Truth's directions? "Gather *first* the tares and bind them to burn them." Error must be disposed of first. This law we will consider in our next study.

"Gather the wheat into my barn." All good is eternal. All error shall be consumed. "For behold the day cometh that shall burn as an oven." (Mal 4:1). The "Day" is the Divine Light; it shall "burn as an oven," for "Our God is a consuming fire," consuming all unlike good. The Light is also the fire, for the Light of Truth destroys all error belief.

Jesus again illustrates this judgment, in Matt 25:31. Truth is the Judge; sitting upon his "throne," represents the Truth enthroned within our consciousness. Then is judgment passed upon all conditions, and separation is made by Divine Thoughts, for the "holy angels" are in this picture. The "sheep" are placed upon the right, the "goats" upon the left. The sheep go into life eternal, the goats into the everlasting fire.

These all teach us of the purifying each soul receives, when it falls into the hands of Truth. Every belief of sin, error, evil, or any opposite to God, shall be dissolved in the consciousness that the One is All.

"I will turn my hand upon thee, and purely purge away thy dross." (Isa 1:28)

Practical Suggestions

When we look into faces around us, we find traces of anxiety and care in all. Anxious thought has written its marks over most faces.

What are we anxious about? Some fear haunts us. We seem afraid of so many things. Afraid of *falling* into something that will hurt us, or somebody else. Suppose now, that we just *let ourselves fall!* Rest awhile by saying, "I have no concern about what happens. I am not anxious. I have no responsibility." It will be well for us to try falling for a time. We have been on such a strain, trying to *hold ourselves up*, to keep from falling; let us now yield, give up the strain, fall! What then? Where is there to fall but into God?

"Underneath are the everlasting arms." We have never rested upon them, because we have been trying to keep *ourselves* up. When we "let go" we shall feel all about us, these strong arms."

All threats of what may happen to us, will be *proven* powerless when we give up resistance. Let come what will, for only God can come!

We may begin to destroy claims of fear and anxiety by saying often: "I am not afraid, for there is nothing to be afraid of. "God hath not given me a spirit of fear. Perfect Love casts out all fear."

I am love, for God is Love. I am peace, for God is Peace. I am understanding, for God is Understanding. I am not afraid.

In the judgment of Truth, we are led to surrender past conceptions, that we may follow the light of a new consciousness. "And another of his disciples said, 'Lord, suffer me first to go and bury my father.' But Jesus said 'Follow me; let *the dead* bury their dead.' So, likewise, whosoever he be of you that forsaketh not all that he hath, he cannot be my disciple.

"If any man come to me, and hate not his father and mother, and wife, and children, and brethren, and sisters, yea, and his own life also, he cannot be my disciple.

"The kingdom of heaven is like unto treasure hid in a field, the which when a man hath found, he selleth all that he hath, and buyeth the field."—Jesus' words.

Martha was cumbered about much serving; and Jesus said to her, "Thou art careful and troubled about many things. But one thing is needful; and Mary hath chosen that good part which shall not be taken away from her."

We cannot receive the Divine Idea of All-good, until we have given up many opinions and beliefs.

Fasting

"WE shall all stand before the judgment seat of Christ." (Rom 14; 10) That which cannot "stand" or remain, before Truth's judgment, is not of Truth.

"*We shall all stand*" before this judgment, is a blessed assurance, that there is Truth enough in all, to abide the trial by Truth! And Paul adds right here, Rom 14:11, as if this is what was in his thought, "For it is written, As I live, saith the Lord, *every* knee shall bow to me, and *every* tongue shall confess to God."

"Judgment day" comes, when the Light of Divinity is so bright in the soul, that it detects all that is of Truth and all that is not of Truth— all that is of the Divine, and all that is not.

In this time, or consciousness, sinners "tremble" because all sense of error is about to be destroyed; only that which is of Divine image and likeness, shall "remain," or "stand," in this increase of Light.

So it is written, Psl 1:5, "The ungodly, shall not *stand* in the judgment," but "*We* shall *all* stand!" All that is ungodly anywhere, shall be wiped out! Truth shall search out all wickedness until none is found.

(Psl 10:1) "The wicked shall be turned into hell," (Psl 9:17) that is, into the purifying fire which is Divine Love.

"For yet a little while and the wicked *shall not be*. Yea, thou shalt diligently consider *his place*, and *it shall not be*" (Psl 37:10). Because in the very place that we saw wickedness, Light and Truth have shown God to be! Omnipresent Good. In this light the wicked shall not stand or remain in any place at all. Omnipresence is the "Consuming fire."

"As wax melteth before the fire, so let the wicked *perish*, at the presence of God." (Psl 68 :2)

"When the Lord shall have washed away the *dross* of the daughters of Zion, and shall have purged the blood of Jerusalem from the midst thereof, by the spirit of judgment, and by the spirit of burning." (Isa 4:4)

"The sinners in Zion are afraid. Who among us shall *dwell* ("stand") with the devouring fire? Who among us *dwell* with the everlasting burnings? He that walketh uprightly and speaketh righteously, he that stoppeth his ears from *hearing* of blood and shutteth his eyes from seeing evil." (Isa 11:14-15)

When the time of judgment or separation comes, the sinners are represented as being "afraid," or "trembling," or being in great rage, because their end is near. As in Rev 12:12: "The devil is come down unto you, having great wrath, because he knoweth that he hath but a short time". Later on in the book, we see the devil cast into the "Lake of fire." The Greatness of Divine Love, at last consumes the most boasted power of evil.

The purifying fire, then, is a process in each soul by which all false conceptions are destroyed. Paul tells all about it in Cor 3:11-16. Upon one foundation, which is Truth, men are building two ideas of life; one is of Divine Nature, therefore is the eternal Substance, designated as "Gold, silver, and precious stones." The other is not of the Divine Nature, Changeless Truth, and it is designated as "Hay, wood, and stubble," because of its perishable nature.

The testing time comes. "The day shall declare it." Divine Light shall show the true or false nature of all things, of all opinions and all works. "The fire shall try every man's work of what sort it is."

If man's idea of life is based upon the true and eternal, his thought and word, his soul and body, is representative of Truth, is the image and likeness of God. This building "abides," "dwells," "stands" in the midst of Light and fire.

If man's ideas of life are contrary to that which is good, his thought and word, soul and body, is representative of error. This *building* "shall be burned" in the consuming fire. All the false ideas of life shall be destroyed; all that this soul has "built" shall be swept away, in order that his thought may be purified, for it is declared,

"But *he himself* shall be saved, yet as by fire."

This judgment day, by the "light" of which we are able to discern what is of Truth's nature and what is not, and therefore to separate the true from the false claim, does not break suddenly upon us, but comes at the end of a process within our consciousness.

It is the "Day of the Lord," which spiritually interpreted signifies the "Light of the Divine Nature," the light in which Divine Nature is clearly seen.

It is a day of destruction, which we welcome when we understand it, because the many false ideas which our ignorance has invented are destroyed by the true light.

This judgment day comes near the "End of the World," because in its light, our conception of the world passes away and we enter into a new consciousness of the world. Thought is ready to see heaven and earth by a new light, is prepared to receive a new idea of heaven and earth; this is the end of *our* world!

John saw in his vision, the "Great and small" appear before God to be judged. In this judgment he saw heaven and earth pass away; he also saw "Death and hell cast into the lake of fire." Later, he declares that he saw a "New heaven and a new earth," but speaks not of seeing a "new hell" after its destruction!

The devil spoke to Jesus, "All these things will I give thee if thou wilt *worship me*." Worship acknowledges a power and presence. Every day this temptation meets us, as it did Jesus; evil appearances appeal to us, to acknowledge the reality of evil, to admit its power and presence!

But Jesus answered, "It is written, Thou shalt worship the Lord thy God, and Him only shalt thou serve." Truth replies to claims of error, God alone is power and presence; this only do I acknowledge. Then "the devil leaveth him and angels come."

We recall the story of the Saint, who was so lost in contemplation of Divine Love, as to be filled completely with its Holy Presence. In the midst of his bright vision arose a dark figure, whom he knew to be "Satan." Looking upon it a moment, with the light of Love filling his soul, he exclaimed, "Satan, thee too I love." Immediately the dark form disappeared, and Light Divine, shone in the very place where darkness had been.

To look at every appearance, with thought aglow in the consciousness of Divine Presence and Power as all, is to dispel every opposite claim.

Peter expresses this idea of the judgment day when he says, "The day of the Lord shall come as a thief in the night." A thief does not *announce* his coming with noise of trumpet and commotion! He steals upon us so silently, that we are not aware of his presence, until we see what *his work* has been!

So does Divine Light quietly take possession of our thoughts, stealing away our treasures of earth. As is added, "In which the heavens shall pass away with a great noise, and the elements (of the world) shall melt with fervent heat, and the works that are therein shall be burned up."

The Light is the thief; we now long for its coming! though we shall find all our old and highly valued ideas of heaven and earth "done away."

Understanding the work of Light, even its destroying power, we no longer rebel, but gladly lay in its consuming power, all that is not of Divine Nature. "He shall baptize you with the Holy Ghost and with fire." Christ's baptism upon us, immerses us in Divine Consciousness, which purifies us from our beliefs in something beside God.

We noted how Truth said in this harvest, or sifting time, "Gather first the tares, to burn them."

First then, we will search truly among our conceptions, and separate, by the light of judgment, based upon Spirit as All Life, Mind, and Substance, all that *claims* to be, or that we have believed to be a truth, a life, and a mind not God.

We can do this when touched by Divine Knowledge, for "He that is spiritual judgeth all things."

Standing in the Presence of Truth, let us witness what separation is made between the Divine, and the not Divine.

On one hand we have:	On the other:
The Divine Nature.	The claim of mortal nature.
Born of God.	Not born of God.
Cannot sin.	Full of sin.
Perfect health.	Full of sickness.
Perfect love.	Full of fear.
Perfect peace.	Full of discord.
The immortal.	The mortal.
The living.	Dying.
The loving.	Hating.
Rest.	Unrest.
The incorruptible.	The corruptible.
The wheat.	The tares.
The sheep.	The goats.
Truth speaks to these,	To these Truth says,
"Enter thou into the joy	"Depart from me, I
of thy Lord."	never knew you."

That which Truth *never knew*, has *no truth in it*, is therefore falsehood. *All Truth belongs* in the *Divine Nature*, and here we find, in the separation taking place within us, Peace, Perfection, Life, Health, Strength, and all Good, hence we declare these to be truth. *All untruth belongs* in the *claim of a mortal nature*, and here we find arrayed, discord, imperfection, sin, sickness and death, all evil.

In the Divine Nature, God, Spirit, Infinite Mind is seen as the Master sowing Good seed only; here is the "Wheat." In the claim of a mortal nature, man has fallen asleep to Truth, and his dreams, which seem so real, while he is in them, are of suffering, death, evil and darkness.

He begins to be aroused by the voice of Truth saying, "Awake, thou that sleepest, and arise from the dead, and Christ shall give thee light." (Eph 4:14)

"It is high time to awake out of sleep, for now is our salvation nearer than when we believed. The night is far spent, the *day is at hand*" (Rom 13:11). The "deep sleep" that fell upon Adam, has held the race in dullness until this day. But it is written, "As in Adam *all* die, so in Christ shall *all* be made alive." Not in some far off Adam, any more than a far off Christ! In the ignorant thought *within us*, is belief of separation and death. Also in the consciousness of sonship within us, is knowledge of oneness and life eternal for all.

In this "sleep," the whole race has believed in separation from God, which means separation from Peace, from Life, from Spirit and Wisdom, from Strength and Wholeness. We have the "fruit" of that belief. It appears as our world of sin and suffering.

In the awaking, we begin to see the falseness of these universal, or race beliefs; we see there is no separation from God, no world of our own, no mind of our own, no life separate from God; no power, no presence, no knowledge but God Mind.

But, as when we awaken from a deep sleep, we do not in a moment throw off the spell of the sleep and its dream, so we do not at once and for all, give up that which has held us so long. We are not at first *wide awake*; sometimes we indulge in a little more sleep, and go back into our dream! But "morning" has come, the "day" has dawned, darkness is disappearing, and we *must* arise.

After we are fully aroused, we often smile at the absurdity of our dreams; sometimes we are so glad to know that they are *not true*. How much more satisfaction shall we feel when we "awake to righteousness," which is right thinking; "I shall be satisfied when I awake with thy likeness." (Prov 17:15) When I *awake* to the truth of being in thy likeness, or of being Divine Nature.

What will help us to arouse quickly from our dream of error and evil? To cease to believe in error and evil, because we see Truth and Goodness as *All in all*. But we have seen the opposite so long it is hard to throw it off.

For this very reason we must not fall asleep again; the first awakening is the hardest; be persistent, be positive. What will help us to be positive?

First, "Bind the tares in bundles to burn them." We have bound them in bundles under Truth's directions. The race beliefs, the claim of a mortal nature, of something not born of God. All appearances of evil result from these beliefs, for we have seen how all sorrow and suffering follow in this train. How shall we "burn" these? "Cast out the bond woman and her son." "The grace of God (which is light within) that bringeth salvation hath appeared to all men, *teaching* us that, *denying* ungodliness and worldly lusts, we should live soberly, righteously and godly in *this present* world." (Titus 2:12)

The surest way to become free from evil is to *deny* it a place; deny all that is un-godlike. We can do this when we know God is all. Begin and deny each claim separately. "There is no truth in the claim of a mortal nature. There is nothing that is not of God. There is no separation from God. There is, therefore, no world of sin, sickness, discord, or fear. "God hath not given us a spirit of fear." (Tim 1:7) There is no death. There is no hate. There is no suffering in the world; for:

> There is no mind but Immortal Mind.
> There is no power in any claim of evil.
> There is no power in the false race beliefs.
> There is no place for evil or error.
> There is no self apart from God."

When we deny the race beliefs the universal opinions about fear, trouble, sickness and death, which bind us, until by Truth, we see our freedom; we have handled the strongest claim of error there is, one of the largest "bundles."

Remember, error and evil are only claims, resulting from ignorance of God, and belief of separation; deny ignorance, it does not belong to Divine Mind, and Divine Mind is All-Presence.

Deny separation—there is none. All are in the One. While we have not *seen* God everywhere, we have *believed* in seeing something *not* God. This belief is that which must be "cast out," and is cast out by our denials; because as we deny, we cease to believe in it.

Jacob, in his sleep, saw a ladder reaching from heaven to earth. Angels ascended and descended. So in sleep have we believed in the visitation of "angels," but God's presence was at the other end of the ladder.

When "morning" came and "day" dawned to Jacob, he saw differently. "When Jacob *awaked* out of *his sleep* he said, Surely the Lord *is in this place*, and I knew it not. *This* is none other but the house of God, and this is the gate of heaven." (Gen 28:16, 17)

When the disciples questioned Jesus about their inability to heal a certain case, he said it was because of their *unbelief.* He added these words: "Howbeit this kind goeth not out, but by prayer and fasting." This is just as true today. We must fast and pray without ceasing.

Fasting in its inner sense, is the soul's denial of all the claims of sense; denying the old mortal idea of life and of self, that the Divine Idea may more fully possess our thoughts.

"The Lord is in the midst of thee, thine eye shall not see evil anymore."

Deny Thyself

I have no *self* apart from God.
There is no Mind, Life, Power, or Substance, apart from God.
There is no Mind or Power of darkness, or evil.
There is no reality or power in fear.
"God hath not given us fear." There is no fear.
There is no evil. There is no death.
There is no cause of suffering or sorrow.
These claims are not found in the Source of All.

Man is not born of flesh.

Man does not inherit from flesh.

Man is not heir to ills of flesh.

There is no flesh, for all is Spirit.

I am not "conceived in sin," nor "shapen in iniquity."

God only is my Father, my Lifegiver, my Source.

I am not affected by universal beliefs of sin, evil and death.

There is no universal mortal mind.

I have no past outside of God.

I have no doubt, anxiety, or fear.

I have no uncertainty of Life.

I have no ignorance.

I am nothing of myself. I am all in God.

The Truth hath made me free.

Prayer

FASTING, in its spiritual sense, is breaking away from all that binds or limits. We may do this by ejection of past ideas which contain belief of *any opposite* to God.

"Is not this the fast which I have chosen: To *loose* the bands of wickedness, to *undo* the heavy burdens, to let the oppressed *go free*, and that ye *break every yoke?* . . . Then shall thy light break forth as the morning and thy health spring forth speedily." (Isa 58:6, 8)

When the light of true judgment has illumined our consciousness, we know how to fulfill this "fast."

"Ye cannot serve two Masters," Jesus said; which is to say: Ye cannot acknowledge two powers. Because we have done so, we must now break the yoke of bondage to one or the other; shall we acknowledge the power of Spirit only? If so, we must free ourselves from the belief of bondage to the flesh. "There is no power but of God; no power but Spirit," may be our denial for this. Jesus said: "Now is the axe laid at the root of the tree, and every plant that my Father *hath not planted* shall be *rooted up.*"

Cause of evil and error must be struck at, not the outer effect. Cause of sickness and sorrow must be destroyed, and not just the appearance. Truth cuts *deep*, and roots out "Every plant which my Father hath not planted;" because Truth reveals that whatever the Father hath not planted, has *no reality, no cause*; this understanding *destroys* the *cause* of sin, sickness and death. There is no cause of evil; when we see this, a blow has been made at the *root*, which shall finally destroy the entire plant." (Isa 52:2, 5)

To clear our garden of weeds, we clean them out root and all, for if we cut away only the tops we shall have an abundant crop again. To heal the sickness of the body is like cutting off the tops of our weeds, and leaving all the roots to put forth again in new growth.

Science goes always into Cause; and as there is but One Cause to go into, and that forever Good, it soon eliminates the *cause* of *evil,* seeing it has none! The only supposed cause of evil and suffering is the thought of separation from Good. There *is no* separation from God. Truth destroys *this* "cause."

Fasting is "casting down imaginations" or false images thought is holding. "And every high thing that exalteth itself against the knowledge of God: and bringing into captivity *every thought*, to the obedience of Christ." (Cor 10:5)

That which sees things contrary to God is imagination. "And God saw that . . . every imagination of the thoughts of man's heart was only evil continually." (Gen 6:5) This condition caused the "flood," and within each of us, the flood shall come, that shall destroy these imaginations. When the soul is flooded with the light of Truth and Love, "The world of the ungodly" perishes; the imagination that there is an ungodly world is destroyed. Righteous thought—Noah (Gen 6:5) is separated from all unrighteousness, that ungodliness may be destroyed.

Fasting is "shutting the door" when thought enters into communion with All-Spirit. It shuts out everything but Spirit, seeing that Spirit is all. Hence fasting *prepares the way* for prayer; it empties thought, making it ready for, or receptive to refilling. "Empty that he might fill me," expresses the idea of fasting and prayer.

Thought emptied of its own opinions and ideas, is cleansed, and prepared to be filled with Divine Idea.

Prayer is the complement of fasting. After the emptying must come the filling; after the rooting out, comes the re-sowing; after tearing down, we want to build; after fasting we must pray.

As a new idea of Truth dawns in our understanding, one of the first questions it stirs up is, How shall I pray?, which shows that our prayer changes as our consciousness changes.

As Jesus opened the disciples' eyes to more Spiritual understanding, we hear them asking at once, "Lord, teach us how to pray."

As consciousness increases, prayer assumes new meaning, and the words of our childhood—the "milk" that belonged to babyhood—no longer satisfy our fuller grown thought.

To find a more helpful idea of prayer, which our new consciousness demands, we first must know what the purpose of prayer is.

Prayer cannot, and has never changed God. We read, in Isaiah 51:9, the prayer of Israel, calling upon God, to awake. "Awake, awake, put on strength, O arm of the Lord." This is the prayer of childhood, and the answer comes back (Isa 52:1) "Awake, awake, put on *thy strength*, O Zion." "Zion" needs to awake, not God.

As soon as we understand that the *All* is Ever present, that we live in It, and that "All things are ours," we see that the purpose of prayer is not to bring anything to us, is not to induce the Divine to grant us, what it would otherwise not have given, but to bring us into a realization of the Fullness of Good, that is everywhere present, so that we may *accept* the Eternal gift of Love.

One says, "God has given all of Himself to each one. He has nothing more to give." And when Truth declares, "Before they call I will answer," it is as much as to say, everything is given them, before they ask for it. Asking does not then bring anything to us, but earnest seeking helps us to find and receive that which is always "at hand."

God's Omnipresence makes us sure of all good here and now, and when this consciousness is ours, prayer changes. We have no more pleading to do, but we desire only to have *our eyes opened*, to see what is here for us in Truth.

When Hagar wept and "Lifted up her voice," praying for water, that her son might live, "*God opened her eyes*, and she *saw* a well of water." (Gen 21:19)

Prayer opens our eyes to see God's ever present supply, and we see there is no lack. Because "Eye hath not *seen*" and "Ear hath not *heard*" we have been "hungry" and "thirsty" in the midst of full supply. "Prayer is not overcoming God's reluctance; it is *laying hold* of His Highest willingness."

In this understanding, Jesus' words come to us with clear meaning, "Therefore all things whatsoever ye ask and pray for, believe that ye *have received*, and ye shall have." (Mark 11:24) (Rev)

No more pleading when our eyes and ears are opened to see and hear the good that is all around us that is ours as "Heirs of God."

If we pray as Jesus here directs, our petitions will be changed to thanksgiving, as we recognize that we "have received" all things!

Jesus' prayer at the tomb of Lazarus, before he had called upon him to come forth from the dead, should be ours in all that we desire: "Father, I thank Thee that Thou *hast heard* me, and I know that Thou hearest me always."

It is also written: "If we *know that he heareth us*, we also *know* that we *have* the petitions that we desired of Him." (John5:15) When we know that He "heareth us always," we will joyfully declare this, as Jesus did, rather than plead, as of old: "*Hear* our prayer, good Lord." Our manner of praying will be, then, according to our understanding of God, and man's relation to God.

While we believe in God as a Great Personality, seated in some far off heaven, arbitrary in will and purpose, swayed by man's pleadings, moved by his desires, sending good gifts as a reward, withholding good as a punishment, we will send up our petitions and pleadings without cessation.

When we know God as Changeless Power and Presence, always Love, forever Good, Eternal Fullness, "Without shadow of turning," *filling full* heaven and earth; that the kingdom of All Good is within us; that this Infinite Good-Presence does not change, because it is always

Perfection; does not make *special gifts*, but forever *gives all* to all; then we pray according to this knowledge.

We know that every good thing is ready and waiting for us to accept with loving gratitude, that in the "Son" we are heirs to this All-good, ever present. We hear Spirit saying to Its Own Begotten in us: "Son, *all that I have is thine*"; and we answer: "All mine are thine, and all thine are mine." Blind ignorance only has kept us from receiving all good; we have not *seen*.

It is written (Fer 17:5-8) "Cursed be the man that trusteth in man and maketh flesh his arm"; that trusteth in man's opinions; that believes in Life and Understanding apart from God. "For he shall be like the heath in the desert, and shall not *see when good cometh*. Blessed is the man that trusteth in the Lord, for he shall be as a tree planted by the waters and shalt not *see when heat cometh*."

So we need not ask God to be near us; Good cannot come any nearer than it always is! Let us then seek to *realize how near* God is. We will not ask for more life, more strength, more health, to be given us; but will try to appreciate and accept the changeless Life and Strength, the perfect Health in which we live. "Shall we plead for *more* at the open Fount, which already pours forth more than we can" (or know how) "to receive"? What then shall we ask for? Only that our eyes may be opened to see what eternally is.

Consciousness of God enables us to claim what is; to recognize our Father's good gifts and good will. The prayer then of a higher understanding is *recognition* of Truth, and willing thanksgiving.

> "In happy childhood, at a father's call,
> Trusting we walk wherever He may lead.
> We say not: 'Father, do not let me fall
> Down this steep hill.' We feel so safe, that all
> We think is to enjoy his loving heed.
> We never plead: 'Do not forget, I pray,
> To give me food and drink enough to-day.'
> Why should we with a heavenly Father plead?"

In a better consciousness, the pleading of God's children, gives place to joyful recognition. Many, at this point, call attention to the "Lord's Prayer," and ask, is not that full of petition? Granted that it is, we must remember that Jesus himself, admitted his restriction in speaking, because of lack of understanding in his hearers. He must give the prayer which the consciousness of his hearers could receive. The Spirit of Truth is revealing the "many things" that Jesus could not then tell about; and clearer consciousness can receive them.

But we notice that in the Lord's Prayer there is *no "if."* It seems that the greatest hindrance to answer of prayer has been because of that little word "if," which Jesus never directed us to use. Webster defines "if" to mean, "In case that, or supposing that." Then "if" implies doubt, and doubting prayer is not answered. "He that wavereth is like a wave of the sea. . . . Let not that man think that he shall receive anything of the Lord." (James 1:6, 7)

Jesus indicated the need of perfect confidence when he said, "Whosoever shall *say* to this mountain, *Be thou* removed, and shall not doubt in his heart, but shall believe *that what he saith* comes to pass, he shall have it." Here we are authorized to speak positively, which we never do when we put an "if" in.

When we know that "The word which I speak is not mine, but the Father's," we will also know that it "Shall not return unto me void."

But one will say, "I pray, if it be thy will, because I am not sure whether it is God's will or not." In such a case, we had better at once enlighten ourselves about God's will; there is no excuse for not knowing it. As Paul says: "Be not foolish, but know what the will of the Lord is." (Eph 5:17)

"The Lord *shall* preserve thee from all evil." (Psl 121:7) is a statement in His Word, and makes plain God's will towards us. Again, it is told us clearly in Gal 1-4, "Who gave himself for our sins, that he might deliver us from this *present evil world, according* to the *will of God.*" One came to Jesus saying: "Lord, *if* Thou *wilt,* thou *canst* make me clean." Not doubting his power—I know thou canst—but uncertain about his *willingness.* Jesus' answer to this one is the answer for all in such doubt, "*I will*: be thou clean." God is always more willing to give than we are to receive!

When we understand God's will, as Jesus did, how gladly will we say, "Not my will, but Thine," for as one says: "The 'I will' in Truth is God's will." This we see, when we know that the *One* is *All*; One Mind; One Intelligence; One Will.

Jesus said: "Abide in me"; be firm or fixed in consciousness of the One that I am, "And ye shall ask what ye will, and it shall be done unto you," for it is then the One Will. "It is God that worketh in me both *to will* and to do of His good pleasure," after I have given up all belief of separateness.

Jesus again said: "If ye ask *anything* in my name, I will do it"; does not say in these boundless promises, "I will do it if it is best for you," but simply, I will do it. Do what? "*Anything*" you wish, but seek it "*in my name.*" This is the secret. We may find everything in that wonderful Divine Name, *I am*, which is also Divine Nature. In the Divine Nature we have all things we desire: Peace, Health, Strength, All-good is there, and is ours in that Nature, which I am. We can feel no doubt, nor say an "if" when we understand asking "in his name."

"Open thy mouth *wide* and I will *fill* it." (Psl 81:10) Make plenty of room to receive, the Divine sets no limit. If thought is half filled with belief of evil, it cannot be more than *half* filled with good. If thought is emptied of all belief of evil, it can be filled *full* of good.

'Prove me now, saith the Lord, if I will not open the *windows* of heaven (open your spiritual eyes to see) and pour out a blessing that there shall not be room enough." (Mal 3:10)

What we receive is not limited by the Giver, but by our capacity to receive.

"When the poor widow applied to Elisha for aid, he met her need by increasing the oil she had in the house; and the limit of increase was set, not by the Giver of every good gift, not by Elisha, through whom the blessing came, but by the widow who *measured for herself!* The oil ran until it filled every vessel *she had set* to contain it! And when there was not a vessel more, the oil stayed."

As one says, "our failure to receive comes from self made limitations."

What shall we ask for? Jesus told us, when he said, "Seek ye first the kingdom of heaven." And David gave us the right idea of prayer when he declared, "One thing have I desired of the Lord, that will I seek after; that I may dwell in the house of the Lord forever." (Psl 27:4)

The kingdom of God is also God's house; David was seeking the kingdom of God, or to dwell in God's presence. To become conscious of God's All-Presence is to dwell in that Presence. If we declare God's Presence as all, we help our thought to dwell in that consciousness to dwell in God's "House."

Jesus said (Luke 10:42): "But one thing is needful." This one thing is to recognize the ever present God or Good.

Can we concentrate our desires to "one thing?" When we do, we shall find in that "one thing" whatever we would ask for. It is His Holy Name or Nature; it is His One Only Presence and Power, which we are to joyfully acknowledge and accept.

Our past praying, has been so mixed with doubt, because we have not seen God's will clearly, and could not understand that the All-Good was ours before we began to pray, so we never felt certain of the answer! This need not discourage us, because when we know better, we shall pray better!

When Peter was imprisoned by Herod, we read that "Prayer was made without ceasing, of the church unto God for him." On the night of his delivery he went to a house where "Many were gathered together praying." Peter knocked at the door, and the maid, who knew Peter's voice, ran in to those praying, and "Told them how Peter stood before the gate." And they said unto her, "Thou art mad!" But she constantly affirmed that it was even so. "Then," said they, "it is his angel!" The need, just as truly now as then, is to have *more faith* in our prayers! And knowledge will give us that faith. In clearer understanding we will revise our form of prayer. Our old and well loved "Now I lay me," has new strength and meaning in its "new" form:

A Child's Prayer

"Now I lay me down to sleep,
I *know* that God His child doth keep,
I *know* that God my life is nigh,
I *live* in Him, I cannot die.
God is my Health, I can't be sick,
God is my Strength, unfailing, quick.
God is my All, I know no fear,
Since Life, and Truth, and Love are here."
"Oh, Thou All-seeing, and All-knowing One,
Whom we call 'Father,' 'God,' 'Creator,' to Thee
We pray, not as of old when ignorance of Thy laws
And Thee, did bid us supplicate, entreat,
Implore for things we most desired.
But in the higher understanding
With which our great Teacher bade us pray;
He who said: 'When thou prayest, *believe*
That things desired by thee, are thine!
For thy Father knoweth *all thy heart*,
And gives thee all good blessings, *e'er thy prayer
Is uttered!* God is perfection, law itself,
And *He* no changing needs. But we, His children,
Heirs by birth and inheritance, have lived
So long in doubt of our estate, cannot receive;
Our spiritual ears, eyes and thoughts are silent;
So we the changing need,
Now when we pray, we will not say:
'Dear Father, hear our prayer;' but *know*
That Thou *dost hear*, and answer!
We will not plead, 'Be near us,'
But *know* that *space* filled by *Thee alone*!
And surely Thou art here as *everywhere*.
We will not *plead* that Spirit's power,

May us encompass and protect,
We *know* that spirit never leaves us day or night.
We'll let each breath, and thought, and word,
A *recognition* be, our lives be hid in Thee.
Content in *Thee*, we find our heaven *now*,
And *nothing* have to fear,
Since God is 'All in All,' and God is *good*."

I And My Father Are One

One in Life, in Mind, in Idea, in Consciousness;
One in Truth, in Freedom, in Fullness, in Wisdom;
One in Strength, in Wholeness, in Peace, and Rest.
God, my Source, is Omnipresent, Omnipotent, Omniscient Life
and Love.
I (my name, or my patient's name) express the Omnipresent,
Omnipotent, Omniscient Life and Love.
I, (patient's name), the individual, express all the Truth of the
Universal Divine Man.
The Universal says: I *am* Divine Man, one with God; one with
Life, Truth, and Love.
The individual says: I express the Whole Truth of Divine Man; his
Perfection, Peace, Wholeness, Ease,
Understanding, Harmony, Goodness, and Love.
The Spirit of Love fills the universe of God.
I live in the full Power and Presence of Love.
Spirit fills all time and all places.
Every moment is brimming full of Life Eternal and Changeless.
Because God is Life, I (patient's name) express life; because God
is Wholeness, I express health; because God is Peace, I express
peace and ease.
(After emptying thought by the denials given, fill it with these
Divine affirmations).

Growth
The Power of the Word

"FOR by thy words thou shalt be justified and, by thy words thou shalt be condemned."(Matt 12:37)

Science turns about (converts) our thoughts from the outward to the inward; from the visible to the invisible; from appearances to righteous judgment; from the body to Spirit; from the word to Mind; from the fruit to the Vine; from effect to Cause. By thus looking beyond appearances, I can see by Divine Light, what I am.

Before I can judge righteously, and *appear* right, I must know what it is to *be* right.

The spoken word is, as Webster defines it: A sign or symbol of an idea in Mind. Every word spoken, which also signifies every *visible thing*—has an idea back of it in which it originated. The idea is the unspoken word; the spoken word is the idea expressed. The idea is first, therefore is the power that is in the word. Hence all power is in Mind, and the word expresses that power.

In Divine Mind is the Eternal Idea of all things. "The word that was in the beginning with God, and was God." This word is complete in God, *before* it is *spoken forth*; for it is God's complete Idea, which is All-Good, All-Perfection, All-Truth. So when we speak the Word of Truth, we speak of *finished work*, that which is eternally done in God; hence our speaking does not *make* any truth, but it expresses, or brings forth, the Truth that *is*, and that was, *before* we spoke.

This explains many verses in the Bible, as Gen. 2:4-5, "In the day that the Lord God made every plant of the field *before* it was *in* the earth, and every herb of the field, *before* it *grew!*" And again, in Heb 4:3, "For we which have believed do enter into *rest*. . . The works were *finished* from the foundation of the world"; or Eph 2:9, "Not of works lest any man should boast."

> My Eternal Life is a finished fact.
> My Health is a finished fact.
> My Peace is a finished fact.

We can never in Truth assume that individually we have done anything; not even can we claim by *our* understanding, to have accomplished aught. *Divine* Understanding enlightens our thought to see that which is *eternally finished in Truth.* And as soon as we see it, we begin to think it, and to declare it: this is to be our work. Our part is to believe in the *finished* Truth of all things in God.

The Truth that thus presents itself to us is God's Divine Idea; we have called it the Christ always Full and Complete. We are to *believe in* this Fullness and Completeness of all things, and this helps us to understand that, which Jesus declares to be the "work" which God requires of each soul. (John 6:29), "This is the work of God, that ye *believe* on him whom He hath sent." We are to believe on, and to be positive about the finished work of God the Divine that He hath sent into all.

Now, I desire to be good, where shall I begin? Shall I try to make myself good by *acting* good? This would be trying individually to make something, which is impossible. If I want a beautiful lily, do I try to make the flower *first?* or do I plant deep out of sight, a lily bulb, which in due time sends forth stems, out of which burst the blossom? All of us can plant a bulb and have a lily. The bulb contains within it the perfect lily; the flower is the result of the perfect life and substance that is in the bulb.

This bulb may represent to us our Divine Nature. The planting of it in mother earth, may remind us to see our Divine Nature implanted within the Whole Divine Life, the Mother, Father, God Source of all; Power in and through all; "Your life is hid with Christ in God."(Col 3:3)

To understand my life buried with Truth in God, is to plant the bulb of my existence, the starting point of all outward expression of good.

The "stem" and "flower" represent to us this outward expression, put forth from within the bulb, *after it is buried.* When we look from the visible to the Invisible Life, from the act to the Actor, or Power of Action, Divine Life stirs up our souls, by pushing out Its own action, and the *result* comes into the visible *act* of goodness.

With faith in the bulb, and what it can do, we plant it, and *wait*. With faith in Divine Nature, and what it can do, we *believe in it*, and wait. "For we have need of patience that after we have *done the will*, we may receive the promise."

The Divine Soul is the budding out of the Spirit of Life, Truth, and Love. The Divine Body is the development of this bud into the perfect flower.

When thought is truly converted, it sees that we cannot *make* perfect lives, but we can *be* the Perfect Life in God, and thus let *it* put forth its perfection, peace, and beauty, into soul and body.

We cannot make good acts that are genuine; they must unfold from within good thoughts, which rest, or are positive in Good Being. All Truth must come from Source.

We cannot then make good health! There is just One Law of making or expressing anything.

We must go into Source and Cause, and *see* Good Health as an eternal fact—a finished Truth—then we *will believe* in good health only, and wait. By the law we have seen, this bud of good health, shall unfold into the perfect expression.

We cannot make the body well permanently, while thought is based upon ill-health as a truth. If we desire a well body, we must "Work as the Father works", which is to say we must recognize the Divine Law and method.

First, a well mind. As there is but One Mind, and that the Infinite, we can easily see that Mind is well! There is no Mind of disease.

Second, a well thought—and this comes naturally from a sound Mind.

Third, a well body—the sure result of a sound Mind and Thought.

"God hath not given us a Spirit of fear, but (God hath given us a Spirit) of love, and of power, and of a sound mind." (2 Tim 1:7) Therefore claim, "I have a sound mind, a sound thought, and a well body." This is the way to look to God for our good health. Joyfully recognize "What God *hath* prepared" for us. My good health is finished in God, is waiting for me to *accept*.

This is the whole Law of expression, which means the law of growth. It is always from within, outward.

"Consider the lilies how they grow; they toil not, neither do they spin." "Which of you, by taking thought, can add one cubit unto his stature." (Matt 6: 27, 28) These words contain such a wonderful secret: the whole mystery of growth is wrapped up in them.

Toil not, labor not *to grow*. Growth is never promoted in that way; busy thought never adds to your stature, and yet thought was made to be busy, for thought is the action of Mind!

It is natural to grow, and we grow without effort. If we use thought as a cause of growth, we make a mistake; thought is only the *method* by which growth is accomplished; the impelling power is in Mind which moves thought on to do its will. Thought is the servant, not Master; the action, not the Actor; the expression, not the Expresser.

Thought does not add to my stature, because I am that I am, eternally. Thought may *see* what I am, and seeing, declare it. The work of thought is not to make me anything, but to continually express what I am.

"Their strength is to *sit still*." In the outer, be passive, but in the inner, to "sit still" is to be brimful of the consciousness of Omnipotence! Be positive.

"For thus saith the Lord...in returning and rest shall ye be saved; in quiet and confidence shall be your strength; and ye whole not." (Isa 30:7-15)

"O, Jerusalem, . . .how often would I have gathered thy children together, even as a hen gathereth her chickens under her wings, and we would not." (Matt 23-37)

"Ye will not come unto me that ye might have life." (John 5:40)

We cannot "sit still" in Life, in Truth, and in Love, until we have come into Christ, come into knowledge of being Divine. Then I rest in *Being*; I direct thoughts to express the truth of my Being Divine, and the word, or visible result of thought, will follow. Growth, then, is not making myself *become* anything, it is becoming more and more conscious of what I am.

Because we have not recognized the truth of our Life and Being, thought has become filled with images of false being, which have obscured the true idea. Our visible world rests under the shadow of such false belief; for it is an acknowledged fact, by many thinkers, that creation, or the visible, is mysteriously linked with man's thought.

"The student of nature observes that all things in nature—the animals, mountains, seas, and stones—have a secret relation to man's thought and his life. Nature gives him a *copy* of every mood and shade in his character and mind. Every object he beholds is the mask of man. Nature is the *immense shadow* of man." Victor Hugo.

"The soul spreads *its own hue* over everything; the shroud or wedding garment of nature is woven in the loom of our own feelings." F. W. Robertson.

The visible world *returns to us* our own opinions and beliefs.

"There is nothing either good or bad, but thinking makes it so." Shakespeare.

"There is nothing unclean of itself; but *to him* that esteemeth a thing to be unclean, to him it is unclean."—Paul. His *thinking* makes it so to himself. We may as truly say, "There is nothing hurtful of itself but to him that esteemeth a thing to be hurtful, to him it is hurtful."

To change our world, therefore, we must change our *thoughts* about it. "The things that *are seen* are temporal," because *our way* of seeing things shall change!

"The creation is on wheels, always passing into something else, streaming into something *higher,* everything undressing and stealing away from its old into new forms. Thin or solid everything is in flight." Emerson. The outer is uplifted, as thought is enlightened by the Truth, to see the true nature of all things.

"A pure inward life, may transform the outward shape, and turn it by degrees, to the soul's essence, till all be made immortal." "Be ye transformed by the renewing of your minds."

The whole world is to be transformed by the making new of our thoughts of the world. When our belief of the world is darkness, the shadow of sin, sickness and death, or the absence of Purity, Health and Life seem to be.

A little girl, when asked what made the daylight on the earth truthfully replied: "The side of the earth that is turned to the sun." But when asked again what makes the night? Naturally replied, "The side of the earth that is turned to *darkness*." There is no darkness for the earth to turn towards! The darkness comes to the side of the earth that is turned *away from the light*. And still more, it is the earth's *own shadow* that creates darkness! If the earth were transparent, the light of the sun would penetrate it through and through, and shine into it and beyond it everywhere. The *opaqueness* of the earth, throws the shadow or darkness.

So the denseness of our thought, throws darkness over our world; these dense thoughts stand between the "Light that lighteth every man," and the world of *Truth*, casting their shadow on all things. This is how "We see through a glass darkly."

If our thoughts were clear, filled with light, then we would see "face to face"; or see everything as it is; for the light would penetrate our thoughts through and through, and shine upon all things.

These shadows cast from ignorant, dark thought make our world *seem* enveloped in darkness, doubt, fear, error and evil; of this it is written: "For all that is in the world—the lust of the flesh, and the lust of the eyes, and the pride of life, is not of the Father, (not God's world), but is of the world" (your own idea of the world). "And the world *passeth away*, and the lust thereof; but he that doeth the will of God abideth forever."(John 2:16-17) It is descriptive of a mental state, opposed to spirituality, which shall pass away, as spirit is known to be all.

Of this "world" (our own ideas, in belief of separation) Jesus spoke when he said, "In the world ye shall have tribulation, but be of good cheer, I have overcome the world. Ye are not of the world, even as I am not of the world."

Our first, or infant ideas of things, shall pass away, as thought matures. "The first man is of the earth earthy"; this represents the earliest idea man has of himself. "But the second man is the Lord from heaven;" the latest, or last idea that man has of himself, when the "new" is "put on," "Created in righteousness and true holiness." Man is to grow into this knowledge of himself, and the seed of such knowledge must be planted in the soil of Divine Mind, put forth through thought, and last *of all* spoken out in word.

Hence to improve the world, we would not in Science begin our work with the world—not work to change the outer; "Not by might, nor by power, but by my Spirit, saith the Lord." Change the beliefs of thought into right knowledge; and this must be done, not by saying "I will," but by hearing the voice of Wisdom within saying "I am." Begin always with Divine Nature, let it reveal itself. This is what all creation is waiting for, as it is written: "The whole creation groaneth; *waiting* for the *manifestation* of the sons of God." (Rom 8:22-19)

"Be still," is not slothfulness, but stilling mortal opinion, to let Divine Will have its full action. Be still, but *expectant*, wide awake, looking! "For to as many as *look for him*, he shall appear, without sin unto salvation. "We receive what we look for, since that only have we 'eyes' for. If we do not look for or expect good, we 'shall not *see* when good cometh!'" So of Health, of Life, and Strength, Peace and all good.

Two who had spent some time in India upon different missions met, and each told his experience. The Missionary recounted his triumphs, and rejoiced in the number of converts; the hunter replied, "I do not believe there is a Christian in India, for I was there for months without *seeing* one."

Then the hunter told his story, and spoke of the number of bears he had seen and shot; the Minister replied, "I do not believe there is a bear in India, for I was there for years and never *saw* one."

We all *see* what we *look for*. As long as we say, "We must look for trials and sufferings, and sickness, and death, while we are in this world," we shall find just these. And we cannot but notice now, how busy people are looking for tribulations!

Let us consider a practical illustration of how to obtain good results by going into Source, rather than working with effect. I feel tired, my body rebels against further effort. I lie down, or lay the body down to rest it. I rise refreshed, but only for a time; soon again the body demands rest; it is right, it should have rest! Again I lay it down to rest;

soon again it asks for rest, and it will continue to cry out for rest, until we learn how to give it true and permanent rest. How shall we do this? Go to where rest eternal is. "Come unto me, and rest." Enter into the Consciousness that *I* am Rest; my thought expresses the Rest that I am, and my body shows it forth this is the only lasting rest; and the body will continually demand it, until we give it its own! The tired body then is a warning voice to us. "Give me my true rest."

Let us be willing to grow up into our Divine Nature in all things. Which means that in every place we recognize that the Divine is, and is the rewarder of all that seek it.

A Study of the Trinity

Three is the sign, or symbol, of completeness.
"Three in One," indicates the Complete One.
Mind is a Trinity in Unity, or is complete as

Mind, Idea, and Consciousness.

This is Infinite Mind, in Stillness and Fullness, but with all Power of action. It "creates," or manifests Itself in Its own likeness. Therefore we find the "Three in One" in all creation; and God-Mind includes the whole creation, and holds it in oneness with Itself.

In the Trinity we may say there is one, two, three.
The One is the Infinite Mind.
The Two is the *action* of the One Infinite.
The Three is the *result* of this action of the One.
The One is the Creator.
The two and three, or action and result, is the creation. In the parable of the Vine, we find an illustration:
The One is the Vine.
The two and three are the branches and fruit; and Vine (Creator) includes and holds in oneness with itself, its branches and fruit (creation).

So there is but One in the universe Mind, the Actor; and creation, the unfolding of Mind.

Mind, the "Head"	Creation, the "body"	All One
1. Infinite Mind	1. Infinite Spirit	1. The One
2. Its thought	2. Its Soul	2. Its Action
3. Its Word	3. Its Body	3. Its Result
1. Creator	1. Infinite Cause	1. The Vine
2. Its image	2. Its Heavens	2. Its Branches
3. Its Likeness	3. Its Earth	3. Its Fruit

"Upon the summit of each mountain-thought
Worship thou God; for Deity is seen
From every elevation of the soul."
"They shall not hurt nor destroy in all my holy mountain;
for the earth shall be full of the knowledge of the Lord,
as the waters cover the sea." (Isa 11:9)

The Mountain of the Lord

AND it shall come to pass in the last days, that the mountain of the Lord's house shall be established *in the top* of *the mountains*, and shall be exalted above the hills, and all nations shall flow into it. And many people shall go and say, Come ye, and let us go up to the Mountain of the Lord." (Isa 2:2)

Mountain is the symbol of clear consciousness, or perfect spiritual realization. As we ascend a mountain our vision is extended; we rise above the earth nearer heaven; we see more clearly. So does consciousness lift us above "earthiness," and give us plainer, broader vision. The "Mountain of the Lord's house," represents consciousness of God's presence, and the promise is, that in the "last days," or fuller light, the knowledge of God's presence shall be established above all other knowledge, and all others shall come into *it*.

This indicates plainly to us, that in due time, all things shall be brought into the Consciousness of Love, Life, and Truth. "For the knowledge of the Lord shall cover the earth, as the waters cover the sea." This Consciousness of Divinity as all in all, is now beginning to be our refuge. "Beautiful for situation is Mount Zion, God is known in her palaces for a refuge." (Psl 47:2, 3) "Flee as a bird to your mountain, thou who are weary of sin." In perfect understanding, sin is not known!

"O Zion, that bringeth good tidings, get thee up into the high mountain." We know how Jesus went up into the mountain to pray; and it was in "an exceeding high mountain" that he met and conquered the strongest claims of the flesh! We need to be established in the highest consciousness, to be able to deny the allurements of sense, or appearances. In the Old Testament stories peculiar reference is made to mountains; and by finding the spiritual significance, most helpful truths are gleaned from the narratives.

"The ark rested upon the mountains," lifted up by the waters that had destroyed the "World of the ungodly." Our ark of safety finds its resting place in Divine Consciousness, borne upward upon the flood of light and Truth, that has destroyed our beliefs of darkness and error.

Moses went into the Mountain to receive the commands of the Lord. We likewise meet the Divine, face to face, when we rise into pure consciousness. John says that he was carried away in Spirit "To a great and high mountain," where he saw "The holy Jerusalem descending out of heaven from God." (Rev 21:10) When in the Spirit we are lifted into "a great and high" consciousness the same vision awaits us. We see in this high consciousness, heaven and earth as one heaven, and hear Truth saying, of this new heaven and earth, "And God shall wipe away all tears from their eyes, and there shall be no more death, neither sorrow, nor crying, neither shall there be any more pain, . . . and there shall be no more curse, . . . And there shall be no night there, . . . for the Lord God giveth them light." (Rev 21:4, 22:3-5) We cannot see this except from the height of pure Consciousness, even in "His holy mountain."

The Mount of Consciousness

EACH one stands now, somewhere on the "Mount of Consciousness." One may be lingering at the foot of this mount, where his vision is shut in, limited. Here his seeing is likely to be obscured by the mists of the valley; into this low spot, the sunlight reaches for only a few brief hours, the "shadows," therefore, fall long and deep. In the "valley" is the "shadow of death." (Psl 23:4)

We hear this one praying for deliverance from these deep shadows and blinding mists. The answer comes, "Work out your own salvation. If you are seeing clouds and shadows, it proves that you are standing on low ground. Your only deliverance is, to *rise above* the *place* of mists and darkness. In the valley must ever be deep shadows and clouds, they belong to the valley; but I have told you that 'There shall be no hurt in all my holy mountain.' Ascend, come *up*; and soon you will be lifted to where there are no shadows. 'Follow me.'"

Now the willing one, obedient to the guiding voice, begins to turn away from the valley, and to seek the mountain path; soon he sees a way that has been opened by the One who first ascended, and who now calls from the heights to all below him, "Come unto me"; "Come and be with me, where I am; come from the depths of your doubt and fear in the valley, to this summit of Light, where I stand. I have gone before and prepared a way for you. I wait to receive you here. I have overcome, by coming up over all doubts and darkness, and because I did this, you may also. The way is 'straight and narrow,' it leads *directly* to me."

This voice is heard even by those halting in the valley; and he who heeds, begins at once the ascent, although the way is not familiar at first.

But soon an exclamation of surprise is heard; as this one advances in the new way, he cries, "How my view is broadening, how much freer I feel, how pure is the atmosphere becoming, how much clearer is the sunlight, how less dense the shadows! From where I now stand, I 'see' what I never even conceived of while I was in the valley!"

From above a voice is heard, "And I, if I be lifted up, will draw all men unto me." And this ascending one, begins to understand the drawing power that is giving him strength to rise in consciousness.

So, all along, from the base to the summit of the mountain, are those who have left the valley, in obedience to the voice, and are attempting to attain the heights. Each speaks *his view*, from *his* standpoint, for the view changes with every upward step; and so we hear views given, differing according to the height reached in consciousness.

Some of these travelers move slowly, others rapidly. We see one who halts and hesitates, and learn that it is because he fears to go *too fast*; he wishes to be sure of every step of the way, before he takes it; he is so occupied with his own thoughts and beliefs, that he hears not clearly the voice that says "come," and feels uncertain as to just the direction from which it speaks. In his confusion he is sometimes led to believe that he must not try to rise higher, and then he halts. He does not realize that by going on up, his seeing will be clearer, and he will draw nearer to the voice that calls him, for it comes from the very summit of the mountain.

Another progress, slowly, as if burdened. We find that this one is trying to carry with him up the mountain, a remembrance of the "clouds and shadows" he has seen in the valley! He is so engrossed with trying to hold on to these memories, that he cannot hear the voice above saying, "Thy sins and thy iniquities, will I remember no more." He sighing says, "Whom the Lord loveth he chasteneth." He does not realize that the chastening means the purifying from all doubts and clouds, and an uplifting into Light! He does not know that all the "Scourging" comes in the clouds of the valley, because Love would draw us above them. "To him that overcometh (which is 'cometh up over') will I grant to sit with me in my throne." (Rev 3:21) This one does not "*Forget* the things that are being left behind," though it is written, "Remember ye not the former things, neither consider the things of old." (Isa 43:18) So his progress in consciousness is hindered.

We meet another steadily pressing upward, and we hear him joyfully singing, "I will look unto the *hills* whence cometh my help. Who shall dwell in thy holy hill? He that walketh *uprightly*. I have set the Lord *always* before me. I shall not be moved. Thou wilt show me the path of life; in thy presence is fullness of joy," and we notice as these words are uttered, that the upward progress of this one, is rapid and easy; we remember it is written, "The joy of the Lord shall be your strength." And all who catch the echo of this rejoicing one, are strengthened to push on.

As we go higher, we see that all the other hills and mountains begin to disappear, as we are being exalted above them. All the hills of difficulty, which once arose so threateningly above us, now seem to be leveled, when looked *down* upon from this highest of mountains. Also as we look, the very valley we left is lifted up, and is seen no more as a valley! Now is the prophesy of Isaiah understood, "Every valley shall be exalted and every mountain and hill shall be made low."(Isa 40:4) Fulfilled when the soul has reached the heights of Pure Consciousness, or the Consciousness of Purity filling all. "To the pure, all things are pure." This is the summit of the Mount, the Christ-consciousness towards which each soul on the Mount has been pressing, from the "beginning."

One says, "To get *above* the clouds you must ascend the mountain; so with the soul; it must rise to where it is lighted by Supreme Truth, before the mists of error and ignorance vanish."

"Behold the day of the Lord cometh, and it shall not be clear in some places, and dark in other places of the world, but it shall be one day which shall be known to the Lord." (Zech 14:1, 6, 7) "There shall be one fold, one shepherd."

The Law of Heredity

IN the second commandment it is written: "Visiting the iniquity of the fathers upon the children unto the third and fourth generation of them that hate me; and showing mercy unto thousands of them that love me and keep my commandments."

Upon these words, the universal belief in heredity is based. Even

Christians claim its threat, of the visiting of iniquity upon the children of the Fathers that *hate me!* They claim for their children the inheritance of an evil habit, or a weak body from some ancestor, even though for generations back they have been God-loving people. They entirely forget that the assertion is, that the sins of iniquity shall be visited upon those that "*hate* me," but mercy is shown to "Those that love me." Certainly, Christians should insist upon freedom from heredity by this very second commandment.

To love God is to be conscious of God. Hate is the opposite of Love; hence to hate God, is to be unconscious of God. Whenever we see evil, or see the absence of Good, we, in a sense, "hate" God, for we cannot see any absence of God, without being unconscious of God! Where we see absence, God is; therefore, to see evil, is to be unconscious of God's all presence, and this is to "hate" God.

In this understanding we can see the truth contained in the words above quoted.

"Visiting the iniquity of the fathers upon the children... of them that are unconscious of me; but showing mercy unto them that are conscious of me." To believe that man inherits any evil, is indeed an indication that thought is unconscious of Truth and Good; hence "The Truth shall make you free," for to become conscious of the Truth of Good only, is to be free in thought, from belief of evil inheritance.

In Ezekiel, eighteenth chapter, we read, long after the commandments had been given: "What mean ye by using this proverb . . . saying. The fathers have eaten sour grapes, and the children's teeth have been set on edge? As I live, saith the Lord, ye shall not have occasion any more to use this proverb in Israel. The son shall not bear the iniquity of the father, neither shall the father bear the iniquity of the son," etc.

Later on, when Jesus spoke from still more perfect understanding, we hear him say, and now know his meaning: "Call no man on the earth your father; for one is your Father, even God." This forever settles the question! Man is child of God only; his Father is the Infinite Spirit of Perfection and Peace; now does he know what his inheritance is; and knowing, he claims it; and claiming, he possesses it, for it is his for the knowing. Therefore, in the Light of true Knowledge we say: Infinite Mind is the Only Source or Cause. I am in that Source eternally, and am of its Perfect Changeless Nature.

I am born of Spirit only, and am Spirit. This is my new birth, or new consciousness of birth. My inheritance is goodness and perfection in mind, thought, and body. I was made *whole*.

There is no source, or cause, of disease, weakness, or lack of any kind. I am eternally of Divine nature, and am filled full of all Truth from my Source.

What I Am Not

God, or Good, is in everything.
There is nothing to be afraid of.
I am not afraid of any kind of weather,
I am not afraid of rain or wind,
I am not affected by cloud or sunshine,
I am not affected by anything *external*.
I am not afraid of anything I do.
I am not afraid of anything I eat.
I do not believe there is anything to hurt me.
I do not believe in two Minds or two Powers,
I do not believe in two Substances,
I am not bound by universal beliefs of fear and evil,
I am not influenced by individual claims of fear or evil.
I am free.

"The value of a thought cannot be told.
He lives most who thinks most.
It is much less what we do, than
What we think, that fits us for the future."

Festus.

"Christian experiences are not the work of magic, but come under the law of Cause and effect. Joy is as much a matter of Cause and effect, as pain. There is no mystery about Happiness whatever. Put in the ingredients and it must come out. All fruits *grow*, whether in the soil, or in the soul. Spend the time you have spent in sighing for fruits, in fulfilling the conditions of their growth. We have hitherto paid immense attention to *effects*. Henceforth let us deal with Causes.

Do not imagine that you have got these things because you know how to get them. As well try to feed upon a cookery book. What more need I add but this: *test the method by experiment,*" Drummond.

Conclusion

"THERE is no new thing under the sun." —Solomon. All Truth is Eternal; but man illumined by the increasing light of Spirit within, progresses in *consciousness*, and perceives Truth more and more distinctly; he is on his way to the "perfect day"; that is, to perfect understanding. One says: "Man is on his way to God, not by mere lapse of time, but through various stages of illumination." Man comes to God, by seeing God more and more clearly.

"Open Thou mine eyes, that I may behold wondrous things out of thy law."(Psl 119:18)

When Gehazi, the servant of Elisha, saw the city encompassed by the enemy, he said to Elisha: "Alas my master, what shall we do?" And Elisha prayed and said: "Lord, I pray thee *open his eyes* that he may *see*; and behold the mountain was full of the horses and chariots of fire round about Elisha". As soon as his eyes were opened, he saw the truth of Divine protection.

What were these "horses and chariots round about Elisha?" We read, in Psl 68:17, "The chariots of the Lord are twenty thousand, even many thousands of *angels*; the Lord is among them."

"The angel of the Lord encampeth round about them that fear (or acknowledge) him and delivereth them." (Psl 34:7) Angels are Divine Thoughts: whisperings of Truth and Love in the soul. These tell us of the Omnipresent Power of Good, and deliver us from all fear. When our eyes are opened to see, we too are made conscious of the Divine that surrounds us, and can say, "I will fear no evil, for Thou art with me."

"Because thou hast made the Lord thy habitation," "Because thou hast seen the Divine as thy dwelling place" "There shall no evil befall thee, nor any plague come nigh thy *dwelling*." Certainly not, for neither evil nor plague can come near to God. "For He shall give His angels charge over thee, to keep thee. . . They shall bear thee up, lest thou dash thy foot against a stone."(Psl 91:9:12)

May we not trust in this, when we come to the rough, steep places in life's journey, that just "at hand" is the "chariot of the Lord," to bear us up above all hardship; that if we enter into Divine thinking, or thinking of the Divine Presence, All in all, nothing can be "hard" to us?

Let us not wait, however, until confronted by appearances that claim to be evil, before we establish our thoughts in Divine Consciousness. Begin at once, and continually try to see Divinity always at hand, within you; deny all other presence, power, or knowledge, a place. Do this while all seems well; then are you fortified when you see the "enemy all around."

We know that when a train approaches a tunnel, the lamps are all lighted while the train is still in daylight; then when it plunges into the darkness of the tunnel, it is all *light within.* If the lighting of the car were left to be done after the train had entered the tunnel, there would be much confusion, for it is too dark to see even how to make a light!

So we find many who have made just this mistake, and feel discouraged because in the darkness they could not find their light; in sickness they tried, but could not find their health!

We should carry our health, our light, our peace, always *burning* within us; and if we suddenly rush into a claim of sickness, it is all health within. If we plunge without warning into discord, it is all peace within.

If the within is fixed in health and peace, the without will soon be restored to harmony.

We need but to know the truth to be free, because we *are* free already from every mortal claim, and we only need to know it. "Open my eyes to see the Infinite Truth," is our prayer; and the answer comes, "Say to them that are of a fearful heart, fear not: the eyes of the blind *shall* be opened, and the ears of the deaf shall be unstopped. *Then* shall the lame man leap as the heart, and the tongue of the dumb sing. They shall obtain joy and gladness, and sorrow and sighing shall flee away." (Isa 35:4-10)

How much we are able to "see," depends upon the height we have reached in Consciousness. A new understanding is our need, and not a new thing. "There *is* no new thing."

One says: "Our measure of Consciousness is our measure of life"; which is to say that we have all the life we are conscious of; and as truly may we say, we have all the good we are conscious of; our health is measured by our consciousness of Health; our strength by our consciousness of Strength; our rest, by our consciousness of Rest.

Our Life, Health, Strength, Goodness, and Rest are limitless—we have all that we know how to claim.

Today a deep and new idea of Truth is dawning in our consciousness; it does not appeal to material sense, for it is the Spirit of Truth that is leading us into this new consciousness, and as we read, "The natural man receiveth not the things of the Spirit of God, for they are foolishness unto him; neither can he know them, because they are *spiritually* discerned."(Cor 2:14)

"The world, weary and disappointed, is wooed to listen to the more excellent way, which promises better results."

If we have worked a long problem in mathematics, and at the end find a mistake in our answer, how do we correct it? Are we willing to change the *figures* in our *result*, without going back over our work to see where the mistake began? Would a teacher allow a pupil to correct his mistake in that way, by simply changing his figures in the *answer*? Never! The scholar must learn what his mistake was, that in future he may, with better understanding, work more correctly, and be sure of correct results.

All our conditions of life, may be likened to the worked out example in mathematics. There is a Principle of Life, back of all examples in the visible, to be understood and demonstrated in living. We learn the Principle; the First Cause, the Source of every visible thing; we find that from this starting point, which is Infinite Mind, all things are brought forth. Our thought recognizes the Way and the Truth to be followed in its working, or reasoning. All things that come from this First Cause, or Source, must *agree* with It in nature; must be like It; must express Its Truth, Light, Goodness, Peace, and Wholeness. Our living, which includes all our conditions, should be an example, or proof, of its Source and Cause: for "The fruit of *Spirit* (of Principle, Mind, or Infinite Cause) is in all goodness," etc. Such would be a *perfect example* of Life. Complete, it is:

> Perfect Mind, as Cause;
> Perfect Thought, and
> Perfect Body; as effect or result.

We have found a Cause, or Principle, and know that when we rightly understand it, and work in accord with its Truth, by thinking rightly of the Life and Peace it contains for all, we shall have in all our *conditions*, rightness, peace, love, health, etc.

But now we are finding in our examples, conditions of not good, not peace, not health! Without much consideration of the *right* way, we have tried to fix up this incorrect example by *changing its figures!* We have taken the sick body, which is one wrong figure, and tried to make it a well body by working to change the outer. This is just like changing our result in mathematics by altering the figures in the *answer*.

We call this in school children, a dishonest method. I look on some other little girl's paper, who always gets her answers right, and I see I have gotten nine as an answer, and it ought to be ten. I just erase the nine and put ten in its place. Have I been helped by this? Only temporarily. I have been carried over a hard place.

So I may patch up the sick body for the time, but have gained nothing until I learn the mistake that produced the sick body, and find the antidote for all such conditions, in Divine Source.

To understand true healing, then, is to know, as exactly as in mathematics, what the *Principle of Health* is; what's its law of demonstration, in order that I may always express this true condition?

"With all things, a right beginning is essential to a correct ending." It is then all important to know and understand the source of all things. One says: "To hold a false idea of God is to worship a false God." And to be ignorant of the True and Only Source, is to misunderstand our Life, and all its conditions. To know anything about our lives we must go into the Source of Life; to understand our health and strength and peace, we must go into the Source of Health, Strength and Peace, and *work it out* from there!

If then, "figures" or conditions appear in our answer to the "problem of Life," that do not harmonize with the Principle of Life, in goodness and peace, we may conclude that our work is wrong somewhere, and our wisest course is to do just as an honest scholar in mathematics does, erase our work and begin all over again.

It seems hard to some, that after having been religious all their lives, they are made to begin so far back, when they turn to Divine Science! But they come with anxious minds and sick bodies, which often have grown rebellious against former methods, and refuse to be improved thereby; so that they *must* have a better way, and in their earnest desire, they submit to the new method.

They are carried at once to the *Beginning* of all things, are shown the True and Eternal Nature of their own soul and body, in changeless Being or Spirit; are persuaded to rub out their past work, or method of reasoning from appearances, to go into Invisible Source, where all Good has its Beginning, and to bring forth by Divine Law or method, from Mind, through thought, into visible things, the Perfection and Truth of Divinity.

This is Divine Science. An exact knowledge of Being Divine; or Being perfect as Source is, in Mind, thought, and body; perfect in Strength, in Health; complete in Love and Truth and Life.

This is the true condition of the I am that I am, and I learn that as I think truly of the *I am*, knowing that "I and my Father are one",

one in Life, in Mind, in Idea, and Consciousness; one in Substance, one in Spirit or Being, as I *think* of this, beholding the glory of the *One Only I Am*, I must become individually in Its *image*, and express Its Omnipresent, Omnipotent, Life, and Goodness.

As I think in my heart, I shall manifest in my world, this is the law. If I think holiness, my world will be holy—whole—complete. If I think not of holiness, my world will lack.

If I believe not in the unity of all things with Source, I see separation from God, and consequently a world *lacking* Ease, Light, Truth, and Love; it is the shadow of my own thought, and the wrong "figures" in the living example, all come from this.

The remedy is to enlighten thought, show it the One that is All and in All. "If thine eye be single, thy whole body shall be full of light." If my thought sees but One and that all light, then must my body be "full of light."

When we turn to the Infinite Source, we find It is Light. All that comes from Light is Light. We find It is Love, and all that comes from Love is Love. We find It is Mind or Spirit, and "That which is born of Spirit, is Spirit." It is Strength, Life, Health, and All Good; that which comes from It, is likewise Strength, Life, Health, and All Good.

If in any living thing there is a lack of Life, Intelligence, Strength, Wholeness, Peace and Good, these are the wrong "figures," because they give no representation of the Source, or Principle of Truth. If the Good made all things and made them good, as the Word declares, and if without Good "Was nothing made that was made," then every true thing is good, and all that seems not good, is a false result from a false reasoning, or thinking.

Evil is not of God, therefore has no Source or Cause in Truth. Our mistakes put it there; our right knowledge will wash it out.

To Spiritual Being and Consciousness, there is no darkness, no error, no pain or disease, no evil. I am spiritual consciousness in Divine Mind, and I know the Divine and Perfect Idea of all things. This knowledge is the Light of my Spirit within me, which judges righteous judgment.

It separates from me, all claims of *Being* weak, erring, sinful, sick and dying. *It* says to these claims, "You are no part of the Divine Me. Depart from me into everlasting fire." The Light within becomes the consuming fire to all error.

We have let good and evil, Truth and error, Life and death, Peace and discord, Health and sickness, share our faith. Now we refuse to do so! We *deny* the *truth* of evil appearances; because we do not find cause for them in the One Source, the One Life, the One Mind, the One Truth, we reject them; this is erasing our old wrong example, in order to write new and truer figures.

We find that by denials, our thought is freed from faith or belief in the power and presence of evil, or of anything not Good, and we are made ready to think wholly upon God as Omnipresent, Omnipotent, Omniscient Truth.

We can make these denials even in the face of appearances, when we have received clearly the Divine Truth, called the statement of Being: *"All* is Infinite Mind and Its manifestation," which means, that Infinite Mind with Its thought and word, Infinite Spirit with Its soul and body, Infinite Source with Its *image* and *likeness*, is all there is in the universe. Or, as another states the same truth, "God, and God manifest is *all there is.*" The same is declared by Paul in these words: "God is All and in all."

"Since God is *All,* there is no room for any opposite."

"To see the Divine Nature as *filling all,* is the destruction of every opposite claim."

One says that all our trouble comes from the use of two little words, "mine" and "thine." These certainly admit a claim of separation. When we learn to speak the "I am" in consciousness of oneness, we will know how to say with Jesus, "All thine are mine, and all mine are thine."

It has been written in one of the sacred books, "This is the great enemy, the my-ness in me." My thought of separation from God and from my fellow being, causes all belief of enmity.

Let us *deny* separateness, and declare oneness. The Great Source of Life and Light, pushes Itself into expression, just as the sun sheds its light in all directions. God's expression is man, and as the rays of light are forever joined to their Source, and shine by its light, not as separate rays, but blended into *one body* of light, so man is always united with his Source, and lives its Life, and is one Mind, soul, and body, with all expressions of Life.

Christ—Divine Nature—is the Head, the Foundation, the Beginning of all things. And all things are the "body" of Christ—the form of Divine Nature. As such, let us receive all things, as being in the nature of the Divine, whose Presence and Power, whose Light and Knowledge is *All*, and embraces all.

One Substance is the Substance of all things. There is no hurt for us in anything. Every breeze that blows, whispers of good; everything that moves, tells of Divine Life and Presence. We have nothing to fear, therefore, "whether we eat or drink, or whatever we do, do all for the glory of God."

> "May not the lofty mountains and the hills
> Be voice of God? His song the gentle flowers,
> His chant the stars' procession; and, alas!
> His only sigh these human hearts of ours."

In full consciousness, there shall be no more pain or crying, for former idea of things is passed away. "Behold, all things are new."

What I Am

"God worketh through me to will and to do of His good pleasure."
"In Him I live, move, and have my Being."
I am Life within Eternal Life.
I am Substance within the Eternal Substance.
I am Strength within the Infinite Strength.
I am Mind within the Divine Mind.
I am Idea within the Divine Idea.
I am Consciousness within Divine Consciousness.

I am Truth. I am Freedom. I am Fullness. I am that I am.
My life is complete now. I am eternally perfect.
My Health is a finished fact.
My Freedom is a changeless reality,
My Strength is Omnipotence.
My Understanding is Omniscience.

I now accept my always Perfect Health, my Changeless Freedom, my Unlimited Strength, my Divine Understanding and my Spiritual Substance from Thee, my Source.

"All souls shall be in God, and shall be God, and nothing but God be." Festus.

Some Final Words

We learn, then, in Science, the futility of trying to better conditions, by working to change the *outer*, without reaching the inner Cause.

One has said, that although our streets were swept and kept as clean as the streets of heaven, and man's thoughts remained the same, every known disease would be repeated within a generation!

The outer is not a cause of anything; all cause is invisible; the visible is the effect, or result, of a cause.

To work scientifically, and this means to work with certain knowledge, and to be *certain* of results, we must begin with Source and Cause.

In Divine Science, we accept that the Source of all things is Divinity; that all Cause is Divine Mind. We follow the method of Divine Mind in expressing Itself, and know that Its first expression, or activity, is Divine Thought, and that the result of Divine Thought is Divine Word, or Body. As this Divine Mind is Omnipresent, and Its expression is always with It, we have *everywhere* the Divine, with Its image and likeness; Its expression and manifestation; Its thought and word; Its soul and body.

We do not pretend to *bring out* the expression and manifestation of Divine Mind into the visible, but we go into the Source and *follow* It out; see that it does *fill all* with Its perfect Presence, Invisible and visible. As soon as we are willing to see the Omnipresence, Omnipotence, and Omniscience of Divine Mind, our "Whole body shall be *full* of light," for the visible will be seen in its true relation to the Invisible; it will be known as the result, or fruit, of Invisible Cause, which is Light.

As soon as we know the Truth, we shall begin to be freed from all false ideas about the visible.

We look to *Source* only to find the *Truth* of things; for that which is in Source is all reality. We look upon disease; immediately we ask, "Has it a place in Source and Cause?" No; Divine Mind is Perfect Ease, and can therefore, as *Source of all*, send forth only *ease*. Disease (of any kind) has no existence in Source; it has no place in Mind, hence no place in "thought," and no place in "body"; for thought and body are image and likeness, expression and manifestation of Divine Mind, their Source.

There is, therefore, no truth in the *claim* of disease, no cause for disease. There is no disease in the world of God, or in the expression and manifestation of God.

We find that these *denials* of any opposite to God, or Good; any opposite to Ease, or Life, cleanse thought of its belief in fear and evil, and prepare it to believe only in God. Moreover, we have learned that as this change takes place in thought, appearances change; sickness, sorrow, and pain, fear, hate, and all discord, disappear. Then we know that there is no opposite to Good except in *our thought* and when its belief is destroyed, the Cause or root of evil is touched, and the whole outgrowth of that belief begins to wither and die! Seeing but One Cause, and that All-Good, we can say there is *no cause* for evil, and its appearances begin to go.

One says, "Regeneration means work." If we receive from these studies in Divine Science, only a beautiful *theory*, we have gained but little. Unless we put into practice, according to the rules given, its Divine Principle meeting every condition in life with true judgment, by letting Divine Truth as seen in Source, settle every question for us; by daily *cleansing* thought of mortal claims—universal and individual, knowing that there is no mortal *Being*, the Only Being is the Divine; no mortal mind with its opinions, the Only Mind is the Immortal therefore denying the claims of mortality any place; then stating or affirming the Truth of the I am until we are sure of what I am unless we do this regularly and earnestly, we shall never know the freedom that is ours in Truth, of which these studies bear witness.

"He that willeth to do the will, shall know of the doctrine." (Rev)

"Let each man think himself an act of God,
His mind a thought, his life a breath of God,
And let each try by great thoughts and good deeds,
To show the most of heaven he hath in him."

Realization for Health

ALL reality is in God and like God. There is no reality in darkness, doubt, fear, or evil.

I am that I am, for my Life is in God, my Being; my Strength is in God; my Health is in God; my Understanding and Wisdom is in God; therefore, my Life is Divine and Perfect; my Strength can never fail; my Health is always the same; my Understanding is complete.

I am expression of Perfect Life and Good, and I am kept by Divine Power, forever in the Truth.

I can never be separated from Truth, Life, and Love. I can never be out of Health, out of Peace, or out of Light. There is no darkness; there is no doubt or anxiety about anything; God is always my Light.

There is no disease in God. There is no truth in the world's claim of disease and death, such a thought has no reality. God is the Only Mind; there is no Mind of error, evil, or suffering. There is no *place* for error, disease, or pain, for God fills all.

There is no truth at all in the claim of sin or sickness; we cannot find these in the Source of all, and only that which is contained in Source is true. All Truth is in God.

That which is born of God, is the image of God, and cannot have any sickness or discord in it. The Divine *fills* all, hence, there is no place for pain or disease in my mind, my thought, or my body. I have no belief in pain. I am the Mind that knows all Peace. In Truth I am now *free* from every claim of ignorance, or error, for these are not to be found in God, and I am in God.

How to Realize Illumination, or Understanding

FIRST, realize what I am.

I am Strength and Understanding. I am Light. I am that I am. I am Mind, I am Idea, I am Consciousness. I am all Wisdom within myself, for myself is God's Divine Idea.

There is no lack in the universe. God fills it all. There is no need of anything. There is no ignorance. Mind has no lack in It, and All is Mind.

There is no Mind of darkness or misunderstanding—no Mind of fear or error.

There is no fear. There is no cause of fear. There is nothing to be afraid of.

Light fills all for Light is God.

Understanding is all in all.

I live, move and have my being in Light. I express perfect understanding.

I am Light, in Mind, in thought, and in body. I am all Light. I am complete. I am satisfied now.

I am filled full of the Fullness that filleth all. Life, Truth, Light, Love, and Understanding, are all mine in God.

Victoria Woodhull 1838-1927
Suffragette & in 1827 first woman candidate for president.

Nona L. Brooks

(1861-1945)

Co-founder of Divine Science

Nona L. Brooks was born in Louisville, Kentucky, on March 22, 1861 at the start of the Civil War. She was born into a large, prosperous family which had ventured from Virginia to Kentucky. Nona was educated in a private school in Louisville, later graduating from the Charleston Female Academy. A typical daughter of an upper middle class family, she entered fully into the social life of the time and the community. She really wanted to marry and rear a family, but none of the men who courted her attracted her sufficiently. Her mother's health required a change of climate, so the family moved to Colorado. Her father's business was suddenly swept away by competition, so he entered a new business, mining. Worried and frustrated by the effort required, he suffered a heart attack and died, leaving the family almost penniless. (1)

They were now in Pueblo, Colorado, living in a very much lowered standard. Several of the family were in extremely poor health. Nona Brooks herself developed a serious throat ailment, and finding it difficult to eat solid foods was losing weight steadily. She was under the care of a Pueblo physician, who tried by various remedies to stop the disease; but instead it got steadily worse. (1)

In 1887, encouraged by her sister, Althea Brooks Small, Nona Brooks attended classes taught by Kate Bingham, proponent of the New Thought philosophy. Bingham had worked with Emma Curtis Hopkins and was healed of a physical condition. She in turn invited Nona and her sister Fannie Brooks (later to be Mrs. Fannie James) to attend classes that she began to teach in which she taught what she had learned from Mrs. Hopkins. While attending these classes, Brooks "found herself healed of a persistent throat infection" and shortly thereafter Brooks and Small began to heal others. (2)

Nona wasn't conscious of just when the healing occurred. But suddenly, she knew that she was healed. It was like the light, she said afterward. The whole room was filled with light. She thought everyone saw it. She simply knew that she was healed. That evening at supper for the first time in months she ate what the rest of the family ate. She had actually been healed.

Through Mrs. Bingham, Emma Curtis Hopkins had once more touched a life and given a start to one who was to make New Thought History, for Nona Brooks was the cofounder of Divine Science.

In December 1898, Brooks was ordained by Malinda Cramer as a minister in the Church of Divine Science and founded the Denver Divine Science College. Shortly thereafter, she inaugurated the Divine Science Church of Denver, holding its initial service on January 1, 1899 at the Plymouth Hotel in Denver, in the process becoming the first woman pastor in Denver. (1)

"By 1918 there were Divine Science churches in San Francisco, Denver, Seattle, Los Angeles, Oakland California, Boston, Portland, Spokane and St. Louis, and by 1925 churches had been opened in San Diego, Sacramento, California; Topeka, Kansas; Washington, D.C.; two in Illinois; one each in Iowa and Cleveland, Ohio; and two additional ones in the State of Washington. The movement was expanding steadily and almost as popular as the Home of Truth." (1)

Nona Brooks was often asked to speak at important gatherings. In 1927 she was given a trip abroad by her friends, and spoke in various foreign centers. She received important recognition at home as well. She was asked to serve on Boards for various civic and philanthropic purposes. For years she was a member of the State Prison Board.

At the height of her popularity, she decided to resign as minister of her church. Against great opposition, and only after a man had been found who might replace her temporarily, she was permitted a leave of absence from the church. For a time she was undecided what to do. Then came an opportunity to go to Australia, and she spent a year there, working in Melbourne, Sidney and Adelaide. This was a memorable visit to the Australian New Thought Movement. After that Miss Brooks spent some time in Chicago, serving there in one of the centers; spoke often in summer conferences of New Thought; and spent her winters in San Antonio, Texas which is the site of a burgeoning new denomination of Divine Science called United Divine Science.

In 1938 she was invited to Divine Science College in Denver, and served as President of the College until 1943. It was that year that Dr. Raymond Charles Barker, then president of the International New Thought Alliance, introduced her to a great congress meeting as "Our best loved leader," to the enthusiastic applause of the entire gathering. Two years later, on March 14, 1945, only eight days before her eighty-fourth birthday, Nona Brooks passed away. (1)

Following are excerpts from her book *MYSTERIES*, first published in Denver, Colorado in 1924.

Links & Acknowledgements
1. Nona Brooks Home Page: nonabrooks.wwwhubs.com
2. http:en.wikipedia.orgwikiNona_L._Brooks

Mysteries

First Edition 1924,
Denver, Colorado
(Excerpts)

There is mystery from the point of view of the wonder of it all, but there is nothing unexplainable to the one who is willing to see from the standpoint of unity that the Universe, and all that is in it, is One.

What is a Mystery?
The Mystery of God
The Mystery of Life
The Mystery of Matter
The Mystery of Suffering
The Mystery Of Healing
The Mystery of Human Characteristics
The Mystery of Thought Transference
The Mystery of Prayer
The Mystery of Success
The Mystery of Individual Unfoldment

What Is a Mystery?

DOWN through the ages men have been accustomed to call that which to them was unknown, unexplained, or uncomprehended —a mystery. There has been a tendency to wrap veils of mystery around natural phenomena, also around the causes of daily experience in the lives of men, and even around God. That which is in any particular, out of what we have called the usual and the commonplace, has aroused a sense of the supernatural or the mysterious in relation to it. Mankind has relegated much to the realm of the mysterious which is explainable under the light that true thinking throws upon the experiences. There rises the question, why is this? Long, long ago, in the childhood of the race, before men thought intelligently about life and living, they felt within themselves an impelling urge for something higher than their daily experiences. They naturally looked to that which was above them, and found it beyond their power to understand. So it came about that while these primitive men were still a great way off, the greater experiences of life looked weird and incomprehensible to them. They were thinking in terms of separation; hence all greater experiences were mysterious to them.

It has been our custom to meditate upon those experiences which touch us as individuals most closely. Hence we hear the world asking, "What is the reason for illness, evil, poverty, old age, and death?" There is an answer in Divine Science to many as yet unanswered questions. With the omnipresence of God as our basic principle, we Divine Scientists feel that we are speaking with authority. We shall endeavor to answer all questions from the point of view of omnipresent good.

Much of the thinking of the race has been negative. Men have seen evil, sickness, poverty, suffering, decrepitude, in human experience; and judging from appearances they have been unwilling to accept a philosophy that proclaims God as all, visible and invisible. "God must be the invisible power, but he must remain in the unseen, for if he is in the visible, how can you account for the wrongs of the world?" is the question that we hear repeated so often. Men have said for ages, "This is a mystery." They have accordingly continued to visualize places and conditions where God is not.

Do the appearances of disharmony that men call sickness, poverty, evil, and death, deny the principle of Omnipresence? From which side are you thinking—the inner or the outer? To many the outer is more real than the inner; to such I can only say, "Detach your thought from that which is without and fasten it to that which is within." We have lived in the external for so long that it seems much more real to many of us than the internal or external. We have lived with our eyes fixed upon phenomena, and now we are beginning to look through the phenomenon to find the cause. Detached thinking has done much to lead us farther and farther from reality. We have seen the manifestation—matter—apart from its source. Now we are seeing that cause and effect are one.

There is nothing hidden from him who knows God and God in action as all there is. There is mystery from the point of view of the wonder of it all; but there is nothing unexplainable to the one who is willing to see from the standpoint of unity that the Universe is one. The nature of God is wholeness—holiness. He filleth all with His holy presence; and there is no truth in anything that is unlike God—in anything that seems to limit us. The Father is infinite Spirit; we live in Spirit; we abide in its abundance. The one who sees the holiness of wholeness knows that in the presence of God is fullness of life.

We wonder at the greatness of solar systems; but from the solar system to the grain of sand, there is nothing mysterious to him who sees the meaning of Omnipresence. The grain of sand is a thought of God and so is the solar system; the process that we call life is God in action. Men plant a seed; it takes root, and sprouts; it springs into growth, a living organism. This process of unfoldment is God-Activity in manifestation. The process is perfect, for all that is of God is perfect. Perfection is the nature of the Omnipresent One.

I shall deal in this series with the so-called mysteries of God, life, suffering, old age, death, healing, wrong habits, human characteristics, human relationships, thought transference, power, prayer, success and individual unfoldment. I hope to show you that there is an answer to all questions in the light that the concept of Omnipresence throws upon life. From my angle of vision I see the Universe as One; and I stand in the center of this unified Universe, looking out and saying, "All is good—God." The universe of form is the living presence of God. Law is God in action. There is no chance. The Divine Purpose is expressing as infinite love. We, children of one Father, are sharers in the divine intent; we are working not for divine purpose, but with it.

Thinking true to the presence of God enlarges our vision; it is our ignorance and unwillingness to see truly that holds us out of participation in the glories that open to the one who is faithful in his practice of the Presence. We are troubled about things just so long as we do not see that all life is related. It is ignorance that keeps us in bondage; it is truth that makes us free. Let us cease walking on the shadow side of the path, on the path of human opinions, superstitions, and fears; for in God-Consciousness, the consciousness of wholeness is fullness of light.

If I take my stand in the presence of infinite Love and Power—that Presence—besides which there is no other, I shall solve every mystery. A mystery is a shadowy place in our thought; but in the consciousness of God there are no shadows. There is only light. When I take my stand in Omnipresence, I know that the thought which I think and the good works which I am able to do, are not mine, but His that sent me. God is thinking and expressing through His children. Light is our heritage. There is no darkness at all. Shall sons of God delude themselves into thinking that they live in shadowy places? As long as we do this, we shall be held in the bondage of this unreality and that unreality—this mystery and that mystery. Sons of God are able, if they will, to solve by their thinking and their living those problems and mysteries which have seemed impossible of solution. There is, let me repeat, nothing unknown to the one who knows God. There is nothing incomprehensible to the man who understands the infinitude of the love and power of God. All phenomena are explainable by law—God in action. Where, then, is the mystery?

The Mystery of God

MEN have long believed that they could not know God, and that what the eye of the senses could not behold was an insolvable mystery. Their concept of God was that of an almighty ruler governing the universe invisibly and mysteriously; God had created the world ages ago, and after creation was complete, had departed out of the world, never to be seen of the children of men. He had, however, created the first man and the first woman, before he disappeared from earth to abide far off in the heavens. Hence arose the mystery about God.

When we were children many of us worshiped a different God from the one we are worshiping today. The change is not in God, but in our conception of God. Men conceived a God hidden from his subjects, ruling arbitrarily, and visiting the sins of the fathers upon the children from generation to generation.

The conception of God is changing from this limited belief into the vision of an almighty, loving Father including His world. We are conceiving of God as infinite Life, Love, Intelligence, Power, Joy, bringing forth His Universe by law. Natural science, modern ethics, and true religion, emphasize law as the principle of the Universe upon which all life rests. Law is the unchanging method by which God is expressing; it is always true to Divine Being. Law is the basis upon which truth rests. It is the assurance that God is expressing; law is our assurance of good. Our lives, then, are based upon the certainty of the unfailing principle of omnipresent good.

> "If I take the wings of the morning, and dwell
> in the uttermost parts of the sea;
> Even there shall thy hand lead me, and thy
> right hand shall hold me."

We find that it is comparatively easy for the thought of the twentieth century to understand the concept of the infinitude of God. The infinite universe of form is God in action. God is infinite changeless abundance. The Universe abounds not only in infinite love and power, but in those things needed every day from the greatest unto the least, from the most important to the seemingly least significant. We are awaking to the immediacy of God also. This infinite nearness of God is more difficult of comprehension, however. We can see God in measureless distances and mighty systems, but to see God in the tiny flower and to come to recognize that there is no point in space or on earth where God is not is more difficult. The concept of the immediacy of

God reveals to us that God is in the smallest details of daily living, as well as in the greatest events of the progress of man.

Natural science is marching hand in hand with modern religious conception; one, it is true, uses scientific expression; the other, religious expression. There is, however, small import in terms; according to both conceptions there is one substance. We Divine Scientists spell Substance with a capital; for to us the universe is Substance and Substance in action. Astronomy shows us that God is responsible not only for the forming, but for the revolution of the planet in its orbit. Chemistry and physics reveal a reign of law, also; biology stands for integrity of expression. Let us not fall short in our thinking; let us keep steadfast, and each hour will show us more of God in action on every hand. The most vivid of life's experiences is found in the consciousness of the omnipresence of God—love, power, abundance, integrity. To know that the breath of life is the breath of God, that the loving word and deed are God in action, that your strength and my strength are limitless in God, that our gifts and our joys are God's intent for us, that every right thought and every corresponding action of ours are approved of God, is the greatest of experiences.

The God of integrity is the God of love. God is love, means that God is in action; and God in action is law as well as love. In the light of the unfolding concept of God as love and integrity, we see that all law is beneficent. The God of love knows no unforgiveness. Jesus, through whom we see the Father working, showed in his living and in his teaching what it means to love perfectly; he showed us how to forgive. Jesus taught that the quality of our love for the Father is shown forth in the way we love our fellow men.

Recall the words of the wise in the hours of stress and in times of meditation: "Behold, do I not fill heaven and earth, saith the Lord?" Whither, then, shall we flee from Spirit? We are always in the presence of God. It is true, our ideal is so great that our shortcomings stand out in vivid contrast—a contrast which causes us to lose heart at times, and think that we have wandered far from Spirit and truth. This, however, is not true. We are in the presence of God, even though we know it not. Our failings are evidence of separation in our thinking only. It is in the hard experiences, and at times of discouragement, that we should be able to use what we know of truth in order to discern between the true and the false, and to see that God does fill heaven and earth, with His presence, His life, and His abundance. Let us train our thought to realize the immediacy of God, and also to think out with understanding faith into the great expanse of universality. We see God as He is when we learn to see wholeness instead of separation. Might it not be that we shall come to know the Father as He knows himself when our vision grows more nearly complete? Then shall we know the fullness that filleth all.

Let us bring God as near as we can get Him. When we do this we shall see reality instead of appearance. When there is something unsightly in that which we see before us, what should be our reaction? So often the seeming defect is all that we see. Our first impulse is to think that God is not there. Why not look through the unsightliness? It is only our concept of the experience—our misconception. True insight proves to us that what we are seeing imperfectly, God is seeing perfectly. The one Creator is bringing forth perfectly. We are worshiping today a perfect God. Let us keep true to the ideal of perfection in every experience as well as in every thought. It is necessary to see perfection in process and in form, and not to weaken when we see imperfection, for there is no truth in it. Always ask yourself this question, "Is the difficulty in the condition, or is it in my seeing?" The answer will come immediately, if you have kept your attitude true. "I am looking upon that which is by nature perfect." It is our responsibility to keep our vision true to what we know. What is the reaction then of God to His world? He is His world; He includes it; He is expressing as His world. The true vision reveals God-Life everywhere.

I look upon the desk in my study. It has served me well. I touch it; my senses, true to the old conception of form, report in a certain way. I was trained to see my desk as something entirely different in substance from myself, and to think of matter and Spirit as separate and distinct. From this point of view I have called my desk lifeless. It has always seemed to resist my touch; hence I have called it hard—a solid. I look at the desk, and I see with these two eyes an unbeautiful mass, dull, lifeless, static; I say to you, "This is inanimate matter." In the old way of looking at the outer manifestations there is no connection between this desk and me, a living organism, except that subject to my will it serves me. Through this kind of thinking the misconception, duality, arose.

The one who is well informed in recent discoveries in the scientific world says to me in answer to my recital of these facts concerning my desk, "You do not understand matter according to the new concept. Nothing that you have said of your desk is true. The senses can never illumine you, even though the eyes see and the touch feels. The mentality is bound by statements long worn out. This desk is not a solid, lifeless mass; it is a center of activity composed of tiny, intelligent, whirling bodies called atoms held in the form which we call a desk by the law of attraction. Matter is a mode of motion; all form is living, intelligent activity."

There comes to me new meaning in the words of Jesus, "According to your faith be it unto you." Then, the proverb, "As a man thinketh in his heart so is he," flashes through my thought. Is it not true that as a man believes about the universe of form and the world of experiences, so is the universe to him; so does he experience? I see my desk in a new light; I see the blade of grass by the wayside with new comprehension. Each is a center of motion, of intelligent activity in the great expanse of universal ether. I no longer perceive deadness but livingness, not matter subject to decay and death, but living substance radiant with the life-principle of universal activity. I see Life as God himself in action. The words of natural science are being heard throughout the land, for scientists are speaking with no uncertain voice, and these words are being received with wondering approval.

We are hearing other voices speaking with authority also. Divine Scientists are saying, "The explanations of natural science accord with our deepest perception of truth. We see God everywhere. We know the Universe as the One Substance in action. A universal God must be present in His creation." When we say this, we imply all that the natural scientist says about creation or form. We like to say, "There is only God and God in action." God in action is form; God in action is law. God is infinitely intelligent, and is bringing forth according to His perfect idea. The intelligence of God is evidenced in the law and order of the universe and is manifested as living forms. There is no inanimate matter, for matter, according to Divine Science, is Substance in action. Substance, as we see it, cannot be subject to mishaps and corruption. I like to quote these words of Jesus, "I, if I be lifted up, will draw all unto me." He saw that when thought is lifted up in you and in me, we lift all that is around us. As we lift our thoughts the world around us arises to meet these. All nature and all men are seen in the light of wholeness as perfect expressions of the infinite Creator. Being is perfect. We are Being in manifestation. "In thy light shall we see light." In this light shall we look upon all that God is making, and with God call it good?

How shall we look at God? With the eyes of Spirit! How shall we think of God? As Universal Expansion; yes, this is easy; but I am making a special plea to all of us to acknowledge God in all our ways—in all expression; to accustom ourselves to the concept of the nearness of God, to the immediacy of the Presence of perfection. When we look at the objects around us, at our bodies, at all nature, let us see to it that the wrong conception shall not dominate, but that we shall perceive with inner vision only intelligent, loving, powerful, harmonious activity—God in action. God is all, both visible and invisible. Let us see as God sees; God sees by the understanding of His love. He knows reality, and never swerves. He sees you and me as perfect expressions of His own idea. God sees us as living soul. He sees our bodies as form, His own Substance in action. Our lives are in God.

The old beliefs are passing; the New Revelation is showing us God in action in every expression of the universe of form. God is His universe. If we raise our eyes to the stars we see the light of God shining through; if we watch for the glory of the sunlight we see God again. Mother Earth and all of her children show us God—Activity radiating love. Nature is God in action; what about the affairs of men? Is God active in these, too? God is working out His universal plan in the affairs of men. Are we cooperating? God is not a ruler of men; He is the very life of men. God works by means of you and me, and of all other people on the earth. Let us be by choice co-workers in the kingdom. There is neither first nor last here. All men are one.

There are neither mysteries nor miracles in the kingdom of God; there is cause and effect, which Divine Science thinks of as one. This is the truth of every day. There are no places where God is not. Our ignorance of the principle of universal love accounts for the lack that we sometimes feel. There is only one way; it is the way to life eternal. The light of truth is ever shining on this path, which leads to reality. The light of truth shows us that there is one Presence and Power, and that this Presence is the only Presence, this Spirit, the only Substance; this Mind, the only Intelligence; this Love, the Universal Nature; this Activity, the only Activity—God.

In God there are no mysteries; there is only light.

The Mystery of Life

THE origin and the process of life have seemed to many the greatest of mysteries. "What is life, and how can it persist in such a variety and under so many different conditions?" are common questions. There have been so many problems in the thought of the race concerning causes and effects that all thinkers have been searching for solutions. Much of this research has not afforded us very much light on the solution of our problems, because students have thought they were dealing with two powers—matter and Spirit. The concept of an unknown power which is directing the process of life has given rise to the assertion, "We can take you so far, and no farther." This assertion is the last word of many scientists, philosophers, and religionists. God has been thought of through the centuries by students in various phases of human knowledge as the Great Unknown—hence, the mystery of life!

How are we thinking about the great word Life? Are we taking it in its highest meaning? The word may be written in two different ways. Divine Science usually writes it with a capital letter; popular usage spells the word with a small letter and thinks of life as meaning everyday existence, the passing show, outer relations and activities. Out of this conception many questions arise, such as, "Why did this happen to him? What is the reason for this tragedy? Why are the lives of so many people on this earth seemingly miserable?"

Divine Science holds out a solution for all problems and an answer to all questions in a conception which interprets Life as God in action. Life written with a capital stands for the Activity of God. God is Omni-active; and what God is must come forth in His activity. Since God is good, the activity of the universe of form is good; since God is love, all activity is loving; since God is power, all activity is powerful for good. God-Activity is what natural science calls the universal energy. In God-Activity you and I live, move, and have our Being. As we function in this consciousness of the oneness of the Universe, we lift the thought of the world around us. "I, if I be lifted up, will draw all unto me." Jesus' words prove his faith in the power of right thinking.

Since the Presence which we call the I AM is the only Presence and Power, let us lift ourselves into that consciousness of oneness through our daily living which brings those around us into the concept of wholeness. Our thinking must be based on the affirmation, "God is all, both visible and invisible."

We are likely to think of God in the highest and the best that we know, but let us not fail to see God in the least of the things of Life; there are no high and no low in the Kingdom of God-Life, and when we think of man in the Absolute, we see that by nature, he must be Godlike, for is not man the highest expression of an infinite, all-powerful Creator? Let us apply this concept to ourselves, our families, and our friends, as well as to all the world of men; it is our obligation to keep ourselves in the most positive attitude toward the Divinity of all Life. Each one has the power to attain to the realm of Divine Consciousness, if we hold true to the vision of our unity with God.

See truth; stand for truth; affirm truth in your lives step by step. Such statements as the following show us the Divinity of Life:

God is Life.
What God is comes forth in Divine Activity.
We live, move, and have our Being in God-Life.
By Divine Power we are alive now.
I know that Life is perfect, for God is All.
Man is Living Soul, brought forth perfect in nature.
Man is divine, because he is one with God.
Man has the power to realize the truth of Being, and to accomplish the best in every relation and activity.
Consciousness of God is the light of the world.

Why not spell Life with a capital letter? Does not Divinity include all? I am asked, "How can you say that God is all that is visible, when there is so much disharmony and imperfection in the visible?" Are you looking with the outer eye of the senses, or are you seeing with the inner eye of Spirit? It is with the inner eye that we see truth. Appearances of disharmony are the results of wrong conceptions. When the inner vision comes, we see that God is the only Creator, and that we live by the power of His consciousness, and that we are brought forth by the impelling Spirit of His Love. When you and I see imperfection, it does not mean that in this place God is working imperfectly. It is we who are seeing imperfection. God's work is perfect; man's conception of it is often imperfect or partial. Imperfect seeing, then, is the cause of our list of sorrows and evils.

When in the hour of silence or in the time of activity, it is possible for us to free our mentality from beliefs of limitation, and the soul, standing conscious of its oneness with God, looks out upon the universe with the God-Vision, it realizes truth. We see that the temporal experiences of sorrow and lack are the results of ignorance and are unimportant compared with the real experiences. In our earnest attempt to dissolve these misconceptions, we see that after all temporal experience is like a little shadow passing across the face of the sun. You and I are coming into the understanding of the affirmation, God is All. God is His world.

> God-Mind is speaking through us.
> God is working by means of man.
> Divine Love is radiating through us.
> God-Light is the light of the world.
> There is no darkness in the Light that is
> illumining the Universe.
> We live to serve; true service means
> cooperating with God in His activity.

Let us be sure that we are true to Life in its highest meaning. This very moment is the testing time; it is our opportunity to prove ourselves true by thinking to our highest and by translating our thinking into doing. Remember, it is living the Life that counts. Are you practicing the Presence? Am I? We know that God is active in this place as Living Soul; since God is active here, there is no other power to interfere with perfect expression this moment; let us not falter. Let us face the situation whatever it may be, with knowledge that the Father is doing the work. God is in this place now; hence there is no room for sickness, weakness, sin, or lack.

God is in action; hence all is Life. Life is the fullness that filleth all. We live because God lives. God is living us this moment. It is easy to fall short, if we are living in the lesser conception of life which deals with outer things only, and are basing our decisions on every day happenings. If a man seems to be walking in darkness, we may be sure that it is because he is unwilling to see the light. Jesus said, "He that followeth me shall not walk in darkness, but shall have the light of life."

I read an interesting sermon recently in which the author says that you and I have a rendezvous with Life and that we must keep our engagement. What does this mean? It means that we have a rendezvous with Truth, and it lies with you and me to keep our engagement. We may exist for many years without living at all. "Clinging to existence, we may, nevertheless, refuse Life." Laziness, fear, prejudices may prevent our keeping true to our obligation. We must be alert and vital now in order to give our best. We miss Life itself through mental indolence. Fear keeps us bound to petty experiences; we are afraid to rise. Many of us have a pet rut; let us welcome the mental earthquake that comes and shakes us out of it; but why wait for the earthquake? I do not wish Life to have to force me out of my limited conceptions; I must make the effort to rise. Spiritual initiative is necessary to true living.

Life is one with truth, beauty, love, wisdom, power, joy; it is a rendezvous with goodness, courage, kindness, faithfulness, service, and it is calling you and me to action. Life is, above all, a rendezvous with God; if we do not keep it, we miss the joy of living.

What, then, is the origin of Life? Are you ready to answer the question? Infinite Wisdom, Knowledge, and Understanding is the origin. Hence we use a capital to emphasize the Divinity of Life. What is the process? Process is God in action. It is the working out of the universal plan. Life is all-powerful. It is God. God is not unknown or unknowable. Hence, there is no mystery; there is only infinite Love and Power in action; the expression is by law; there is no chance; neither is there a secret process. God is revealed as Life.

The Mystery of Matter

WHAT is matter? For ages men have asked this question. Philosophers and scientists have been making earnest endeavors to answer the question satisfactorily, to explain away the mystery of that which we have called matter. There is always a mystery associated with what we do not understand—hence, the mystery of matter. It has been a phenomenon that we have not understood. Many scientists and philosophers of all schools and of all times have touched on the truth of matter, but we as Divine Scientists believe that there is one great step which must be taken before a satisfactory answer can be given by any of the thinkers of the world. They must see God in action as manifestation.

We are moving toward the concept of oneness. This is a most hopeful sign. The belief of dualism is passing; monism is taking its place. The concept of two powers and two substances—Spirit and matter, one having control over the other, is evolving into a greater vision which is revealing a Universe of One Substance. Divine Scientists translate the philosophy of monism into terms of religion; our basis is Omnipresence. We have taken the one great step; instead of seeing the world as a multiplicity of unrelated phenomena, we are seeing these phenomena in terms of the whole.

The dualistic conception separated the effect from its cause, the manifestation from its source, and creation from the Creator; hence there arose a belief in two powers, Spirit and matter, good and evil, life and death, sickness and health. Naturally that which was separate from the perfection of Spirit was thought of as subject to all kinds of ills. Now we see no separation in any phase of expression. We believe in the continuity of life, and we know that nothing is ever lost. Although the One Substance is manifested in myriad forms, the fundamental remains unchanged. Natural science tells us also that there is nothing lost in this universe of form, and that we are seeing the universal ether, the one substance, in millions of forms. Is it true, then, that the mysteries of life are only contradictions in our thinking?

What is called matter, Divine Science looks upon as Substance, or Spirit visible. We shall in these chapters use the word form instead of matter, not because there is any objection to calling the Substance involved in form, matter, but because there has always been connected with the term matter, a conception that it was something susceptible to disease, decay, and death.

At the outset let us declare the truth of the Universe; it is God and God in action, as the Whole. The universe of form and force is creation. Form and force are God in action, the One Spirit visible. There is no process of separation evident in all the diversity of universal expression to the one who sees form as Divine Idea being expressed. The God-Method of thinking infinitude into form, we call the law of expression. To us law is God in action.

God is ever expressing His Ideas in an infinite variety of manifestations, for is not God infinite in potentiality?

Omnipresence is our foundation; we shall be building from it always. It is the only one upon which to base our thinking. If we are true to our Basis, contradictions will fade out of our thought process, and the old beliefs will begin to scatter like clouds before the sun after a summer rain. To us who use the word divine in relation to the science of life, the universe of form is God in action, Substance in manifestation, Infinite Intelligence in expression. The new heaven and the new earth are one; creation is the outspoken word of God. Is it true that a new universe is revealed to him who sees God in action in all manifestations?

Through the new understanding that form is not an outline confining a solid entity, but according to natural science a grouping of self-determining electrons, the natural scientist is traveling far from the traditional concept of an inanimate universe. There is nothing that is not living; all is life and activity in the natural scientist's concept of the universe. In the Divine Scientist's there is nothing which is not perfect by nature, since all form is God in action, for is not Life, God in action, the universal power? All activity is by law in both phases of science, natural and divine. There is no chance. Natural science calls this the law of cause and effect; Divine Science calls it God in action.

It is vital that you and I get the truth of form firmly fixed in our thought. A new universe is being revealed by natural science as a unity of Being, expressing by a unity of law. Divine Science is revealing a Universe that is God and God in action—a Universe in which there is nothing but God—a Universe which is God and God-Idea in expression. Form cannot by this concept be susceptible to conditions of disharmony. All of us who have thought of matter or form as opposed to and unlike Spirit have been worshiping other gods besides the One. As a result of misconception as to the nature of form we have thought of our flesh as liable to many ills—sickness, poverty, sin, death, loneliness. We have, of course, conceived a partial God; a great power, it is true, but one limited by another power which men have called evil.

The concept of separation is responsible for the misconception, evil, in the thought of men.

There are those who say in regard to this universe of form that all visibility is unreal; in fact, that it does not exist. This we do not accept. We see the visible as Mind in action, and we see that like its Source, the visible is perfect by nature. We declare that right thinking leads to realization of perfection, and that the truth of life is revealed to the man with the single eye. If thine eye be single, if it sees only the One Presence and One Power at work in the universe of form, thy body shall be full of health; thy thought shall be filled with light.

Since God is omnipresent and includes all as well as being the Creator of all, creation is by its very nature, whole and good. God sees only wholeness; he is infinitely conscious of His creation, for is God any less a creator than He was in the days when the wise man of old said of Him, "And God saw everything that he had made, and behold, it was very good."? In the Infinite there is no past or future; there is only the living present—the Now. There is no place for a false creation in a universe of form that is Infinite Mind in action; there is no false world except in man's misconception. Let us clear out our subconscious; a mental house-cleaning is a valuable exercise in this day and age of the New Revelation.

We are perfect and complete in God; all form is Substance in action. God is expressing as living form; these living forms, then, are Divine Ideas in manifestation. Do you see that all life is one? When we are true to Omnipresence, we see that there is no place, not a dot on earth or in the heavens, the size of a pin point, where God is not. Substance—God—is everywhere; hence, activity, Substance expressing as form, is the universe of form and force. Where the Spirit is, and it is in all places at all times, there is freedom, love, health, power, truth, life, joy.

We no longer dwell on imperfection; we do not think of form as something played upon or molded by individual mind; we know form as Infinite Substance in activity. We agree with the natural scientist in his conception of form or matter as a mode of intelligent motion. We see this motion as God Activity. The vibration of the natural scientist is the Divine Activity of the Divine Scientist. It is God's method of expression.

There are various beliefs about the relation of Mind to its manifestation. Some people say that if we keep our thinking true the body will respond. There is much danger attendant upon this conception—the one of giving too much power to what men call the human mind. Those who believe that everything depends upon their mental power, naturally become too strenuous in their efforts to bring about the desired conditions, and employ formulation and suggestion. The method is wrong; it is not based upon principle, but on opinions. We go through life contending with two powers. Mind and body become separated in our thinking, and there follows a struggle which emphasizes the power of the mentality. We think in terms of a material force and of a spiritual power, and we are placing our faith in both. This kind of thinking gives rise to a dualistic conception, and to a practice of mental suggestion which is often harmful. There are times when we seem to experience an absence of God in our lives, when we allow ourselves to form thought habits of mental and autosuggestion. Divine Science teaches that the body, a God-Expression, is perfect by the nature of its Source. We teach the eternal perfection of all manifestation or form. This assertion of the eternal perfection of form we base upon the fact of the perfection of God, the Father. Since form is God's creation, it is not affected by human conception about it. The body, as God's manifestation, can be neither repaired nor impaired by human effort.

The moment we take our stand in Omnipresence, the One Universal Power and Presence of perfection, we see everything in terms of its nature; there is only One Substance to him who sees. He is seeing God in action; God is ever thinking himself forth as the universe of form according to a pattern in Divine Mind. Perfect Idea is resting eternally in God-Mind, and is also expressing as visibility. It manifests as perfect form. The Aristotelian philosophy teaches that the universe is a thought in God—Mind—God, The Thinker—His Thought, The Universe! Let us be well content in the assurance that all form is a thought of God, for

He that keepeth the world as Idea in Mind-Universal is living us now; there is no instant of separation. Substance is Spirit; Spirit in action is Creation; matter or form is Substance or Spirit in action.

The analogy between what we call natural and what we call Divine Science is heartening. Natural science speaks in terms of varying rates of vibration; Divine Science accounts for the vibration by seeing it as God-Activity. God is expressing, as the tiniest particle and the mightiest solar system; hence we are conceiving the immediacy of God as well as the universality. We see God as the Infinite Being who is including men and all other forms of manifestation in His love. The old human conception of separation and limitation is truly giving place to the consciousness of the universality of God in the hearts of men.

Whereas, the word matter has implied inactivity and inertness; in the newer modes of thought it implies continuous activity; and to the Divine Scientist it is form, God in manifestation. The rock by the wayside was dead to the thinker of old, but man was alive. The loveliest flower that grows was thought of as insensitive, unconscious of its surroundings, while the animal was supposed to be capable of feeling. Everything which did not have the sense organs with which men and animals are equipped was thought to be lacking in the power of consciousness. The thought habit of separating differing expressions in the world grew in proportions until it proclaimed dead matter and living substance. Today when we say, I, we include the whole. All life is one. Body is one with Spirit; it is whole, beautiful, and wonderful in its mechanism. There is truly one body in Christ. Let us glory in the universe of form which God is creating, and know that he who loses his limited conception of matter or form for truth's sake, shall find all life—forms one. He shall see God in action.

Why do we speak of matter? Why not think and speak only of God? It is through our understanding of form that there comes release from bondage—the bondage of sickness and sin. When we see that form is perfect activity, that it is the God-Mind in manifestation, we are free from world opinions about ourselves and about all other forms of God-Expression. You see, I am sure, why the mystery of matter has persisted so long. It had its inception in a dualistic conception of the universe. We have emphasized the outer and minimized the inner values for so long that the old mysteries have quite a hold on our thought today.

The poet says that, if we understand the flower in the crannied wall, we should understand God and all things. As we come into an understanding of the simplest expressions, the Universe is revealed as one. We are beginning to see truly—to see God in action. In a universe in which we can interpret form as Spirit made manifest or visible, a universe wholly one, there are not two powers or two substances; but there is Substance and motion. There is only God and God in action. That which we think of as evil is only the result of our imperfect concept; thought images become very real to us. Let us be careful which kind of form. What I believe I shall see. Just so long as we hold a belief in the imperfection of form, we shall see imperfection everywhere. Let us endeavor to raise our thinking out of the current of personal opinions ever flowing around us. He that sitteth in the heavens, in the harmony of the realization of oneness, laughs at appearances. He sees them in their true perspective.

Divine Science teaches eternal progression; there is no final revelation. The Spirit of Truth is our guide. Natural science begins at the visible and works toward the invisible, the cause; Divine Science begins with the invisible and works from Cause to effect, but it sees these as one. Both groups see the unity of the Universe of form and force. The natural scientist is telling us that the nature of matter is continuous activity; the Divine Scientist says that this activity is God in action. There is no mystery about matter to us; God is Creator and Creation. Just as the light of far away stars reaches us after centuries of traveling through infinitude, unchanged in its constituent elements, so today the light of the truth of Being that has shone from the universe of form and force through the ages, not comprehended by the many, seems to be growing brighter, because we are beginning to see with the eye of Spirit. The consciousness of Omnipresence is the light of the world, and the mystery of matter is solved.

The Mystery of Suffering

LET us be sure that we are gaining a clearer understanding of the term matter as we consider the pages of this small volume; for without more light on matter, we shall not come nearer to a solution of the problems that confront us in our daily lives. Of these that of suffering is one of the most insistent, whether it takes the form of evil or of pain. What is suffering? What is evil? In order to approach a satisfactory answer to these questions, it is necessary to study carefully the meaning of form or matter.

What has been our concept of form? Something manifesting in limitation, and subject to disharmony and decay, is perhaps as clear an answer as most of us could give. The visible has been thought of as that which is separate from the invisible. We have been dealing with what we conceived to be two phases in the life process—a visible and an invisible existence, only one of which, the invisible, has been thought of as perfect. Imperfection has always clung to that which is manifested. Why should this be? Belief in separation is the answer. Let us make sure that we see form as Living Substance in manifestation, expressing according to the law of unity in infinite variety. To the one who sees this truth, the mystery of suffering begins to clear. What is the conclusion that thinkers in the realm of natural science are moving toward? It is a conclusion that has already been reached and accepted by Divine Scientists—that the universe of form is alive—that it is One Universal Intelligence in expression. We say that God is Spirit and that the universe of form is God in action. As natural science teaches one source or power, so we teach one Cause in the Universe of Spirit, which is Love Universal. We have learned that cause and effect are one, hence the expression of perfect cause is by nature, perfect. Whence the seeming imperfection? What is suffering? What we believe we experience in regard to our bodies and to all kinds of form. Wrong believing gives rise to untrue seeing; and imperfect seeing is the cause of that which we call imperfection. Where, then, shall we look for an answer to the mystery of why we suffer and why we sin in a universe of form which is God in action? You will see that we must turn to the thought realm where we have been harboring misconceptions as to the nature of form; through thought training we can learn to see truth.

What shall we think about form? The natural scientist says that all form is vibration; he accounts for different forms by speaking of these as varying rates of vibration; but he deals with a universal substance which he calls ether. The discovery that matter is a mode of motion leads to the truth, that the universe of form is God-Activity. Infinite-Activity is form. We are told in Genesis that God saw His creation and called it very good. In the knowledge that time is only a concept in our thinking shall we change this great truth into the present tense to meet the views of the present day? God sees His creation and calls it very good. God is true to himself; He sees us and all that He is expressing, as one with Infinite-Life, hence, as whole. God is not expressing that which is unlike himself in nature, since cause and effect are one. What of suffering? Why do we suffer? Surely not because we are by nature intended to suffer, but because we have been as a race unwilling to consecrate our thinking to the God-Standard.

Picture a world filled with God-Love and every one in it radiating, out streaming goodwill. Would there be any suffering? Would there be any evil? There could be neither suffering nor evil if all men were thinking true to God-Thought. Wars would end; greed would go; self-ishness would cease; destruction would give place to constructiveness. We should see only God in action if the world were thinking true thoughts. It is only in the thought realm that we find suffering and evil, for it is here that we believe in separation, while the truth of life is oneness. As we think, so do we experience. Therefore, let us watch our thinking, for it is through the process of true thinking that we unfold into the consciousness of God and God in action as all there is. True thinking is the basis of all development; it is the key that unlocks the gates of the kingdom—the gates that our thoughts have been locking for us through misconceiving the true meaning of life.

We shall begin to solve the mystery of individual suffering and evils when we believe with all faith that God is thinking forth His own Ideas as perfect, complete, intelligent forms. This is the truth of creation. As we make this truth the basis of our thinking about the universe of form and of all human experiences, darkness, doubt, fear, and all other human limitations will vanish. Think of the universe of form as a living organism, by nature perfect, and you will draw the world of form around you, into the realm of your thought. Natural science tells us that the universe is a living organism controlled by mind; we believe that the Universe is Mind and Mind in action, and that every expression is conscious to a degree. Mind is manifesting everywhere; the flower evidences this; and so does the tiniest insect that crawls, as well as the mightiest solar system. The mind of the molecule is the God-Mind in manifestation; there is no other mind. Every cell thinks because it is Mind in expression. Mind, universal cause, is revealed by every expression in the universe of form. Universal Mind thinks only truth and wholeness; it is thinking you and me, as it is thinking the solar systems and the grains of sand. This infinite variety of activity shown forth in myriad forms of manifestation is all after a pattern in Divine Mind; each form has its part in God's mighty design of his activity—the universe of form. The Universe is glorified in God.

What of suffering from the standpoint of Omnipresence? It is purely mental. Pain is caused by fear; and there is nothing in Universal Mind to fear, for all is perfection. It is when we believe in another mind and power that our sufferings begin. Get back to God. Remember the foundation word—oneness. God above all, through all, in all!

You and I must decide as to whether we shall suffer and be sick. The choice is ours. Our attitude will determine what the effect of that which comes to us shall be. After our decision to stand true to Basis is made, we begin to grow in understanding, and the Universe becomes illumined for us with the light of God. We see that the Infinite Being is all and includes all. What God is, is wherever you and I are. Why should we suffer when God is through us and in us? Our own thinking must be at fault! Man, the spoken word of God, is in reality always divine and whole; consequently, in the real of him he does not suffer. It is through belief in separation that he suffers. There is only one God-

Expression, and that is good, for God brings forth only that which is like unto himself. Each form of the infinite variety of God-Expression is inherently good. Each of us is always being brought forth by the power of his own consciousness. Expression is eternal; it is always good. We are alive in God. Can God suffer and be sick? Since the good is eternal, what about evil? Has it any place in the plan of existence? Could it really exist? Like suffering, evil is in the thought realm.

Tolstoi says, "God is That All, That Infinite All, of which I am conscious of being a part." Another has said, "God is the totalized consciousness of the whole."

Natural science is fast working out of the concept of a dead material universe tossed about by various forces, to a universe all force, life, and soul thought. God is not half dead, but wholly alive; hence the Universe is wholly good. In form, God the Infinite is called finite, because infinity is centered and located in the visible expression of invisibility. The man who is conscious of this intimate relationship between himself and God is blessed indeed. There is no material universe in the sense of a universe apart from God.

Our suffering is purely mental; it is induced by belief in another power than the power of good. As soon as we separate ourselves in the thought realm from the realization of the eternal and ever present goodness of Life, we suffer. As long as men believe in two powers, they will suffer. Suffering and sin are the results of wrong thinking. Are these experiences mysterious? They are only the result of our unwillingness to face the full import of the law of cause and effect.

The mystery of evil is allied with the mystery of suffering. How can there be evil in a universe of form that is wholly good? Again I say, evil, like suffering, is in our thinking. There is no principle of evil, for principle is eternal, and evil is temporal. Where, then, does it originate? Whither does it go? That which has its inception in a wrong mental attitude really comes from ignorance and returns to nothing. Evil is a temporary condition of the mentality which can be banished when we choose to live aright, for since the power of good is at the foundation of all expression, evil has no real hold upon the individual. The power of good is the power inherent in the development of the world; it is all-powerful in civilization. Evil is being overcome by the setting of a higher thought standard for the race. Jesus overcame evil with good; this he did by his thinking. His love, deep, true, and steadfast, has touched humanity in a way that no other love ever has. We do not overcome evil by denying it with the lips; we must overcome it as Jesus did, with good.

Nine-tenths of the wrongs and sufferings of the world come from man's inhumanity to man. All conditions of evil, such as the sweat shop, unjust labor conditions, all immoral conditions, could be banished from the face of the earth, if men would turn their thought to universal love, for the evils of the world would fade away in the light of good.

There is no evil to the one who lives with the vision of God before him. Evil is the outer result of a mental condition of fear, ignorance, doubt, unbelief. As fear is the cause of suffering, so is it the cause of evil. We fix our attention on the dark places because we fear these; we emphasize darkness instead of light. Our world becomes peopled with fears, doubts, misgivings, and our birthright of health, peace, power, and joy seems to desert us. But does it really leave us? No, that cannot be. Since power, love, health, wisdom, and joy are the truth of us, these cannot really desert us, except when we turn our thought away from these to false images of sin and suffering; then we seem to lose our heritage of good for a time. True thinking brings us back to the good. We are by nature children of righteousness and truth. That evil is not one of the eternal realities is evidenced by the instability of its nature. Even though there are numerous world conditions which are obviously evil, such as war, jealousy, dishonesty, injustice, suspicion, it is also evident that these conditions have no place in the universal plan. God does not know these. Since God is all, evil must be a temporary condition without power. Evil always vanishes when you and I take a strong enough stand in God-Consciousness.

How is it, then, that we continue to believe in the power of evil and suffering in a Universe which is God and God in action? I believe that men are brought forth, children in consciousness, in order that they may have the opportunity of working out their own salvation. The intent of the Father for his children is that they shall attain; hence they are brought forth perfect, divinely capable of unfolding. Great is the privilege of development! Men are left to make their own decisions, and to exercise their own free-will as to how and when to attain. God must desire the companionship of His children or He would not have created them capable of Divine understanding. God knows about each one and shares in the development of the individual; every true thought you and I think is approved of God. Upon our decision to choose God as our comrade in every experience of life depends our well being. It is the Spirit which preserves us from all evil.

Ignorance keeps before us pictures of unrealities called evil and suffering, and fear keeps us bound to these. Knowledge of truth frees us from bondage, and right thinking makes us free from evil and suffering. These are mysteries only in so far as we give them power to shape the lives of individuals. Why do we suffer? Why do we sin? The same answer suffices for both questions. Our thinking is not true to the foundation principle of Life; the Universe of form is God in action. God is infinite Love, and in Love there is only light; there is no mystery.

The Mystery of Healing

MANKIND has looked upon healing as a bodily process, and there has always been a sense of the mysterious attached to it. Among primitive peoples there are rites and medicinal herbs that are thought to hold within themselves the power of restoring men to health. As you see, faith in something is necessary. While men are believing in these means of restoration, they are shrouding them in mystery. How we have worked to take life out of the natural and to surround its observances with the supernatural. Now we are coming to see that there is no supernatural, for the natural is God in action.

Divine Science is revealing to us two things: first, that healing is not a physical process but, spiritual realization; and second, that health is not a condition of physical well-being only but the realization of a state of wholeness in the individual. Healing is the turning from the belief in disease to the realization of God's Presence and Perfect Activity. God is health. Do I hear you asking, "Since God is health and God is omnipresent, what is there to be healed?" There is only one condition to be healed—our mis-conceptions.

When we understand form, our point of view on healing becomes clearer. In the old thought what was called form or matter was considered susceptible to all kinds of ills. Healing, consequently, meant a righting of wrong conditions, a changing of disease into health. Divine Science holds that Substance is God and that form is Substance in manifestation; hence, form is declared incorruptible because by nature it is perfect. God is being rediscovered. In the light of Divine Science, we see omnipresent Spirit manifesting in an infinite variety of forms. We believe in the perfection of the manifest because God is everywhere. We know that imperfection is only our misconception. Form is the expression of God; it is Spirit manifest, and Spirit is perfect, true, and harmonious.

As the misconception, dualism passes, and the true conception of One Presence and Power takes its place, the unity of all life is being revealed as well as the perfect nature of all God manifestation—and there is no other. Divine Science recognizes the unity of the universe, and form and Spirit, not as two, but as one. Just so long as we persist in thinking in terms of two powers, there will be a mystery about all manifestation. So long as we emphasize the power of mind over matter, we are holding on to a dualistic conception; we are proclaiming the existence of two powers. There is danger in this; it retards our development.

While healing to the mental scientist is brought about by exercising the power of mind over body; to the Divine Scientist health is the natural state of the individual and is only waiting for his realization of perfection as his divine heritage. Health always is universal, but we do not always realize it. Mental healing does not differ so much from the old conception of healing the body by external means, for the mental power of one person is supposed to restore another to health. Spiritual healing is realization; it does not bring about anything but realizes what is already there. The greatest thinkers are agreeing that there is only one Power and its activity is the Universe and that we are one with this activity everywhere.

Divine Science sees God's creation like its Creator, eternally perfect, and untouched by human thought. The creation of God is eternal; the misconception about it is temporal. Spirit is always expressing in terms of perfection; there is nothing that needs healing in God-Life. Where God is, there Substance is, whole and perfect, and God is in all places at all times. There is no place where God is not. What is it, then, that is ill and sinful? It is only our thought of the body; it is not the Body, the temple of the living God; and remember there is only One Body—the God-Body. Divine Science knows one Substance—Spirit—and one Mind—Universal Intelligence. You and I are included in this Mind. All that we see with true vision is Spirit brought forth.

Men are not creators; there is but one Creator—God. Men are sharers in creation which is the very presence of God-Power: Wisdom, Love, Truth, and Light. We see what we believe; we believe in imperfection of all kinds, and we see it; hence, there is to you and to me, sickness, lack, sin, as long as we see these. If you are seeing with a limited vision, God seems limited to you. God seems to be a fluctuating power, sometimes in the ascendancy, other times under the domination of another power called evil. It is as we think that we experience.

Divine Science teaches that men cannot recreate or rebuild tissue. Tissue is always perfect and does not need restoring; neither can they reshape or restore a body to health. The body does not need this, for it is always perfect. They can, however, accomplish wonderful results by right thinking, and glorify the world with great healing power by consecrated thinking which brings realization of perfection. Body is Mind in manifestation. Do we believe this? If we do, you and I are healed. Body is perfect as its Source; it cannot suffer, be sick, or die. Jesus said, "Be ye perfect, as your Father in heaven is perfect." He meant this. Since ye are perfect, why not realize your perfection. Right thinking restores us in consciousness to our normal state—perfection, although we seem to have been straying far from it.

We are responsible for our wrong thinking as well as our wrong doing. Difficult experiences are the results of misconceptions about our bodies and our affairs. Ignorance is blindness; it is darkness. And in the darkness, yes, even in the twilight, things assume grotesque shapes; a tree stump takes on the semblance of a huge bear, and until our vision is cleared, we fear the bear on the path before us as much as if it were a bear. To us it is. So it is with the body when we see it through the shades of twilight-thinking; it seems to have many ills; it does not look to us in the half-light like the God-Body. Why? Is it the Body or is it our misconception of it? Since we believe that there is only One Substance, God, and that our bodies are Substance in action, these are in truth perfect. We see the body imperfectly and say that it is sick, when we look through the dimmers of sense experiences. Remember always that the senses give us only a partial report of the true state of anything. Let us look with the eye of Spirit, the single eye, and our bodies shall be full of light.

Misconceptions are shadows that fall across sunlit paths only to flicker away. We are emerging into the full light of truth to see that man is perfect Being. When we realize this, we are healed. Faith in God makes us whole; health is wholeness, and it is our normal state. There is no mystery in healing for God is Health.

The Mystery of Human Characteristics

THE race has been acquiring undesirable characteristics through the centuries instead of turning to the divine inherencies: wisdom, love, knowledge, understanding, power, life, and joy. All of these are inherent in God-Life, and Divine Love is sharing these with you and me. In considering every subject we should turn our attention toward our foundation; we cannot then go very far astray. For example, the question is often asked: "Why do these undesirable human characteristics persist after we have learned that, in the light of truth, we are divinely endowed?" This is a practical question; and a satisfactory answer to it will be most helpful to those who are seeking to serve more efficiently by living truer lives.

We are children of God, heirs of God, and we truly inherit a nature that is divine. Let us see then, why we have this fault and that fault, this virtue and that virtue. We are wondering the same things about our neighbors as we do about ourselves. Are we not? The assertion that human traits are transmitted from father to son, which is so generally accepted, shows that we really believe in a human source. This concept is deeply rooted in the thought of the race, and like all racial concepts is not easily dissolved. It seems that if we view these human characteristics from the point of view of the Universal Presence and Power of Good, the mystery of them should fall away. God is living us and God is manifesting perfection. What does it mean to be alive? It means that Infinite Love is expressing as form, and that you and I as God-Expressions are destined to realize God-Life—that Life which is powerful, true, pure, and joyous. Nothing is thrust upon you and me, however, as children of an Almighty Love; we are free to choose which kind of thoughts we shall think.

Do you see what our foundation is? Men are wonderfully and eternally good by nature. We are sharers of Life Divine; we partake of the Nature of God. Universal Love is expressing as the individual; the Father is working in us to will and to do. The same Power that brings my work to me, helps me to do it well, for Divine Power is radiating through me. Since it is the only power, why do we give power to so many things?

It is true that we do not all move forward toward the realization of our Divinity at an even pace even though our destiny is unchangeable. We shall ultimately know truth, and this knowledge shall set us free from the limitations of the human characteristics that seem to keep us from realizing our destiny. There is in reality no standing still, and no going backwards. Each one is progressing to some degree. Did the prodigal son retrograde during his journey in the Far Country? It does not seem so, for did he not rise out of the experience of separation from

God in his thinking, and return to the Father's house? The Father did not force the prodigal to return; but he loved him all of the time he was away.

There is no ruling power that forces us into realization of our heritage; we may wander far and suffer many tribulations before we decide to return to a right attitude—one that will put us in harmony with good. Divine Love is always sharing its warmth, glory, and beauty. It impels the individual to do better things, but it does not compel him to live to his highest. Man is a free agent in so far as his power of choice to realize the good that is always his is concerned. We cannot as individuals by using our personal wills change the truth of what we are in God. A child of God cannot change his nature for it is divine. He can, however, neglect to cooperate with Divine Activity, and thereby retard his own progress. Those who through ignorance deny their divine nature live in limitation until they change the trend of their thinking. We seem so eager for the worldly inheritance, and correspondingly indifferent to the Divine Inheritance.

What you and I think does not change the truth of Life. Divine Law is working irrespective of our opinions; let us cooperate with the working of law. If we depend upon our inner heritage, the outer will take care of itself. If we choose the right way, we shall move forward at a much more rapid rate. The choice of the ignorant way means the retarding of our unfoldment. Fullness of life for us depends upon our decisions; we must decide for ourselves what our reactions to experiences shall be. Are we moved and changed by outer things? Is the trend of your life and of mine to be determined by circumstances and conditions? Or shall we say with Paul, "None of these things move me?" The decision lies with you and me.

Jesus believed in freewill; he believed that man's destiny is realization of the whole, but that the rate of his progress is determined by the kind of thinking he chooses to do. He shows us that we are truer companions of God because we are endowed with the power of choice. The victory is much greater if we choose the way of truth as free agents. Although our destiny is chosen for us, our rate of development toward this realization is a matter of our decision. Jesus brings out this truth in the Parable of the Talents. Shall we use the Divine Inheritance that is ours, or shall we bury the riches of it under a load of fear and material limitations? Again the choice is left with us. Shall we follow the example of Jesus, and merge the personal into the Divine? This means progress. It means acceptance of Omnipresence as a working basis for life. As we accept the Allness of God, so do we prosper in every phase of our expression.

How shall we make use of the acceptance of Omnipresence as a basis for the overcoming of wrong human characteristics? First of all, let us apply to our dispositions the fact that harmony is God's way. Do these need changing for the better? It lies within us to make all necessary changes; we may turn a gloomy disposition into a joyous one, or a selfish one to an unselfish one. We can overcome evil with good. The person who looks out upon human experience from the standpoint of the eternal presence of God as the background of his life is the one who comes up over limitation. He overcomes hardship with understanding, foolish ways with wise ones, ignorance with knowledge, separation with love, weakness and inefficiency with power, sorrow with joy, and death with Life Eternal. We are much concerned about our temperaments and those of our children and our friends; psychologists are planning ways and means for overcoming undesirable temperaments by outer methods. Why do we not turn to the true method of overcoming—to the understanding of the truth of Being? By this truth we see that we are inherently whole; we are neither weak nor are we sinful.

Some of us are easily discouraged. I hear people say that after years of the study of truth they are still facing conditions of limitation such as weakness, temper, selfishness, depression, hatred of others. This simply means that your victory is not won; be steadfast; keep the faith. Life is eternal progression. You are perfect in nature as the Father is perfect, for you are his expression. The human characteristics that you are holding up in contrast to the divine, and grieving over, are only misconceptions of that which really belongs to you and me by our true nature. He who knows that strength is inherent in his Being cannot be weak for long; if you believe that God is Love, you cannot hate. The one who sees God as harmonious activity cannot lack self-control. Those who know that Life is God—joyous and free, cannot be depressed and fearful.

Do not deplore your weaknesses; work with yourself until these go. You are the one to decide whether or not the human failings shall persist. Be sure that you are not falling below God's high intent for you, his child. If you inherit a temper according to the thought of the race from someone who has gone before you, turn to this affirmation: I inherit poise from my only Source of inheritance, God. If you are afraid of life's experiences, say to yourself, I know that God is Life. The Life-Principle is infinitely strong; I will trust it. To the sensitive person I say, "Affirm your part in the universal plan as a child of God, and know that there is only the spirit of love in the realm of you and of those who seem to hurt you. Bless the one who tries to do you an injury in word or deed. Know that all Life is One. Sensitiveness is self-centered thinking; think out into the universe; get yourself out of the way and you will see more clearly."

Do not concentrate on your faults; centralize your thinking around God-Life. Know yourself as God in manifestation. You will overcome by the very process of your thinking; the weak traits will vanish. Ask yourself at some moment when you seemed to lose control, "Why was I angry? Why did I criticize? Why was I thoughtless? Why was I hurt?" In the old way of thinking you may believe that you have answers to these questions that are satisfactory. Have you? Let us see. I was angry, because another was unjust. I was critical, because another was in the wrong. I was thoughtless, because I forgot. I was busy attending to concerns of my own. I was hurt, because another did me harm. Is anything that you have said true? You are receiving only what you open yourself to receive. Another cannot hurt you. You are self-centered and open to discordant thoughts; therefore you receive these. Remember, too, that there is no explanation that is satisfactory for destructive criticism or for lack of consideration; your responsibility is to do your part, not to try to do your neighbor's. Thoughtlessness is always selfish; you are thinking only of the personal self, not of the principle involved. Ask yourself, "What is my part?" You will receive an answer.

Are you thinking, "Why was I not put forward as she was or as he was? I am just as capable of doing this greater work." Perhaps you are, but the law of life is working for your good and for the good of all your fellow men. You who believe in law will see that your place is best for you; there is neither high nor low in God's sight. "All work ranks the same with God."

Are you feeling separation? Are you condemning others? Are you at odds with your work? Are you interpreting everything that comes on the dark side? Are you wondering where these disastrous traits come from in a child of God? From you, not from God, I assure you. You and I come into this phase of Eternal Life as little children in development; we are not fully aware of our heritage even after many years of growth and unfoldment. We feel the force of race beliefs, and we find these beliefs persisting in us. These human characteristics that have caused us so much trouble—fear, loneliness, despondency, discontent, envy—we carry over from the race owing to our misconceptions about our heritage. These are deeply fixed in us, and it takes definite work— also illumined work—to eliminate them.

It is well for us to face failures squarely; we should know where we fall down, and repent according to the true meaning of the word, repentance, by turning our thoughts in the direction of the truth of Being. What human characteristics have you? Face these without fear, and begin the work of substitution at once. For every limiting trait substitute a universal one. Begin now to strengthen your thinking; this is not difficult. We live only a moment at a time; overcoming means faithfulness. We are not subject to race beliefs; for since we are children of God, the power of God is active within us. We inherit from God only divine characteristics. Let us refuse to acknowledge the power of anything unlike God. We are free by the power of God. Failings and weaknesses do not belong to us; these have no part in divine Life. Failure does not belong to the one who knows his Source; neither does fear.

Universal Life is infinitely powerful. By cooperating with it we can come up over the undesirable human characteristics that have limited us. Let us rejoice that our real inheritance is the inherencies of God-Life. Our method of realization is right thinking.

The mystery of human characteristics is soon cleared away when we view these from the point of view of our true endowment as children of God. Our characteristics are limiting only in so far as we give them power over us. It is the right use of the power within us that makes us powerful. Weakness is a misconception of our potentiality; loneliness is our own thought of separation affecting us; depression is fear of what may happen to us as individuals; temper is misdirected power. We cover our divine power with loads of material limitations, and then, we wonder that we are burdened in a world that is divine, by human characteristics. A few hours of reflection should set us right. There is no mystery about our characteristics; it is our attitude towards these that has caused us to be mystified by their presence.

The Mystery of Thought Transference

WE say, "How wonderful! What marvelous things the brain of man conceives," as each new invention takes its place among the marvels of the century. "What next?" we ask. It is not the brain of man in the accepted sense of the word brain that is producing the wonders of the age; it is the Mind of God working through the brain of man. All of this development that so often seems to us mysterious comes by law; there is no chance in it to the one who sees life as eternal progression. Although the latest invention seems greater than the one before it, each has its own place in the line of development that man is following. We think of great achievements as mysterious. How can man think out such wonderful things? Divine Science teaches us not to marvel at the brain power of men, but to recognize the One Mind in action through these men who are cooperating with the great forces of the Universe.

The trend of modern invention is toward the annihilation or elimination of time and space. To the one who believes in the unity of life this is a hopeful sign; for by means of the great mechanical devices of this era of development men are steadily being brought nearer and nearer together. We are today closer to those on the other side of the world owing to the great discoveries of radio and wireless than we were a hundred years ago to those a few miles away. This is all part of the law of progression.

I thrill when I hear that a heart beat in Schenectady was heard recently in San Antonio. We shall not need assembly rooms always; we shall sit in our homes, and hear the Sunday morning sermon, as well as the great musical programs, the operas, and speeches that are being broadcast now. From present indication we shall sit in our homes, some day in the not very distant future, and see the actors, as well as hear them, give their lines.

We who have watched the onward movement of natural science and invention with spiritual insight have known that greater and still greater developments would follow. The world is becoming truly one. Let us by our thinking and living speed the day when the oneness of mankind will be not only theorized over but practiced. It is the bringing together of men in common sympathy and clearer understanding that is the great ideal for the world to follow. The elimination of time and space by mechanical means is wonderfully significant of the unifying process that is working in the Law of Life.

We are almost tempted at times to think that in the greatness of recent discoveries we have heard the last words spoken in the development of different phases of human progress. Is there nothing more to be said? I believe that there are greater things still. When an inventor produced the amplifier for the radio which made it possible for ten thousand persons to hear what ten had heard before, we thought a final word had been spoken; then came the microphone, another invention which is so sensitive that it registers the sound if I drop a crumb of bread upon my table. This sound is registered many miles away. Some of us are saying, "There can be nothing greater than this." I say that there are greater things in our midst right now.

The idea of radio is not new; the practical application of it is. The next step in the application of the principle is mental radio, no doubt. This is thought transference or telepathy. The psychologists are testing out the method of the transference of thought—and are proving that it can be done. Mental radio has been known by many people for years, but they have said little about their experience because they were awaiting further developments. The natural scientific men are not alone in their discovery of thought transference; the spiritual scientific women have seen this possibility for a long time. Their experiences have proved to them that thought messages can be sent without any mechanical means. Women have a deep insight into the things of the Spirit; this does not mean that men do not, but they are more concerned with the outer than women are—of necessity, of course. They are focusing thought upon that which is taking place in the outer conditions of daily existence. It was a woman, you remember, who first recognized the Christ; and she found it difficult to convince the men.

Mental telepathy means that thought messages sent out by me are caught by you. When thought messages were broadcast by mental radio in years gone by, the phenomenon was considered supernatural. In the light of recent discoveries we find that this is not outside of the law. A great step had been taken; the scientific world is depending less upon material means.

There are two ways of contacting others metaphysically. We may reach them by mental concentration; this method is used by workers in applied psychology and mental science. It has its analogy in radio. The other method of contact is spiritual. In this method we reach another by knowing that there is only one Mind, and commune with him through this realization of unity. Let us for a moment assume the office of the one who forecasts. The spiritual method is the way of the future. It will be applied more and more as we think in terms of unity. The elimination of distance and time in our thought takes place as soon as we are established in the consciousness of the One Mind.

There is most helpful work being done today by the Spiritual scientists who are giving messages of the truth of Being to all the world. We in our treatments and silences are doing what wireless telegraphy is accomplishing by mechanical means. The effect of our thinking is felt not only in our midst and among the loved ones of our home group; these thought messages reach the uttermost parts of the earth. We have no way of measuring the power of thought; we know, however, that it is the mightiest force in existence. No one lives to himself alone. There is a universal radio system. Any one may listen in whose thought instrument is attuned. It is becoming recognized among natural scientists that every man is a radio station, and that we are constantly sending and receiving in the realm of thought. The psychologists are testing thought with instruments in order to prove to the world that thoughts are things. This is well; for the reports that come from learned men in great universities will be accepted by the world at large.

Divine Science teaches that since there is only one Mind, the transference of thought is by law; it is the natural method of communication among men. I like to think that we send thought blessings even to what the world has called the dark continent. I am sure that the natives in Africa can be reached by thought messages and blessed by these. Many of them are tuning in.

Luther Burbank tells many interesting incidents of thought transference in a recent magazine article in which he says that his mother was able to receive and send out thought messages. Mrs. Burbank was at one time attending a wedding at some distance from her home; she had intended to remain in this town during the night. Suddenly she became aware that her son had broken his arm. She returned to her home at once, to find that Luther's arm had been broken at just the time the mental message had been received. Mr. Burbank says that his sister, according to tests made at the University of California, was able seven times out of ten, to receive messages sent to her telepathically. He says that weak thoughts must soon fall flat, while strong ones may travel to the ends of the earth, and that thoughts held in common by large numbers of people must "swell into a tremendous chorus." Think of the privilege that is ours as individuals—that of lifting up the thought of the world. Every positive thought is an uplifting power. The ideal for the race is unity of thought. Is it true that the confused condition of the world today can be traced to the negative thoughts that the human race has been and still is generating and transmitting? We might well heed these words. We do not give sufficient attention to the power of our thoughts.

Mr. B.F. Mills told an amusing incident of thought transference which proves that we must not be too strenuous in our attempts to get a message across. Mr. Mills and a friend of his, by the name of Thompson, who were especially congenial mentally, decided to try an experiment in thought transference. They agreed that the experiment should be made at ten that evening. About six-thirty Mr. Mills was planning casually what message he should send to his friend. I will ask him when he last heard from his friend Anthony, and tell him to write to Anthony at once. Mr. Mills then dismissed the subject. At ten o'clock he set to work to concentrate with great vigor on the message to Mr. Thompson. He felt assured that such strenuous thought-work could not be done without results. At ten-thirty they were in communication. "Well, Thompson, what did you get?" asked Mr. Mills. "Not much of anything," was his friend's reply. Mr. Mills was greatly disappointed. "Well, didn't you get something?" Mr. Thompson in a vague way answered, "I got something about an automobile. What did you really send?"

"I asked you when you had heard from Anthony, and added that you must write to him at once." "That's queer," said Mr. Thompson, "at six-thirty I seized with the greatest desire to write to Anthony, and I did." It was at six-thirty that Mr. Mills was planning his message to Mr. Thompson in a casual, easy way. The ten o'clock message had been blocked by the strenuous efforts of the sender to get it across.

Healing and all thought transference should be carried on with lack of effort, quiet certainty and confidence. Do not treat with screwed up faces and try to send out thought messages by making strenuous efforts. When our thought is directed toward the right thing, the realization of the truth of Being, we shall not be troubled by outer conditions. Let us not be diverted from the Big Thing by the lesser thing, the phenomenon. We should fix our thought upon the truth of the experience, not upon the experience itself. The truth is that good is omnipresent, and that he who is attuned to the harmonious activity of the universe of form will receive and likewise send out worth-while messages. Are we using the perfect thought power which is God-Mind in action? Are we ever more or less disturbed by the thought that there are many negative messages out on the waves of ether? We are told that this is true. We need not be disturbed, however, by these waves of thought; we shall not be affected by these unless we open ourselves to them. The great broadcasting process is ever at work; let us cooperate in the universal system by opening ourselves only to that which is true and by sending out only that which is positive.

I look back now upon the experiences my grandmother had in thought transference; her power was considered supernatural at that time. My grandfather with four other pioneers started out to explore the unbroken West. He had reached what we now call Missouri. This part of our continent seemed far away then; it took three weeks to get a letter from the West in my grandfather's day. Grandmother dreamed one night that my grandfather had passed on; those in her family who tried to comfort her with the thought that it was only a dream after all, were assured that her dream was true. In three weeks a letter bearing the news of my grandfather's passing was received. In those days what to many seemed supernatural, to me seems the most natural thing in the world.

Another instance of thought transference interested me. Four of us were driving around Denver in the days of open carriages; two of our party were strangers out to see the city. In the midst of a conversation in which we were all engaging, one of the guests said, "Pardon me, I am called upon to give a treatment; please go right on with your conversation." After a time of silence she joined in the conversation again, and nothing more was said about the incident. Sometime after this I met my friend, and she told me that at the time when she dropped out of the conversation the day of our drive, she did so because a call had come from her husband who seemed to be in great need. She responded to his call for help by beginning to treat at once. Her help had been needed; for she received word from her husband that at the time of receiving the impression of his need the walls of the mine in which he was working had caved in. He was buried in the dirt for a time, but after being carried out regained consciousness, and was found to have escaped injury.

Right thinking is the basis of powerful living. When we are tempted to think a thought of criticism, hatred, fear, envy, let us immediately meet the temptation, and come up over it. Someone else might be likewise tempted to open himself to the negative, and our wrong thought may find lodgment and do more harm than we think. While we are in a negative condition mentally, we are open to what we call the evil messages of others. But as long as we are positive in our thinking, we are safe in the Good.

I have had innumerable experiences in thought transference; in fact, they are daily occurrences. When we think of ourselves as broadcasting and receiving stations, is there not a thrill that comes with the thought? Reflect for a moment on the privilege that is ours—that of helping to uplift the world. Let us keep our station in tune with the good and the true; then none of the negative thoughts can possibly reach us. Negative thoughts are evils—temporal of course. I would prefer, however, to face one good-sized devil than a thousand sneaking ones in the form of wrong thoughts. If only the race would wake up to the truth, and guard its thinking, for there seems to be what we may call race thought—an attitude toward life that is infixed in the race. Some psychologists have much to say about what they call the subconscious—the reservoir of race conceptions that seem to be a force in the world. What kind of thoughts are you and I contributing to the race consciousness? Remember that our responsibility is that all of our thinking be constructive. The world needs lifting up out of the concept of separation into the realization of love.

The greatest of all methods of thought transference is spiritual realization of the unity of all men. There are many of our brothers seeking the best; let it come persistently from you and me. I often think, as I speak, and look into the eager faces of the audience before me, of our

invisible audiences in other cities and other countrie،
searching to find God. Let us feed the spiritually hung
cooperation with the law of love. There are seekers ev،
homes, schools, and offices —and there are broadcasters
Remember that we can broadcast truth from the kitchen ۔s
from the platform. Let us be sure that we are receiving our ،nessages
from Spirit, and then, broadcast these and no others to the world.

The Mystery of Prayer

PRAYER has seemed a mystery to men because they have not understood the nature of the relation between God and man. When God
was thought of as abiding in heaven and ruling the earth from a throne
on high far from the homes of men, there was reason in belief that he
did not know the thoughts, needs, and ideals of earth-dwellers. For
centuries our thinking has been in terms of space and time; hence,
heaven seemed a long distance from us, and the time when God walked
with Adam in the garden at the close of the day seemed an eternity.
According to this conception, God had visited the world after creating it, but He had withdrawn His mighty presence to become a ruling
power; hence, in order to reach this presence, it was necessary that
men become subservient as they did in relation to earthly kings, and
implore the mercy of this heavenly king. Some among the children of
this earth seemed favored by this ruling power; others were less favored,
or in fact, were is disfavor—hence, the mystery. Men sought to reach
the mighty one by various methods; sacrifice of possessions, expiation
or individual repentance, and supplication were the most commonly
employed means. It is the relation of supplication to the newer form of
prayer that we shall discuss in this chapter.

In the old prayer, men sought to get that which they needed and
desired; in the new prayer, men seek to give of themselves, to commune
with God that His perfect will may be known to them, and to give
of themselves to their fellow men according to this Purpose; in other
words they seek to cooperate with God, the Giver of all good gifts.

nstead of beseeching a far away power, they are affirming the immediate presence of an abiding Power. Instead of begging for bounty, they are working to realize the abundance that is theirs by divine heritage. The great lesson of prayer today is that God and man are one; the high purpose of prayer is to establish this relationship in men's thinking. Instead of the old conception of a God who is reluctantly withholding his favors from the lives of men, and who, therefore, must be appeased and besought in order that he may grant favors, there is a new concept—Infinite Spirit sharing its all.

The new conception of God requires a new method of prayer in which men do not ask for things but seek light and more light. This is the powerful prayer, if it is backed by conviction. The new prayer, then, is for realization. From the dawn of consciousness that something within has sought That Something Bigger; it is the Divine Urge impelling men to seek the good and to find it. Prayer is the method by which the sons of God come to realize the immediate Presence and Power of God in their lives. No matter by what method men have prayed, however, if their prayers were backed by faith, these have proved effective. Worship and prayer have a reflective benefit upon the one who worships and prays; prayer is not for God's benefit except as the Father finds satisfaction in direct communion and companionship with his children.

The Indians of Colorado in times long past believed that the Great Spirit lived upon the top of Pikes Peak, and they would march for many miles in order to camp in sight of this mighty mountain, that they might offer their prayers directly to the Great Spirit. These children of the race watched for signs; if the sun shone, the Spirit was commending their plans; if clouds covered the top of the peak, he was saying no, and they would abandon their project. The yes of the Great Spirit meant courage to these children, and they went forth prepared to carry through their purpose.

Today many of us believe that we are praying a larger prayer than our forefathers did; we must remember, however, that our prayer is larger and more powerful, because they prayed before us the prayer of supplication with great faith. The consciousness that lies back of prayer is dynamic. Faith is the great motivating power. I look back to the first time that I was directly conscious of the power of prayer. My mother was going to visit my grandmother and my aunt; I was to be left at home. Now, to visit my grandmother's home was the height of my dreams. My brothers were to be taken. I saw why later. It was easier and safer to leave the girls at home without paternal guidance than it was to leave the boys. I was heart-broken for the first time in my six years of life. What was I to do? I had been told to pray for what I believed that I should have. I resolved to pray a special prayer. I did not put my supplication into the regular morning and evening prayer, but I had a time set apart. I would break away from my play over and over again to hasten to my room; there I would kneel at my bedside and ask the Father to let me go to visit my grandmother. I kept my prayers secret; but I silently prepared my doll's clothes for a trip. The day before my mother left, she decided to take me. My prayer had been backed by conviction; it was effective.

Prayer is fundamental in life. Whether we know it or not, we are continually praying. Every aspiration, all worthwhile desire, and all true attitude are prayers. All praise to God and all appreciation of his goodness to the children of men is prayer. True service is prayer. Highest prayer is that prayer which is based upon great principles; it is the prayer that is in accord with the nature of the Universe; it is the prayer that aligns itself with Truth. Knowing and living the truth of the Infinite is the highest prayer.

The prayer of affirmation is most powerful; in the old way I asked God to heal me and to give me what I needed; in the new way, I affirm that God is Health and Abundance. I know that wholeness and abundance are God's will for me; I know that I am well, whole and perfect. It makes no difference what I think about it; human conception does not determine the state of my Being; Truth does this. I do not plead, but I train my thinking to realize that in God-Mind I have my Being; this Mind is always manifesting. Mind and Mind in action is the Universe. Before I call for health, God has answered by being

Health, Love, and Harmony. The new prayer is affirmation of fullness. All things are possible to the one who prays the prayer that is in accord with principle. There will not be one thing that seems to be wrong that cannot and will not be righted, when we identify our thinking with God-Thought.

Faith is the dynamic power, remember. Above all, pray. The praying life is the life of power; Jesus lived it. The new prayer is the prayer of illumined faith, and of the acknowledgment of God's Presence and Power. It is the foundation of all true seeing and believing; and through it comes the greatest of all joys, the realized [comradeship between God and man. Through praying the larger prayer we become constantly more conscious of God and God in action, and of Infinite Mind everywhere in all life experience.

Sometimes one longs to pray the old prayer—to ask the Father for something very near to the deepest desires and aspirations of the heart. I have felt this, and I have known that God has understood. Even though we do not consider that the prayer of supplication is that of the highest vision, still, we know that it has brought satisfaction to the lives of many men. Sometimes a few words like these spoken from the heart bring comfort and rest: "Dear Father, you know for what I am praying, and I trust you to help me to realize that which is best about it." Prayer is the essential. I recall the evolution of prayer in my own life. First I prayed for things; then, there began to come within me a deep longing for a greater Something; at first I did not know for what. One Sunday morning when I was ten or eleven years old, all of the family were at church; I went out into the garden, and walked up and down between two old-fashioned flower beds, gay with flowers that my mother loved. I can see again the glow of sunshine that flooded the garden; it was there that I had my first deep religious experience. I prayed, "Oh, Father, make me good; I want to know You—to come close to You, Father." The aspiration which awoke in my heart that morning is the fundamental aspiration of my life today; this great desire underneath every act of my life, this aspiration to get closer to God, has been a constant experience. God answered my prayer; although I could not see then in what way the answer would come. This desire within me to know God has been steadily realized; it is supreme above everything in my life.

Our prayers are answered; the fundamental things come to us in answer to our deeper prayers; while those things which are not essential, and do not further our development in deeper realization are withheld. Prayer prepares us for bigger things. That which is best for our development comes to us by the eternal working of the Law of Life. At one time I prayed for light; and light came. I felt that I was touching God; I was alive in God. I am living my answered prayer now. I do not ask for this and that; I seek realization. The larger prayer in my life grew out of years of deep inner longing, without my knowing what the results would be. The way was opened for me to come into a greater revelation of truth. I was led to study; I entered the first class held in Pueblo thirty-six years ago; in that class my prayer of the years was answered. I found God. I saw my first great light; it has been growing deeper, clearer, and more powerful ever since. In this light there is no darkness. I was one of a simple little group searching for more of truth when I saw this great light; how well I recall that afternoon in the class when radiant glory filled the room. I knew that I was healed. I felt the Spirit's blessing upon me; I had touched God.

We have been taught to pray without ceasing. What does this mean? It means true aspiring, high thinking, being infinitely patient, keeping the faith, trusting deeply, serving with integrity of purpose. Prayer is not a matter of words merely; it is a treatment, an affirmation, a thought of love, an assertion of faith; these establish within us an attitude of certainty and of confidence in the goodness of God-Law and Love which is the most powerful prayer. When I am going on a journey, I do not say that this or that must be done; I rest in the certainty that Spirit is going before me to prepare the way. Your ways and my ways are divinely directed; all is well. When I rise to speak before a strange audience, I know that only the Spirit is speaking; I get myself out of the way. These are some of the ways of praying without ceasing.

We are agreed, I trust, that all prayer is powerful; its effect is always uplifting. It reacts for good upon the one offering it. The one who knows that he is praying according to the nature of the Universe, and whose affirmations are backed by faith, prays the dynamic prayer, and it reacts wholesomely upon him. The man who lives the praying life is not moved by outer conditions; he is able to solve these. He says with Paul, "None of these things move me." The praying life is the powerful life, for it touches all the fundamental principles and is able to apply these. To him who knows himself one with all Life only good comes; all of his prayers are answered; his thoughts, words, and deeds are worthwhile. The praying attitude was the Jesus attitude; he identified in his thinking with Spirit, and showed us the meaning of praying without ceasing.

There is no longer mystery about the perfect communion of God and man that we call prayer. We have found the key that unlocks all of the mysteries in the concept of Omnipresence. In the light of Omnipresence we see that God and man are One; that heaven and earth are One; it is this established attitude that is our most powerful prayer. Time and space vanish from our thinking as we grow in the re-alization of Truth. We see now that the garden in which Adam walked at the close of day was itself Infinite Mind in manifestation, and that as we walk among the flowers, we walk with God. Sincere that there is no separation, there is no true need, uplifted thought, or loving aspiration, of which God is not aware. Instead of asking to be given more, let us make the best use of what we have—the gift of God within us. What is the powerful prayer? It is the life lived in the realization that God and man are one.

The Mystery of Success

WHY have we always looked upon successful people of the world with wonder in our eyes? Perhaps, we have even added in a whisper, "How did they do it?" Our tendency has been to wrap veils of mystery around success, and to think of it as an achievement of a favored few. Now we know that man is, by nature, a success, because he is a son of God. Success is the normal; it is the rule in the kingdom of God;

hence, the successful man is a normal man. As long as we are thinking in terms of the visible only, we are likely to look upon everything that is not common to most men as a mystery. Achievement and attainment are synonyms of success; falling short is an antonym. The question is, in which phase of Life Universal must we succeed in order to be thought of as a success? Sometimes you and I pass the successful man by without a nod of recognition, because he has no outer accumulations of material possessions to mark him in the eyes of the world. Let us learn to know success, when we see it; we find true success in the lives that are lived with highest purpose.

We feel that we are very certain of the mission of man as man, the generic man. Wilberforce says, "Man is the outburst of God." I like to think that we are spontaneous expressions of Divine Love because this love could not contain itself for joy—the joy of giving. Man must be a wondrous outburst, when we remember that God can bring forth nothing unlike himself. Divinity has a divine mission to fulfill; man by nature of his Divinity is here to cooperate. We must have faith in the process of daily living, for we are impelled by the Power within to work up and on until we reach a fuller realization of truth. Every man is responsible for living his own life to the highest that he knows, and he has even a greater opportunity and obligation that this, that of taking his part in the fulfillment of the mission of the whole. Humanity cannot fulfill its mission perfectly, unless you and I do our parts. The good of the whole is the purpose of the life of the individual.

There is also a special something for which individual life is destined. Everyone has his or her particular mission. Each one of us has his significance in the plan of the Universal. There is this danger in the thought process of the man who believes that he has a mission; he may think that he is intended for a big work, something important in the eyes of the world, and that fulfilling of his mission means journeying into far places, when the greatest work he can do lies right at his door. A mission sounds like a call to something greater than we are doing in our daily lives, while it really means realizing more definitely the truth that we know just where we are.

There are many men fulfilling their missions out of sight of the world. Always take into consideration when you are endeavoring to understand the meaning of success, that he who lives quietly and steadfastly true to the truth that he knows is attaining as much and is as important a part of the universal plan, as is the platform speaker or any other outstanding man. Jesus more than anyone else knew his mission and fulfilled it. His was the successful life. Best of all he fulfilled his mission in his daily living; it was in the experiences of the day that he proved himself a son of God. He did not fail in the little things, those details which many of us consider insignificant.

I like to think of Jesus at the carpenter's bench with his difficulties much like ours—a normal lad learning of his father, preparing to do his work, and after his father is gone, feeling as the eldest son of the family, the responsibility for his mother and brothers and sisters. I know that Jesus did his part; he did not falter in the carrying out of his part in the domestic conditions, nor did he consider this responsibility a handicap. I picture him at his work which, I am sure, was always done accurately. As Jesus stood at the carpenter's bench he doubtless knew that there would come a time when his life would open into wider service; but he did not neglect the thing at hand for the vision of the thing beyond. Integrity and love were applied to every experience of his life.

Think of the mark Jesus left upon the world in three short years of public ministry. I like to think of the way he attained to the great influence he has left upon daily living. I enjoy thinking of him in his free times, wandering in joyousness over the hills of Galilee, loving all that God had made and was making. What was the mission of Jesus? Isaiah gives it as the office of the Christ—to be a light unto the world; to do the will of God; to preach the gospel to the poor; to bind up the broken-hearted; to proclaim liberty to the captives. This is the mission of the Christ in every man, but Jesus fulfilled his perfectly. What is the individual mission as we analyze it? I am the light of the world—it is then our part to shine forth in the radiance of love. Are we doing it? Jesus told us that he came into the world that men might have life and have it more abundantly. Did not you and I come into the world for this purpose? Are we realizing life for ourselves and for others more abundantly? There are broken hearts to bind up, and there are also broken world conditions to be mended. Let us help bind up the wounds by living true, thinking true, and speaking true to the principle of Omnipresence. Are we so living that our lives are preaching deliverance to the captives—those who are bound by limitations of sin, sickness, poverty and fear? We have been sent to attain. There is for us a Divine Intent; our lives must show it forth. It is your and my mission to stand forth and live truth. You and I are centers of light; keep the light shining. We are witnesses of the truth of God's immediate Presence as life, health, beauty, goodness, truth, and joy. We can never bind up the broken hearted by weeping with them over their wounds; but we can heal their wounds by realizing truth for them. We must not weep over the sins of the world, if we would release those that are bound in the prison house of sin. We must greet them with love that is triumphant over all else. Jesus says, "Be of good cheer, I have overcome the world."

Truly as children of God we have a right to health, supply, happiness, position, and all else that is good. Are we thinking in terms of real success? Have we ever thought that there might be a secondary success? Are we sacrificing the real success for it? It is the getting of outer things that obscures our vision often. If we can keep our vision clear and true, we shall see true success—the inner triumph that comes from realization. When we understand the true success, we shall choose that line of work which gives most to the world instead of to us as individuals. When an experience that comes to us makes it necessary that we should decide upon a course of action, we shall have the wisdom to choose that course which leads us to the good of the whole.

Faithfulness is essential to the successful life. We are told that those who are faithful unto the end shall receive a crown of life. Death is the word used, but I believe that it can be interpreted to mean the end of a process of life. The overcoming of self-seeking, of wrong habits, of temper, of instability, is accomplished by faithfulness. That something which does not really belong to you will pass, if you are faithful to the end of the process of overcoming. What is this crown of life that is promised to us? It is the realization of life more abundant, more glorious, more deeply understanding. It is the certainty that all power in heaven and earth is ours, if we are true to the principle of Omnipresence. Success, the normal state of a son of God, is your heritage and mine, and the successful life is the one that realizes the glory of its heritage. The man who fulfills his mission realizes his oneness with God in all his ways, and solves the mystery of success.

The Mystery of Individual Unfoldment

MYSTERIES are shadows; only he who looks down sees the dark places. Tradition and superstition cast their shadows around them; but truth and wisdom dispel the gloom. Men have lingered too long in the dark places; truth is calling us into the light. Some of us are tempted to stay a little longer in the valleys of ignorance, even though the sunlit stretches of open country lie just above. There seems to be something that holds us in the valley, and Something that calls us to come up out of the limited places into the full light. The something that tells us to stay seems to be the voice of the self which race thought has implanted in us; and sometimes we stay a little longer becoming more mystified while we wait.

There has been an attempt in this volume to solve some of what the world calls the greatest mysteries by directing the searcher to follow the highway that leads to God.

Are you saying, "Yes, I can see that there is a solution for the mysteries connected with the general experiences of mankind—life, death, matter, sin, sickness, old age; but what about the mysteries connected with the personal experiences in the individual lives"? What are the answers to questions like the following: Why did this come to me and not to you? I am not responsible for this condition, why should I suffer? Why did my loved one have to leave me? Why, why, why? Are you trying to see why this experience came to you because it was you who was affected? Is one of these the mystery for which you demand a solution? The first step to take in solving what we call the personal mysteries is that of shifting our center of interest from the continual stress on self to a contemplation of the good of the whole. Instead of asking the question, why did this come to me; let our query be, what can I do with this situation? It is an opportunity for some kind of service or for a step in my development. It is by rising out of the personal self into the consciousness of our oneness with universal Life, that we solve all mysteries. Infinite Mind does not work in mysterious ways but in open and infinite ways, its wonders to perform. There is always the rising process we call the Resurrection. What is the goal to which we are lifting our lives? It is God-Consciousness.

The closing chapter of this book tells the story of the resurrection as attained by Jesus, a true son of God. I trust that we shall find here a practical method of coming up over limitation into the consciousness of resurrection. Resurrection, the greatest event in the individual's story, is also the greatest event in the history of the race. If we understood the principle back of the resurrection, we should touch truth universal which applies to every one of us at the present day. Jesus reached the culmination of life process in the individual.

Resurrection is the culmination of life process in the one who lives in the resurrection consciousness; it is the end of one process and the beginning of another. Since the process of resurrection is taking place in every one of us, the event which we speak of as the Resurrection is especially significant to each individual. We all feel the Law of Life working within us; it is urging us upward and on. As we are led by the spirit of light into more and more truth, our vision broadens, and we come into a clearer realization of what it means to live truth as Jesus did. There is great comfort and joy in knowing that we, too, share in the process of resurrection, and are capable of attaining to the glory of even a resurrection morn, as Jesus did.

The story of Jesus reveals to us the history of the life process from its earthly beginning to its glorious outcome, from the manger to the cross, through the sepulchre to resurrection, from the babe to the risen Jesus. The man Jesus attained as you and I must attain; he rose out of limitation moment by moment. Is it not interesting to watch Jesus' unfoldment as a lesson for our own lives. Think of the glory of the culmination—through the sepulchre into the resurrection morn.

How did Jesus accomplish the resurrection? He taught, "I am the way, the truth, and the life." He lived true to God-Presence; he realized the immediacy of the Presence. What do we mean by the immediate Presence and Power of God? It means knowing and feeling the Presence of God active in every moment of our lives. It means the realization of God's Presence in the smallest experiences of life as well as in the greatest. God's Presence is Life. As God was a father to Jesus and the source of his living and of his thinking, so let it be with us. God was also the companion of Jesus always; therefore Jesus was never alone. You and I need never be alone either, if we think as Jesus thought. Jesus saw himself as God's opportunity for expression; he, the individual, was an opportunity for the expression of God—Wisdom, Love, Power, Life, Joy. Jesus was certain of God; hence when something came that needed a special exercise of power and love, Jesus spoke the word with authority. He knew the Father as immediate Presence, as the Source of all his individual power. His attitude was one of intimate association with the Father. There was one dark moment on the cross, and probably a short time in the struggle at Gethsemane when he may have felt a fleeting moment of separation. However, these experiences were so rare that they need not be dwelt upon.

Out of Jesus' deep love for God grew his first commandment, and out of his all inclusive love for his fellow men grew his second commandment. Jesus' love for God was expressed in his love for men. He understood the meaning of the great word love; we so often miss the true meaning of this most wonderful of all words. Love is God; and to touch a life radiant with love is to touch God. This greatest of all lives that was ever lived was radiant with love and beauty, power and joy. The two commandments which this great teacher gave us are the basis of all true living.

Jesus lived the most powerful life the world has ever known, because he kept these two commandments in letter and in spirit. Jesus was interested in the multitude; he was also interested in the individual. When he touched the multitude, his heart yearned over them; he was so eager to show all of his brother men the meaning of the great realization that he had come into. Some were not ready for his message, it is true; but nothing was lost. Through his living, Jesus put something into the race which has been the foundation of all the greatest movements that have arisen in the development of mankind. His teaching is embodied in all of the great ideals of mankind. The Christ ideal is steadily expanding into more and more practical movements for the benefit of mankind. There is a constant increase in the number of those who are consecrating their lives in human service. People are seeing the truth of the human family, and are realizing a greater love for its individual members. The message of brotherhood is being carried to the ends of the earth by followers of Jesus, the friend of God and man. We are getting together; even though there are wide distances still apparent. The coming together movement holds out great promise.

The teachings of Jesus are being embodied in more movements today than ever before. The Christ principle is practiced by many persons who are not church members. There is at present a feeling among many that the church is not fulfilling its mission. I like to attend general meetings even if there is opposition to the churches expressed by the speakers who feel that the church does not see and embody the message of Jesus.

There are many indictments against the church which accuse us of teaching Jesus but not living according to his precepts. If these indictments are true the church must listen to the charge, and change its methods. The ministers and the people are responsible for righting the wrong; we must see to it that the Christ principle is practiced as well as preached. It is interesting that in meetings and all kinds of gatherings where the church is criticized, one never hears a word against Jesus, the man. Everyone agrees that the practice of the principles which he taught would accomplish immeasurable good. I listen to those who say that the church is not fulfilling its mission among men, and I feel that there is truth in what they are saying. However, I believe that it is not nearly so much a matter of not understanding the teachings of Jesus, as it is of not being willing to live up to as much as we understand, that gives ground for the charge.

Doubtless we are not living up to the best that we know; but there is this to be said: the fundamental principle of true living is eternal progression. There is no final attainment in progressive achieving. There is always the next achievement and the next. If we were satisfied that we are living up completely to the principles that Jesus taught, there would be no more steps to take. Our vision would not be as high as we in our ideal of eternal unfoldment in consciousness would have it. As I listen to what is being said of the Christian church today, I feel a greater call within me to hold up before our people the Christ principles and the Christ life, in order that we may be resurrecting our lives day by day with greater power.

The two great outstanding principles of Resurrection are conscious oneness with God and love of our fellow men. Establishing a steady realization of the immediate presence of God is the essential of true living. It is true that all Life is one; we must live up to this truth, and meet men as brothers in every experience of the day. You remember that Jesus fed the multitude spiritually, but also that when they hungered physically he gave them food. Some of us attain to a vivid consciousness of love for humanity; but others say to me, "Oh yes, I love all people, but there are certain individuals toward whom I cannot feel love." I say to you that there is still something else for you to accomplish. What are you going to do about the unlovable ones? We must love them as Jesus did, if we hope to attain to the resurrection consciousness. Jesus could never have attained to this consciousness, if he had divided people into two classes: those he loved and those he did not. Do you remember how patient Jesus was with Nicodemus, a ruler of the Jews? He tried to give him a message of truth in a loving way. I like to think of the understanding that Jesus expressed for the woman of Samaria, and also for the loving spirit he showed toward the rich young man who appeared so eager to inherit eternal life, but who was so unwilling to give up his personal possessions. Again, I like to picture that day in Jerusalem, when Zaccheus, chief among the publicans, hence unpopular among the people, being small of stature but very eager to see Jesus as he passed that way, climbed a sycamore tree in order that he might have a better view of the great teacher. There was evidently in this man a deep desire to come into touch with Jesus; hence, he took this way of making his purpose sure. Can you imagine Zaccheus' surprise when Jesus, looking up and seeing him, said, "Make haste, and come down, for today I must abide at thy house"? Do you still say to me, "I love everybody—well, almost everybody"? I suppose that we would put Zaccheus into the almost everybody class; from the external he was not lovable, it is true, but he needed Jesus more than anyone else in the group; and this great one who always lived by principle, knew the need and acted accordingly. This is what I mean be love—a love that pours itself out, an all-inclusive love. If we are to attain to the resurrection consciousness, we, too, must have it.

The resurrection consciousness is the consciousness that raises the body from a belief in mortality to a certainty of Life Eternal. It is the consciousness of Universal Love. Love on the lips is good as far as it goes; but love in the heart, the love that calls Zaccheus and goes with him to his home, is necessary in order to attain. The love that met the need of everyone around him is the love that Jesus felt and practiced and taught. As this love illumined the life of Jesus, so does it illumine yours and mine. It is the true light of the world.

Jesus met every human need. The fact that he experienced all phases of what we call our human problems brings him closer to us. The dark hour in Gethsemane, when he went alone to pray at the time of deep need, touches our hearts and shows us that the Master was human, too. After the struggle in Gethsemane Jesus arose and went forth, saying, "Father, not my will, but thine be done." Can we follow him in this experience? It was his great resurrection moment. He had come up over personal feelings, and was standing in the consciousness of Divine Will. He yielded himself to the cross to show humanity the glory of the resurrection process. Perfect consecration and absolute faith were essential in his development, as they are in ours. Shall we rise with him up to that triumphant moment when none of the outer things can touch us?

Peter, who had not reached the resurrection consciousness, when the soldiers came to take Jesus, saw only the outer injustice of the proceeding and cut off a soldier's ear. Jesus, with great love, healed the ear. When just preceding the crucifixion the accusers of Jesus tried to humiliate him, Jesus met them with the same unswerving love. They did not really touch him. On the cross at the time when most of us would be saying, "Why, why, are they crucifying me? Why, why, why?" Jesus, who knew that why is a sign of unbelief, said, entirely free from any rebellious feeling, "Father forgive them, they know not what they do!" Are we forgiving as Jesus was? Are we praying that our ignorance may be lifted? Only then shall we know the truth of Being. Are we thinking of others with love and consideration? Do we see them as our brothers? When Jesus looked down from the cross, and saw his mother standing beside the disciple whom he loved, he said to her, "Woman, behold thy son." And to the beloved disciple he said, "Son, behold thy mother." Jesus saw that his mother would be lonely, and consequently he was entrusting her to his friend's care. Even on the cross Jesus' first thought was for others. He never failed to apply the principle of universal love; Jesus was consistent. His was the resurrection love.

When Jesus saw Mary weeping before the empty tomb, although he knew that if she could see the whole in the process, she would not weep, he sympathized with her human loneliness, and comforted her with the assurance, "I ascend unto my Father and your Father; and to my God and your God." Jesus, who had passed through the darkness of the sepulchre guided by Love supreme, still understood the human love of Mary. Because of this conscious love there came that first resurrection morning, the blessedness of which has been felt ever since.

The world today needs resurrection. Just as there was first century resurrection, so let there be a twentieth century resurrection. This resurrection time will be brought about by the spirit of consecration in your heart and in mine which says with Jesus, "Thy will be done in us." Resurrection will be brought about by our own thought process.

It is that consciousness which loves without wavering. The resurrection consciousness is the complete consciousness; it includes the whole man—soul and body.

I hope that many of us who read this chapter will find that today is a day of resurrection—a day in which our lives are being lived closer to Divine Consciousness than ever before; as we attain to the resurrection consciousness our lives become radiations of unwavering love for our fellow men. Is this a day of resurrection for you? Test your attitude toward God and man—then answer to yourself. He who attains the resurrection consciousness becomes a saviour in whatever age he lives. Let us become twentieth century saviours. God is working through us; let us give Him an opportunity to speak and act through us to His highest purpose. We are God's opportunities. Consider well. Out streaming love shining from our lives is proof that our day of resurrection is here. If we meet all demands of the days with love we shall rise out of our limitations for Love is Resurrection.

It is by the process of resurrection that we rise out of the contemplation of that which is hidden, the mysteries as we have called these, into the full light where everything is made clear. There is nothing hidden that shall not be revealed to the one who sees the unity of Life. We are rising into a recognition of the glory of process when we stand before a blade of grass and see that even this is wonderful. Are we leaving the mysteries behind us as we rise, or are we lifting these old mysteries into the wonder of it all!

Stump Speaking
Library of Congress Prints and Photographs Division
Washington, D.C. 20540

Malinda Cramer

(1844-1906)

Co-Founder of Divine Science, teacher and healer.

Probably the most understated and overlooked early leader of the New Thought movement, Malinda Cramer, founder of Divine Science, was indeed ahead of her time.

Malinda Elliott Cramer was born in a large family of eleven children. Her parents were Quakers. When Malinda was fifteen she developed a disease which the doctors declared incurable and she became an invalid. Later the family moved to San Francisco in hopes the good weather would cure Malinda. It didn't.

"In 1902 Mrs. Malinda Cramer, the co-founder of Divine Science, published her own healing narrative. She had been an invalid for twenty-three years. Her case had 'baffled the best physicians.'…In 1885 Cramer turned to prayer…and received 'an immediate and all convincing reply. Instantly Omnipresent Spirit was realized and everything was transformed into Spirit…I at once saw the unreality of the conditions of dis-ease and was free from the belief that they had any power or could control for either good or ill.'" (*Each Mind a Kingdom,* pg 97) Within two years she was completely healed.

In common with many of the other early New Thought leaders, she studied with the "teacher of teachers," Emma Curtis Hopkins. Classes and healing treatments developed as a result of sharing her experience with others. In truth, she became a New Thought wayshower. She understood her role as a teacher and healer. She recognized that the Power of healing was God.

Over 113 years ago Malinda Cramer's spiritual career began at age 40. As Mrs. Malinda Cramer studied, taught and traveled to reach more people with her newly found truth, she did so in great earnest. She lectured and traveled extensively even to Australia and the United Kingdom.

She founded the Divine Science Home School on May 4, 1888. Mrs. Cramer organized the International Divine Science Association on May 17, 1892 and this was the forerunner of International New Thought Alliance. Malinda first published the Harmony Magazine in August, 1888. This magazine is considered historically as one of the earliest and most significant New Thought publications.

Mrs. Cramer inspired many of the great early New Thought leaders whose ministries and books are still held in high esteem. She incurred an injury during the great San Francisco earthquake at the age of 62 and a few months later on August 2, 1906, the great lady made her transition.

During the earthquake, the Divine Home School and all its contents were destroyed. Many of the original writings of the Divine Science movement were lost.

Over the years many churches were founded under the name of Divine Science but all were autonomous and none were part of her original school. The Divine Science movement appeared to weaken even to a point of near extinction in terms of numbers of thriving churches, and Divine Science achieved virtually no name recognition even within the New Thought movement. Bearing those facts in mind and coupled with the overwhelming desire to return to the original teachings of Malinda Cramer, Dr. J. William Trainor and Dr. Anne Kunath founded United Divine Science Ministries International in February 1999 in San Antonio, Texas. The word "United" was included as a part of the new Divine Science organization in order to create a forum to bring together all people dedicated to the original principles and teachings of Malinda Cramer. (1)

Link & Acknowledgement
    1.   Malinda Cramer Home Page: http:malindacramer.wwwhubs.com

Lessons in the Science of Infinite Spirit and the Christ Method of Healing

1890
"Come unto Me, all ye that labor and are heavy laden
and I will give you rest."

Short Lessons and Meditations
Want, Love, And Works

"Be not conformed to this World; but be ye transformed by the renewal of your mind; that ye may prove what is that good and acceptable, and the perfect will of God."(Rom. xii: 2)

There is an essential requirement, threefold in its nature, to be fulfilled by every student of Divine Science if they realize the absolute consciousness of the esoteric truth underlying the expressions or creations of Infinite Spirit, and how to work with the law of expression. Existence is the result of understanding. We know and express the attributes of Divine Mind by receiving and expressing them within our own thoughts and mentality. Think divinely, and we are at once conscious of feeling as we think; think loving thoughts, and we feel loving.

To be permanently conscious of the presence of Divine good is to be unwavering in Divine thinking. To be able to hold steadily to truth, with undivided faith in good, is to be renewed in the Spirit of the mind, which transforms every external expression, word, deed and feeling, into "that good and acceptable and perfect will of God." Truth is harmony, and when held in thought it is a messenger of peace, bringing glad tidings from the unmanifest Spirit into the form of word and outer expression. Truth is life, and when spoken it is health and ease—not disease.

"He knoweth the way that I take."(Job xxiii: 10) The first requirement on the way to a realization of eternal life—the permanent good—is to *wait*. The student must want to hold the truth because it is truth; want it sufficiently to put away preconceived opinions and beliefs, and work to attain it; want the truth sufficiently to be energetic in refusing error's claim, and in casting out intellectual rubbish that does not harmonize with the great central and "all-saving truth," the basic principle of Divine Science.

Another requirement is *Love*—Love for all truth, because it is truth—Love and regard for the Omnipresent, silent and invisible God, the only source of life and power. "Except ye become as little children ye can in no wise enter the kingdom of heaven." This means that unless we consult "the Father," the One Principle of good underlying all expression, and are governed by Him in our thought, we can in no wise express perfect harmony, which is true happiness or heaven; for heaven is a condition and is within each one of us, and to think truth, is to realize that we are the eternal, ever present.

The third requirement is that of *Works*. Not until the student wants the truth, and loves it because it is truth, will he perceive it with reference to himself, and to his relation, the Infinite One. He will see with the eye of understanding when he dares to draw the line between the Creator and the created—the Manifestor and the manifestation— between himself as immortal and the mortal body and his beliefs. When he dares to think of self as invisible, immortal, and divine here and now; that he in being is now what he ever will be, and that his manifestations and mortal body are only visible to him on the sense plane. Man can only be spiritually perceived and understood; and until he reverses his decisions of himself he will not perceive himself and understand his relations to Divine Being. The student must dare to rise up and throw off all beliefs of limitation and disharmony, instead of waiting for them to desert him: he must banish from mentality the accustomed mode of thought concerning self, and all beliefs that are opposed to the spiritual and clear realization of himself as immortal. Then identify himself with all manifest life, and know of his union with the One eternal Spirit in which all live. Yes, dare to think that by doing the Will of Spirit, and speaking its Word, he can conquer selfish personality—beliefs of separateness and limitation.

The way to strengthen the will is to sacrifice the individual will to the permanent good, by acting, under all circumstances, in obedience to the law of good, and by daring to realize Self as Immortal—a divine reality now; and by facing and conquering life's seeming difficulties as they come. Our expressions are ever changing and passing away, and are therefore mortal. Hold fast to the invisible and immutable—the Soul, or Life, behind this veil of shows! If the student of Divine Science wants to know the truth, because it is truth, and if he loves the truth for the same reason, and lives it as rapidly as he recognizes it, he is taught of the Spirit or Christ within, and the Spirit will lead him into all Truth.

The Law

All systems of religious or divine teaching should point the way by which individuals can perceive the truth for themselves. Unless we see for ourselves and understand, we have no conviction; and without conviction we cannot have perfect faith; and without perfect faith our expressions are weak and inharmonious. Even the teachings of the world's great masters—unimpeachable as they are—and the sacred and unalterable truths taught by a Christ or Buddha can only instruct. We must take the steps upon the ladder of progress for ourselves.

Teachers can point the way of Truth and Life in silent thought and spoken word. Sometimes it is better for the student to have the silent instruction of the words of Life as given in healing in connection with the oral lesson; especially if it seems difficult to understand the science of Spirit, or in thought to hold the true consciousness.

All must see and know the truth, and depend upon its practice if they would have permanent health and harmony. To state this in another way, all must come to know that they are Divine and Permanent, and speak the unalterable truth for themselves. We must look beyond the temporal kingdom if we would find the Staff of Life that never fails us; we must seek the permanent kingdom if we would be conscious of eternal life. "Seek, and ye shall find." Retain whatever of truth you perceive by practicing it, and it will act as a magnet consciously relating you mentally to more and more of truth. Then, with energetic effort in Truth's practice, and with aspirations attuned to harmony by the truth, the Spirit will lead to all truth. The mentality will expand to receive more and more of that which is permanent.

If the individual be obedient to "the Law"—Love—then perversity is overcome; and the student will hold with divine steadfastness to truth, and rapid will be his growth into the consciousness of Spirit. He will be surprised how quickly he will surmount life's seeming difficulties and pass the border line of elemental thought, from the mortal to the immortal, from belief to knowledge, from error and disease to truth and ease; from a belief in death to that of life, and from all illusion resulting from not knowing, into the light of understanding.

That which is called the evolution or progression of the soul is the process of demonstrating that God is within; or the process of individual effort to consciously realize that which is, and is permanent; resulting there from is unwavering and perfected faith, based upon the knowledge that we are one with the Father, and that we are in and of the kingdom, the power, and the glory. For when our thoughts and expressions are reconciled or adjusted to the good, the person or face of man is at one with Universal Harmony.

The Ever New

The impersonal path is the path of unity. And the way of unity leadeth to a knowledge of "The One" which lives beyond "The Gates of Gold." Unity is the way which leadeth into the presence of the Ever Present.

All who travel this way will find their life, and what true being is.

Now is the eternal. Now is life.

Now is truth. Now is love.

Now is the time to know that being is what it ever will be.

Now is the time to turn to the Spirit, and awaken and acknowledge the ever-present goodness.

Death, is going away from "*The One.*" The way of death is the way of the past. It is death to righteousness to hold the past in memory.

Regrets of the past are crystallization.

Temporal things fade away, places change and are no more; time passes and leaves us naught but the present. All that we have been or ever will be we are now. All that is, is now. Dear friends, we have all now, for we are in the presence of the all, and that presence is all.

The old is passing away; let it pass, bearing with it all memory of error. "Let the dead bury its dead."

Let every belief that temporary things are real go with it.

Assign them to the dead past and live in the presence of the One that is ever present.

"Lift up your eyes and look on the fields, for they are white already to harvest."

Welcome the ever new and beautiful gospel, renewed by the spirit of truth.

Welcome the presence of the all good by recognizing it.

Welcome the Spirit by speaking its word with love, and you will gather fruit that is eternal.

The prevailing thought at the close of an old year, that there is much to be done ere it passes and the new year comes to greet us, is what should be held in consciousness throughout the entire year; we should act—act in the living present, recognizing God within and God o'erhead, and each hour will find us further on the way to a full realization of the ever-present kingdom, power and glory, in which we live and have our being. The ever-present is the time to be happy and to be true to Being. The habit of holding gloomy and despondent thought can be broken and given up by thinking. "I forgot my real self; this is my time to be happy and satisfied." The present is the eternal; we cannot draw the line in time—the future is ever merging into the present, and the present into the past. We should resolve to recognize the presence of peace and harmony ere the present merges into the past, and the future finds our thought unfruitful; ere the present passes, bearing no record of truth spoken, or good manifest, and the future finds us unillumined with the light of truth and understanding. Our prayer for all is, that you awaken to the truth and know that you are free; so that the way to knowledge of the all good will be recognized by you. May the Spirit reveal to you higher possibilities than you have yet conceived! May truth clothe you with its white robe, ornamented with the gold of wisdom! May your thoughts and hearts be illumined and warmed by divine truth and love, and may your actions rest upon Divine Justice! May the Dove of Peace rest upon you now and forever!

Divine Love and Unity

"The hour cometh and now is when the true worshipper shall worship the Father in Spirit and in truth." As the Spirit of God is One and is Truth—if we worship in Spirit and in Truth, it is necessary that we fulfill the law of Unity, *which is Love.* The command of the Spirit of Unity is, "Thou shalt love thy neighbour as thyself." This command can only be understandingly fulfilled by perceiving One Spirit in all; and then by thinking and feeling toward all just as we think of and feel for ourselves. The time cometh, and now is for humanity to see beyond the visible Universe—this veil of shadows—and pass out of appearances and beyond seeming differentiations of matter into the Spirit of Unity, which is in all places forever and ever, and thus free mentality of deception and delusion. As there is now a general awakening to the consciousness of unity, it is the time for earnest recognition and practice of divine truth according to principle.

As we realize that the law of love is written in the fleshy tablets of our hearts, and that it is working therein, so do we endeavor to keep the Spirit of Unity in the bonds of peace in our dealings one with another. To see with understanding is to see that unity *is,* for understanding sees that unity which forever is, even where diversity appears. There is but one Infinite Spirit, but there are myriads of images or creations within The One, living and moving in it.

So the apparent diversity in creation is the result of unity; therefore we find that all Cause is unity, and all effect the result of unity. There are myriads of thoughts formed in every individual; but with this diversity of thought there is but one being. "There is one body and one spirit, even as ye are called in the hope of your calling." As there can be but one Infinite Spirit, there can be in fact or truth but one Principle to demonstrate, hence one body and one calling. By the light of unity we perceive that the purpose of the one Spirit is the purpose of all; the high calling of one belongs to all. But to keep the Spirit of unity in the bonds of peace, it is necessary to perceive that we are called by the Spirit, in the faith of one calling; and that every individual is working out his or her own salvation according to the Spirit of Unity or divine truth. As the one Spirit is all, all are called to seek and know their own source.

In the external appearance of this plane of manifestation there seems to be a great diversity in our callings, but this diversity is only seeming. Humanity, like a hive of bees, is working to accomplish one common purpose. Bees go out from their hives in various directions, seeking the variety of flowers, for the one purpose of gathering honey. When seen at work away from the hive, intent upon their purpose, they seem to have different callings; but when they return to the hive it is seen there is but one purpose. So it is with humanity; every individual has his or her origin in Spirit, and, like the bees, each goes out from the Father to do mental and visible work. But when busy about our daily work—for the one purpose of demonstrating innate possibilities—we look upon each other as separate and apart from the Father; the seeming is, that we have different callings and destiny.

This judgment is according to sense and is erroneous; for when we return home to the Father—withdraw mentality from our work—it is seen there is one purpose, one calling, which is that of gaining individual experience and knowledge of God. Then it is that we see all humanity as belonging to God, and as in the hands of Omnipotent Goodness. Then it is that personal desire and will about humanity that ceases, for we are willing to trust Omnipresent Goodness. When the individual holds humanity in Truth, administering to all as if only to one, he begins to know what is meant by worshipping in Spirit and in Truth; he has entered into the true communion.

Necessity is the child of unity, and unity is the father of necessity. We intend to show you that unity is in all seeming diversity of business life. The healer is essential to the patient, and the patient to the healer, that God may be made manifest; and this is the unity of necessity. The artist supplies a need to the student and lover of art. The need of every individual is at one with the want of the dentist or with his profession; and he supplies a want in every person. The merchant, tailor, and dressmaker's calling are at one with the universal demand for bodily covering or clothing; and a universal demand for clothing is at one with their business. The business of the architect, contractor and builder, is in unison with the race-belief that houses are a necessity; and property owners and tenants are in unison with their business. The music and songs so perfectly rendered in this age of illumination, to which all listen, and enjoy with unity of interest, is the melodious expression of the unity of spirit, or, we may say, it is the art of combining sound in a manner to symbol the harmony of the spheres, which is the spirit pervading all. Music meets with and calls forth harmony in and from every soul. The baker and fruit-merchant are necessary to the housekeeper; and the housekeeper is in harmony with their calling. The restaurant-keeper supplies a universal necessity, a necessity often felt by every individual. All can testify to unity in the demand for physical food. And yet, partaking of physical food is but a symbol of truth. Truth is the food of which, if ye eat, ye shall not hunger.

Blessedness

"Blessed *are* they which do hunger and thirst after righteousness, for they shall be filled."

"Be ye perfect, even as your Father in Heaven is perfect."

"Blessed are they which do partake of the Righteousness of the One ever present."

Filled are they who drink of the water from the fountain ever present.

Righteous is it to perceive and live the perfection of the ever-present One.

Filled are they who partake of the perfection of the ever-present One.

Perfect was the consciousness which perceived the idea of being perfect.

Perfect is the understanding which perceives that the Father's perfection is possible.

To purity all is pure.

To goodness all is good.

God comprehends Himself as Infinite: The Whole. . Perfect and complete from eternity is God, and we through holding truthful thought, express more and more of His perfection and completeness; perfect and complete from eternity is the *I am* of every one, and through the cycles of eternity we shall realize more and more of the *I am,* and of self in expression.

Judge Not

"Judge not that ye be not judged: for with what judgment ye judge, ye shall be judged."(Matt vii: i 2) "For wherein thou judgest another, thou condemnest thyself; for thou that judgest doest the same things."

It is our thought and motive which is manifest, when we judge or condemn another and that thought and motive is our condemnation. That which we do is our own, begotten of our thought, motive, and belief. If we have aught against another, attention should be first given to the mote that is in our own eye; not until we forgive are we forgiven; the act of forgiving is forgiveness; in condemning another we are condemned.

"Speak not evil one of another, brethren. He that speaketh evil of his brother, and judgeth his brother, speaketh evil of the law, and judgeth the law; but if thou judge the law thou art not a doer of the law." "The judgment of God is according to truth." When we speak the truth we do well. To be a doer of the law and not a judge is to think of others and of self, as one with all good, which we are in being. To be a judge of the law—or of another, and not a doer, is to think of others and of self as one with appearance or expression, which is temporary—mortal.

Witness Of Truth

"To this end was I born, and for this came I into the world, that I should bear witness unto the truth. Everyone that is of the truth heareth my voice."

What is truth? The question is being asked daily and hourly by earnest seekers, and was asked by Pilate, more than eighteen hundred years ago. Christ, who came to bear witness of the truth, bore witness of it by demonstration in word and deed.

They who work in concert with the Law of Being, fulfill the law and purpose of creation, and demonstrate the same truth as did Jesus.

To bear witness of the truth is to heal the sick.

To cast out devils (erroneous thought, selfish desire, and erase false belief), is evidence of the presence of truth. To open the eyes of the mentally blind to understanding is evidence of the possession of truth. The evidence of the realization and freedom of Truth is the raising of the dead, and awakening from unconsciousness to consciousness, the spirit of Truth.

To be raised from the dead is to understandingly enter into eternal life, permanent health, and infinite harmony.

"Know the truth, and the truth shall make you free." Free from what? Free from beliefs of disharmony, of feelings of selfishness (or separateness), free from mental darkness and unconsciousness of the real and permanent, and from the effects of false believing, which are erroneously called sorrow, sin, sickness and death.

The evidence that the truth was manifest in Jesus, was that in his presence, through his teaching and works, they who were in mental darkness—from ignoring the presence of Spirit for the letter—were illumined, and caused to perceive the truth which was manifest in him. "That the people who sat in darkness saw great light; and to them which sat in the region and shadow of death light is sprung up."

Where truth is manifest, there are no appearances called error. Where light is perceived, there is no darkness. A perception of truth is knowledge; hence, Jesus was an illuminator or light of the world. "Ye are the light of the world."

Jesus bore witness of the truth, by declaring his oneness with God, the Father of all, and he did the works of the Father, by obeying His silent voice. It is thus that the goodness and power of Spirit is ever demonstrated. The principle of goodness and harmony is Truth; it is formless, invisible and silent; by truthful thought it is formed, made visible, and spoken, or manifest.

God being the Principle of all good, necessity requires that thought be in the image and likeness of God, or Principle, if He or It be manifest in us. The way of truth is one—it is straight and narrow; in it there are no differences. It being that which knows not limitation, it is free, and for this reason it frees; hence is the comforter. Truth reveals the truth to us, that all are in the Father and that the Father is in all, and it guides to consciousness of life eternal.

Are we not, dear friends, manifesting in this world of effect, for the same purpose as did Jesus? Are we not in the world to bear witness of the truth? Should we not clothe ourselves in purity with the same purpose and intent as did he? "For by being clothed in purity, and being unsullied and enlightened, binds the sinless soul to happiness and truth." Jesus bore witness of the truth that life, peace and reality are only to be found in God, Goodness. That God or Goodness is Infinite and "To Know Thee, the only true God." is life eternal.

As we cannot serve two masters, are we not to choose which we shall serve, cause or effect? Not until we decide—as did our Great Teacher—to serve the Spirit, or First Cause, and nothing but the Spirit, or First Cause, can we manifest power over external things, and control thought and deed; nor do we consciously surrender mentality to the Living Spirit or Goodness, in and by which we live. To bear witness of and to serve the Spirit is to work in unison with Spirit and thus fulfill the law and purpose of creation.

In interpreting the plan of Salvation, the simple truth as taught by Jesus has been obscured, and Salvation made to appear difficult to attain, for the reason that the ever present God, and Kingdom of Heaven, have been rejected, by placing God and Heaven in the distance to be gained in the future. Thus the truth of the at-one-ment of the soul with God is unperceived, and Heaven unenjoyed.

There is a straight and narrow way which leadeth out of darkness into light, out of all seeming difficulty into a realization of the Kingdom of God and his righteousness. God knoweth the way thereof, and his silent voice is heard to say: recognition, acknowledgement and faith, they are the way. They who come to know the real must believe that it is, and that the Spirit sought is a rewarder of those who diligently seek it. Through a constant recognition of that which is real and permanent, Peace, like a dove, settles upon us and baptizes with the inner consciousness (Holy Ghost); and the heaven within opens to us, and we enter and find that it is not a locality nor a place to be gained at the dissolution of the body, but is a condition to be enjoyed when re-cognized and made ours by right expression.

Why does truth free or heal?

Truth frees or heals for the reason that truth is freedom. To know that which is free, and to live it, is freedom.

Knowledge and being are one; to know the real and Eternal is to know self. The truth is all that is free, and false is the belief that any are bound, for a belief in bondage is false of the real, or truth. To turn from falsehood to truth is the way to freedom. Healing by the power of truth or God is healing by the Christ method; hence, the practitioner of truth is a disciple of Christ. Truth or Christ, knowledge or life, are one, and One is Unity, fullness; never is it otherwise. To have knowledge of Being, is to know that we are that which is above limitation and external environment, or effect. Or to have knowledge of what we are is to free the intellect of beliefs of limitation. This is freedom.

"He that believeth shall do the things that I do, for I go to my Father." They who understand the teachings of Christ, and believe in him, understand truth and believe in omnipresent Spirit (for they are one); such a one should bear witness of and demonstrate the truth as did Christ. Not until falsehood is erased, and misinterpretation ceases, will doubt and fear be dispelled—fear of losing the material body—nor will we know the truth when it is manifest in the flesh. The powers that be, and the Spirit which is, are manifest through truthful interpretation. Truth manifest in the flesh is an understanding of the Oneness of life, or of the Unity of the whole. To know that the One living presence, or Holy One, works through us to will and to do, and to understand how to work in unison with the One, is freedom, power and glory.

It is the One Spirit, or I Am, in different individuals which perceives at one time in different parts of the universe the principle underlying mathematical demonstration. It is the One Spirit of truth in different individuals which perceives its own truth at all times, in different parts of the universe. In truth there is no difference; whenever and wherever perceived it is one. Think of truth as infinite and as indivisible, then will faith in the power of truthful thought be perfect; so will you know that God's thought cannot be hindered, and that its demonstration or witness will remove mountains of difficulties, for it is harmony. Truth perceived is faith based aright; in the presence of knowledge, ignorance ends. The substance of faith dispels doubt. Where there is understanding, misunderstanding is not.

Walk In The Light

Attachment for mortal things; ambition for worldly fame; desire for what is called worldly comfort, blinds to the true interest and inward happiness. They are the clouds which darken the way that leads to a realization of life eternal and union with all Good.

Feed not upon husks, for the forms of the world are but symbols of the real, which is substance and truth. "There is therefore, now no condemnation to them which are in Christ Jesus, who walk not after the flesh but after the Spirit."

All goodness that is recognized is enjoyed; that which is, and is unrecognized, is unenjoyed. Postpone not the time for re-cognizing the Kingdom of Heaven, which is always at hand. They, who recognize and enter there, rest in faith and certainty.

"And With What Measure Ye Mete,
It Shall Be Meted To You Again."

What man thinketh in his heart is his belief. Fixed beliefs are imaged in mentality and made manifest by thought; and resultant from beliefs and habits of thought, are word, deed, and sensation. Therefore, with what measure we mete, the same is meted to us again, or is manifest by us, for our measure is our belief, or our present state of thought. If our thought measures the idea of wholeness and perfection for others and for self—it measures that idea from the Infinite Spirit, and thus wholeness and perfection is measured to us, for the same is our measure. But if our belief and thought measures limitation and imperfection for others and for self, then limitation and imperfection is measured to us, for the same is our measure. Therefore, in proportion as we recognize and affirm Truth, to that degree do we manifest it, and measure forth the possibilities of the invisible I am.

For not until our ideas measure wholeness, have we cast out the beam from our own eye, nor is it single to Truth —which is light; nor do we clearly see to pluck the mote from our brother's eye. As we must ever see through our own eyes, that is, according to conclusions that we draw, therefore, as long as the beam of error or belief in imperfection remains, we see in part with the eye of error or belief in imperfection, as through a glass darkly, for the belief in imperfection cannot perceive or realize perfection. "Blessed are the pure in heart, for they shall see God." Purity perceives and acknowledges its own. It being omnipresent, recognizes the truth that it is omnipresent, and sees Itself in all, with the eye of purity or perfect understanding. The beam of doubt, which is hesitation, leads not to understanding; it is not a cause for, neither is it a guide to, perfect perception of the unity and wholeness of Being. Therefore, it must be erased from, or cast out of the mental vision, before thought can receive and produce a true image of the perfect idea of God, the Father. The beam of judging according to sense, which is made apparent in beliefs of uncharitableness, criticism, and fault finding, must be cast out of the mental sphere before we can see face to face the absolute truth of the omnipotence of the ever-present Good. For as long as we have belief in imperfection, we have belief that there is something that is the opposite of God, for God is *Infinite perfection,* and through that belief we see imperfectly, for our judgment is not of Truth, nor is our measure that of wholeness; it is through such believing that error and imperfection is seen in others. By allowing appearances to become a cause for judgment, we yield thought to obey appearances, and through criticism thought confirms and confines mentality to error.

The acknowledgement of the whole truth that God, or Goodness, is infinite: All in All, and that there can be but one Infinite or one All, is the one thing needful to lead from earth to heaven, from error to truth. To some the thought may arise, this is a road too short to be good, a truth too simple to be true. Nevertheless, when this acknowledgment is made, or this step taken, and we find the kingdom, and the truth is realized that we are in God, or Goodness, and that God, or Goodness, is in us, and that the two are one in Being, the greatest truth has come; and "when that which is perfect is come, that which is in part shall be done away." When this truth is perceived, we must lay off the garb of sensuous judgment with all carnal thought, and make the eye single to the all-inclusive truth of the Unity of Being: that is reconcile and conform our expressions to it, if we would gain a full realization of the wealth and power of the kingdom in which we live, and clothe ourselves in the incorruptible garb of immortality, and wear the pearl of greatest price, which is perfect illumination. Not until a perfect understanding reveals the Unity of Being, will the expression in earth, the body, be that of the fullness of power.

They who would hasten toward Goodness or God, must cease false interpretation and perceive the true worth and position of Spirit; that is, worship in *Spirit* and *Truth,* or in *single, fervid faith, by holding all in Spirit, and by thinking and speaking truthfully of Spirit, as the truth was spoken by Jesus.* And if mentality be illumined by truthful thought, the realizations are light and life manifest or made apparent. If the intellect be not darkened by false belief and erroneous thought, the ever-present truth will illumine it with understanding, and take from it the dead branches which bear not fruit of the Spirit. When we rise above delusion, to us there is no delusion, and as we have plucked the beam from our own eye, we are therefore able to remove false belief from others; that is, we are able to and clearly see to take the mote from our brother's eye.

"Be ye perfect, even as your Father in heaven is perfect," is a commandment that may be fulfilled by a perfect perception of truth. If we would realize the meaning of this perception, it is essential to understand that we cannot have or gain knowledge of imperfection, for knowledge is a clear and certain perception of truth, and truth is perfection.

The principle of mathematics, or the idea which underlies all mental problems, is not revealed or made manifest in error of calculation, but the principle of truth is revealed and made manifest by correct calculation or statement of the principle or idea. In no way is it possible for us to demonstrate knowledge of principle through a misstatement or false representation of principle. The mistake or error made in the problem is false calculation, and has no true relation to the principle or idea, for it does not represent or symbol it; hence nothing is manifested unless principle is truthfully stated.

The Infinite Spirit which underlies all manifestation, is not revealed or made manifest in false interpretation, but it is revealed and made manifest by correct and truthful interpretation of itself. In no way is it possible for us to demonstrate knowledge of the Father through mis-representation of Him.

Statements void of principle are in no way related to Spirit; they do not express or symbol forth anything that truly is, for when the Infinite is not manifest or apparent, nothing is manifest or apparent; but in every truthful statement of truth, the Infinite is manifest or apparent.

Meditations
What is Justice?

The Uncreated, Unmanifest Being, is Justice, and this Justice is manifest in all creation. Prior to manifestation, Justice is, and is the at-tribute of being just, right and impartial, the attribute which measures wholeness and gives to all according to their works. It weighs in the bal-ance our inmost thought and the expression of thought; and if found wanting in the Spirit of Goodness, or if not in the image and likeness of the attributes of Infinite Spirit, they are cast into the fire (spirit) and consumed. The imperfect is of short duration—appearance only.

Justice renders to everyone his or her due, and to every expression according to measure, or the thought and motive producing it. The method of Infinite Spirit is now operating in creation, and is exact justice; therefore, the science of the expression of Infinite Being is exact justice. The science of mathematics is exact justice. Divine Truth ex-pressed, is exact justice. Just and right is The One—The All.

Conformity to truth in thought, word, and deed is Justice mani-fest. Thoughts of love are just and righteous; they are the fulfilling of the law. "To refuse Justice and bestow love is an affectation of mercy and reality of insult."

A manifestation under the name of love, without justice, is pretense—false. Love, the Royal law of Being, is administered with exact justice. It recognizes neither friend nor foe—all are one to it. The manifestation of justice has no attachment; it is passionless, unaffected by emotion or sensation. It is that which finally brings all to re-cognize first and final truth, which is harmony. It acts not that it may receive affection, gain nor hate. The just act free from self desire; they are humble, yet steadfast and unwavering in truth and right, content to be just, without seeming content to do right, and practice truth without fame for the love of right or truth. The practice of Divine and unchanging truth, is justice to God and man.

Harmony

Harmony is the divine and orderly method of the Infinite in creation. The endless variety of created things in the Universe is the harmonious expression of the Infinite One. Knowledge reveals harmony. Ignorance veils harmony to the intellect. Truth is harmony; and never varies or changes. The truth is always truth—its foundation is knowledge and wisdom. Error or falsehood is seeming disharmony, and is ever changing; its foundation is ignorance and folly. The perception of the true relation of nature to God is the perception of harmony. In truth there is no disharmony. The method of the Creator, now operating in creation, which is contained within Himself is perfect harmony, and the Perfect knows no imperfection.

"Good citizens live in harmony." They, who are thoroughly conscious of the presence of Goodness, do not give place to seeming disharmony. Good is in harmony with all goodness. A goodly act or deed is in harmony with good or truthful thought; good or truthful thought is in harmony with the goodness of the thinker, or Being. If thought be in the image and likeness of Being, the act will be in harmony with the thought and with the thinker. This is the method of proving the harmony of Being in creation. Harmony is wisdom's way of expressing truth. It is the perfect adaptation of a part to the whole, or of expression to the expressor. It is infinite order, and there is no other.

"'There is none good but One. "

One is the number of Unity; and Unity is the order of, and is as permanent as, The One. There is but One all, hence all good is that One; therefore there is none good but One. Infinite Being means that which is, was, and ever will be. It is interior and anterior to the finite, which is the expression of the Infinite. Being and the good are one; therefore, to be is to be good, that which is, and is uncreated and unmanifest. A knowledge of what being is, furnishes a basis that prepares us for just and harmonious thought and action; without this knowledge individuals are at a loss to know how to control thought and action—hence "they are like a wave tossed to and fro by every wind of doctrine." Not until we become stable and unwavering in our thought and action is it possible to understand and work with the orderly and harmonious method with which the law of Being works. When thought is adjusted to and is representative of Being, the *endemic order* is maintained in consciousness; then all expression is dressed and kept in order, for if thought be adjusted to God, the effect there from is harmonious and pleasant: this is reconciliation—regeneration—or atonement. Thus the individual will becomes a manifestation of universal faith, and love expands to include all. God, or Goodness, made everything that was made, and pronounced it good. It is race belief—a personal opinion— a false and perverse method of interpretation, which presumes to claim and clothe self with the corruptible, the opposite of God, or Good. When false interpretation ceases, we shall see as Spirit sees, that all is good. All of anything is one, and there can be but one All, which is goodness; therefore, there is none good but one.

"Thy faith hath saved thee."

If by faith one was saved and made whole, by faith all are saved and made whole. All are alike under one divine law, and all error is subject to that law, for truth is that law. As all are saved by faith, from what are they saved? Not from truth, for truth is the law and is itself salvation. Is

it not clear that we are to be saved from error, which is false interpretation, erroneous belief and action, or from taking things for what they
are not? Is it not clear that Spirit perception, truthful interpretation,
and right action can alone erase, save and set free?

How is Spirit perception gained? They who would witness within
themselves the perception of Spirit, should lay aside blinding prejudice,
and accept truth when and wherever expressed. If you do not willingly
accept truth whenever and wherever expressed, you do not accept the
manifest Christ. Acceptation of truth is faith based aright, and is life,
substance and harmony. By accepting the present truth perceived, and
demonstrating it in word and deed, we make it our own, or in thought
we accept that which we are in being, and thus the way is opened to all
truth. They who would climb the ladder of progress, which leads from
earth to Heaven, or which guides from the letter to Spirit, from error
to truth, must climb it step by step; thus it is necessary that they accept
truth perceived, and stand firm therein and adjust the thought and
act to it, before they can ascend to the next round or advance a step.
Through spirit perception, and thought made perfect, all is adjusted to
the source of Divine Being. This is the faith which saves. They who fulfill the law are in love with truth; and when all are loved, all *is* forgiven;
but to whom little is forgiven, *the same* loveth little.

Freedom

Freedom is the state of being free. It is that which is exempt from
control, and which is unlimited and unenvironed. That which is free,
is not under the law of being, but is the law. Can it be said that the
visible universe or any visible thing therein contained, is exempt from
control? Or, is not subject to its source? Verily, that which is made is
subject to its maker.

Manifestation and appearance of every kind, be it the physical
form, or that of health or disease, joy or sorrow, truth or falsehood, love
or hate, knowledge or ignorance, is subject to the manifestor, which is
not apparent. That which is uncreated and which creates is unlimited

freedom. All Being is uncreated, hence to be is to be free, and not to be subject to the created; therefore, "whoso looketh into the perfect law of liberty and continueth therein, he being not a forgetful hearer, but a doer of the work, this man shall be blessed in his deed." They who *forget not* what Being is, and what they are, will come to realize the freedom of Being. Forgetting is losing consciousness of the immortal self, the real, and is the cause of all belief in limitations. To know ourselves is to know that we are free, one with the unlimited and boundless. Dear friends, they who try to realize these truths seek in the right direction for true freedom, and they who thus seek, find. "Blessed Are They which Do Hunger And Thirst After Righteousness." It is written that they which do hunger and thirst after righteousness are blessed, for they shall be filled.

Righteousness is a state of thought and consciousness, which is in unity with, or conformity to, Divine love, the law of God. To hunger and thirst after righteousness is a desire to work with the law, and to realize oneness with God, the whole Spirit of Goodness. If they who have that desire also have sincere belief and faith, they have the necessary receptivity and substance for success, and are seeking to know and to fulfill the whole law of God, or Goodness. When seeking that which is, which is the Infinite, we enter the straightway that leadeth to exact knowledge—perfect faith or power. To be receptive to Omnipresent Goodness is to quench the thirst at the fountain of Life. So to hunger and thirst after righteousness is a blessed condition, because it is the condition which precedes its attainment.

It is blessed to seek and blissful to find. We cannot expect to find unless we seek. So, "to do truth is to practice God's command." His truth reveals the adjustment of all to himself; His word is Goodness manifest, or made apparent.

Hope

Hope is where the affections are. That which we are attracted to we hope to attain, and hope causes the necessary effort for its attainment;

in other words, if we have a desire or aspiration and make an effort to attain it, it is hope that prompts us to make that effort. If it were not for hope, effort or seeking would cease. Faith is the silent and absolute power or substance of hope, effort, or seeking. St. Paul said, "we are saved by hope: but hope that is seen is not hope; for what a man seeth, why doth he yet hope for; but if we hope for that we see not, then do we with patience wait for it." So when we work diligently and patiently, as if already possessing what we hope for, faith is manifest which brings the condition desired. If our hope be in God, or Goodness, we hope for that which is, and is for us. If it be not in God, or Goodness, it is based in negation or denial of Him; verily both bring their reward. What we sow the same do we reap.

Faith Or Divine Will

Faith, or Divine Will, is the substance or power of Infinite Spirit or Mind, and is prior to thought, and is that which prompts mind to act or think, and which causes us to express thought in word and deed; so it is the substance of thought, word, and deed, and of things hoped for. It makes manifest and proves the unseen.

Through faith worlds are framed, and forms are created; without it, is not anything made that is made. As there is but one parent source or uncreated cause, there can be but one method of creation or manifestation. The method of the Parent Source is manifest in the son of man: they who understand this, consciously work with the Father, and do His will; then the Father's will and perfect faith is manifest. Faith is the power which enables us to successfully perform our every day duties; by it we think, speak, act, and move our bodies from place to place; by faith we accomplish all that is accomplished. It is faith in our ability to succeed that causes success in all our undertakings of life. All our works are done in faith; beside it there is no power. Consider the lilies how they grow, they toil not, neither do they spin, faith grows the flower; it is fullness of power or substance, and is manifest in all things; it knows not fear or anxiety; the more we live in the fullness of power, the more powerful we are in manifestation. They who have watched a little child making its first effort to walk, have witnessed the increase of power, as it expressed faith with each successive step, with the result that in a few days it walked about the house with perfect faith in its ability to do so. And this simple, child-like faith, which wavers not in effort, is the power which removes mountains, and enables us to rise to the pinnacle of the temple and to mountain tops in consciousness and understanding, above temptation and the limited view of sense, into eternal freedom and power. Without this high perception and faith, it is impossible to realize the parent source and do what we see the Father doing. Inexhaustible is the fountain of faith, therefore exercise it daily and hourly.

How Should Desire Be Overcome?

To desire is to long for the enjoyment or possession of something, to feel the want of, to mourn the loss of. So, desires result from a sense of limitation, which is attention fixed in and limited to manifestation. They who do not know themselves desire much, and great are their beliefs in sorrow and affliction.

In the universe there is the unmanifest, and the manifest. The unmanifest is one and inseparable, perfect and complete, from eternity to eternity; and in the manifest there seems to be many—this seeming is limitation. So when the attention is based in manifestation, it is focused to the limited, and thus come the delusions which arise from sense and beliefs in separateness, which prevents us from realizing that the whole Parent Source is the life of all. Desire is caused by not having true knowledge, and can only be overcome by gaining it. True knowledge consists in perceiving one inseparable, omnipresent Spirit, manifest in all that lives, or in creation—one Creator. Desire should be overcome by making what we find to do accord with the Spirit of Truth, and by unremitting effort to realize that we are the unmanifest and one with the all, which possesses all things. When we realize what we are, desire is overcome; we do not hunger and thirst after righteousness when we are filled. With this consciousness, deeds are not performed with the hope of reward, nor with anxiety as to results. Truth is the food which feeds the hungry Soul. Partake of it freely, and desire and anxiety will be done away, and all things made new.

"Come Unto Me"

The purpose of silent meditation should be, to realize what Being is, and what its possibilities are.

If the attributes be expressed in thought, the will of Spirit done, and the motive based aright, resultant there from are visible expressions of Being, which is harmony manifested; this is the way to illumination of understanding.

Meditation on any subject should be for the purpose of realizing the principle underlying the subject, of which words can only be symbolic or representative. Not until we arrive at an understanding of the meaning of Being can we know that creation or expression is symbolic and represent-ative, for we cannot be certain as to what visible things are, until we find the Cause which produces them. Therefore, not until we find Being, and perceive from the plane of Being, is it possible for us to distinguish between Being and existence: *i.e.*, between ourselves and our expressions; therefore, all endeavour should be for the purpose of getting understanding of the reality underlying the subject on which we meditate or think.

"Come unto Me," is an invitation by the speaker to move hither-ward, to draw near to that which is first. "If we draw nigh unto God, He will draw nigh unto us." Me, means Reality, the invisible Speaker, or the "I Am." Therefore the meaning of this subject is, that all are asked to come unto Spirit and learn of It, and find rest from labor, or from the burdens which arise from a denial or negation of the Me.

Though Spirit be omnipresent, the only way to accept the invitation, and "come unto Me," Spirit, is to act with undivided faith, and right motive; and they who come in this way will find rest in the realization of Oneness with the Omnipresent.

Jesus spoke not of himself as the body, nor did he act as if His expressions were himself, and in this he has revealed *the way* to us, and they who think and act truthfully, will think and act as did he, and with the same intent; not because the personal Jesus thus spake and acted, but because he, the Spirit, revealed the true way of life, by which every one may manifest the same truth and come unto me. The invitation to "Come unto Me," would be meaningless, if it meant no more than that one material form should appear in the presence of another material form.

We may as justly and truthfully expect that because the furniture of a room is associated together while in that room, or that because a row of houses are resting on a certain block of land, that they can give life and power to each other, as to expect that physical contact, or that the association of physical forms, can give life, peace, or rest. They who labour, and are heavy laden, do so because they do not come unto "Me," Spirit, and recognize and claim to be life, peace, and rest; such are seeking in effects, expecting to realize life, peace, and rest there from; such expectation is negation, and never is it otherwise. We cannot manifest the gifts of Spirit, unless we go to the Spirit for them. We do not find them in expression, for the reason that expression has them not. Spirit is *"the way, the truth, and the life;"* then to find the Me, the Invisible Speaker, is to find God, and in Him eternal truth, life, and rest.

The yoke of Truth is easy; union with God—Goodness—makes all burdens light. The Spirit of truth, which is wholeness, gives all, yet it labors not, neither is it heavy laden. Therefore, to "Come unto Me," is to get understanding and awaken to truth; and *everyone* who comes, finds. And they who live in a full consciousness of Being, can give to others rest, by imparting to them the truth that brings them into the same consciousness; therefore the awakened can point the way, because they know that they are the way of wisdom, and all who follow in that way no longer labor, or are heavy laden. But they who continue in the error of believing their manifestations to be themselves, or that which is made is real, and that visible things are a cause for happiness, are trying to make visible things serve as the cause for what the invisible Spirit alone can give. And not until they cease to partake of this forbidden fruit and place the true worth on Spirit, and see existence by the light of truth, can such know self, or "Come unto Me." Not until we cease believing the manifest and unreal to be ourselves, and believe ourselves to be the Unmanifest and real, can we know and reveal the wealth and power of Being. Neither have we "worshipped in Spirit and in Truth" until we have placed the true worth and value on Spirit, by acknowledging in all our ways, the Me—which is prior to expression.

What is Mesmerism?

A definition common to all is, that "mesmerism is a supposed influence or emanation by means of which one person can act upon another, producing wonderful effects upon the body and controlling his action and thought." "Or, the art of inducing an extraordinary, or abnormal state of the nervous system, in which the actor claims to control the action, and communes directly with the mind of the recipient."

If we would know by what means one individual seems to control the action of another, we must first learn the cause of action, and the means by which we control our own action.

The science of expression teaches that thought precedes all visible action, and that Being precedes all interior motive or action of thought; hence it is true that the mental constitution, which is born of Being, is the means through which this visible plane is made, and is the action thereof; for thought, will, and motive is our action, the controller of the body; therefore it is the thought, will, and motive that seems to control the action of the mesmeric subject.

The subject enters what is called the mesmeric state, by yielding the thought and will to that of the operator, and the control is due to the fact, that the subject changes his own thought and will to harmonize with the operator's.

Individual thought and will cannot be used to control the thought and will of one whose consciousness is universal, nor can such a one become a mesmeric subject. To think and act as the operator dictates is to yield the thoughts to obey or work in unison with his. It is therefore the subject's own thought and will, acting in concert with, or according to the operator's, that produces that which is called the mesmeric state or condition; both conditions are temporary and mortal.

They who live in a full consciousness of Being, or truth, are exempt from the influence and control of individual thought and will, for when the absolute is come to the individual consciousness, it has come for the reason that the thought and will have become that of the universal, or of Being.

And when that which is absolute is perceived, that which is in part rules not.

"Jesus Wept"

As it is a truth that men to whom the word of God came clothed the truth in language descriptive of things natural, so the words of our text are purely symbolic.

"He groaned in his spirit, and was troubled." "Jesus wept."(St. John xi: 33-35)

To groan means to strive after earnestly, as with groans. Thus, to groan in Spirit, is symbolic of effort made to concentrate in thought, and express the power of Spirit. "And he troubled himself," symbolizes the fact that he exerted himself to raise Lazarus, and thus do his Father's work. Christ raising Lazarus from the dead symbolizes the purpose for which he came into the world: *i.e.,* to raise from the dead the mental conditions of the race, into a living realization and consciousness of Truth and Life Eternal.

The Spirit of God, which is eternal, is fullness, stillness, and goodness; and is brought forth or manifested by the power of faith, and the interior action of thought. Therefore, groaning in Spirit, or weeping (in Scriptural language), is symbolic of effort made for the bringing forth into manifestation the power of Spirit; it is symbolic of preparation for the birth of great power, which precedes the joy that comes to all who are raised from the dead, that is, from form into consciousness;

also of the joy that is for those who are privileged to be witnesses to
the raising up, or they who see truth face to face in the expression of
the power of Spirit. In no way could Jesus have wept, according to the
unillumined definition generally given to the word, and to the text of
the disciple. The fourteenth and fifteenth verses of the same chapter
read as follows: "Then said Jesus unto them plainly, Lazarus is dead."

"And I am glad for your sakes that I was not there, to the intent ye
may believe; nevertheless, let us go unto him."

Again Jesus saith unto Martha, "Thy brother shall rise again." He
also said, "I am the resurrection and the life," which means, I am that
which rises again, and am the life which causes to rise. "He that believeth in me, though he were dead, yet shall he live." "I am the Truth
and the Life." They, who believe in Christ, believe that Truth and Life
is the maker of everything that is made. They who thus believe, though
they were dead to the consciousness and understanding of truth, yet
shall they rise up and live, or return to truth and live in understanding.

For that which we believe in, we are conscious of, and to believe
in the power of truth and life, is to awaken, and be conscious of Truth
and Life, and the awakened know that they have eternal life with God.

'Seek and Ye Shall Find'

To seek is to go in search or quest of, to endeavor to find. It would
be as useless to search for something that we believed did not exist, or
that we knew was not for us, as it would be to seek God without believing that what we seek is, and is for us.

So, if our seeking be in faith, we will believe that what we seek for
is, and is for us; then we have a definite idea of where and what it is we
wish to attain and manifest.

And as God, the giver of all is omnipresent, if we seek in truth we
must recognize that what we wish to manifest is at hand, and in this
thought we realize that we possess what we seek.

"Seek and ye shall find;" this promise is fulfilled in everyone that
truly seeks. To find is to gain a knowledge and to have a realization of

Infinite Spirit. And this knowledge, or realization, is only to be gained by true seeking: that is, through the acknowledgment of the presence of the ever-present Wisdom Spirit working in us, and by adjusting and conforming our will and way to it.

For if we would act from the Spirit, we must not be unconscious of its presence and of what it is, but must be able to acknowledge It unmanifest, and recognize It manifest in all our ways. "Canst thou by seeking find out God?" True seeking will bring to us a full consciousness of God, for we ever realize what we recognize, believe in, and conform our thoughts and words to.

Therefore, acknowledgment is the way of conformity to the Spirit, and is reconciliation, regeneration, and atonement.

Understanding and Its Realization

Understanding is knowledge or discernment of truth. The word comes from the Latin verb, *"sto,"* to stand, and "under," meaning under, below, after. Understanding is therefore an attribute of the Reality or Spirit which underlies and supports all existence; is a perception or consciousness of the Supreme Deity—it is absolute and unchangeable. So, to realize that we have understanding is to know that we are one with the Eternal.

The word realization is derived from the root, "real," and the suffix, "ize," to become, and "ion," the act of. Hence the act of becoming conscious that we are the real is the process of turning from error to truth, from nature to Spirit, or from the example to the Principle; and thus realization is gained that we are the real that understands the absolute truth, and that we cannot understand that which we are not; therefore we are truth.

Realization is the Truth of Spirit understood or made manifest; so to know that we are the Spirit of truth, which knowledge we realize in manifesting it, is divine understanding. Nothing but Spirit can understand the truth of Spirit—which is its own—for truth manifest is the only begotten of God.

The creature cannot understand the creator, but the creator which pervades the creature, understands itself and the creature. The creature is a symbol or example of an idea in the creator. Power is not given to the example in mathematics to understand and demonstrate the principle, but the power is in the principle to understand and demonstrate itself. The question will arise, if the finite be that which is manifest by the Infinite, and it cannot understand the Infinite or the absolute truth, how are we, as separate individuals, to understand the Infinite or the absolute truth? As it is not given to the belief of separateness, to understand unity and wholeness, so it is impossible for one to realize and know the Spirit, until they cease to look through the false belief of separateness that would say, I am separate from God, and from all that is made. Not until we acknowledge in thought the same relationship with God, as did Christ, that "I and my Father are one"—and hold steadfastly to this truth, sustaining this relationship by truthful word and deed—is the eye and ear of understanding opened, or are our manifestations universal. In other words—not until the individual knows that he is immersed in the Universal Spirit, is thought entirely freed from the belief that we are the creature, or example. To be free from this belief, is to know that we do understand the universal Spirit; that we are that which we understand, and that which is manifest, is the manifestation of Spirit, or the I Am.

We may have faith to know that if we practice the truth of God, we will come to realize that we have the understanding that Christ had. Be the law of love, and manifest it, and you will know God, for God is love; be one with Infinite truth and manifest it, and you will realize that you understand God, for God is truth. If we acknowledge that God is Infinite Being, Spirit, or Mind, and that there is no finite being, spirit or mind, then we know that there is but one Mind to perceive its truth; as that Mind is Infinite and is perfect, it admits of no error or imperfection. Then we are that Being or Mind, or else we are an existing creature without Spirit, Being, or Mind, hence without truth, reality, or immortality. Therefore it is an eternal truth that no one knoweth the things of God; or naught but the Spirit of Goodness can realize or manifest the Spirit of Goodness.

Like comprehends like; to realize the above statements, is the understanding of Spirit or Mind realized; and upon this rock we may build a structure of truth against which the gates of negation or false belief cannot prevail. Understanding and its realization means the Infinite or divine idea manifest. The absolute understanding of the Infinite is realized in the expression of every truth.

Great Religious Teachers

The great teachers of religion are the men and women who in their daily lives have demonstrated divine love and truth according to the Spirit of Truth, thus proving their faith by their works. Religion is defined to mean, to collect anew, to bind back; properly interpreted, it means bound back, relationship, or unity with God, or Goodness. This carries with it the meaning that that which is bound back must have been bound before. As individuality has its origin in God, to be bound back is in thought to return or be returned to God. It is the individual thought that wanders out into the wilderness of material effects, which is virtually an effort to put the example where principle should be. It is therefore deceived by the senses, not knowing the unreality of effects; this is unconsciousness of truth.

Therefore it is the individual thought that returns to God and binds mentality anew to the universal. This is to be accomplished by a divine and orderly method of thinking, by adjusting all conclusions to God, as all problems in mathematics are adjusted to the principle; and thus it consciously returns to God, knowing that every decision is based in Goodness.

And so we come to realize that we are the I am, and were never lost; that from eternity we were in the bosom of the Universal, the Father. And though thought be veiled by sense, yet the I am is never veiled from the presence of the eternal Father. Religion is subjective, and designates our unity with Good in word, feeling, and deed. It also designates the oneness of will, thought, love and motive, with God or Goodness.

A great religious teacher is one who teaches humanity that it can be as perfect as its Father in Heaven is perfect, one who teaches the way by which it can recognize the same Mind within itself that was in Christ Jesus. For it is written, "Let this Mind be in you which was also in Christ Jesus; who being in the form of God thought it not robbery to be equal with God." A great teacher of religion is one who reveals the unity of the way of Truth and Life; he is one who teaches that God is Infinite Spirit, and reveals the way by which we can worship in Spirit and in Truth, and how to be like Him in all our ways, prefacing all our ways with truthful thought.

The greatest of all in the kingdom of heaven, or in divine realization, is one who without omission thinketh Truth, and speaketh it in word and deed. One who without omission manifests the love of God for neighbor as for self, and whose worship consists in the practice of Truth.

Take My Yoke Upon You

A yoke is a bond of connection; a chain or link which connects or unites. The yoke or bond of union of which Christ spake was his consciousness of the truth of his union with God, or absolute Goodness. Hence he said; take *this* yoke upon you, which means this oneness or atonement, and you will realize what I realize, and find rest unto your souls. The consciousness that understood the truth of the unity of Being, and perceived the idea of being perfect as Spirit, or Goodness, is perfect, is one that realized that it understood the idea of Spirit, or Goodness.

As personality and false belief cannot comprehend the impersonal truth and life, so form cannot understand the impersonal. None but the meek and lowly who are willing to love all alike, who have turned from pride, ambition and worldly desire, can come to realize the full meaning of the divine and impersonal idea of God. The consciousness that "I and my Father are one," is the yoke that connects our expressions to all Goodness, to all truth, to all life. Therefore, if we take the yoke of truth and life, the Christ, upon us, it will make all seeming burdens easy and light; it will give peace and rest to the weary. We, as he, should not deem it robbery to be equal with the truth and Spirit of Goodness, we should not deem it robbery to put on the whole armor of righteousness, the whole armor of truth, the whole armor of perfection.

None but the meek and lowly in personality can take this yoke upon them and learn of Spirit, or consciously realize their unity with the Infinite. But they who through meekness rise above personality, or beliefs of selfishness, distinction or separateness, will be able to take this yoke or realization of truth upon them, which is freedom from limitation and rest from fear. Unity, and not division, is the pathway of truth and life. Be not divided in consciousness by sense-seeing, and you will cease to labor with the shadows or symbols of life; give up the testimony of the senses and all the things of sense for truth and life, and dominion will be gained over the world of sense, and you will know, as did Christ, that you are the truth and life.

The same consciousness and truth that bound Christ to God, or Goodness, is the yoke that connects all to God, or Goodness. Therefore take this yoke upon you, and you will let that mind be in you that was in Christ Jesus, and have nothing between you and God; this is rest.

Eternal Punishment

To solve this question, which has troubled the thought of so many persons, and which has caused so much fear, doubt and anxiety—that bear not fruit of the Spirit, because they are the opposite of love, faith and rest—it is necessary that we learn what the word "eternal" means, and what that is, which is eternal.

All are agreed that life, love, truth, that power, wisdom and goodness are eternal; or that Mind, idea, or Spirit is eternal; the word represents that which is without beginning or end—without end of being or duration—the state of being the same at all times. Then naught but the unchangeable is eternal; and naught but the eternal is unchangeable.

No existing thing or form is without change. The action of thought is a continuous or never-ending change. Therefore it is unthinkable that that which is eternal and which is unchangeable love and goodness, can create or manifest, or cause to be manifest, that which is not in the image and likeness of itself.

Universal love, which has no respect to person, cannot inflict eternal punishment on anything that it makes, for all that it makes is good, and is like unto itself, which is Goodness. Punishment is supposed to be inflicted upon immortal souls for the violation of divine law, and as God's law is infinite love, if He were to inflict eternal punishment upon any of His creations for not fulfilling the law of love, He would violate His own law thereby.

Then, dear friends, consider the meaning of the word "eternal," and you will clearly perceive and know that that which is real cannot punish or be punished, cannot afflict or be afflicted, for that which is in the image and likeness of Spirit is in perfect harmony with Spirit, as the mental problem is in perfect harmony with the principle. It is an eternal truth, however, that the testimony of the senses, when unillumined by spirit perception, testifies against the Spirit, or all that is eternal; and this has ever been and will ever be the same. As thought is ever based in the premise from which we draw our conclusions, so if the testimony of the senses be taken as authority, the thought is based in effect, not in Spirit; and thus we calculate from our incorrect work, and not from principle. It is truth that we ever feel our own thought, and it is the source of our pleasure or pain. From a false premise, one that is ever changing, we cannot draw truthful conclusions, and feeling or sensation will ever suffer or be punished, as it were, at the hand of sense judgment; this is eternally true, or ever the same. It is fear, doubt, anxiety, falsehood, or all negation of God that will weep and wail when they are cast into the fiery furnace of eternal truth, to be consumed; and not the reality, or immortal soul.

Again, it is an eternal truth, that sensible conclusions—conclusions of sense—or false beliefs, which are neither reasonable nor truthful, are the punishments inflicted, and this is ever the source of suffering. But as thought is continually changing, so everyone who is instructed into the Kingdom of Heaven, bringeth forth divine love in their thought, and by fulfilling the law—love—are in Heaven, in a realization of the presence of God, or Goodness, for God is love.

Paragraphs

Statements of Truth are never cutting to those who are in Truth.

Shrink not from identifying yourself with *God,* "in which you live," for this is the truth that frees from beliefs of limitation and suffering.

Christian Healing is healing by the power of Infinite Spirit. Spiritual healing is healing as Christ did; therefore the two are one.

The object of Buddha's investigation was to find the cause of misery, and the remedy for it. Gautama Buddha found the cause to be ignorance; Christ Jesus demonstrated the remedy to be understanding.

As long as the individual believes that he has two natures, one good and the other evil, thought presents sometimes one belief and sometimes the other; and just so long will there be doubt, uncertainty, no knowledge of the Permanent.

The word of God is the truth of Spirit, and can only be spiritually understood. Attempting to understand scriptural teaching or the truth of Infinite Spirit by intellectual, or sense seeing, is like trying to measure the Infinite by personality.

Through sense seeing, personal will and desire, mentality is veiled from a perception of truth and perfect understanding. The perception of truth is light, in which there is no darkness.

Expressions of life are in powerful thought. That which is called death is a denial of life, or power. That which is loved, is held in thought and bears fruit.

The ear that heareth the silent voice is understanding. To maintain a deaf ear to the senses is to open it to the silence. We are taught from life eternal, the Spirit of Truth.

Image God in thy thought, and thus wilt thou prove thy faith, peace, and truth to thyself. Compare thy deed with the goodness of the

Father, and thus wilt thou know the Master thou servest. The faithful servant doeth the will of the master, and thus is the edenic order maintained.

He who heareth the reproof of truth and rejecteth it not, but abideth in its decision, is in the way that leadeth to a realization of eternal freedom.

To account for our existence is to solve the problem of life.

The awakened are those who have become conscious that it is not they, personally, or individually, who live, but the Father in them.

The law of nature is love in its harmonious and regular order of action, that by which God governs the universe.

To give alms before men to be seen of them, is to give for vain and selfish motive, with desire for reward; and if a gift be offered with such motive or purpose, the reward cannot be from the Spirit of Goodness, because the motive is not based therein. When the motive or purpose be like unto God, then God is manifest in it. "Verily, all receive their reward."

To hold all in love and truth, is to do what the Father doeth; so, the recompense at the resurrection of the just is justice. "With what measure ye mete, it shall be meted to you again."

Consciousness of Truth is eternal Life. Truthful thoughts make truthful statements, which bud, bloom, and produce the fruit of Spirit.

The Aura, or thought emanations of the awakened, electrifies the atmosphere with the healing balm of Truth, for all who come within their mental sphere, as the flowers extend their fragrance to all who come within their sphere.

Love is our being; and this we seek to manifest by our thoughts. Thus we may base our love either in the spirit or in the material. That is, we thus think we are Spirit, or Matter. In the one case we decide we are Goodness; in the other case we decide we are its forms. We cannot serve *both* God and Mammon.

Divine Law Is Love

"He that loveth, knoweth God, for God is love;" the same is

obedient to the law of his being. As thought is an expression of the thinker, or is the action of being: hence the expression or thought must be obedient to the law, Love, if *its* expressions be harmonious. The Sons of God love all life and all things; they are like the Sun that shines equally upon the seeming evil and upon the good, and like the rain that comes to the just and unjust alike. To be a Son is to do what the Father doeth. The awakened know what they possess, and their purpose is to give continually, that the law may be fulfilled.

Read Between the Lines

When we speak the word of Spirit, we speak to all, for all.
When we commune with Spirit, we commune with all; for all.
Such speaking and communing are impersonal.
When our speaking is personal, we commune with like mental states, which is in part, but "when that which is perfect is come, that which is in part shall be done away."

The Way of Approval

If it be difficult for us to love our neighbours and acquaintances because of something they may have said or done which we did not see fit to approve, then to love them is the thing we most need to do; we should never allow the error of a sister or brother to prevent us from expressing the all-saving power of love toward them; we cannot expect to be strong in good and be healed ourselves until we arise and do things that are difficult. "To him that overcometh will I give to wear the crown of life."

To judge of our true condition by examination of the physical body, is morally wrong. To judge of our capabilities by the present degree of manifested truth, is mental darkness and limitation. It is setting up our present manifestations against the government of Infinite Spirit. Error is without the reality of truth, therefore it is without reality. As we awaken to the reality of Spirit, we lose thought of matter as profiting anything; and the less we think about bodies, the more harmony do we express.

Truth is the bread of life, for it is the remedy for all misconceptions and seeming *disharmony.* Know the truth and live in it, and it will free you from all limitations.

Just as much of Truth as we recognize, just so much—and neither more nor less—do we manifest. To each one is given according to the measure of the gift of Christ. To the degree that we think truth, to that degree do we manifest Christ.

Not until we claim the truth of Infinite Being as the truth of all being, shall be known for ourselves that God is in us, or have we perceived righteous judgment.

The harvest of Truth is always ripe; postpone not gathering in your harvest, thinking that in weeks or months it will be ripe. To-morrow never comes—today is the harvesting time.

Illumination
The Way and Will of Universal Spirit
Revealed to the Individual

1. In the silent, soundless Presence, there is a still small voice which speaks and says, "Be thou (O Son of my Being), instructed in wisdom's way; know thou this truth, that I am forever and forever One, Infinite, and indivisible; and *the way of One* is the way of unity forever more. If thy thought doth abide in the Unity of my way, thy decisions will be illumined with mine own truth, which leadeth into my kingdom of perfect Goodness, where all good doth abide forever and forever.

2. Live thou in the way of truth; it forsaketh thee never, and surely doth it lead unto Me; so shalt thou come unto, and dwell safely in me, and thou shalt share the wealth of my kingdom. My love, and my faith, and my goodness, shall be thine now and forevermore; nor wilt thou know fear, nor pain, nor sorrow.

3. Unite thy way to wisdom's way, and more and more shall thine understanding increase into a perfect whole. So shalt thou truly dwell

in the land of freedom, where reality and perfection doth abide forever and forever.

4. Let not thy thought depart from Me, and wander in the fertile land of effects. Image My love and My truth in thought, seal it to Me, as reality is sealed to Me, as father and son, or mother and child, are sealed, the one to the other; as Infinite Mind and idea, and idea and thought, are sealed, the one to the other. So shalt thy way be clear, and thy charge be light.

5. Thou wilt ever gather fruit from the way in which attention is directed by thy thought—by the way in which it lights thy mental vision. Let not thy thought turn from understanding, out of wisdom's way, for unity leadeth into My kingdom; so shalt thou enter by that way, and gather the golden fruit thereof in thine experience. Full is that consciousness which understands that I am All in All, and that it is in Me and I in it. In this truth all is contained: on this tree of life hangs the golden fruit of My kingdom, which is for all who will partake.

6. Oh son of my Being, if thou wouldst be instructed further in the way of Unity and wisdom, know thou this truth: that My love and will, My purpose, and My thought, must be made thine; I, being Infinite, cannot be less than All. My idea can be known only as perfect and Infinite. My expressions are images like unto Myself, nor canst thou abide in truth, and justice, and love, without consciously abiding in My way.

7. Adjust thou all thy ways unto Me; hold thy thought in the perfect idea and consciousness: so, verily shalt thou come unto Me, and dwell safely in Me, and know that as thou art in Me, and that *I am in thee,* much fruit will result therefrom, to feed my children which do hunger and thirst after righteousness. I am One, and My kingdom is one. Walk thou, dear one, in the way of Unity, and thou shalt know the wholeness of My Being, and the harmony of My way, which is Unity, Love, Oneness and Atonement, now and forever.

Suffragettes 1919

Annie Rix Militz

(1856-1924)

Founder of the Home of Truth

Annie Rix Militz will always be regarded as one of the "greats" of New Thought. Her editing and publishing of *Master Mind*, one of the earlier and more outstanding New Thought magazines, from its beginning in 1911 until her death in 1924, would ensure that. She was also a key figure in the early days of the Unity movement.

She was a magnetic speaker, a leader of far vision, a valued counselor in organizational matters in the International New Thought Alliance, and an inspiring teacher. She founded one of the early New Thought groups, Home of Truth, which, beginning as a local institution, came to have centers in a number of places, chiefly on the West Coast, but also elsewhere in the United States. Like a number of other groups it was the result of influences set at work by that remarkable New Thought "teacher of teachers," Emma Curtis Hopkins. It was in one of her classes in San Francisco in 1887 that Mrs. Annie Rix became one of her students and found her life work, as she told her sister, Harriet Rix, after the third lesson.

A fellow-member of the class, a Mrs. Gorey, had a small metaphysical bookshop, and when this woman asked Annie Rix to give up her teaching—she was a public school teacher—and join her in the bookstore, she did so, and began soon to conduct classes there in what was essentially the teachings of Mrs. Hopkins.

Her work in the bookstore gave her opportunity to read widely in the metaphysical field, and she absorbed a great deal from her reading. It was perhaps this experience which accounted, in part at least, for her broad tolerance and sympathy for the thought of others who differed from her. She was never creedily bound by any one teaching, though she herself held profound views as to the nature of the universe, of God, and of man. Her one basic belief she said, was in "The Allness of God," no matter where or how she found it.

On June 1, 1891, a group of leading New Thought students, including the Fillmores (who later co-founded Unity), Annie Rix, and Paul Militz, were ordained as Christian Science ministers by Hopkins. Shortly after their ordination, Annie Rix married Paul Militz and became Annie Rix Militz.

Mrs. Militz and Mrs. Gorey quickly outgrew the bookshop and secured a new place of several rooms over a store. Growth of their work soon led them to take over the store and convert it into a hall where they could hold their meetings. They called their Center "Christian Science Home," but later abandoned the use of that name most likely due to the fact that Christian Science had come to be associated with

Mary Baker Eddy's denomination. In any event, the name Home of Truth was substituted for that of Christian Science Home.

Mrs. Militz worked in the "Home" for several years, then she was called to teach as a member of the faculty of Mrs. Hopkins' Christian Science Theological Seminary, in Chicago. She left the San Francisco Home in charge of her sister, Harriet Rix, and Miss Eva Fulton. When, in 1893, Mrs. Militz returned to the West Coast, she found the Home of Truth ministry in excellent shape. Harriet Rix and Miss Fulton had not only purchased a handsome residence at 1232 Pine St.—where the main San Francisco Home of Truth would be located for years—but Harriet had organized a second Home across the bay in Alameda. Annie Militz could see that the work was proceeding well in San Francisco, and, in early 1894, she decided to move to Los Angeles to start a new center. The movement spread to other cities. Soon there were Homes of Truth all up and down the coast from San Diego, California, to Victoria, British Columbia.

In August 1893, the long and important professional association between Annie Rix Militz and the Fillmores, founders of Unity School of Christianity, began with the publication of her first article in *Unity* magazine entitled "Manifestation of God Through Judas Iscariot." Mrs. Militz was to have much involvement within the Unity movement in the years to come.

Between the latter years of the 1890s and the early 1900s, Militz's "Bible Lessons" were the major teaching articles in *Unity* magazine. These lessons were extremely important to the Unity movement and formed a basis for many of its teachings. The Fillmores openly acknowledged their appreciation of Militz as a writer, teacher and healer. She continued her association with Unity right up until 1911.

Mrs. Militz was much in demand as a lecturer and teacher. She taught the monthly class at Unity headquarters in Kansas City in 1900 and traveled widely both at home and abroad. She became very active in the National (later International) New Thought Alliance also, and founded the University of Christ in Los Angeles (along with a major metaphysical library) to train New Thought teachers. She traveled the globe as an officer of the New Thought Alliance spreading the metaphysical gospel; and served as president of the New Thought Exposition Committee which organized the New Thought Day (August 28, 1915). She wrote numerous books and articles applying metaphysical precepts to a wide variety of local, national, and international social concerns.

In the Spring of 1911, an announcement in *Unity* signaled the end of the intermediate years in the career of Annie Rix Militz and her separation, physically and creatively, from the Unity movement. Though the parting was obviously amicable, Militz had cut her ties with Unity and was prepared to fully develop her Home of Truth movement in Los Angeles, and concentrate on her *Master Mind* magazine which comprised of articles, poetry, lessons and other discussions on theology, study of the bible, prosperity, immortality, soul communion, planet healing, healing circles, the home ministry and other various spiritual topics, which she continued to do until her passing on June 22, 1924. (1)

Link & Acknowledgement
1. annierixmilitz.wwwhubs.com

Concentration

Crusader Publications, Boston Massechusetts

I. *The Nature of Concentration*
The Common Center

THE simplest definition of concentration is that found in the dictionary, namely, "to gather to one common center," for it defines that which is spiritual as well as that which is material.

We need only to consider what is the common center in order to put concentration into its right place. That common center is within you and its name is One, whether we call it the name of the Lord, as we read in the book of the prophet Malachi, as to the great Manifestation that finally shall be in this world, that "there shall be one Lord and His name One," or whether we call it the mathematical one. It is sufficient that we see the common center of our spiritual thoughts and of our material thoughts as one thought, one manifestation.

The Way of Creation

Concentration is the formative way of creation. Creation is manifested by the power of divine mind working upon thoughts, ordering them and being obeyed, so that they gather around one common center; thus we have that expression, called the Solar System, or a world.

If we turn to the scientific theories of the formation of this universe, we have that nebulous mass which finds its center in some nucleus about which all is gathered. This formative power of divinity within you is that which brings everything to its essence. The common center of your being is the essence of God, your divine self. To begin to make your eye single to that central self, that divine I, is to feel your mastery.

The reason why people are so disturbed, upset, mixed and lacking in concentration, is because they have forgotten. They have ceased to look to that One, and they must return, and remember the One that is the source of our life; the power that holds us together; the great means by which we can order our lives and manifest the works of God—works of healing, of mastery, of self-control and the restoration of memory. Thus can you be a power like the sun, radiating power to transform your whole world, according to your own idea, to the light that dwells within you, bringing forth all that which is right, and that which is a blessing.

A Gauge of Intelligence

The power of concentration has always been a gauge of intelligence. It is an indicator of intelligence, whether it be expressed in the animal realm, or in the human, in the babe, or in a Socrates.

When a trainer wishes to select animals of intelligence, he will note their power of concentration. A famous trainer of dogs would gather together a number of these animals from everywhere; sometimes they would be very common dogs, for he found that it was not always dogs of the best breed that showed the most intelligence; sometimes it would be but a yellow cur that would make the best trick dog. After association with their master long enough to become familiar with his voice, it was the practice of this trainer to test their powers of concentration. He would gather them together and holding up some object, would demand the attention of all the dogs to that thing. One by one, the dogs dropped their eyes, turned away their heads and sought some other interest, only a few remained alert and waiting and these were the dogs that the trainer chose to become performers on his stage.

And so we can take the babe. The babe that "takes notice" very quickly and very steadily, we count of much intelligence. This is also true of ourselves, we find that the times, when we can hold our mind to certain things, are the times of greatest accomplishment—when we manifest the greatest intelligence—and finally, we shall see this as a power so supreme that one might, like another Socrates, stand in the midst of the market place absorbed in a revelation, and even stand for hours. It is said this great philosopher once stood a whole day and night, while the people surged around about him. Were you or I able so to stand, we also might present to the world such a philosophy as he gave. Socrates represents intelligence of the highest degree, and it expresses itself in this power of concentration. There is no greater pursuit than that of the knowledge and understanding by which you can express your intelligence in concentration.

Natural Concentration

It has been found that those who follow the spiritual life, devoting all their time and attention to it, have no difficulty in concentrating. Healers easily center their thought; can easily be at peace, be self-possessed, poised and fearless in some of the hardest problems and the most distracting situations. Therefore if you simply pursue this truth, putting it into practice in your daily living, seeking ever to help people and lighten their burdens by your power of thought, you will manifest concentration without an effort. You are even now exercising that power in centering your minds upon what I am saying. I have had speakers, who have been on the platform with me, express themselves with wonderment at the attention that is given me—the silence, the peace, the freedom from restlessness. It is all a marvelous expression of concentration, because the subject that I present is so vital and of such power that it naturally unites our thoughts and you concentrate naturally—without an effort.

Special Concentration

We know the advantages of the ordinary concentration, how it gives you peace and self-control, and the masterly, orderly expression that invites confidence. But there is a special advantage in *the concentration that is based upon principle.* Have you discovered that what you concentrate upon, you become one with? That it is possible for you to enter into the heart—into the very essence of a thing and get its secret and make it reveal its nature and its meaning? Some of you have had this experience that when you wanted to know a thing, you simply centered your mind steadily on it, and presently it was opened up to you and you found yourself knowing without the ordinary efforts of getting information. One man told me this, as a common experience with himself in school. He was a boy of fine intelligence, but he was lazy, and oftentimes did not have his lesson, but when his turn came to answer the question put to him, he would think toward the Professor, and say (mentally) to him: "You know the answer; it is right in your mind this moment," and while he would think that, the answer came to him. He did this so often that he knew that he had fulfilled some law.

Again, let me remind you of the little newsboy that I saw guessing the dates on the coins, which another boy held in his hand. Steadily his eye rested upon each copper cent, and three times he gave the correct date, imprinted on the underside, which none of us knew until after each coin was examined.

It is a good illustration of power that is in us which we exercise, even when we do not know the nature of it nor how we have it. You think it is by coincidence or chance. You think that something called your attention to the fact, and you dismiss the experience in a material- istic way, even with doubt. But it is a power called "psychometry," now acknowledged by scientists. Maeterlinck says, "The existence of this faculty is no longer seriously denied." It is orderly; it is right; we have this power, we need only to exercise it. But to do so, we must take care of our thoughts, dismiss certain kinds of thinking and hold to certain other kinds of thinking.

Thoughts of Evil, Rubbish

In the first place, we cannot afford to "clutter" our mentalities with thoughts of evil. It is a homely word but it is literally so. You clutter your mind, filling your brain cells with what the physicians call "dirt," and this is all because of erroneous thinking—thinking upon wrongs and upon evils, revenge, fear and worriment. Everything that has its root in the belief of evil must utterly pass from our mentality and pass forever, and we become like a little child, with pure, clean brain-cells, because we have no false thoughts or ill feelings, but are filled with love, and purity and goodness. So the very organ of your mentality, the brain, can be orderly and free, without congestion of blood, without any piling up of that foreign material which the physician calls "dirt," and when you wish to think upon a thing, you will not have to use your human will power but just wait and rest, and naturally it will spring to the front and you will have wasted no effort, but have concentrated easily and with power.

Memory Restored

This is the way for the restoration of your memory. The reason why people lose their memories and find their mental faculties getting out of order, is because they try to hold thoughts in their minds that do not belong there; they will be so disconcerted if they forget dates, or events that should be counted nothing at all. Why should you remember the old past, and why should you dwell on the things of yesterday? *Now* is the only time. Live in the present. Dismiss thoughts of yesterday; those thoughts of the past. Be as though you were born this morning. Begin every day anew.

Some may say: "I have been so wronged by everybody; people impose upon me and it will not do for me to forget or I'll be wronged again." There is "a more excellent way," by which these experiences shall not be repeated, than remembering the wrongs of the past. This excellent way is to begin to fill your mind with meditations upon God, the Good. Even though it be so simple as this reasoning—that there is the One that is the source of all and that One is God the good; that One is omnipresent; therefore good is everywhere. Then insist upon seeing it everywhere, upon believing it, dwelling upon it continually— Good *is the only real presence.* Do this in place of the evil thinking; do it persistently. How do you put out darkness? Not by dealing with darkness! So you cannot put out evil memories by dealing with them themselves. You put out darkness by bringing in the light, and you put out evil memories by bringing in good ones.

Faithful Practice

This means an exercise as faithfully practiced as the beginning of the study of music. When you began to learn music, you pursued practices that were tiresome, but your teacher said it was necessary. When you began to learn a physical exercise, like rowing a boat, you went through simple actions and pursuits, and some were very wearisome, but these simple things were most essential. Begin your practice of concentration by centering your mind upon the thought that the *good is all there really is,* and learn to crowd out the opposite thoughts with that one thought. It will prove itself true, presently.

Such was the case of a young boy who had run away from his home in Portland, Ore., and became stranded in San Francisco. Through a lady, who learned his story, he began coming to the Home of Truth. There he learned to hold the thought: *Good is all there really is.*

He desired to get back home, and a purser on an Oregon steamer told him to be at the dock on the Sunday morning that the steamer would sail, and he, the purser, would come ashore and get him, and he could work his passage home again.

The boy was there but the purser never appeared. The steamer sailed, leaving the boy in rage and despair. Then he remembered that he was to say, "Good is all." In bitterness, almost sarcasm, he began to repeat the words. Soon he calmed down and found himself walking toward the Home of Truth. There, on the steps, he met a lady who began to inquire why he had not gone. He reluctantly told her his bad luck, with the result that she handed him the fare to go on the train to Portland, and he arrived there before the steamer reached that city. He proved quickly "the power of the word."

Worldly Success

Worldly success is one of the out-picturings of the power of concentration. Those who have made material success will tell you that it has come by concentration upon their business, and devoting all their strength and time to it. The secret of Paderewski's skill with the piano was this, that he gave himself to eighteen hours practice at a time. A certain rich man, who was very successful with railway stocks, gave it as his secret, that he studied the manual of railways, night and day; would read it before he would go to sleep, then the first thing in the morning before meals, after meals—all the time. And when someone asked him the secret of his success, he said it was concentration—studying night and day upon that in which he was successful.

Oh, but Paderewski can be thrown off with the injury of a finger; the railway man can receive a little blow on the head, and it all counts for nothing. Those who concentrate upon material things have but a temporal success, for if they try to concentrate upon anything else, they find they have not power in that direction, and it sometimes seems like beginning life over again. This was illustrated in the experience of a man who had been a most successful business man, as a commercial traveler, commanding a high salary and finally becoming a partner in the company, though still pursuing his own efficient line.

Finally, he had accumulated such a snug little fortune, owning a pretty home and ten acres in one of California's loveliest towns that his wife and daughter persuaded him to retire from business.

What they meant to be freedom and a joy to him proved to be the greatest mistake. He tried to lead a quiet life and, for activity, to become interested in the pursuits of his society-neighbors. But his mind was ever off on the familiar routes that he had followed for over fifty years. He could not center his thoughts on the new life and the result soon was "softening of the brain," the beginning of dissolution.

Fortunately, his wife and daughter, understanding Truth, brought his case under spiritual treatment and his mind was saved, and he was able to hew out a new way of concentration, by utterly abandoning the material for the spiritual.

The Oriental Yoga

The Hindus call the practice of spiritual concentration, "Yoga," which means "union," and comes from the same root as our word "yoke". The Aryan language is at the root of all civilized languages, and our word yoke and their word yoga have a common root, and it means to unite—to join. "Take my yoke upon you, for my yoke is easy and my burden is light." This is the Christ teaching of yoga, that we shall have such a power of concentration that there shall be no burdens at all, but all life shall be full of ease and freedom. The Christian Yoga is "taking on Christ," being one with him, which is the easy way of concentration. Hindu devotees spend whole lives in the study and practice of Yoga, because by means of right concentration, they look for all power, all knowledge and all bliss here in this life. The text-book of Hindu practice is *"The Yoga Aphorisms of Patanjali,"* in which is displayed most subtle and wonderful understanding of the human mind and its workings, and the way of deliverance from its errors by right knowledge and practice of concentration.

Knowledge and Love

There are two forms of thinking which make the way easy for concentration. One is knowing; keep on knowing; never rest content with ignorance; get knowledge and get understanding. The other is love. Begin with the love of truth; love truth for its own sake. My friends, if you will only "fall in love with truth," you need not have another lesson; you will concentrate and no one can stop you.

There are people who think truth night and day, in their dreams, and in the ordinary things of life, and the consequence is that they are joyously and powerfully in the consciousness of concentration. Of course they are in love with truth. If anybody is in love with another you do not need to tell them to think about the other one; if you are in love with another, you simply cannot help thinking of that one. It would sound ridiculous to say to a real lover, "If you expect to win her, you must think of her night and day." "How can I help it!" says the lover. The advice is not needed. A lover has a wonderful power of concentration, and if there is no mixture of resentment, of hatred or jealousy, there is a perfect feeling of peace and power. Pure love is a power for concentration in itself, and so to be in love with truth is to be able to concentrate without a thought. Love is faithful.

Express your love by obediently practicing this first rule of concentration, the use of the silent word. Often practice saying, "Good is all there really is."

II. *The Power of Repose*

Let us unite in silence, taking the words found in Psalms. *"Be still and know that I am God."*

Be still in every way, relaxing yourself and letting the I AM be your stilling power. Rest in the Divine Mind that knows itself (which is yourself), the great I AM that dwells in the midst of you.

We remember that "God" is the name of our good, and whatever your desire may be—for peace, for health, for happiness, for freedom, it is the very desire of your heart that speaks and says, "Be still and know that I am God"—be still and know that I am. This is our silence.

The Effortless Way

TWO great principles are at the root of the power of concentration. One of them is *Knowing* and the other is *Loving.*

Knowing might be considered the active principle and loving the passive, or still principle, in this that knowing is associated with activity, pursuing, seeking, grasping, and so on, while loving is associated with *being.* Love comes without effort. It is the effortless way to love, and if you are in love with truth, you concentrate without effort. And this effortless way is the happy way of concentration.

By loving truth, you enter true wisdom's ways, which are pleasantness, and you find the path which is peace. So you must love truth with your whole being, seeking it, not for what it will bring you, not for its reward, its healing, its peace, even for its power of concentration, but for it, itself—loving truth for its own self.

This is the orderly, masterful, efficient way of attaining concentration. Learn to concentrate upon *truth,* and having acquired that power in the realm of reality, you will have no difficulty in centering your mind upon whatever you will in the realm of appearances. For always you will stand upon the Rock of right reasoning; and if you turn aside from concentrating upon exact truth you can look at symbols, as symbols, and let them hold your attention, so long as you will, because you see the connection between them and truth. Whereas, the things that distract, that break up the mentality and spoil concentration will not invite your attention. You can refuse to center your mind upon evil, fear, worry, foolishness, for these are the things that distract and they are spoilers of concentration.

No Suppression by Human Will

The worldly methods of thought-control by strenuous effort of the human will are to be put completely aside. Use no will power to concentrate. This mistake has been made by certain young metaphysicians, and even old ones. Those who have been long in this life have practiced and pursued ways that are strenuous and congesting; have inflamed and disturbed even their brain cells by dwelling upon some word which has little or no meaning in itself, repeating it over and over again, thinking that to hold a thought, one must exercise human will. No, the real holding of thought is as a cup holds water; through being still and letting the thought rest in your mind, and the power by which you do that is *the power of repose.*

Repose is not something you do not already have. It is within you, and it needs only meditation and acknowledgment of it, to bring it forth. The way to uncover it is by, first of all, knowing yourself.

Know Thyself

You cannot know yourself perfectly without knowing God. For this personal self, which has been called yourself, is but a *reflection,* a shadow of your Real Self which is one with God. Knowing the Real Self, you will understand this shadow, this reflection, just as one, knowing about a material thing will also understand its shadow. Recognizing the power that is in you to cast a shadow, you know how to manage the shadow—that of your hand on the wall, for instance; you can control the shadow because you know how to manage the hand. Thus, if you know your Real Mind and its processes, you will understand its shadow, and doing what you will with your Real Mind, you can reflect or shadow it forth in appearance, just as you wish it to appear.

The Real Mind, is God Mind. It moves upon itself in all manifestations. It is the actor and the one acted upon. It is God, the actor, and God, that which is acted upon—it being all God. The mind that shadows it, which has been called by various names,—the carnal mind, mortal mind, mentality, mind-stuff and so on—also acts upon itself, imaging, reflecting the laws of the divine Mind.

Mentality and Mind-Stuff

Let us call the actor of this mortal mind "mentality," and that which is acted upon, "the mind-stuff." To know how to conform your mentality to the great Actor, the divine One, and to act upon the mind-stuff according to the Divine Law, is to have a power that will heal, and thoughts with which nothing can interfere, so that you need never be confused nor disturbed, nor lose your poise or your peace, no matter what you face or are passing through.

Sometimes the mind-stuff, which is the great mass of thoughts that are going hither and thither within us and round about us, has been compared to a lake, and the mentality to the breeze that blows upon the lake. When this mind-stuff is still and the mentality is quite at peace, then we have a lake all clear and free to reflect perfectly. Whatever is then held over that lake will be imaged forth as it should be, not distorted nor false, but true. Although inverted, it will be clear and its form correct, a perfect image of that which is held over it.

Upon a still lake, the ship that floats on its surface will show forth all its beauty, form and graceful movements, giving a perfect image of itself. But when the lake of your thoughts is disturbed and agitated, then your mentality is like the wind that blows and lashes the waves. Then the mind-stuff is thrown into foam and becomes roiled and disturbed and it is not strange that you cannot reflect what you wish. You must become still again. The lake must subside and the wind must calm, that perfect repose may be manifest, that you may reflect what you wish and show forth the concentration which you desire.

Christ in the Ship

The One in you which can still your mentality is the Christ-self. To try to still the wind and waves without the Christ-self is a long process with more or less sense of failure. The Christ may appear to be asleep in the ship, as we read in that story about the disciples, who were crossing the Sea of Galilee and a great storm came upon them and the ship was in danger of sinking; of how they went to the Christ, asleep in the hold of the ship—not Christ really, but the form, Jesus, for the Christ is "the Lord that slumbers not, nor sleeps." It is but the form of that Christ-presence which seems to be hidden and inactive for a time. Your Lord-self never sleeps nor loses consciousness, but if it seems to you that you have no Lord-self, that you cannot think of yourself as divine or spiritual, then you need to arouse and awaken yourself, even with a cry of prayer, "Awake thou that sleepest!" or as the Psalmist calls, "Why sleepest thou, O Lord?" The disciples went and called Jesus from his sleep and he came forward and rebuked the wind and waves and all was still. So, no matter how agitated you seem to be—no matter how roiled the waters are or contrary the wind, in an instant, by remembering your God-self, the whole lake will quiet and you will quickly find yourself at peace.

This Christ-self is your power of repose. It is that part that abides in peace. It is the great immobility by which all things are moved. If you can find that Holy of Holies, that still place within, you will take hold upon a power of concentration which will remain with you forever.

Purity, Essential to Clear Thinking

The lake—the mind-stuff that fills your personality and surrounds it—must not only be still, but clear. Our living true to principle and fulfilling the moral law tends to purify this mind-stuff; sincerity, purity of life, freedom from deceit—freedom from doubleness in action, thought, word and deed— clarify this lake and make it pure. This means a life of freedom from "the three qualities" that the Hindu describes as: *Tamas, Rajas* and *Sattvas*.

The Three Bonds

The Tamas quality is described thus: it is that state of lethargy and inertia, deadness, dullness and laziness which lies back of stagnation. If you feel spiritually lazy at times, or physically lazy, you can rise above that appearance by remembering the divine life, which is always alert, active, sparkling even in its stillness. You are God's active self, full of life, full of alertness, full of power and God. State these things for yourself and put away that stagnation which will make the waters of the mentality grow dark and thick with scum and not able to reflect what is held over them.

The second quality, the Rajas, is that of passion. It is the opposite to the Tamas quality for it stirs and muddies our thought-realm. Greed, jealousy, envy, anger, lust are things that move one to excess and upset one, so as to muddy the water of the mind-stuff, that it cannot reflect. Watch yourself. The moment you begin to find yourself wandering off into this state, being moved by anger and other forms of passion—the power of concentration is needed, the power of *self-control*, which is the next lesson we will take up especially.

The third quality is Sattvas, a sense of goodness often so personal as to be self-righteousness. The human ego says, "I am good, why should I not have perfect health? I have always done right, why should I suffer?" It feels that certain things are owing to it. This ego longs for praise and approval. It says, "I must be regarded," and again "I have been insulted," or "I have been neglected." Such thoughts are very disturbing. You may be leading a very pure life, may be fulfilling the laws so that you are counted very good and very lovable. Yet, if your face is full of fine wrinkles, or you have nerves unstrung, and there is a trembling or an agitation in your body, you lack in concentration.

The human ego can dwell upon its "rights," its "superiority" and its ambitions and achievements until unbalanced. "Insanity is egotism gone to seed." Insanity is simply *the lack* of concentration, reaching its ultimate.

It is the Christ that brings you to yourself, out of the three qualities, giving you perfect peace and repose, as you are in the divine Mind.

Repose a State of Mind

Repose is a state of mind. We commonly associate it with our surroundings, and our relations. We think, "Oh, when I can get into a place where there is no more noise; when I can relax in body; when I can get off on my vacation; when I can have a change, then I shall rest and find repose." These things are but symbols of that which is the real cause of repose, the restful state of mind. All the time it is your mind that gives you the repose; even though it seems to be the bed, or a vacation, or something else external.

If the mind is not at peace, you can have weeks of vacation and be as upset and disturbed at the end as you were in the beginning. If your mind is not at peace, you can lie down upon your bed hour after hour and even go to sleep, and at the end of it you will feel as though you had had no rest. Why? Because the mind did not take hold of the idea. Yet, on the contrary, there are people who have no vacations, but who are just as fresh at the end of the day as in the morning, full of energy, resolution, full of power for work, and they never grow tired. Why? Because their minds are at peace. They love the activity, and there is nothing at cross purposes with them. The man who has been working hard all day will dance all night, but have no sense of weariness at all. His dancing was according to his mind. There was peace in it, there was a poise, there was a sense of refreshment and rest.

The Art of Decomposing

The philosopher, Delsarte, taught a way of acting and living, which he associated with thinking—so much so, that those who are the best students of this philosopher never separate the mind from an exercise, but always associate the mentality with whatever one is doing. Thus, he gives practices for what he called "decomposing"; to relax the muscles; to decompose the strained, fixed expressions, inward or outward. But the decomposing begins in your thought—in your mind—you may shake your hands, like tassels on the end of a whip-cord, but you will not decompose you wrists until your mind relaxes itself.

Practice relaxing every hour of the day, realizing that to be still is just as important as to act, that these two are to be rightly married through all your expressions —stillness and activity, rest and motion. These are to meet and associate perpetually in your life.

There are certain ways of relaxing yourself which you can practice, no matter where you ate. Let out the muscles of your face. Have you ever thought of the muscles around your mouth, your lips pressed together, oftentimes strained with thought of precision or rectitude? Relax the muscles around your eyes. Perhaps you are contracting them with the thought that the light is too strong. Realize the power of the spirit to temper the light and to take care of all your affairs.

Whenever you have opportunity, let out the muscles in your body. Perhaps you are sitting in a car, clutching your bundles, when you can just as well lay them down and loosen the muscles of your arms. Perhaps your whole body is tense, and thinking of the end of your journey you are pushing the car mentally. If you find yourself growing tense in any of your muscles, loosen them by relaxing your mind and taking the words: "Be still and know that I am God."

Have the same consciousness that the motorman has, as he sits, turns his levers and applies the power, or takes it off. He is not pushing the car, or pulling it, but he is knowing that the greater power is established and fully centralized, and he is in perfect connection with it, and all that he has to do is to turn the lever, on or off, without an effort. This is our true consciousness of ease. It brings us peace and rest and satisfaction in and about our affairs. Go on, you need have no concern about anything.

The Power of Silence

The great philosophy of this silence is that there is in you a mighty nothing, a quietness that has been from the great forever and always will be. It is the master of goodness, that still place, that Holy of Holies. It is your power of abandonment, your child-likeness, and in that, it rests, waiting for you to move. It is a mighty vacuum that causes all motion but in itself does not move. Oh, that being nothing—nothing of yourself! When that feeling of having so much to do, of being so important, and you must do things or they will not be done, rises up, about that time let go and enter into your own sweet nothingness. Stop thinking. You can do it. Just remember there is a power to stop thinking, and if suddenly you should find your mind a blank, know then, you are practicing the perfect concentration of repose.

Practice not thinking, non-thinking. Practice being nothing—especially when you feel like asserting yourself. Be like the mirror, as to your human mentality. The mirror is nothing of itself, but it can take in all things. The mirror is a marvelous symbol. In the religion of Japan, the Shinto religion, they have only two symbols in their temples; one is a mirror, the other a bell. The mirror is the nothing, the wonderful nothing, by which God is reflected.

To be a perfect reflector, a mirror must be still. If you wish to see yourself in a mirror and it is moving back and forth all the time, you have to take hold of it and steady it, in order to get a good reflection. So with your mentality. In order to reflect your Godhead you must be still. True, the mirror must also be clean, it must be true. There are other things besides stillness; nevertheless, even the mentality, to be true and clean, must be well controlled and well trained—you must hold it still and steady.

The Christ-Door, the Nothing

"I am the door," said the Master. A door is useful as an entrance, through being nothing. We commonly call that which closes up, "the door," but the door is the empty space; and a door, to be perfect, must be unobstructed—an unobstructed entrance. So, when the Christ says, "I am the door," he is referring to that power of being nothing.

When you are perfectly still, you feel the nothingness; you are not thinking; you cannot even feel your body. There are certain of you that have experienced this lightness when there was a loss of the sense of being a body, of being a personality, and then came the great cosmic consciousness. You entered the universal. You did not lose consciousness. You gained the great consciousness, beside which the other seems trivial. If you could be perfectly still as to your human thinking, then the great divine consciousness would be your thinking and your life forever.

It was so with Tennyson. He could enter into cosmic consciousness by centering himself upon his own name and losing all thought of the little self. He entered into the great Idea for which his name stands. He saw only the great immortal self, and he describes it as losing all consciousness of being a body or a personality, a little man among things. It was an entering into the universal mind, feeling himself the whole mind; knowing all things without beginning of time and without limitation of space.

"BE STILL BEFORE GOD AND LET HIM MOULD THEE"

III. *Self-Control*

Let us unite in silence with these words: "I, if I be lifted up from the earth, will draw all unto me." These are the words of Jesus Christ spoken from the central I. For this I to be lifted up from the earthy thoughts, the earthy associations, is to lift up all the thoughts so that they work for peace and not pain, for harmony and not discord. So we take the statement as our very own: *"I, if I be lifted up from the earth, will draw all unto me."*

The Three Bonds Broken

The Hindu philosophers are among the deepest students of psychology, understanding the subjective nature so well, that we can take their description of the bonds that hold and rule unregenerate humanity, as sufficiently reliable, for our inquiry into concentration.

Let us briefly review the three great causes of the mortal manifestation. The first of the three bonds that hold humanity is the quality of dullness, deadness, torpor, drifting, blankness, ignorance. It is the lack of knowledge—inertia, laziness. It is that which causes us to drift along the old lines and take no step progressively, the *Tamas* quality. It is back of laziness—whether physical, mental or spiritual.

The second quality is just the opposite—passion, that which causes great action, hurrying, struggling, striving, worrying, agitation and disturbance in general, the passionate quality, *Rajas.*

And the third quality, *Sattvas,* is that which is counted the best in us, that of which we may be proud, that which is self-assertive, self-righteousness, that in which we feel that we are good. It is called the goodness of the race and by other good names, such as virtue, enlightenment, knowledge, etc. Nevertheless it acts as a bond with people who claim reward; that think they have earned a right to good things. They may be bound by that feeling, and perhaps filled with self-righteous pity or self-excuses from the basis of their righteousness. They may feel themselves wronged and misunderstood, and suffer from sensitiveness and, worst of all, from egotism, for there is where the ego stands, the I of us; which, seeing from a personal standpoint, believes itself to be the good.

Now, according to the psychology of the Hindus, these three bonds must be broken. The sages among them have learned that they are not broken by violence, but by knowledge; knowing the nature of them, that they are delusion, that they are not real, but are shadows and reflections. They have no real strength and no real place, and by the mind keeping single to the Real back of each, their substance and strength in the Spirit, they can be surmounted and used for the Highest.

Repose Not Inertia Nor Laziness

The Real of the *Tamas* quality is the power of repose, of being still and poised and quiet, that of resting in the Lord. Sometimes people condemn that passivity and quietness, and call it by unregenerate names through not understanding it. Let us learn that persons may sit with folded hands, apparently having nothing to engage their action, and yet not be lazy, but be bringing forth a great and wonderful stillness which is back of all the moving of activity. It is the power behind the throne, what the mystic Eckhart calls, "that immobility by which all things are moved," and we must learn to cultivate that righteous stillness.

Certain active things may carry out the *Tamas* quality, such as being busy doing nothing or foolishness; much talking that is only chatter; a dullness and conventionality that is simply a drifting along with the rest of the race. A number of our activities arise from the thought that we must 'be doing something all of the time, because of this belief that if we are not doing something we are lazy. Yet in this we are wrong, for there is a virtue in not doing, which we must take hold upon for repose. If you find your fingers twitching, that you are chattering and talking too much—about that time, relax and be still.

If we come under the accusation of laziness from ourselves or from others, let us enter into the repose of our spirit and realize that we are not lazy, that in truth, we are not lacking in energy. Our sweet stillness is more powerful and a greater cause of manifestation, than much of the activity round about us that has no principle in it.

The Great Self in Control

Who is the self that controls and what is that which is controlled? Again, the Hindus teach us:

"Upraise the self by the self; do not sink the self. For the self is the friend of the self, and even the self is the enemy of the self." (Bhagavad Gita)

Raise, uplift, or "upraise" the self by the self; self-control is control of the self by the Self. Divinity says, "I control myself." The Self that controls is God in the Highest, and the self that is being controlled is that appearance which is called ourselves, but which is only the shadow or the reflection of the Great Self.

There is no one that should control you but yourself, and in truth, there has never been any one controlling you but yourself. If you think that others have controlled you, there is something that has consented to it within you; that is, blindly and weakly consented because there was, to your ignorance, no way out of it, or else you have knowingly consented at the time, even though you afterwards desired to recall your consent.

Therefore, begin with yourself and speak the truth: "I am the one, that controls myself. I am the only one that controls myself."

Soon you will prove that you can no longer ascribe things in your life to anything or anybody outside yourself. Declare, "I am my own Master and I rule myself," and be delivered from the apparent influence of circumstances and people and other outside things.

World Mastery

You begin with your own feelings and thoughts, and see them as your little selves to be ruled by your dominant Self, and controlling this *microcosm* or little world, you will exercise your true Control upon the outer world, as yourself enlarged, realizing the *macrocosm* to be yours as well as the microcosm.

But this ruling yourself is by love not by force, with knowledge not in ignorance. It is the second quality that we meet with this power of self-control, the *Rajas* quality, or the passions that seem so active and disturbing. These are to be put into their right place and become subject to ourselves. So we guard against our feelings running away with us; against being confused by the desires and passions of others. Because we have found control over ourselves and our own feelings and thoughts, we cannot be interfered with by the feelings and thoughts of others.

Ruling the Passions

The passions, that are counted the most influential in disturbing one's peace, are anger, lust, and hatred. If one will take up these three and put them into their right place by finding the reality of them, and see to it that everything which springs from evil, or the belief in evil, is put under foot, then we shall have broken the bond of that *Rajas* quality which was interfering with our perfect concentration. You know that when you are agitated, disturbed, or begin to feel the passions of others stealing over you—you are not in the peace and poise of perfect concentration.

And it is for you, in the midst of the storm, when things seem to be going against you and there is a rising in you of passion from the uncontrolled nature, to prove yourself master and keep your peace. The way to do this is to begin to understand and control these primitive passions.

First of all, we must take the right stand or viewpoint of these passions. We must not condemn our selves when we have repented of our false ways, no matter what we have done. It matters not where you find yourself, or what perverted passions are controlling you, the moment you discover the condition, it can be brought under control if you will not condemn yourself. Condemning yourself is confusing and weakening.

No Self-Condemnation

Never condemn in yourself what you do not condemn in any one else. You will have the same fruit for yourself that you deal out to others. "With what measure you mete" to others, you will measure to yourself. And whatever attitude you wish others to take toward you, practice it toward others. So, when you find criticism rising within you and you are losing your repose—your feelings are being disturbed on account of the actions and words of others—take warning. Bring yourself quickly to yourself. "Come to yourself" and remember that "there is now no condemnation to them that are in Christ Jesus"— neither condemnation of self nor condemnation of others. So long as we condemn others there is an entering wedge of self-condemnation, and sometimes there is nothing so powerfully bitter and withering as one's own criticism of oneself. Better can you bear the sting of the tongues of others than you can the criticism of yourself. Saints have been spoiled by it in their realization of the kingdom of heaven here. They have thought it right to put the stripes upon their own backs, torment themselves, turn the screws tighter, so long as it was their own bodies that suffered, and they have spent a whole lifetime keeping themselves out of the kingdom of heaven, which "as for them and into which they could have entered, if they had not justified this false position."

One way for you to cease from condemnation is to remember that it is not your real self which you condemn, but your shadow or representation, that personality which you call yourself, upon which you have been willing to put your divine I AM. It is to be cared for as tenderly as your little babes; with the same mercy and kindness with which you look after your beast of burden, for it is the vehicle of your life, and it cannot do well if you are at enmity with it. If you are finding fault with it, forgetting it, hating it and mistreating it, all because it is your own, from the feeling "I can do with my own as I choose," what better are you than one who mistreats his wife, or the mother who misuses her child from that same standpoint?

Be Merciful to Yourself

Bless yourself and do not curse it; uplift, do not degrade it; do not make it your slave, but your good servant. Servants cannot do their best when one is finding fault with them all the time. So, see to it that you look at this which has been called the carnal nature, the mortal mind, with kindly eyes, tolerant and generous, and best of all, with knowledge.

If an animal is natural, you don't condemn it. You simply say it is an animal, and animals will always act that way. So you should see your carnal nature. As long as it is not open to the spiritual overshadowing, it will act its own natural self from its own natural basis, and should not be whipped nor condemned on account of it. But, you may say, it ought to know the law, and be obedient.

Paul says, "The carnal mind or natural man receiveth not the things of God and is not subject to the law of God, neither indeed can be." (Cor. 2:14 and Rom. 8:7). Well, if it cannot, why punish it? Why find fault with it? Why condemn it? Be wise. See that nature as it is, and instead of finding fault with it, help it. For truly your carnal nature wants your happiness, wants to be abiding in the peace of your higher nature, and it is your privilege to instruct it on its own plane continually and to exact obedience. And when you see that it repents, that it wishes it had not done that, then let it not accuse itself nor condemn itself, but be at peace.

Not Destruction Nor Suppression

Do not think to have control over your passions by destroying them. You cannot destroy the life of your passions. "Kill out desire" are words, which spring from the belief that the kingdom of heaven can be seized by violence, but the truth is, you never can kill anything, not even "desire." If you think you can kill you are deceived and you will have to do your work over again. So, we do not think of *destroying* our passions, neither on the other hand, of suppressing them, for there are people who have a certain amount of self-control through suppressing themselves. Sometimes they suffer great distress through crowding back their desires until they are like a mighty dynamo of power. Sometimes there follows a bursting, an explosion—a lawless act through a mighty desire for freedom and a crashing fall of a nature overborne with ascetic restraint.

Transmutation

No, transmute your desires. Lift them up to the spirit and have the spirit take hold of them. Transmute them through the renewing of your mind. The anger that you have held back and crowded down, suppressing your words, pressing your lips together, and yet justifying; the cause of your anger will one day burst out in words most painful, if you do not take it in charge and give it to the spirit. Give no place to righteous indignation—not given as the wrath of God, for there is no such thing. That is a figment of the imagination, making God in the image of the mortal—an idol which men have bowed down to, content in their own lack of peace and power through justifying the wrath of God. There is no place for anger in love, and so, if you find this rising even in the slightest, give it over to the Spirit. Say some little words, like *"Thou only"* or pray a prayer. Realizing that fear of anger within you, you begin to give it over to divine love. Love takes it. Love uses it. Do not try to think anything else until that old form of "righteous indignation" begins to pass away.

And so with lust. When thoughts that you have counted impure, and desires which you have felt to be unregenerate and unclean rise within you, instead of being filled with self-condemnation, or the false thought that those desires must be gratified because of the ignorant teaching of the world, take hold of the passion and lift it up to God. Whenever you feel the accusation of being impure, immediately hold, "I am pure! I am pure!" Thus will you use this mighty passion for rising to spiritual heights; for getting joy in the life of regeneration; for the mastery over yourself.

In the same way, if you have a revengeful and hateful feeling and a memory of wrongs, and if malice tries to impose itself upon you, remember *to pray the Lord's Prayer,* "Forgive us our debts as we forgive our debtors." Say, "I let all my feelings be used by the Spirit of Love, by the Almighty God, and no revengeful, hard or bitter thought of hatred can work through me." This is the stand to take, instead of crowding things back and suppressing them, as though they were realities, and ready to burst forth at any moment.

Counter-Thoughts

We remember that the transforming is all done from the mind, from the inner nature, "Be ye transformed by the renewing of your mind." Some have used certain external practices such as holding the breath. Controlling the breath reads upon the thought, for the breath moves with the thought, and acts by reflection or "reflex action" upon the mentality. Some of these practices have been good up to a certain point, but eventually it is the mind that does the work. Even when you control your breath.

These are aids, but they have their limitations. There are other aids, ways of counteracting these thoughts, feelings, words and deeds by setting up counteracting thoughts. Thus, when one is being stirred by sonic passion, which naturally would burst forth in violent words or rough actions, one can say, sing, or do something gentle and harmonious. There are some people who, when angered easily slam doors and throw things. If you feel like stomping your foot, (and probably you justify it, it seems so harmless), put that foot down gently.

You who would have perfect control over yourself and always be poised and full of power and peace, manage your mortal nature as a man manages a horse or art engine, or whatever he wills. Use all the devices that come into your mind to get the upper hand of your passionate nature. Remember that passion is not evil in itself.

Texts and Mantrams

The committing of verses and *mantrams* and reciting them is one of the outward ways to aid in concentration. The Hindu call them mantrams; we call them texts. There are some that have a pacifying effect and bring a realization very quickly of the control exercised by your divine self. Take a single thought and raise it above your other thoughts, like a Moses in the wilderness raised up to head the children of Israel out of the old slavery into the land of eternal freedom and happiness. I know one who took "*Thou only*" as her statement, and every time she found herself having thoughts and feelings that were not desirable she would say, "*Thou only.*"

There are those who have taken "*Thy Will is done in me,*" with the result of giving up the human will and knowing there is but one will working in and through them. Some take the twenty-third Psalm, others the Lord's Prayers. Whatever appeals to you, in verses or single words, use them as Leaders about which to gather your wayward and scattered thoughts.

If you love this life and are pursuing it all the time, some Truth is always presenting itself and you can have a variety in your spiritual diet. As I have said before, whoever is living this life, uplifting others and talking truth, is concentrating without an effort, and I must continually call your attention to this way—this effortless way *of loving truth for its* own sake, for when you are in love with truth, you cannot help but think of it night and day, and thus the power of concentration becomes as natural to you as your breath.

IV. *Concentration in the Daily Life*

Let us unify in silence, taking with us the word of power found in Zachariah 4:6. 'Not by might nor by power, but by my spirit, saith the Lord of Hosts.'

We understand that the "might" spoken of here and the "power" refers to the human will and mere external power. This statement is one of the very best to bring you to the consciousness of effortless concentration, that you do all things, not by might nor by power, but by My Spirit, saith the Lord of Hosts or Forces.

Leader Thoughts

By way of review, I will remind you that in entering into concentration whether for a few moments or a regular half hour or more, it is well to have a leading thought just as in the gathering together of people, a leader is most essential—not that the leader is superior necessarily, but is simply good as a leader

There are spiritual thoughts that appeal to you and certain thoughts do not; again, there are times when the same thought will appeal to you much more than at other times. Select your leading thought by that divine sense within; you will know when you have found the right word or the right statement by the same sense of satisfaction that you have when you taste anything and it tastes just right. It is the same with the Scriptures, that the mind "trieth words, as the mouth tasteth meat." Thus we try sentences—words of truth—and accept certain statements at the time as the very best to hold. That which we have just held in the silence, "Not by might nor by power, but by my spirit, saith the Lord of Hosts," is an excellent leader almost any time.

Illustration: Overcoming Worriment

And this is what I mean by taking a leading thought. You may sit down full of worriment, of belief that there is so much to do and so little time to do it in and that much effort is necessary. Then that thought of not by effort "but by my spirit, saith the Lord," dropped among the other thoughts about the necessity of effort and rush and confusion, will pacify and quiet, and give you rest by its cool, calming realization, so essential to do the things necessary to be done in the time that you have.

What is true of Worriment in its character of distraction and confusion, might be said of fear and other perverted passions, like jealousy and hatred. But we will not dwell upon these as positive things—no evil thought is positive. Sometimes one gets an idea about evils, that they are so real and have so much power, that they so interfere and spoil things, that that very thought is followed by panic. A person is almost afraid to be afraid and worries about worrying. Put away that suggestion this moment by realizing that all these evil thoughts are mere negations, mere emptiness. They have no real power in themselves, only as they are emphasized. Some metaphysicians have so enlarged upon the power of evil thinking that they have made a new devil. I have heard many people say that they would rather believe in the old-fashioned kind of a devil than this kind, known as "m. a. m."—or "malicious animal magnetism."

It is for us to prove that such influence has no real power, no real place.

Emptiness of Error-Thoughts

Let us take up these things in the right way as nothingness; worriment is negation, fear is a kind of emptiness. Fill in the place of these negatives (worriment or fear) the opposite thoughts which are positive. Here you will need to use discretion and discernment to select your opposite thought, but the mere act of feeling after God, the seeking of the Word, is itself beneficial. The very attempt to find the opposite sometimes will do the work—just the attempt.

Perhaps, whenever you have thought of a certain person you have had a sweep of hatred go over you, and you have justified it. You felt you had done right to hate that person for he had been the embodiment of wickedness and vice; there was no good in him. You had made up your mind that he didn't even have a soul and there was nothing to save about him, and he might as well be out of the world as in it. I am describing something that may not apply to any of you, but there are a great many people who think that way. They dwell upon the thing so long *that they justify murder, and then someone is killing somebody else.*

You have come into the Truth, and if you have had an old hatred for some people, now you have learned to dismiss them from your mind, for they were so uncomfortable to think about. You have learned that you cannot hold them altogether evil, but then you sometimes justify hating the sin because you think that God hates sin, and that wrath against sin is legitimate. But in love, there is no hatred at all. God is love, and love knows no wrath, knows no hatred, not for one second. Therefore there is nothing in hating sin; sin is nothing; what is there to hate?

You reason with yourself and this reasoning is good. It takes you from that distracting thought, that dividing, breaking, insane thought of hatred. For hatred leads to insanity. So when that person comes into mind, you should know a thought that neutralizes the old one of hatred—something just opposite to hatred.

Exercise by the Audience

By way of exercise let all this audience think upon an opposite thought to hatred.

Audience: "Love."

Speaker: Perhaps you start with love: "I love you. Love is the only presence and the only power."

It sounds, perhaps, like a lot of words; you don't want to spoil your thought about love, so you drop it.

"It is a little too much," perhaps you are thinking; "I don't see how I ever can love that one."

Then some other thought had better be introduced.

Audience: "Tolerance."

Speaker: "I will be tolerant." Perhaps you take a little pride in it. Perhaps *charity* would be better. You are beginning to climb. Charity. Yes, perhaps I can find some excuse. There is a kind of mildness about that charity. It works. Perhaps you begin to find your word empty. Then you think *peace,* and you grow a little less agitated. Every time that image rises and the thought of hatred and the old sense of justifying it, you say, "Tolerance, Charity, Peace," and you lead up to "Love." Soon you find yourself saying, "God is Love. Love in me forgives;" and you go on in power, and presently you can speak the whole truth, for you are large enough to understand the old mortal mind, its nature, and why it acted that way, and you have come to your peace.

Let us continue this exercise. Supposing that you find yourself full of fear and you are agitated. Now fear is a negation. Give me some opposite word.

Audience: "Faith!" "Confidence!" "Assurance!" "Courage!" "Trust!"

Trust is a very good word. Now give me something the opposite to jealousy.

Audience: "Confidence!" "Understanding!"

You understand what I mean. Every one of these evil things are like emptiness; that is all. And you need only to take the opposite—the opposite which *appeals* to you at the time—to begin and fill in that emptiness.

Concern About Tomorrow

Sometimes you are under a pressure to fill in with the substance of faith for a demonstration that is coming. You find yourself worrying tonight about tomorrow. You don't know what you are going to do tomorrow, and in the old days, you would lie upon your pillow and keep awake thinking:

"What can I do? Where shall I go? What is the next step?" and perhaps remain awake all night or, if you fell asleep, you would awake exhausted, still with that awful sense of fear and worriment, feeling you had not slept at all.

What is the meaning of it? You need more faith. You are going to have a special demand for the manifestation of your prosperity or protection. Therefore begin to radiate this substance, faith, and meet that thought of worriment with:

"I trust in the great principle of my life. I trust in the All-Good, working in and through my life. My Good is coming to me. I know what to do. I always do the right thing. I speak the right words. I am inspired." Words like that, until you fall asleep. You will wake in the morning without a sense of burden, with a wonderful calm and peace. Why? Because last night you laid up treasures in heaven.

The landlady comes in for her rent—suppose this was the coming demonstration which was to be made. You are able to face her with, "Will you wait a little while?" There is such a confidence in your voice that she says, "Very well!" Then in some unlooked for way, *as surely as you laid up substance the night before for a manifestation of it at the right time, the money comes. This is the way it works. We have seen it again and again.*

Concentrating Where You Are

In this talk I am taking up concentration in the daily life, right where you are—not in some other place or among other people, or by yourself. Where you find yourself, there you are to know concentration, self-control, poise, self-possession, peace and power. The old idea that we must go to a nunnery or to some secluded spot in a mountain, or be by ourselves before we can get control and be at peace we must dismiss.

It is true, you will have moments when you can go to "The Secret Place," and you must recognize such; even though it be only five minutes, you must thank God for that, when you can get off by yourself and hush everything. It may not come until you are at the point of retiring at night, but take advantage of it and thank God that you can be still and forget everything for two minutes. It is enough. Such a minute is "like unto the grain of mustard seed." If you can have the Sabbath-consciousness for one minute in the day, it can solve the whole problem of concentration. "Remember the Sabbath to keep it holy." Remind yourself that you have that minute. Don't say, "I have no time for concentration, for meditation." You might as well say, "I have no time to be useful." You have all the time there is and you can do with it what you will.

In the busy life we learn to concentrate by using the things that we are passing through, which we are contacting, as suggestions of concentration. Whatever you are employed in must be a means of suggestion to you of some spiritual thought of power and goodness which you desire to realize.

The Practice of the Presence of God

There is a little book that I would recommend to you, called *"The Practice of the Presence of God."* It is one of the very best treatments for concentration that has passed down to us. It is over two hundred years old, but it is just as meaty, just as full of substance as it ever was.

It is about a man, who was a lay brother in the Catholic Church, who had not become a monk because he felt too humble even to apply for such advancement, but was content to act as servant. He entered a monastery to do the cooking, the common work. But he had had a touch of the cosmic consciousness, insight of heaven, and he never forgot it. He learned that he could commune with God at other times besides the stated hours when he entered into the form of prayer. He became very familiar with the Divine Presence and it instructed him so that he learned to do everything he did for the Lord. He said if he picked up a straw off the ground, he did it for the Lord. He tells us that "the best rule of a holy life is to practice the presence of God." This means that there is nothing to recognize but the *Divine One in everybody; that there is nothing but peace; nothing but purity; nothing but blessings.*

Practice the presence of your Good. Thus learning to see divinity in and through all things, nothing is impure or unclean to you. Like the poet Herbert, you can pray:

> "Teach me, my God and King,
> In all things thee to see.
> And what I do in anything
> To do it as for thee."

George Herbert was inspired, and it is such things as that that make him dear to us. Truth that he saw over one hundred years ago is just as true today.

Practice the presence of God—in that poor, old woman that you are waiting upon; that miserable man, fault-finding, and unkind, that you are serving. These can become divine in your sight and you can realize that you serve the Lord in them—the spirit in them. That very thought will transform her, and she will grow sweet and patient; and he will begin to be kind and considerate, such is the power of right thought. And when this takes place, you will have known a richness and sweetness in your life that cannot be described in words; you concentrate without any trouble; nothing can distract you. Nothing can move you from your peace when you do everything for the Spirit, and let the Spirit in you do it.

Spiritual Housekeeping

In the little book which I have written on *Spiritual Housekeeping,* I give the spiritual meaning of the daily life of the housekeeper and show how each day can be a suggestion of some manifestation of the spirit. I take you through the seven days, and many of the points that I have given you in this course on concentration will be found in this book.

Monday is for water—Freedom; Tuesday for fire—Love; Wednesday for sewing—Creation; Thursday for general individual work—Grace; Friday for sweeping—Purity, and Saturday for baking, and finishing work—Perfection; and Sunday has its own sweet Peace, the word of satisfaction and rest. Each day can bring forward these divine qualities in yourselves. Perhaps it will mean overcoming that impatience; putting away that temper that upsets things so easily; that besetting sin put under foot, as you know yourself and know what it is that distracts you. You will work with that until you walk at peace with yourself.

Your Special Business

While a person might take that little book upon concentration and see one's self a housekeeper, inasmuch as you are keeping this house— your body, and you are a housekeeper, no matter what you appear to be,—yet some of us would like to be specific as to the business we are in; to know the thought to hold in *order to let that business, which perhaps is disliked by you, be a suggestion as to how you can think and feel while, perhaps, the one* is *calling you to do this, and another that is giving you another piece of work and you feel you must push and pull and give all your strength and knowledge to things material and foreign to the spirit.*

Therefore, let us consider some of the business pursuits that men are in. I know one man that was a carpenter, who was well advanced in the power of concentration; every time he built a house, he thought, "Every nail I drive home, I drive a spiritual thought home, such as 'now the truth sets you free,'" etc. He was talking silently to somebody all during his work or sending out his word in a general way, and he was full of activity and spiritual thoughts, quick to see and full of business alertness and efficiency.

Thus the man in the shop or the real estate dealer, or the promoter can find that each one of these things has a correspondence in the spirit which he can learn by saying often, in his heart, "I am about my Father's business. I am here to do the work of the spirit, and to do divine work."

If he is a promoter, for instance, what is he really promoting? He is promoting the good of humanity; promoting opportunities for individuality to express itself; for the spirit to work through these bodies; to manifest to the greatest advantage to everybody with *whom he comes in contact, not merely promoting his own purse.*

Attracting Your Own

Taking this spiritual position, a man draws to him the very people that should be opened up interiorly. They are ready and waiting, and as truly as those, who have come to this lecture today, have come by the spiritual law, so every man who puts his business under the spiritual law will draw to himself men that mean business, that will not trifle, men that are able, that have substance, that are prosperous and desire what he has to give.

He will draw men that will not try to exploit him, for he is not trying to exploit men. The very best people will be his customers, for they will be like what he thinks about. It may seem at first a slow movement and somewhat mixed, but he will know why because he himself is going on slowly in this spiritual life, and more or less mixed in his thoughts.

This is the way the business life will teach the gospel, will carry it everywhere, and the man who fills himself with spiritual thoughts, no matter what he is engaged in, radiates prosperity and helpfulness, has poise and power and "prospers in whatsoever he puts his hands to." He is inspired and inspires others, being a living Word of God to unite earth with heaven, and usher in the millennial age.

V. *Concentration Through Devotion*

Now let us join in silence, taking the first words of the Psalm 103:

"Bless the Lord, 0 my soul; and all that is within me, bless his holy name."

Most excellent words to remember whenever you have occasion to drop into the Silence. When, perhaps, no other words can come to your mind, these will center you quickly, not by merely wording them, but through realizing their meaning.

We know that the Lord of all needs no blessing from us. Nothing can be added to, nor taken from, the great divine One. But it is everything to your soul to express itself towards this One in the form of blessing, for when you begin to praise the divine One you center yourself and get into the poise, the peace, and the power that belong to right concentration. We are remembering that the Lord is the Good in all and working through all, and to remind yourself of this Good and to be devoted to it is the way of the happiest concentration.

"Bless the Lord, O my soul; and all that is within me"—the demand is not only upon the soul, but upon every faculty that is within you, your mentality, your feeling nature, as well as your soul consciousness. *All* that is within me, bless his holy name—his holy nature—his whole, pure, true being.

With this understanding let us repeat these words in the silence and rest in the spirit of the Holy One.

The Power of Blessing

One of the easiest ways to concentrate in your daily life is mentally to bless everything and everybody. And it is not merely a matter of the lips, for when you speak these words, especially from the heart, silently radiating them, you are transforming people. You are transforming things. You are removing the curse and giving everybody and everything opportunity to express themselves in the best way.

If there is anything that is especially cursing you, bless that until you find its meaning, what it is prompting you, or pressing you to manifest, and thus discover the divinity in everything; that all things are working together for good to them that love the Lord. There is nothing that seems to worry and irritate you, and to cross and oppose you, but what is an instrument in the divine hands to bring forward something right and beautiful, fine and noble that lies in your nature waiting to be expressed. Instead of being irritated and feeling at cross-purposes and upset, thus losing your power of concentration, let nothing defeat or overcome you, but make everything an opportunity for rising and expressing more of your divine self, more the conqueror and captain of your soul.

"Bless them that curse you" was the divine direction, "that ye may be the child of your Father which is in heaven, for He is kind unto the unthankful and the evil." This is the divine character and whoever takes upon himself the divine method and nature is in a masterly control, the power of concentration that is back of the universe.

Healing and Being Healed

Everybody and everything that comes into your life is there for one of two reasons and generally both—*either to be healed or to heal you*—and I am not speaking of disease alone, except in the broadest sense of the word. Disease from "dis" and "ease," means lack of ease, lack of comfort, uncomfortable, and whatever brings discomfort to you could be called disease, whether it is poverty or sorrow, vice or chronic sickness. Whatever is of discomfort comes under the category of disease and can be healed, and your healing is your whole being made whole, holy, hearty, healthy. Everything and everybody is in your life either to press you into more of holiness, or for you to draw out of them more of this holiness or wholeness.

Therefore we learn not to run away from things, not to resist people, not to grow impatient and fret, but to transform, redeem, wholly save, uplift and bless. Just as soon as you have done that, the thing or person changes or passes out of your daily life; they cannot irritate you; they cannot trouble you. Although they may still appear in your life, they only feel harmony toward you and have nothing but blessing for you, when you have fulfilled your part towards them. But if you run away or in other ways try to escape, because they seem so evil, you simply put off the day of salvation, that is all. You must take it up in some future form because of your wrong belief about it.

As long as you believe a thing to be evil that very belief draws that experience into your life until your belief is healed, and you know there is no reality to the evil, that the good is all there really is.

The Way of Devotion

All this is part of the devotion which is one with concentration, because it comes from the love of truth, because you love the true Life, the Source of all good. You love the All Good, you love to express good and are devoted to it, and the first thing you know, you are quite self-possessed, poised and peaceful, and you have never thought about concentration.

The Hindus call concentration "Yoga," and concentration by devotion, Bhakti Yoga. According to their teaching there are four paths which the devotee of right concentration, or "union with God," can take: the path called Bhakti Yoga or the heart way, through loving without reasoning about it, only devoting your whole heart to God; the second way, Raja Yoga, wherein the soul and its psychic powers are given over to devotion, the aspirations and all that is spiritual in us being devoted to the one God; the third, Gnana Yoga, or giving the whole mind, making the union with God through giving all the reasoning or intellect; and the fourth, the way of our strength, our works, called Karma Yoga, wherein one gives one's self to serving the Spirit in our works, doing everything for the Lord, giving all our strength to this Divine One.

The Way of Jesus Christ

"But behold, I show you a more excellent way" than these four, and that is a combination of the four, as described in Jesus' presentation of the first of all the Commandments: "Thou shalt love the Lord thy God with all thy *heart,* and with all thy *soul* and with all thy *mind* and with all thy *strength.* "You take the four: heart, soul, mind and strength and devote every one of them to the Spirit of the Lord. Obeying and fulfilling this commandment, you concentrate wherever you are. You are at peace. You are poised. You are free. It matters not what comes to you. This is the power of devotion.

The Convent of Perpetual Adoration

Those who go to nunneries and monasteries have certain practices of devotion which continually recall them from distraction. We read in Victor Hugo's Les Miserables about the nuns of the Convent of the Perpetual Adoration, that they were reminded of the Holy Life every half hour by the ringing of a bell. Then it mattered not what they were doing, or how much they were engaged at that moment, every nun ceased and repeated over an Ave Maria or other prayer.

Oftentimes the ring came in the midst of a conversation which was causing a nun to be disturbed, distracted and resisting within herself, but they all dropped their eyes as the bell sounded and repeated over the words, that reminded them of the One of whom they were to think perpetually. You can imagine that sometimes, when a nun was losing her temper, she turned within to the quiet place and was immediately poised; that one, perhaps, was beginning to engage in some foolish occupation or conversation, then she was reminded and quickly came to herself. The description is very beautiful of the Convent of Perpetual Adoration, and there is something very high, and strong and noble in this method which commends itself to us, though we do not need to go to convents or monasteries in order to get control of ourselves.

Our Convent-Bell

Certain things in your experience can remind you of your deep Self just as that bell reminded those nuns. Is there something in your life that annoys you? Somebody is continually drumming on the table; or when that one is practicing you begin to get worked up? Let that state be *the bell* and repeat these words: "Bless the Lord, O my soul and all that is within me, bless his holy name."

Perhaps you have been thinking you have no control over yourself as you listen to that practicing, and you will have to complain to the landlord; yet you want to give that person liberty to live in his or her way. Let that practicing be the bell to remind you, that now is the moment of your peace and nothing can move you, as you repeat these words, *"Bless the Lord O my soul and all that is within me bless his holy name."*

The Value of Prayer

It was that man might have this control and self-mastery, to be ready and alert for any emergency in his earthly experiences, that Jesus gave the teaching: *"Pray without ceasing, pray always."* When we consider prayer in its highest meaning, we see that we can be praying continually by reminding ourselves of the All-Good in everything and in everybody. Learn to enter into your closet, retire within yourself and shut the door of the senses. Learn to speak to your Father in secret and your Father in secret will answer you openly. Thus the Master describes the way of prayer.

Meditate upon Emerson's description of prayer, for it also covers the whole ground and is as inspiring as those words of Jesus Christ. Here is Emerson's definition:

"Prayer is the contemplation of the facts of life from the highest point of view; it is the soliloquy of a beholding and jubilant soul; it is the spirit of God pronouncing his work good."

It is a beautiful exposition of prayer, and it takes you from the mere externals into, and up through, your own soul to your Godhood—body, soul and spirit. If you contemplate the facts of life perpetually from the highest point of view, you are ever in prayer according to Emerson. If you lift up your joys into the high places of the soul, then anything that you do, whether you dance or sing, whether you play cards or you run and leap in the sports of the field—your soul can be jubilant, can be talking with God, and there is nothing but what can become a holy action, and a pure and true pastime, as you let your soul uplift it. Prayer is the finishing power and benediction upon the creation of God. It is God in you pronouncing His work good.

Our Desires One With Prayer

Through devotion, all your desires can be turned into declarative power, blessing God that it is so, declaring your desire to be fulfilled now. Sometimes our desires distract us, we are wishing so hard for something and fearing disappointment lest it will not come out just as we want it, and then there is agitation and disturbance. Give all your desires to the Spirit. See that everything—every single desire—is a prayer, and learn to bless God that it is now come to pass. "I thank thee, Father, that thou hast heard me," said Jesus at the tomb of Lazarus, before the work of raising him from the dead was accomplished. Learn to say, *"It is so, it is so, it is so," for every wish of your heart*, and then do not trouble yourself about it but when you see it come to pass, acknowledge it and be glad. So shall you pray the prayer of the righteous man—the right-thinking man—and your devotion, your "prayer without ceasing" be a perpetual accomplishment.

Those who will remember to declare their wishes already come to pass are placing themselves as the instruments of God to benefit this whole world. There comes a wishing that is so righteous and good that is such a blessing for everybody, that when you are wishing for anything, you are simply voicing God's desire. Then you must take the next step for its accomplishment. Declare it is so. It is done now. It is finished. It is, already.

Character, the Garden of the Lord

We are returning to Eden through this devotion that Eden described in the first chapters of Genesis— the plenty of the Lord. Every time you "contemplate the facts of life from the highest point of view" you are cultivating that garden of the Lord within you, your blissful state, and your union with God. You can bring forward that Eden-consciousness by simply remembering it, putting fresh plants into it and cultivating it. If there be weeds in it, fears, doubts or unspirituality, or a serpent still among the trees of subtle suggestion, of something else beside God's good, it is in your power to lift that serpent up, and to redeem the weeds. As Emerson says, "A weed is only a flower whose use has not been found." When you have unworthy thoughts or suggestions that do not belong to the Eden peace, instead of finding fault with yourselves, by saying, "How can I have such thoughts?" rise up and give them to the Spirit, and declare the truth, "I am pure, I am true, I am divine," and your weeds will come under the hand of a spiritual Burbank, who knows how to find use for weeds and to cultivate the best in all.

Seed Thoughts

One way to practice concentration is to see thoughts as seeds and, if you desire certain thoughts, take them and deliberately plant them in your mind. Some seeds you have to watch over very carefully, very tenderly, that they may root and start growing. A strong stream of water must not play upon them, because it will uproot the new plant. It will not do for the sun to come too directly upon some of these tender little plants. There is a wisdom, a marvelous good judgment in planting seeds of truth.

When you want to be healed of certain tendencies, or to develop certain traits, give the work over to the Spirit to cultivate. You will find yourself growing wise and tender and kind to yourself; not finding fault and lashing yourself, feeling that you are so far wrong; such is letting the sun beat down upon your tender plants and pouring the water upon them, when there should be a gentle spray and tender sunlight to those young thoughts, those budding trees that are just coming to their manifestation.

The Practice of Mental Planting

One way to plant these seed thoughts is described in *Primary*

Lessons in Christian Living and Healing, sixth chapter, where a method of concentration is described thus: You take a thought that you wish to cultivate. Say that you desire to manifest Faith—more Faith. Suppose you are feeling shaky about something, some position you desire; you don't know how things are going to turn out, keeping you on tender-hooks, as it were; you are not as self-possessed as you ought to be when going out to take a position, or to undertake a piece of work; you feel nervous and you see you must have more faith and more trust.

Therefore you begin to meditate upon Faith, letting that be your seed thought. It appears nothing but a word to you at first, just a dry seed and you wonder if it will amount to anything, but you proceed to plant that thought of Faith and this is the way you do it:

You mentally repeat the word seven times (I take seven because that is the perfect number). To avoid counting, you repeat it three times, and three times and then once. Then going within yourself you shut the door of the senses and repeat it in your heart:

Faith, faith, faith—faith, faith, faith—faith. Thoughts will begin to rise; you may remember certain texts of scripture; you may begin to feel stronger because it is the law that what you meditate upon you gravitate to. You begin to draw all the mentalities that are filled with faith. You are launched upon a stream of faith. You are contacting the mentalities that have confidence, strength and trust and your faith in yourself grows stronger. Some doubt falls down; some unbelief takes to itself wings. There rises up in you a new consciousness.

This may not take place at first, for sometimes your mind begins to go off into lines that have little or no connection with faith. But so long as your mind is upon a spiritual thought, you are in right meditation. The stems, leaves, branches and fruit may not look like the seed, but eventually there is a seed at the end that is just like the first. It comes as the divine promise. First the seed of the vine, *then the root, stem, branch, flower and fruit, and within the grape is the seed again, complete and perfect.*

If you find your mind going off into other channels not altogether good, bring yourself back to that first thought, just as though you were beginning again. After a while you will be able to cut off those branches that do not bear fruit, with the Word. Keep your vine growing in an orderly way and by the time you have finished your meditation, you will enter into a new consciousness of your seed-thought, whatever it was. If it was Faith, you will be the stronger and the truer and clearer in your consciousness, as to confidence and trust, and ready to express a greater faith than you have ever yet experienced.

Soul Culture

This is *soul culture*. It is fulfilling the work that Adam was created for. "And there was not a man to till the ground," so the Lord God formed man of the dust of the ground, and breathed inspiration into him and he became an immortal soul. And he was there to till the ground. This Bible story is a description of the work of the Spirit in you every day. Every day there is something in you moulded by the Divine Hands; a character coming forth from you that is spiritual, strong, intelligent, loving; and that character is there to cultivate this ground, the earth-consciousness, to till this soil and make the most of it and show it to be an Eden of God.

In your flesh you shall see God; with that body that you have now you can see all that belongs to heaven, peace, health, freedom and every good. This is what you are called to do. It is not merely a privilege, it is a commandment: "Let them have dominion over all the earth."

You are here to do the work which the spirit has given you to do, and that is to be happy, healthy, true, an angel on earth, drawing into the kingdom of heaven just as many as you possibly can. That is the glorious work that you are appointed to do.

Here, to Prove God, the Only Self

In devoting yourself to the Great Self, I would have you remember that it is not a Lord far away, nor a God in opposition to you, but the Great Heart that dwells within you. You are to love your Self, as God. This is the true interpretation of that first commandment, "Thou shalt love the Lord *thy God* with all thy heart and with all thy soul and with all thy mind and with all thy strength." But you cannot love yourself when you think it is this personality. For that is not your true Self. It sometimes seems that in this earthly ego you had taken up your enemy and were working with your enemy. That is why people hate themselves. But you must make friends with yourself, make friends with your enemies, learn to love your enemy-self in the Christ-way and you will heal it, and redeem it.

This one Self is the same God that they are bowing to in India, in China and in the isles of the sea, in the temples of our City. It is You that they worship, and it is the Self of us all, and we are to prove that we are that Self; that there is nothing to us but our great Godhood and we are to prove it in the midst of the flesh, while yet we walk humbly, meekly and in lowly spirit upon this planet.

It is not an occasion for pride, for self-glorification, nor conceit, not that state where they feel their *I Am* is the little personality; that is gross egotism, a form of insanity. No, your Great Self is the Self of the meanest as well as the highest, it is the Self of us all, whom you worship in that other personality just as well as in this, your own, and you are to face it in your neighbor. The second commandment, *"Thou shalt love thy neighbor as thyself,"* is the same as the first. Thou shalt love the Lord thy God in thy neighbor as well as in thyself.

Devote yourself to the All-Good In all. Take the idea of Eden and fulfill it in yourself; learn to contemplate the common facts of life from the highest point of view; let your soul talk to itself, a beholding and jubilant soliloquy; see that the one that we are praising in you is God, and ours is the prayer of affirmation, not beseeching but pronouncing all things good and very good.

VI. *Peace and Bliss*

Let our meditation be the closing words of Psalm 19.

There is no better book of the Bible, wherein to find leading, spiritual thoughts that are good for meditation, than the Book of Psalms. These words were studied by the old Hebrews with the understanding that they had spiritual powers which would ward off trouble and deliver from any predicament in which they might find themselves.

The words Jesus Christ spoke on the cross were almost everywhere to be found in the Psalms. His closing words, "Into thy hands I commend my spirit" are in the 31st Psalm; "My God, why hast thou forsaken me?" the first verse of the 22nd Psalm was the word that loosened up his interior from his exterior body. Death is always the ultimate expression of the sense of separation, and Jesus expressed a sense of separation from his Source and the result was death, but he entered into death only to conquer it by repudiating that thought of separation in his heart, and he rose triumphant over death.

The words which we will take today are affirmations, three-fold. "Thou wilt show me the path of life. In thy presence is fullness of joy. At thy right hand are pleasures forever more." The spirit within us is showing us the path of life; that in this great omnipresence is the fullness of joy; on the right hand or power of the Spirit are pleasures, eternal and unlimited. This was the inspiration of the Psalmist. Let us take it for ourselves.

We Make Our World

We live in a great world of our own creating, for what we meditate upon determines first of all our mental world, and this determines our outer world.

Therefore it is exceedingly important what we meditate upon, since meditations upon peace and bliss determine whether we shall walk in peace and bliss; and on the other hand, meditations upon evil may fill our whole world with evil images.

Wise are we to cease utterly and forever from meditating upon injuries; from meditating upon this little self; from meditating upon poverty. These three are important subjects to eliminate utterly from our consciousness—injuries, the little false self, and poverty. For if we meditate upon these long enough it means insanity. Meditation upon evil is disintegrating, not only distracting, but disintegrating. And if we meditate upon this little self, its injuries, its rights and so on, we develop a false ego, and as someone has said, "Insanity is egotism gone to seed." And that third meditation upon poverty lies back of many of the cases in the insane asylums. People thinking that thieves are after them, that their property has been taken from them, although they may be wealthy; that losses are crowding upon them, and that every man's hand is against them—this is unhealthy meditation, distracting and spoiling.

Therefore we take our stand to repudiate utterly all meditation upon evil or injuries or upon this little, mortal, conceited self or our poverty-ills or lack. We learn to put in their place the good, the beautiful, and the true. This Platonic trinity of the good, and the beautiful, and the true, can counteract all the false meditations that have been set up.

Memory Restored

Your memory is purified by the truth as you learn to dismiss from your mentality all memories of injury, mistakes, sins and sorrows. You deliberately forget these, that your memory may be clean and free and strong and true. It is written, "Thou shalt forget thy misery and remember it as waters that pass away." This is the divine promise and it is fulfilled in the man of right meditation.

Instead of being disturbed because you cannot remember certain dates, names, faces or other temporal, passing things, count them all nothing and you will soon find that you will easily remember just what you should. That list, that date, those evil memories are absolutely non-essential and must be forgotten sometime. Why not now? And as you cease to be agitated and do not congest your brain cells over things, they can slip into your mentality just when they should; and if you are to remember a date, you will remember it quickly; if a number, it will come in good time, and names will come quickly by not worrying over your memory.

The suggestions that you are weak or old or losing some of your faculties dismiss immediately. They are not fit companions to entertain. You did not invite them and they have intruded themselves upon you. Learn to shut the door to such thoughts and say, "I never knew you. I know you not nor whence you came." This is the power of the Christ—the Master of the House (Luke 13:25) who shuts the door upon all these things that would claim place and power in the name of your good.

No suggestion that you are losing your memory should be entertained for a moment, for it is not true. That which is to be remembered by you is there forever and you can call it up at will. This is the truth, and if you will not be deceived into believing that you are losing your memory, you will co-operate with your own Spirit so as to have *the inspired memory*— always thinking the right thing at the right time. Conscientiously dismiss all the false thoughts, the tramps, beggars and impostors that would clutter your mentality. By refusing such thinking you give room for the operation of the true thoughts. This is one of the secrets of peace, that quiet joy that belongs to one who is in the true life.

Serenity by Right Memory

Serenity is yours by right and for you to demonstrate while yet you walk in the flesh, so that no one can take your peace from you. No one can do that if you will not do it yourself. Therefore never concern yourself about remembering injuries or wrongs. Sometimes people make the mistake of taxing themselves with such thoughts as, "Now I must remember that I made a mistake that time and so not repeat it." What you are to remember is that which is not the mistake but the truth, and declare to yourself, "I must remember to walk true here, to speak right there, to act wisely always," etc. Put it into the right affirmation, not the false negative, for what you keep your eye single to, you manifest.

If, when Peter started to walk the waves (Matt 14:29, 30) he had kept his eye on the Christ and had not begun to observe the wind and the waves, he could have walked all the way. It was because he looked down at the seething water and thought of the storm that he began to sink. That was the manifestation of his limited faith, so the Master said, "Why did you doubt—O ye of little faith?"

"They who observe lying vanities, forsake their own mercies." Let us not observe lying vanities, but keep our eye single to our God at all times and under all circumstances. And so it is when we speak to warn others, little ones and people coming to ask counsel of us. Learn to draw their attention to *the way of safety,* not the way of liability. If you were to cross a muddy street, would you look out for the mud? No, you would keep your eyes away from it, looking for the dry places where you could put your foot safely and avoid the mud. Keep your eye single to the good, and the beautiful and the true, and you will avoid their opposites without care.

Freedom From Personality

The second false meditation to be avoided is thinking upon personality. Oh, to have your mind taken off from this little personality! Why, that is the key of self-possession. It is the secret of the little child.

It means that you shall not think of this little personality as yourself, but look at your great Spirit and remember it; to be able to hear anything about one's personality and not be moved—whether it be praise or blame. There are some people, who are immune to blame, and can harden themselves and feel quite at peace when fault is found with them, but who become quite elated and fairly unbalanced when they are praised. And sometimes they get so puffed up, that there comes the pride that goes before a fall, because they are so out of balance. On the other hand, there are people who can stand praise, it seems so natural, but when one little fault in them is pointed out, one little condemnation, they "go all to pieces." They are so sensitive, they grow weak as water before criticism.

Neither praise nor blame should move us. The praise you receive, you can ascribe to your divine Self and silently say, "I give all glory to the universal Life—the Holy Spirit. I am nothing of myself. I am nothing except by this power." Thus you will keep your modesty and your peace, and praise will not be able to move you. And when, on the other hand, you are condemned or blamed, you will not be moved either, because you remember this, that the carnal self can never be anything of itself. Only as the power of the universal Spirit fills it, can it be anything. Why blame it? Why find fault with it?

Simply take every one of these things as a help to further expression of your divinity—as a means of correction, just as artists love to have the master give them "a criticism." They know they advance by it and it does not hurt them, even when he speaks quite sharply and is very sweeping in his condemnation and his general view of their work. It only means that they will correct this and go on further.

Sense of Limitation Lost

As you meditate upon your divine I Am—the Great Self that you are—you may find yourself growing so impersonal that you lose all feeling of this body. If you should have the sense at any time when in meditation, as though you had no body at all and you were very large and very universal, be not concerned. At that time you are entering into your greater consciousness and it is good; and instead of hurrying back to the small consciousness, sit still and grow accustomed to it, for you will observe that you do not lose consciousness but have a more acute sense of being real.

I know one lady who once felt that her material beliefs were standing in her way as a healer, and she determined to have a less material mind. So one day she lay down on her couch and began to hold:

"All is Mind! All is Mind! There is no matter. All is Mind!" And as things would come up before her mentality she would say, "Mind—not matter! That is Mind! Nothing is matter."

As she went on with this, she suddenly found herself to be pure mentality. She could not feel her body; the room had no walls about it; she was one with the whole earth; there was no time—neither past nor future. She knew things to come; she could see the people that she was going to meet as right in the present; she knew the things of the future that would take place in her life.

About that time, somebody knocked at the door suddenly, and she was back in the old consciousness. She had learned the secrets of the prophet, that it was because he had entered into the universal consciousness that he knew no time nor space, and could know what things would take place.

The Cosmic Consciousness

There is nothing that seems to break the limits of the carnal senses so quickly as the denial of matter. For matter is a limited view. That is all. It is nothing *per se,* only a view. Even the material scientists have come to that conclusion, that there is no matter of itself, it is a mode of thinking. Both matter and motion are modes of thinking, and the way to recover from those methods of thinking is to break down the material limitations which one has put upon oneself and upon others. Abiding in this peace and giving yourself to spiritual pursuits and living the life, you find yourself rising to a greater consciousness and a more pleasing realization until suddenly there comes to you the Lord—the *Glory of the Lord,* called the Cosmic Consciousness.

The Cosmic Consciousness is an actual experience, a realization, a joy. It is a taste of your universal knowing, feeling, being. Anyone who has ever tasted of this can never doubt that there is more than the physical sense can testify. Everything in our spiritual experience is preparing us for this baptism, so that when it shall come upon us we shall be able to contain it and be normal. If you are instructed about it, when it comes upon you, you will walk in peace, knowing yourself and the realm of appearances and able to handle things, at the same time abiding in this peace and bliss, the Way of Jesus Christ.

The Heavenly Anesthetic

In the closing days of Jesus' earthly career, He walked through the sorrows and the strife, the ignominy and the crucifixion, calm and serene as one who has taken an anesthetic. The earthly anesthetic is a symbol of this super-conscious state, in which you can pass through anything and everything and be absolutely unmoved and unhurt. But it has none of the deadening effects associated with the material anesthetic, for you have perfect and conscious control over yourself. You are poised, peaceful and blissful—in the world, but not of it—healing, teaching, uplifting and delivering your fellow-beings and yet not implicated in any of these things.

Those who have never heard of Cosmic Consciousness, and yet arrive there may, either through fear or ignorance, do that against which the Buddhists, in these words warn us: "Drive not back the ecstasy of contemplation." Through being instructed about this state, you will not drive back this blissful consciousness by thinking that something is going wrong, but rather will see that you are only just entering into heaven, while yet you walk upon the earth.

The Escape From Insanity

Anyone who meditates upon the beautiful, the good and the true need never fear insanity, for he keeps the mind single to the All-Good, to the Divine Self. When people have seemed to go insane on account of religion, it is because they have had *some belief in evil,* which they did not eliminate from their consciousness as they went on in the spiritual life, and therefore that little grain of dust spoiled their vision.

I saw this illustrated in the case of a woman who had been unbalanced twice before I saw her in this third attack. Religious mania they called it.

A friend of hers, a student of Truth who came to my classes, asked her to come and stay with her. One day, this student was very much concerned, because it seemed as though her friend were on the verge of being unbalanced, so she brought her to my Bible Lesson.

She sat and listened to this lesson, and at the close she rose up in the midst of the students, her face very white, and began to speak words of Scripture.

I had not been told anything about her case, but I saw what the trouble was, and the whole class began to hold her in the One Mind, the Divine Mind.

She said, in a soft, plaintive voice:

"They are all lost, they are all lost, and only I am saved! O my friends! Where are they gone?"

Her friend tried to reassure her with the words, "We are all here!" but she did not hear.

Then I spoke up and said, "I am here!"

And she turned to me, "Yes, but where are the rest?"

I said, "They are eternally safe."

"No," she said, "they are lost forever."

I saw the mania in a moment—that old dogma that some are elected to salvation, but the greater part are to be lost forever. I was able to keep myself in her sight as one who was saved, until she came to herself, standing by my side and began to receive the assurances that everybody was absolutely safe in life.

The outcome of understanding her was, that instead of antagonizing her brothers, who wished her to be placed in a private sanitarium for a while, she agreed with them. It had always been her antagonism that would throw her off her balance. She agreed with them and in perfect co-operation did as they wished, and was afterward dismissed by the physicians of the sanitarium as perfectly sane and of sound mind. I received a letter from her not very long ago, in which she told me that she has always been poised and peaceful from that day, and she now knows she is absolutely safe through the power of the Truth.

We need never fear that we shall be unbalanced so long as we keep the good before us and our eye single to the good. It is the same with our friends that seem to be going aside from the balanced state. Remind them there is but one presence and power working in and through them and everything, and you will make yourself a vehicle—a bridge over which they may pass out of the false, disintegrating concentration into the true.

Openness to the Holy Spirit

It is for each one of us to know the bliss of heaven while we walk upon the earth, and the way is to be instructed by the Holy Spirit within us and learn to hear the little Voice—"the still, small Voice"— and receive its guidance. The object of Jesus' teaching was this very end, that you might be open to your own heavenly Voice and always be able to know just the step to take, when to move, when to be still, how to walk the straightway in peace and poise and power, the Path of Life—"Thou wilt show me the path of life" is what we can declare of the Spirit within us. For there is where the prophets found the Spirit— within—the Lord in themselves, telling them these great truths: "Thou wilt show me the path of life. In thy presence is fullness of joy. At thy right hand are pleasures forever more."

If there has been any earthly sense of ecstasy, whether of seeing or hearing or any other sense, be sure it is as a toy to the real thing, only a taste of the perfect and supreme satisfaction compared to the fullness of the joys that await you. It is written that it has not entered into the heart of man (into our meditation) to know the joys that are prepared for them that love God. But we must dismiss the old satisfactions that we are clinging to, in order to receive the new feelings, as a mother is not a perfect mother, who still clings to her dolls after the little babe has come to her. Many of our pleasures are only toys compared to the real bliss which is ours forever and ever.

Living by Inspiration

You rise above all fear concerning your circumstances, and enter into the inspired life, wherein every step is shown you and you cannot make a mistake. You do not need to plan your life, it is already planned and you slip into the divine way which has been arranged for you, as a car goes on the track smoothly does not need to lay its own track—because everything is already prepared.

This means that you live, putting away all objects—not living even with a purpose or a mission, but like a child. A child has no mission. It is not living for something. It is just living. And so the highest consciousness is planless, objectless, without purpose, and without a mission. And yet it will seem to be fulfilling the greatest mission and the greatest purpose and the most divine plan that could be devised by human beings. This is the highest consciousness of the daily life that is without anxiety.

Be not anxious for anything; not about tomorrow; not anxious to live, to get well, to demonstrate anything. To be without anxiety is the way to get all these. Then your hearing can come easily; that healing comes along without an effort; prosperity and other manifestations of good are as natural as your breath. Whenever you have to make an effort to breathe, you are not very healthy, and when you are breathing with an object in view, you may find yourself in a very weary state. The highest expression is where you have no object. You simply are yourself—the great Divine Self, without an effort. This is the way of bliss, of peace. Walk in this, day by day, for walking with God is abiding in this joy, this fullness of joy forever.

In closing, let us take that meditation which came to Isaiah in a cosmic moment, when he rose to the High Consciousness and heard the angels sing, "Holy! Holy! Holy!" We will enter into the silence and hold these words, finishing with:

"The whole earth is full of His Glory!"
"Holy! Holy! Holy! Lord God Almighty!"

Group of Suffragettes 1920
Library of Congress Prints and Photographs Division
Washington, D.C. 20540

Dr. H. Emilie Cady

(1844-1948)

Doctor, Healer, Metaphysician

Partnered with Charles and Myrtle Fillmore, in the
foundation of the Unity School of Christianity.

"Every man, every woman must take time daily for quiet and meditation. In daily meditation lies the secret of power. No one can grow in
either spiritual knowledge or power without it." ~ Emilie Cady

"All of life is the Breath of God. When God created man…he breathed

into his nostrils the breath of life, and man became a living being."
(Gen. 2:7)

"The spirit of God has made me, and the breath of the Almighty gives
me life." (Job 33:4)

"There is but one kind of life in the universe. All life is divine; all life is
the Breath of God." ~ Emilie Cady

Emilie Cady was one of the pioneers of New Thought. Her
training as a homeopathic physician combined with her insights as
a metaphysician, enabled her to treat patients medically and spiritually. Her approach was simple, clear and rooted in her own experience.
Cady teaches that one's life can be transformed by the power of one's
thoughts, words, and beliefs, encouraging us to find the truth as it is
written in our hearts and then apply these truths in every area of one's
life. (1)

Cady was a student of Emma Curtis Hopkins, the renowned
New Thought "teacher of teachers", a contemporary of popular New
Thought writer Emmett Fox, as well as Ernest Holmes and many other
New Thought greats. Inspired by Biblical teachings and influenced by
the ideas of Ralph Waldo Emerson, she partnered with Charles and
Myrtle Fillmore, in the foundation of the Unity School of Christianity.

Since its first publication in 1896, Unity's textbook *Lessons in Truth*
by H. Emilie Cady has sold over 1.5 million copies. Over the years millions of people have read *Lessons in Truth*. Emilie Cady shared the belief
of the Fillmore's and Albert Grier that "truth should be told not sold."
Thus her books were placed in the public domain for all to discover the
path to inner peace.

Born in 1848 as Harriet Emilie Cady in a farmhouse in Drysden,
Syracuse, a beautiful and prosperous part of upstate New York, she was
the daughter of a hardy pioneer. In her book *How I Used Truth* Cady
relates that her father was well known and respected in their neighbourhood. Cady soon dropped the name Harriet, preferring Emilie.

She spent the early part of her career in her hometown as a school-teacher in a one-room schoolhouse.

Emilie Cady eventually chose a career in medicine in the 1880s, a field that even 120 years later is still dominated by men. She was as an established and successful physician when she first appeared on the Unity scene.

When her booklet *Finding the Christ in Ourselves* came to the attention of Myrtle Fillmore, she gave it to her husband, Charles Fillmore, who lost no time in asking permission to print and distribute the booklet and invited her to write for Unity Magazine. As a result, beginning in 1892, a number of articles by Dr. Cady appeared in the magazine and she later went on to write the Unity textbook, *Lessons in Truth,* which was translated into eleven languages and Braille. From all over the world, from the length and breadth of the continent, letters came, testifying to lives transformed, physical ailments healed, money problems resolved, domestic difficulties dissipated, all through the study of her inspired book and the application of the principles therein.

Few have made a greater contribution or left a more shining monument to a long life of unselfish service than did Dr. H. Emilie Cady, physician and metaphysician. Her work will succor humanity for millennia!

"Healing of the body is beautiful and good. Power to heal is a divine gift, and as such you are fully justified in seeking. But God wants to give you infinitely more." (*Lessons in Truth* by Emilie Cady) (1)

Her writings include:
Finding the Christ in Ourselves
How I Used the Truth
Lessons In Truth
God A Present Help

From Lessons In Truth, Chapter 7, "God's Hand":

"When we have learned that God is our supply, and that from Him comes all our help, we shall no longer care whether 'pay' is rendered for our services or not. We shall simply know that all things are ours now, and out of the fullness of love we shall give freely. God's hand is sure. Your hand is God's hand now, today. It is full now. Give out of it mentally to all who call on you, whatever they need. "Trust also in him, and he will bring it to pass." (2)

Links and Acknowledgments
1. newthoughtlibrary.comcadyEmiliebio_cadyE_3.ht
2. absolute1.nethiut.html#God%27s

First Woman Jury, Los Angeles, Ca 1911
Library of Congress Prints and Photographs Division
Washington, D.C. 20540

How I Used the Truth

(Formerly Miscellaneous Writings)
by H. Emilie Cady

Dedicated

To the many loving friends all over the world who have been cheered and helped by these simple messages.

Why?
Finding the Christ in Ourselves
Neither Do I Condemn Thee
In His Name
Loose Him and Let Him Go
All-Sufficiency in All Things
God's Hand
If thou Knewest
Trusting and Resting
The Spoken Word
Unadulterated Truth
Oneness With God

Foreword

Because of the oft-repeated requests of many friends who have been helped by reading the various booklets and magazine articles of the author, it has seemed best to publish them all under one cover, to offer a convenient way for readers to have the helps always at hand. The papers that make up this volume have been written from time to time as a result of practical daily experience. In none of them is there anything occult or mysterious; neither has there been any attempt at literature. Each chapter is very plain and simple.

In revising the articles herein contained, there have been a few non-essential changes; yet the principle and its application remain the same. Truth is that which is so, and it can never change. Every true statement here is as true and as workable today as it was when these papers were written. We ask no one to believe that which is here written simply because it is presented as Truth. "Prove all things" for yourself; it is possible to prove every statement in this book. Every statement here given was proved before it was written. No person can solve another's problem for him. Each must work out his own salvation. Here are some effectual rules, suggestions, and helps thereto; but results that one obtains from them will depend on how faithfully and persistently one uses the helps given.

The author is grateful for the many words of appreciation that have come to her from time to time. These words are encouraging to one who is trying to solve her own life's problems, as you are trying to solve yours, by the teachings of the Master.

Lessons in Truth, because of its effective helpfulness, has been sought for and published in eleven languages; also in embossed point for the blind: Let us hope that this book, now sent forth with the same object— that of being a practical living help in daily life—may meet a like fate.

H.E.C.

Why?

THE following is a letter written by H. Emilie Cady to Lowell Fillmore. In this letter Doctor Cady says many helpful and inspiring things that we believe will be welcomed by lovers of her book "How I Used Truth."

Dear Mr. Fillmore:

When I sent you, a few weeks ago, a copy of the little pamphlet *All-Sufficiency in All Things,* which you said had been surreptitiously printed by an anonymous publisher, you wondered why I felt so keenly about the fact that the article had been broken up, put under different headings, and so forth. Let me tell you why.

Almost every one of the simply written articles in *How I Used Truth* was born out of the travail of my soul after I had been weeks, months, sometimes years, trying by affirmations, by claiming the promises of

Jesus, and by otherwise faithfully using all of the knowledge of Truth that I then possessed to secure deliverance for myself or others from some distressing bondage that thus far had defied all human help.

One of these cases was that of my own old father, who, though perfectly innocent, had been kept in exile for five years; put there by the wicked machinations of another man. No process of law that I had invoked, no human help, not even the prayers that I had offered had seemed to avail for his deliverance. One day while sitting alone in my room, my hands busy with other things, my heart cried out, "O God, stretch forth Thy hand and deliver!" Instantly the answer came "I have no hands but human hands. Your hand is my hand; stretch it forth spiritually and give whatsoever you will to whom soever you will, and I will establish it."

Unquestioningly I obeyed. From that moment, without any further external help or striving, the way of his release was opened ahead of us more rapidly almost than we could step into it. Within a few days my dear father came home a free man, justified, exonerated, both publicly and privately, beyond anything we could have asked or thought. Then I wrote *God's Hand.*

The case was written up by all the papers in the country in which my father resided as well as in the *New York Sun*. His innocence was clearly established. Once again he sat happily under the trees in his own dooryard and received congratulations. Delegation after delegation came from miles and miles around; friends who had known him from childhood came to assure him that his long life of uprightness had, in their minds, never been questioned. He was seventy-five years of age and, being an honest man, had felt the disgrace deeply. These stanch friends had been unable to help until God moved. The faith of many was renewed by his exoneration.

Another case was that of a dear young friend who had been placed in my care. He was just entering on a life of drinking and dissipation. There were weeks of awful anxiety, as I saw him drinking day by day, before I reached the place where I could "loose him, and let him go." When I did reach that place and stood there steadfastly (in spite of appearances), it required only a few hours to see him so fully healed that although forty years have passed, he has yet to touch a drop of liquor or indulge in any form of dissipation since that time. The lesson *Loose Him and Let Him Go* was then written.

Then came the question of money supply. I had a good profession with plenty of patients paying their bills monthly. But there were also other people coming to me daily for help, people whose visible means of support were gone. These cases of lack, as they presented themselves to me, were like cases of gnawing cancer or painful rheumatism. Therefore, there must be a way out through Truth, and I must find it. As always, instead of rushing to others for help in these tight places, I stayed at home within my own soul and asked God to show me the way. He did. He gave me the clear vision of Himself as *All-Sufficiency in All Things;* and then He said: "Now prove it, so that you can be of real help to the hundreds who do not have a profession or business on which to depend." From that day on, no ministry or work of any kind was ever done by me for "pay." No monthly bills were sent, no office charges made. I saw plainly that I must be working as God works, without expectation or thought of return. A free gift.

For more than two years I worked at this problem, never letting a human being know what I was trying to prove, for had He not said to me, "Prove me now herewith . . . if I will not open you the windows of heaven, and pour you out a blessing, that there shall not be room enough *to receive it?*"

More than once in the ongoing the body was faint for want of food, and yet, so sure was I of what God had shown me that day after day I taught cheerfully and confidently to those who came to my office, the Truth of God as the substance of all supply—and there were many in those days. At the end of two years of apparent failure I suddenly felt that I could not endure the privation any longer. Again, in near desperation from deferred hope of success, I went direct to God and cried Out: "Why, why this failure! You told me in the vision that if I would give up the old way and trust to You alone, You would prove to me Your sufficiency. Why have You failed to do it?"

His answer came flashing back in these words: "God said, Let there be light: and there was light." It was all the answer He gave. At the moment I did not understand. I kept repeating it again and again, the words God said becoming more and more emphasized, until at last they were followed by the words "Without him (the Word) was not anything made that hath been made." That was all I needed. I saw plainly that while I had, for two years, hopefully and happily gone on enduring hardships believing that God would supply, I had not once spoken the word *"it is done. God is now manifested as my supply."*

Believe me, that day I spoke the word of my deliverance. Suffice it to say that the supply problem was ended that day for all time and has never entered my life or mind since. This is the why of the article *The Spoken Word.*

I should like to give one more "Why" of *How I Used Truth.* After days of excruciating pain from a badly sprained ankle, the ankle became enormously swollen, and it was impossible for me to attend to my professional work as an active medical practitioner. Ordinary affirmations of Truth were entirely ineffectual, and I soon struck out for the very highest statement of Truth that I could formulate. It was this: *There is only God; all else is a lie.* I vehemently affirmed it and steadfastly stuck to it. In twenty-four hours all pain and swelling—in fact, the entire "lie"—had disappeared. Out of this experience I wrote *Unadulterated Truth.*

Can you not see, dear Mr. Fillmore, how it is that these simply written articles in *How I Used Truth* are as my children, and how all revision or changing of them seems to me like a violation of something sacred between God and me? I am sure you can. In each case I had proved God before I wrote. I thank the Fillmores that they have kept these messages just as they were written.

Yours in His name,
H. Emilie Cady

Finding the Christ in Ourselves

THROUGHOUT all His teaching Jesus tried to show those who listened to Him, how He was related to the Father, and to teach them that they were related to the same Father in exactly the same way. Over and over again He tried in different ways to explain to them that God lived within them, that He was "not the God of the dead, but of the living." And never once did He assume to do anything as of Himself, always saying: "I can of myself do nothing." "The Father abiding in me doeth his works." But it was very hard then for people to understand, just as it is very hard for us to understand today.

There were, in the person of Jesus, two distinct regions. There was the fleshly, mortal part that was Jesus, the son of man; then there was the central, living, real part that was Spirit, the Son of God—that was the Christ, the Anointed. So each one of us has two regions of being—one the fleshly, mortal part, which is always feeling its weakness and insufficiency in all things, always saying, "I can't." Then at the very center of our being there is a something that, in our highest moments, knows itself more than conqueror over all things; it always says, "I can, and I will." It is the Christ child, the Son of God, the Anointed in us. "Call no man your father on the earth," said Jesus, "for one is your Father, *even* he who is in heaven."

He who created us did not make us and set us apart from Himself, as a workman makes a table or a chair and puts it away as something completed and only to be returned to the maker when it needs repairing. Not at all. God not only created us in the beginning, but He is the very fountain of life ever abiding with us. From this fountain constantly springs new life to recreate these mortal bodies. He is the ever abiding intelligence that fills and renews our mind. His creatures would not exist a moment were He to be, or could He be, separated from them. "We are a temple of the living God; even as God said, I will dwell in them, and walk in them."

Let us suppose that a beautiful fountain is supplied from some hidden but inexhaustible source. At its center it is full of strong, vigorous life, bubbling up continually with great activity, but at the outer edge the water is so nearly motionless as to have become impure and covered with scum. This exactly represents man. He is composed of a substance infinitely more subtle, more real than water. "We are also His offspring." Man is the offspring or the springing forth into visibility—of God the Father. At the center he is pure Spirit, made in the image and likeness of the Father, substance of the Father, one with the Father, fed and renewed continually from the inexhaustible good, which is the Father. "In Him we live, and move, and have our being." At the outer edge, where stagnation has taken place (which is man's body) there is not much that looks Godlike in any way. We get our eyes fixed on the circumference, or external of our being. We lose consciousness of the indwelling, ever active, unchanging God at the center, and we see ourselves sick, weak, and in every way miserable; It is not until we learn to live at the center and to know that we have power to radiate from that center this unceasing, abundant life, that we are well and strong.

Jesus kept His eyes away from the external altogether, and kept His thoughts at the central part of His being, which was the Christ. "Judge not according to appearance," He said, that is according to the external, "but judge righteous judgment," according to the real truth, or judge from Spirit. In Jesus, the Christ, or the central spark that was God, the same that lives in each of us today, was drawn forth to show itself perfectly, over and above the body, or fleshly man. He did all His mighty works, not because He was given some greater or different power from that which God has given us—but just because He was in some different way a Son of God and we only children of God—but just because this same Divine Spark, which the Father has implanted in every child born, had been fanned into a bright flame by His prenatal influences, early surroundings, and by His own later efforts in holding Himself in constant, conscious communion with the Father, the Source of all love, life, and power.

To be tempted does not mean to have things come to you which, however much they may affect others, do not at all affect you, because of some superiority in you. It means to be tried, to suffer and to have to make effort to resist. Hebrews speaks of Jesus as "one that hath been in all points like as we are." And Jesus Himself confessed to having been tempted when He said to His disciples: "Ye are they that have continued with me in my temptations." The humanity of the Nazarene "suffered being tempted," or tried, just as much as you and I suffer today because of temptations and trials, and in exactly the same way.

We know that during His public ministry Jesus spent hours of every day alone with God, and none of us knows what He went through in all the years of His early manhood—just as you and I are doing today—in overcoming the mortal, His fleshly desires, His doubts and fears, until He came into the perfect recognition of this indwelling Presence, this "Father in me," to whom He ascribed the credit for all His wonderful works. He had to learn as we are having to learn; He had to hold fast as we are having today to hold fast; He had to try over and over again to overcome, as we are doing, or else He was not "in all points tempted like as *we are.*"

We all must recognize, I think, that it was the Christ within that made Jesus what He was; and our power now to help ourselves and to help others, lies in our comprehending the truth—for it is a truth, whether we realize it or not—that this same Christ that lived in Jesus lives within us. It is the part of Himself that God has put within us, which ever lives there with an inexpressible love and desire to spring to the circumference of our being, or to our consciousness, as our sufficiency in all things. "Jehovah thy God is in the midst of thee, a mighty one who will save (or He wills to save); he will rejoice over thee with joy; he will rest in his love; he will joy over thee with singing." Christ within us is the "beloved Son," the same as it was in Jesus. It is the "I in them, and thou in me, that they may be perfected" of which Jesus spoke.

In all this explanation we would detract nothing from Jesus. He is still our Saviour, in that He went through suffering unutterable, through the perfect crucifixion of self, that He might lead us to God; that He might show us the way out of our sin, sickness, and trouble; that He might manifest the Father to us and teach us how this same Father loves us and lives in us. We love Jesus and must ever love Him with a love that is greater than all others, and to prove our love, we would follow His teachings and His life closely. In no way can we do this perfectly, except by trying to get at the real meaning of all that He said, and letting the Father work through us as He did through Him, our perfect Elder Brother and Saviour.

Jesus sometimes spoke from the mortal part of Himself, but He lived so almost wholly in the Christ part of Himself, so consciously in the center of His being, where the very essence of the Father was bubbling up in ceaseless activity, that He usually spoke from that part.

When He said, "Come unto me . . . and I will give you rest," He could not have meant to invite mankind to come unto His personal, mortal self, for He knew of the millions of men and women who could never reach Him. He was then speaking from the Christ-self of Him, meaning not "Come unto me, Jesus," but "come unto the Christ"; nor did He mean, "Come unto the Christ living in me," for comparatively few could ever do that. But He said, "The words that I say unto you I speak not from myself, but the Father abiding in me doeth his works." Then it was the Father saying not "Come unto Jesus," but "Come unto me"; that is, "Come up out of the mortal part of you where all is sickness and sorrow and trouble, into the Christ Part where I dwell, and I will give you rest. Come up into the realization that you are one with the Father, that you are surrounded and filled with divine love, that there is nothing in the universe that is real but the good, and that all good is yours, and it will give you rest."

"No one cometh unto the Father, but by me" does not mean that God is a stern Father whom we must coax and conciliate by going to Him through Jesus, His kinder, more easily entreated Son. Did not Jesus say, "He that hath seen me hath seen the Father," or in other words, "As I am in love and gentleness and accessibility, so is the Father"? These words mean that no man can come to the Father except through the Christ part of himself. You cannot come around through some other person or by any outside way. Another may teach you how to come, and assure you of all that is yours if you do come, but you must retire within your own soul, find the Christ there, and look to the father through the Son, for whatever good thing you may need.

Jesus was always trying to get the minds of the people away from His personality, and to fix them on the Father in Him as the source of all His power. And when toward the last, they were clinging to His mortal self, because their eyes had not yet been opened to understand about the Christ within their own souls, He said, "It is expedient for you that I go away; for if I go not away, the Comforter will not come"; that is, if He remained where they could keep looking to His personality all the time, they would never know that the same Spirit of truth and power lived within themselves.

There is a great difference between a Christian life and a Christ life. To live a Christian life is to follow the teachings of Jesus, with the thought that God and Christ are wholly outside of man, to be called on but not always to answer. To live a Christ life is to follow Jesus' teachings in the knowledge that God's indwelling presence, which is always life, love, and power within us, is now ready and waiting to flow forth abundantly, aye, lavishly into our consciousness and through us to others, the moment we open ourselves to it and trustfully expect it. One is a following after Christ, which is beautiful and good so far is it goes, but is always very imperfect; the other is a letting Christ, the Perfect Son of God, be manifested through us. One is an expecting to be saved sometime from sin, sickness, and trouble; the other is a knowing that we are, in reality, saved now from all these errors by the indwelling Christ, and by faith affirming it until the evidence is manifested in our body.

Simply believing that Jesus died on the Cross to appease God's wrath never saved and never can save anyone from present sin, sickness, or want, and was not what Jesus taught. "The demons also believe and shudder," we are told, but they are not saved thereby. There must be something more than this, a living touch of some kind, a sort of intersphereing of our own soul with the divine Source of all good and giving. We are to have faith in the Christ, believe that the Christ lives in us, and is God's Son in us; that this indwelling One has power to save and make us whole; aye, more, that He has made us whole already. For did not the Master say, "All things whatsoever ye pray and ask for, believe that ye receive them, and ye shall have them."

If, then, you are manifesting sickness, you are to ignore the seeming—which is the external, or circumference of the pool where the water is stagnant and the scum has risen—and, speaking from the center of your being, say: "This body is the temple of the living God; the Lord is now in His holy temple; Christ in me is my life; Christ is my health; Christ is my strength; Christ is perfect. Therefore, I am now perfect, because He dwelleth in me as perfect life, health, strength." Say these words with all earnestness, trying to realize what you are saying, and almost immediately the perennial fountain of life at the center of your being will begin to bubble up and continue with rapidly increasing activity, until new life will radiate through pain, sickness, sores, all diseases, to the surface, and your body will show forth the perfect life of Christ.

Suppose it is money that you need. Take the thought, "Christ is my abundant supply. He is here within me now, and greatly desires to manifest Himself as my supply. His desires are fulfilled now." Do not let your thoughts run off into how He is going to do it, but just hold steadily to the thought of the supply here and now, taking your eyes off all other sources, and He will surely honor your faith by manifesting Himself as your supply a hundredfold more abundantly than you have asked or thought. So also with "Whatsoever things ye pray and ask for." But remember the earnest words of James the apostle: "He that doubteth is like the surge of the sea driven by the wind and tossed. For let not that man think that he shall receive anything of the Lord."

Nowhere in the New Testament is the thought conveyed that Jesus came that there might be, after death, a remission of the penalty for sin. That belief is a pure fiction of man's ignorant, carnal mind of later date. In many places in the Bible reference is made to "remission of sins"; and Jesus Himself, according to Luke, said that "repentance and remission of sins should be preached in his name unto all the nations." "Sins, in the original text, does not mean crime deserving punishment. It means any mistake or failure that brings suffering. Jesus came that there might be remission or cessation of sins, of wrongs, of mistakes, which were inevitably followed by suffering. He came to bring "good tidings of great joy which shall be to all the people." Tidings of what?

Tidings of salvation. When? Where? Not salvation from punishment after death, but salvation from mistakes and failures here and now. He came to show us that God, our Creator and Father, longs with yearnings unutterable to be to us, through the Christ, the abundance of all things that we need or desire. But our part is to choose to have Him and then follow His admonition to "hold fast till I come"—not till He comes after death, but just to hold steadily to our faith until He manifests Himself. For instance, in thus looking to Him for health, when by an act of your will you stop looking to any material source, (and this is not always easy to do), and declare the Christ in you to be the only life of the body and always perfect life, it needs but that you hold steadfastly, without wavering, to the thought, in order to become well.

When once you have put any matter into the hands of the indwelling, ever-present Christ, in whom there is at all times an irrepressible desire to spring to our rescue and to do all things for us, do not dare to take it back into your mortal hands again to work out for yourself, for by so doing you simply put off the time of His bringing it to pass. All you have to do in the matter is to hold to the thought: "It is done. It is manifest now." This divine Presence is our sufficiency in all things, and will materialize itself as such in whatever we need or desire, if we but trustfully expect it.

This matter of trusting the Christ within to do all things for us—realizing that we are one with Him and that to Him is given all power—is not something that comes to any of us spontaneously. It comes by persistent effort on our part. We begin by determining that we will trust Him as our present deliverance, as our health, our riches, our wisdom, our all, and we keep on by a labored effort, until we form a kind of spiritual habit. No habit bursts full-grown into our life, but everyone comes from a succession of little acts. When you see anyone doing the works of Christ, healing the sick, loosing the bound, and so forth, by the word of Truth spoken in faith, you may be sure that this faith did not jump to him from some outside source all at once. If you knew the facts, you would probably know of days and nights when with clenched fists and set teeth he held fast to the Christ within, "trusting where they could not trace," until he found himself possessing the very "faith of Jesus."

If we want the Father within, which is the Christ, to manifest Himself as all things through us, we must learn to keep the mortal of us still, to still all its doubts and fears and false beliefs, and to hold rigidly to the "Christ only." In His name we may speak the words of healing, of peace, and of deliverance to others, but as Jesus said of Himself, so we must also say of ourselves: "I can of myself do nothing." "The Father abiding in me doeth his works." He is the ever-present power to overcome all errors, sickness, weakness, ignorance, or whatever they may be. We claim this power, or bring it into our consciousness where it is of practical use, by declaring over and over again that it is ours already. Saying and trying to realize, "Christ is my wisdom, hence I know Truth," will in a short time make us understand spiritual things better than months of study will do. Our saying, *"Christ is my strength, I cannot be weak or frail,"* will make us strong enough to meet any emergency, with calm assurance.

Remember, we do not begin by feeling these things at first, but by earnestly and faithfully saying them, and acting as though they were true—and this is the faith that brings the power into manifestation.

The Christ lives in us always. God, the creative energy, sent His Son first, even before the body was formed, and He ever abides within, "the first born of all creation." But it is with us as it was with the ship on the tempestuous sea after the storm arose: Jesus' being in the vessel did not keep it from rocking, or the angry waves from beating against it; for He was asleep. It was only after He was awakened and brought out to manifest His power that the sea became still and the danger was over.

The Christ in us has been there all the time, but we have not known it, and so our little ships have been tossed about by sickness and poverty and distrust until we have seemed almost lost. I, the true spiritual self of me, am one with the Christ. You, the true spiritual self of you, are one with the Christ. The true self of every person is the child of God, made in His image. "Beloved, now are we children of God, and it is not yet made manifest what we shall be. We know that, if he shall be manifested, we shall be like him." Now, already, we are sons. When He shall appear—not when, sometime after the transition called death, He, some great, glorious Being, shall burst on our view, but when we have learned to still the mortal of us, and let the Father manifest Himself at our surface, through the indwelling Christ—then we shall be like Him, for He only will be visible through us.

"Behold what manner of love the Father hath bestowed upon us, that we should be called children of God." We are not simply reflections or images of God, but expressions (from *ex*, out of, and *premere*, to press or force), hence a forcing out of God, the All-Good, the all-perfect. We are projections of the invisible presence into visibility. God made man one with the Father, even as Jesus was, and just in proportion as we recognize this fact and claim our birthright, the Father in us will be manifested to the world.

Most of us have an innate shrinking from saying, "Thy will be done." Because of false teaching, and from associations, we have believed that this prayer, if answered, would take away from us all that gives us joy or happiness. Surely nothing could be farther from the truth. Oh, how we have tried to crowd the broad love of God into the narrow limits of man's mind! The grandest, most generous, loving father that ever lived is but the least bit of God's fatherhood manifested through the flesh. God's will for us means more love, more purity, more power, more joy in life, every day.

No study of spiritual or material things, no effort, though it be superhuman on our part, could ever be as effectual in making grand, godlike creatures, showing forth the same limitless soul that Jesus showed, as just praying continually the one prayer, "Thy will be done"; for the Father's will is to manifest His perfect Being through us. "Among the creatures, one is better than another, according as the Eternal Good manifesteth itself and worketh more in one than in another. Now that creature in which Eternal Good most manifesteth itself, shineth forth, worketh, is most known and loved, is the best; and that wherein the Eternal Good is least manifested, is least of all creatures" (*Theologia Germanica*). "For it was the good pleasure of the

Father that in him the Christ should all the fullness dwell"—fullness of love, fullness of life, fullness of joy, of power, of All-Good. "And in him ye are made full." Christ is in us, one with us, so we may boldly and with confidence say, *"in Christ all things are mine."* declaring it will make it manifest.

Above all things else, learn to keep to the Christ within yourself, not that within somebody else. Let the Father manifest through you in His own way, though His manifestation differ from that in His other children. Heretofore even the most spiritually enlightened of us have been mere pygmies, because we have, by the action of our conscious thought, limited the divine manifestation to make it conform to the manifestation through someone else. God will make of us spiritual giants if we will but take away all limits and give Him opportunity.

"Although it be good and profitable that we should learn and know what great and good men have wrought and suffered, and how God hath dealt with them, and wrought in them and through them, yet it were a thousand times better that we should in ourselves learn and perceive and understand who we are, how and what our own life is, what God is doing in us, and what He will have us do" (*Theologia Germanica*).

All the blessings promised in the 28th chapter of Deuteronomy are to those who "hearken diligently unto the voice of Jehovah," those who seek the inner voice in their own souls and learn to listen to and obey what it says to them individually, regardless of what it says to any other person, no matter how far he or she may be advanced in spiritual understanding. This voice will not lead you exactly as it leads any other in all the wide world, but, in the infinite variety, there will be perfect harmony, for there is but "one God and Father of all, who is over all, and through all, and in all."

Emerson says: "Every soul is not only the inlet, but may become the outlet of all there is in God." We can only be this by keeping ourselves consciously in open communication with God without the intervention of any other person between Him and us. "The anointing which ye received of him abideth in you, and ye need not that anyone teach you." "But the Comforter, which is the Holy Ghost, whom the Father will send in my name, he shall teach you all things." "Howbeit when he, the Spirit of truth, is come, he shall guide you into all the truth: for he shall not speak from himself; but what things so ever he shall hear, these shall he speak: and he shall declare unto you the things that are to come."

It needs but the one other little word now, firmly and persistently held in the mind, to bring into manifestation through us the highest ideal that we are capable of forming; aye, far higher, for does it not say, "As the heavens are higher than the earth, so are my ways higher than your ways, and my thoughts than your thoughts"? This manifestation through us will be the fulfillment of God's ideal, instead of our limited, mortal ideal, when we learn to let Spirit lead and to hold our conscious mind to the now.

You want to manifest the perfect Christ. Affirm with all your heart and soul and strength that you do so manifest now, that you manifest health and strength and love and Truth and power. Let go of the notion of being or doing anything in the future. God knows no time but the eternal now. You can never know any other time, for there is no other. You cannot live an hour or ten minutes in the future. You cannot live it until you reach it, and then it becomes the now. Saying or believing salvation and deliverance are to be, will forever, and through all the eternal ages, keep them, like a will-o'-the-wisp, just a little ahead of you, always to be reached but never quite realized.

"Now is the acceptable time; behold, now is the day of salvation," said Paul. He said nothing about our being saved from our distresses after death, but always taught a present salvation. God's work is finished in us now. All the fullness abides in the indwelling Christ now. Whatever we persistently declare is done now, is manifested now, we shall see fulfilled.

Questions for Self Study

1. Is Christ lost? Why do we speak of "finding" the Christ in ourselves?
2. Explain how God lives and works.
3. How are you the son of man? How the Son of God?

4. Why does man lose the consciousness of his spiritual identity?
5. How is Jesus the Elder Brother and Saviour of mankind?
6. Explain how your body is "a temple of the living God." What takes place in a temple?
7. In what phase of our nature do truths have to be imbedded before they become for us living principles?
8. What is the distinction between a "reflection of God" and an "expression of God"?
9. Explain fully the "will of God."
10. Is salvation to be ours at some future time in a faraway place, or when is it acceptable? When is man really "saved"?

Neither Do I Condemn Thee

HITHERTO few of us have had any idea of the destructive potency of condemnatory words or thoughts. Even among Truth students who know the power of every spoken word—and because they know it, so much greater is that power—there is a widespread tendency to condemn the churches and all orthodox Christians, to criticize and speak despairingly of students of different schools (as though there could be only one school of Christ), and even to discuss among themselves the failings of individuals who, in ways differing from their own, are earnestly seeking to find the Christ.

Let us stop and see what we are doing. Why should we condemn the churches? Did not Jesus "continue to teach in the synagogues"? He did not withdraw from the church and speak of it contemptuously. Nay, He remained in it, trying to show people wherein they were making mistakes, trying to lead them up to a higher view of God as their Father, and to stimulate them to live more truly righteous lives. If He found hypocrisy in the churches, He did not content Himself with saying, "I am holier than thou," but He remained with them and taught them a more excellent way: that the inside of the platter must be made clean.

Is the servant greater than his Lord? Shall not we, whom the Father has called into such marvelous light, rather help those sitting in darkness, even in the churches, than utter one word of condemnation against them? A loyal son does not condemn his father and his mother because in their day and generation, with the limitations of their day, they did not grow up to his present standard. We do not condemn the tallow candle or the stage coach because we have grown into a knowledge of electricity and steam power. We only see that out of the old grew the new, and that the old was necessary to the new.

God, in His eternal purposes, is carrying every living person on toward a higher knowledge of the Truth, a more perfect evolvement of Himself through the soul. If some are being pushed on into the light of Truth and consequent liberty more rapidly than others, shall they turn and rend those who are walking more slowly but just as surely toward the perfect light? Nay, nay; but let them, praising God for the marvelous revelation of Himself within their own souls, lift up rather than condemn any who are struggling toward the light. Let them become workers together with God, doers of the law, not judges.

Let no man who has been born into a knowledge of God ever dare again to speak or even think disparagingly of or to any who seemingly are behind him in spiritual growth, lest by so doing he be found working against God, who is infinite wisdom as well as love.

Jesus said to the disciples, after they had come into the consciousness of their oneness with the Father by receiving "the Holy Spirit," "Whosoever sins ye forgive they are forgiven unto them; whosoever sins ye retain, they are retained." Oh, with what mighty meaning these words are fraught, in this new light that God has given us! See how our speaking, aye, our very thinking, of the sins or mistakes of others tends to fasten those mistakes on them as realities.

Strong, positive thoughts of condemnation to anyone by any person will strike that one and give him the physical sensation of having been hit in the pit of the stomach with a cobblestone. If he does not immediately rouse himself to throw off the feeling—as he easily can do by looking into his Father's face and saying over and over until it becomes realty to him, "Thou, God, approvest me"—it will destroy for the time being his consciousness of perfect life, and he will fall into a belief of weakness and bitter discourage-ment more quickly than from any other cause.

We read that the eyes of our God are too pure to behold iniquity. An absolutely pure person sees no licentiousness in another. A wholly true person sees no falsity in another. Perfect love responds not to envy, or fear, or jealousy in another. It "thinketh no evil." Jesus said, "The prince of the world cometh: and he hath nothing in me"—that is, nothing to respond to anything in himself. So, unless there is some-thing within us that responds to sin in others we shall not see it in them. "By thy words thou shalt be justified, and by thy words thou shalt be condemned." the moment we begin to criticize or condemn another, we prove ourselves guilty of the same fault to which we are giving cognizance.

All condemnation springs from looking at personality. Personality (Latin, *persona*, a mask) is the outward appearance, not the real self. That anyone utters a word of condemnation of another is the surest proof that he himself is yet living largely in the external of his be-ing, the personality; that he has not yet risen at all beyond the plane of those to whom the pure Nazarene said: "He that is without sin among you, let him first cast a stone at her." Just in proportion as we return to God, as we withdraw from the external to the within of ourselves, keeping our thoughts centered on Him who is perfect, shall we lose sight of personality, of divisions and differences, and become conscious of our oneness with one another and our oneness with God, Our Father.

We are one always and forever, whether we realize it or not. Knowing this, do you not see a new meaning in the words, "Judge not, that ye be not judged. For with what judgment ye judge, ye shall be judged"?

"God sent not the Son into the world to judge the world; but that the world should be saved through him." Yet when Philip said to Jesus, "Show us the Father," Jesus replied, "He that hath seen me hath seen the Father." Then, if God does not condemn, shall we, dare we, even in the smallest things? To each of us the Master says, "What *is that* to thee? Follow thou me."

Not while we are looking at the imperfect either in ourselves or in our brother, but while we "beholding as in a mirror the glory of the Lord, are transformed into the same image from glory to glory, even as from the Lord the Spirit."

Neither Do I Condemn Thee

1. Why is the "spoken word" regarded as having more power than the "unspoken word"?
2. What is the meaning of the word criticize as used here, and how is condemnation related to it?
3. What is "righteous judgment"?
4. Why should there be no condemnation of any person?
5. How does one work against God?
6. Explain: "Whosoever sins ye forgive, they are forgiven unto them, and whosoever sins ye retain, they are retained."
7. In the light of Jesus' teachings how can one handle the attitude of condemning another?
8. What causes a condemnatory attitude of mind?
9. How shall we rid ourselves of a condemnatory habit of mind? Explain the meaning of "habit."
10. How are we one with God and with one another?

In His Name

HAS it ever occurred to you that you are almost daily taking God's name in vain? Unless you are very watchful, very careful, you are doing so.

When God called Moses to lead the Children of Israel out of Egypt, "Moses said unto God, Behold, when I come unto the children of Israel, and shall say unto them, The God of your fathers hath sent me unto you; and they shall say to me, What is his name? What shall I say unto them?

And God said unto Moses, "I AM THAT I AM": and he said, "Thus shall thou say unto the children of Israel, I AM hath sent me unto you."

"This is my name forever, and this is my memorial unto all generations."

"I AM," then, is God's name. Every time you say, "I am sick," "I am weak," "I am discouraged," are you not speaking God's name in vain, falsely?

I AM cannot be sick; I AM cannot be weary, or faint, or powerless; for I AM is all-life, all-power, All-Good.

"I AM," spoken with a downward tendency, is always false, always "in vain." A commandment says, "Thou shalt not take the name of Jehovah thy God in vain; for Jehovah will not hold him guiltless that taketh his name in vain." And Jesus said, "By thy words thou shalt be justified, and by thy words thou shalt be condemned."

If you speak the "I AM" falsely, you will get the result of false speaking. If you say, "I am sick," you will get sickness; if you say, "I am poor," you will get poverty; for the law is, "Whatsoever a man soweth, that shall he also reap." "I AM," spoken upward, toward the good, the true, is sure to out-picture in visible good, in success, in happiness.

Does all this sound foolish to you? Do you doubt that such power goes with the speaking of God's name? If so, just go alone, close your eyes, and in the depth of your own soul say over and over the name "I AM." Soon you will find your whole being filled with a sense of power that you never had before—power to overcome, power to accomplish, power to do all things.

I am because Thou art. I am what Thou art. I am one with Thee, O Thou infinite I AM! I am good. I am holy. I am well. I am, because Thou art.

"The name of Jehovah is a strong tower; the righteous runneth into it, and is safe." They who think rightly about the power of the I AM spoken upward, simply have to run into it, as into a strong tower or fortress, and they are safe.

Did you ever go into a meeting where the drift of all the "testimonies" given was the "I AM" spoken upward—"I am happy to be here," "I am glad I am a Christian," "I am hoping and trusting in God," and so forth? Attend such a gathering, and almost before you know it, you will find yourself lifted entirely above your troubles and anxieties. You leave such a meeting with a feeling of joy and lightness, and a consciousness that you have the power to overcome all the home troubles and worries; you go, singing and confident, toward the very fire which, an hour before, seemed about to consume you.

Dear friends, you who at times feel almost discouraged, you who are being continually "sand-papered" by the petty worries and anxieties of life, just try for one week always saying "I AM" upward, toward the good and see what the result will be. Instead of saying, "I am afraid it will rain," say, "I hope it will not rain"; instead of "I am sorry," say "I would have been glad had it been so and so"; instead of saying, "I am weak and cannot accomplish," say, "I am because Thou art; I can accomplish, because I am." You will be astonished at the result.

The Christ, speaking through Jesus, said to the Jews who were boasting of being descendants of Abraham: "Verily, verily, I say unto you, before Abraham was born, I am." And Paul, writing to Timothy, said: "Let everyone that nameth the name of the Lord depart from unrighteousness." Let everyone who speaks the "I AM" keep it separated from iniquity, or from false speaking. Let it be spoken always upward, never downward. Jesus also said, "If ye shall ask anything of the Father, he will give it you in my name"—that is, in the name I AM. Whenever you desire—not supplicate, but desire, speaking the "I AM" upward—He will give what you ask. Every time you say, "I am happy," you ask in His name for happiness. Every time you say, "I am unhappy," you ask in His flame for unhappiness. "Hitherto," He said to the disciples, "have ye asked nothing in my name: ask, and ye shall receive that your joy may be made full." Is not this just the trouble? Hitherto what we have been asking in His name? Have we been asking for health or for sickness, for happiness or for unhappiness, for riches or for poverty, by the manner of our speaking the name I AM?

Have we spoken it upward, toward the good, or downward toward the not good? That which we have been receiving will tell the story. Jesus said that if they asked rightly in His name, their "joy would be made full." Is your joy full? If not, then give heed to your asking.

The disciples healed "in the name of Jesus Christ." In the name of Jesus Christ is the name of the I AM.

Suppose that a messenger is sent out from the executive mansion at Washington to do certain things in the name of the President of the United States. These three little words, "in his name," invest the messenger with the full power of the President, so far as the performing of that service is concerned.

"Whatsoever ye do, in word or indeed, *do* all in the name of the Lord Jesus, giving thanks to God the Father," said Paul, in writing to the Colossians. Whatever we do heartily and sincerely in the name of Christ or the I AM, carries with it the power of the I AM to accomplish—a power from a higher source, as the presidential messenger receives his power from a higher source. All power is given to Christ. Doing all things "in his name" puts aside our mortal personality and lets the Christ do the work. When Moses, with a sense of his personal insufficiency for so great a work, shrank from it, saying, "Oh, Lord, I am not eloquent . . . I am slow of speech, and of a slow tongue. And Jehovah said unto him, Who hath made man's mouth?...is it not I, Jehovah? Now therefore go, and I will be with thy mouth, and teach thee what thou shalt speak." In Edward Everett Hale's story, "In His Name," a story in a setting of seven hundred years ago, it is no fairy tale that invests the words, "in His Name," with such magic power. This little password carried safely, through the most dangerous places, all who went on errands of good. Locked doors were readily opened at the sound of the words. Soldier, sentry, officer of the guard, all gave way respectfully and instantly before it. Men were willing to leave their homes at a moment's notice and plunge into the greatest hardships "in His name."

Ministering today in His name, I say to you, troubled one, anxious one, weary one: Be strong! Be of good courage! Be hopeful! The world—the mortal—is overcome already. The Christ, the I AM, speaking through Jesus, has spoken, saying: "I have overcome the world."

"To him that overcometh (that is, to him who recognizes that already the world is overcome by the I AM, that there is nothing in all the universe but the I AM) to him will I give of the hidden manna, and I will give him a white stone, and upon the stone a new name written which no one knoweth but he that receiveth it."

"He that overcometh, I will make him a pillar in the temple of my God, and he shall go out thence no more, and I will write upon him the name of my God," even the name I AM.

In His Name

1. What is the purpose of a name?
2. What does God's name designate?
3. Explain the third commandment, "Thou shalt not take the name of Jehovah thy God in vain; for Jehovah will not hold him guiltless that taketh his name in vain."
4. What is the meaning of I AM?
5. Why should one not use such phrases as "I am sorry" and "I am afraid"?
6. How do we ask "in His name"?
7. What did Jesus mean by the statement: "Hitherto have ye asked nothing in my name: ask, and ye shall receive, that your joy may be full"?
8. How can we tell whether or not we are using His name righteously?
9. Explain how all power is given to the Christ.
10. What is an "overcomer," and what is to be overcome?

Loose Him and Let Him Go

ONE of the natural tendencies of the mortal mind is toward proselytizing. The moment we believe something to be true we begin to try to convert others to our belief. In our eagerness we forget that Truth is kaleidoscopic in its forms. We learn to say, with some degree of realization, "God worketh in me to will and to work for His good pleasure," but we quite forget that the same God is working equally in our brother "to will and to work."

Among the wise sayings of the ancient philosopher, Epictetus, we find these words: "Does anyone bathe hastily? Do not say that he does it ill, but hastily. Does anyone drink much wine? Do not say that he does ill, but that he drinks a great deal. For unless you perfectly understand his motives, how should you know if he acts ill? Thus you will not risk yielding to any appearances but such as you fully comprehend."

Every person has an inherent right to freedom of choice, a right to live his life in his own way. One of the surest signs that a person is no longer in bondage himself is his willingness to give others their freedom, to allow others the privilege of seeking and finding God as they will.

Our great basic statement is "All is good, because all is God." In other words, God Is the only intelligence, the only life at the center of every form of existing life. We say that we believe the highest manifestation of God is in man; that God ever abides at the center of man, of all mankind, and is always in process of manifesting more and more of Himself, pure intelligence, perfect love, through man's consciousness until man comes to be consciously one with the Father in all things.

Do you really believe this fundamental statement? If you do believe it, where is there any cause for the anxiety that you feel about your loved ones who are not, as you say, "in the Truth"?

If we truly believed that "all is good," we should not be troubled about those who apparently are going all wrong. They may be going wrong according to our limited conception of right and wrong, but my brother, my sister, you are not your brother's keeper. He that will redeem, aye! He that has already redeemed your brother lives within Him. The Christ, who ever loves at the center of every soul, "will neither slumber nor sleep." God works, or as the original has it, "God is working effectually to perform" in your brother, to bring him to himself just as much as He is working in you and in me. We have absolutely nothing to fear about the eventual success of this worker. God never fails.

You have perhaps come to the flowering or the fruiting season, in your growth out of the darkness of sense belief into the light of spiritual understanding. It is blessed and beautiful to be where you are, and it is hard to human belief to see those whom you love just barely showing their heads above the earth of sin and mistake, or harder still to see them daily going deeper into the earth of an animal life, farther away from your conception of the good than ever before.

But just here is the place for us to cling faithfully and trustingly to our basic statement. "In hope were we saved; but hope that is seen is not hope," said Paul. Faith is not sight. Is our basic statement, "All is good," founded on Principle or on evidence of the senses? If on Principle, then it is immutable, unchangeable. And God is just as surely abiding at the center of your loved husband or son, working in him, when he is drinking, or going down, as when he is coming up.

God is just as much the life of the seed when it is being planted in the dark earth, where, to the human sense, it is dead and all is lost, as He is the life of the new leaf which a few days later bursts into sight. In fact it is because God is there at the center, working in the stillness, unseen, and not at all because of the fussy, noisy outside work that you and I do, that the seed comes forth into newness of life.

"Except a grain of wheat fall into the earth and die, it abideth by itself alone; but if it die, it beareth much fruit."

Thus it would seem that the dying, the failure, the going down of the old is a necessary step in all true salvation. Every man must go down till he strikes his own level, his own self, before there can be any real growth. We may seem to hold another up for a while, but eventually he must walk alone. The time of his walking alone with his own indwelling Christ, his own true self, will depend largely on our letting go of him. No one will seek anything higher than he is today, until he feels the need of something higher. Your dear ones must have the liberty to live out their own lives, and you must let them, or else you are the one who puts off the day of their salvation .

"But," says someone whose heart is aching over the error ways of a loved one, "should you not help anyone? Should you not run after him, and urge him continually to turn into the right way?"

Yes and no. I gladly, joyfully help anyone when he wants help, but I could not urge anyone to leave his own light and walk by my light. Nor would I, like an overly fond mother, pick up another and try to carry him in my arms by continually "treating" him.

A mother may—and sometimes does, mentally and morally, if not physically—through her false conception of love, carry her child until he is twenty years old, lest he, not knowing how to walk, fall and bump his nose a few times. But if she does this until he is a grown man, what will he do? He will turn and rend her, because she has stolen from him his inherent right to become a strong, self-reliant man. She has interposed herself between him and the power within him that was waiting, from his birth, to be strength and sufficiency for him in all things. She should have placed him on his own feet, made him know that there was something in himself that could stand, encouraged and steadied him, and so helped him to be self-reliant and independent.

Hundreds of anxious fathers and mothers, sisters and wives say, "Ah! but I love this one so I cannot stand still and see him rushing on to an inevitable suffering."

Yes, you love him. But I tell you that it takes an infinitely greater, more God-like love to stand still and see your child burn his hand a little, that he may gain self-knowledge, than it does to be a bond-slave to him, ever on the alert to prevent the possibility of his learning through a little suffering. Are you equal to this larger love—to the love that does not hold itself on the *qui vive* to interpose its nagging bodily presence between the dear ones and their own indwelling Lord who is with them "always"? Having come yourself to a knowledge of the mighty truth that "God is all and in all," have you the moral courage to "be still, and know"; to take off all restrictions and rules from others, and to let the God within them, each one, grow them as He will; and, trusting Him to do it in the right way, keep yourself from all anxiety in the matter?

When Jesus preached of a glorious freedom from suffering, through a "kingdom . . . within," He often interspersed His preaching with the words, "He that hath ears, let him hear." In other words, the Gospel message of deliverance is for all who are ready for it. Let him who has come to where he wants it, take it.

No one has any right to coerce another to accept his ideal. Every person has a right to keep his own ideal until he desires to change it.

God is leading your friend by a way you do not and cannot know. It is a safe and sure way; it is the shortest and only way. It is the Christ way; the within way, "I am the door," says the Christ within every man's own soul. "If any man enter in, (that is, by way of the Christ in himself) he shall be saved."

Now you are trying to have your friend enter in through your door. He must enter in through his own Christ, his own desire, and you must let him alone to the workings of that indwelling One, if you want him to manifest good.

"But," you say, "is there nothing I can do when I see my husband, brother, friend, going down?"

Yes, there is something you can do, and a very effectual something, too.

"The sword of the Spirit is the word of God." You can, whenever you think of your friend, speak the word of freedom to him. You can always and in all ways "Loose him, and let him go," not forgetting that the letting him go is as important as the loosing him. You can tell him mentally that Christ lives within him and makes him free, forever free; tell him that he manifests the Holy One wherever he goes and at all times, for there Is nothing else to manifest. And then you see to it that you do not recognize any other manifestation than the good in him.

It is written, "Whosoever sins ye forgive, they are forgiven unto them; whosoever sins ye retain, they are retained." Will you invariably speak the word of remission or loosing to your erring ones? Or will you bind them closer, tighter in the bondage that is breaking your own heart, by speaking the word of retention to them continually?

If you really want your friends to be free, there is but one way for you: Loose them and let them go. For it is the promise of the Father, through the Son, that "Whatsoever thou shalt loose on earth shall be loosed in heaven."

Loose Him and Let Him Go

1. What fact seems particularly difficult for one person to remember in regard to another?
2. What is a sure sign of a free man?

3. How are you your "brother's keeper"?
4. What does proselytizing mean, and why should one not be anxious about the welfare of another man?
5. What causes a person to seek that which is higher than he is today?
6. How do counselors and teachers often stand in the way of a student's attaining a desired consciousness?
7. To whom should each man turn for guidance?
8. What did Jesus mean when He said, "I am the way," and, "I am the door"?
9. Should the one who is apparently going wrong be specifically treated for his "sins"?
10. How do you "loose him and let him go"?

All-Sufficiency in All Things

THERE is that within every human being which is capable of being brought forth into the material, everyday life of any person as the abundance of every good thing that he may desire.

Here and there a man who is consciously abiding in the secret place of the Most High, and being taught by the Spirit of truth, dimly recognizes this, and says, "The Holy Spirit abiding within us is able to do all things for us"; while occasionally a metaphysician, in whom the intuitional is largely developed, is beginning to apprehend it as demonstrable Truth, and carefully avoiding all pious words, lest he be considered in the old rut of religious belief, says, "The outer or visible man has no need that the inner invisible man cannot supply."

Let us not haggle over terms. There need be no schism. Each means the same thing. The only difference is in words. Each one is getting at the same Truth in his own way, and eventually the two will clasp hands in unity and see eye to eye.

The Spirit of the living God within us, fed ever from the Fountainhead, is not only the giver of all good gifts, the supplier of all supply, but is the gift itself. We must come right up to this point.

The giver and the gift are one. God Himself is the fulfillment—or the substance which fills full—of every desire.

Truly our eyes have been beholden, until now, in these later days, we are coming to know of "God in His world"; of Him, the immanent creative Cause of all things, ever dwelling in man, ready and willing at any moment to re-create or renew our body and mind, or to manifest Himself through us as anything needed by us.

The certainty of this manifestation depends on ability to recognize and accept Truth.

One recognizes God within as indwelling purity and holiness. To this one He is sanctification, and just in the proportion to the recognition and the trust with which this divine Presence is regarded as immanent holiness, does it spring forth into the outer, everyday life of a man as holiness, so that even they who run may read a something more than human in him.

Another recognizes and accepts the God within himself as the life of his body, and instantly this divine life, always perfect, strong, and vigorous, and always desiring with the mighty desire of omnipotent love to manifest itself through somebody or something as perfection, begins to flow through his body from center to circumference until his entire body is charged with a fullness of life that is felt even by others who came in contact with him. This is divine healing, and the time required for the process of complete healing depends, not on any changeableness of God—for God knows no time but the eternal now—but entirely on the ability of the person to recognize and trust the power that works in him.

The one who recognizes the indwelling God as his holiness, but cannot mentally grasp any more Truth, lives a holy, beautiful life, but perhaps lives it all through years of bodily disease and sickness. Another who recognizes the same immanent God as his health, and is made both holy and physically well by the recognition and acceptance, stops there, and wonders, when he is well and living a life entirely unselfish and Godlike, why he should always be poor, lacking even the bare necessities of life.

O fools and slow of heart to believe! Can you not see that this same indwelling God, who is your holiness and your health, is also your sustenance and support? Is He not our All-Sufficiency in all things? Is it not the natural impulse of the divine Being to flow forth through us into all things—"Whatsoever ye pray and ask for"? Is there any limit, except as our poor human mind has set? Does He not say, "Every place wherein the sole of your foot shall tread shall be yours"? What does this mean? "Whatsoever you dare to claim, that will I be to you"?

This divine energy is the substance (from *sub,* under, and *stare,* to stand), the real thing that stands under or within the visible or unreal of all things—food and clothing as well as life and health.

How do we get holiness? Not by outside works of purifying ourselves, but by turning to the Holy Spirit within and letting it flow forth into our human nature until we become permeated with the Divine. How is perfect health through divine or spiritual healing obtained? Is it by looking to or trusting external efforts or appliances? Surely not; but rather by ceasing entirely to look to the without, and turning our thoughts and our faith to the Father in us.

How, then, are we to get our abundant supply—aye, even more than we can ask or think (for God gives not according to our need, but "according to his riches" we are told)? "Acquaint now thyself with him, and be at peace: thereby good shall come unto thee. If thou return to the Almighty, thou shalt be built up. And the Almighty will be thy treasure, and precious silver unto thee."

It is not enough to believe simply that God is our supplier—the One who shall by His omnipotent power influence the mind of someone possessing an abundance to divide with us. This is limitation. God's being our health means far more than God's being our healer. God as our supply is infinitely more than God as our supplier. God is the Giver and the gift.

When Elisha multiplied the widow's oil, he did not, recognizing God simply as the supplier, ask, and then for answer receive a few barrels of oil from someone over-rich in that commodity, someone in whose heart the Spirit of God was working. That would have been a good but a very limited way, for had the demand continued, in time not only the village but the whole country around would have been destitute of oil.

Elisha understood the divine law of working, and put himself into harmony with it; then God Himself, the substance of all things, became manifest as the unlimited supply—a supply which could easily have flowed until this time had there been need and vessels enough.

Jesus' increase of the loaves and fishes did not come up from the village in response to some silent word spoken by Him to a person having a quantity. He never recognized that He had any right to seek the surplus possessions of another, even though He was going to use them to benefit others. In order to feed the multitude, He did not reach out after that which belonged to any man, or even that which was already in manifestation. The extra supply was a new and increased manifestation of divine substance as bread and fish. So with the oil of Elisha, who was a man "of like passions with you." In both these cases, nothing came from without to supply the need, but the supply proceeded from within outward.

This divine Substance—call it God, creative energy, or whatever you will—is ever abiding within us, and stands ready today to manifest itself in whatever form you and I need or wish to manifest, just as it did in Elisha's time. It is the same yesterday, today, and forever. Our desire is the cup that shapes the form of its coming, and our trust—the highest form of faith—sets the time and the degree.

Abundant supply by the manifestation of the Father in us, from within outward is as much a legitimate outcome of the Christ life or spiritual understanding as is bodily healing.

The Word—or Spirit—is made flesh (or clothed with materiality) in both cases, and both are equally in God's order. The law of "work-to-earn" is only a schoolmaster beating us with many stripes, breaking us into many pieces when we fall across it in our failures, just to bring us to Christ. "But now that faith is come, we are no longer under a tutor." Then Christ—the Divine in us—becomes the fulfillment of the law.

"I work not for the food which perisheth," said the Nazarene. Cease to work with the one object, viz., for a living or for supply. Be forever free from the law of poverty and want, as you are from the law of sin and disease—through faith in Christ; that is, by taking the indwelling Christ, or Spirit, or invisible man as your abundant supply, and, looking up to no other source, hold to it until it manifests itself as such. Recognize it. Reckon it. Be still and know it. Do not struggle and work and worry while you know it, but just be still. "Be still, and know that I am"—what? Part of God? No. "Know that I am God"—all of God, all of good. I am life. I am health. I am love. I am supply. I am the substance of all that human souls or bodies can need or want.

The law says, "In the sweat of thy face shalt thou eat bread." The Gospel brings "good tidings of great joy which shall be to all the people." The law says: Work out your salvation from sin, sickness, and poverty. The Gospel teaches that Christ, the Father in you, is your salvation. Have faith in Him. The law says: Work all you can, and God will do the rest. The law is a way; Gospel, or Christ, is the Way, "Choose you this day whom ye will serve."

"But," says someone, "will not such teaching that our abundance is not at all dependent on the labor of our hands or head foster selfishness and indolence? Is it not a teaching dangerous to the masses?" Jesus never thought the Gospel dangerous for the masses. It has not proved dangerous to teach that health is a free gift of God to His children—a gift that they need not labor for, but just recognize and accept.

Does anyone attempt to hide away from others, like a talent hidden deep in the earth, the newborn health that is God-manifest in response to recognition and faith? If he does, he soon finds that his health has disappeared, for selfishness and the consciousness of an indwelling God cannot both abide in the same heart.

Let not anyone for a moment suppose that he can use Gospel means for selfish ends. As well suppose he can go west by going east. A thousand times better that a millstone be hanged about his neck and he be drowned in the depths of the sea, than to attempt to use God's free gift for selfish purposes. The divine abundance manifested through you is given you for ministry to others. You can neither receive it indolently, nor retain it selfishly. If you attempt either, the flow of divine oil will be stayed.

In Christ, or in the consciousness of the indwelling divine Spirit, we know that every man and woman is our father and mother, brother and sister; that nothing is our own, but all is God's because all is God.

And because we know this, we give as we work without thought or hope of return, because God flows through us to others. Our giving is our only safety valve. Abundance is often a snare to those who know not God, the indwelling One, who is love. But the abundance that is manifested from within outward is only the material clothing of perfect love, and cannot bring selfishness. "The blessing of Jehovah, it maketh rich; and he addeth no sorrow therewith."

Will God, being manifest as our abundant supply, foster idleness? A thousand times, no! We shall then, more than ever, be co-workers with God, working but not laboring, working always for others. Work is labor only when it is for self. Labor, not work, brings weariness, sorrow, and sickness. Labor not for meat, that is, for any good to yourself. Working as God works does not weary, for then the current of unlimited divine life is always flowing through us anew to bless others.

"There is a river, the streams whereof make glad," but we must always keep the stream flowing from within—the source of its uprising—outward if it is to make glad. When we work in harmony with divine law we have with us the whole force of the stream of living waters to carry us along.

Better than he knew; spoke the poet when he said: "Earth has no sorrow that heaven cannot heal."

Not the faraway heaven after death, when a whole lifetime has been spent in sorrow and trouble, but the "kingdom of heaven is at hand," here, now, today. The mortal, human, earth part of you has no sorrow that cannot be healed, overcome, wiped out at once and forever by this ever indwelling divine Spirit.

If any man would hasten the day of every man's deliverance from all forms of human sorrow and want, let him at once begin to withdraw himself from outside sources and external warfare, and center his thoughts on Christ the Lord within himself.

"Jehovah is in the midst of thee, a mighty one."

"Acquaint now thyself with him, and be at peace: thereby good shall come unto thee."

"Prove me now if I will not pour you out a blessing, that there shall not be room enough *to receive it.*"

Let us prove Him. "Commune with your own heart upon your bed, and be still." Be still and know. Be still and trust. Be still and expect.

"My soul, wait thou in silence for God only. For my expectation is from him."

All Sufficiency In All Things

1. What is it that is capable of supplying each man with the fulfillment of his own particular desires in abundant measure?
2. What do we mean when we speak of God "Immanent" in man and in the universe?
3. What is divine substance, and what is its relation to manifest objects?
4. What is the Holy Spirit, and what is its relation to the Father, and to the Son, or Christ?
5. Explain how God is the supply and the supplier.
6. What governs the "shape" of our supply, and what fixes the "time" and the "quantity" of it?
7. Is it safe to teach that supply is a "gift" and that it does not depend only on the labor of head or hands?
8. What governs the outpouring of divine substance, and what inhibits its flow?
9. In its true sense, what is work?
10. From what phase of our being do we bring our world into manifestation?

God's Hand

THERE is but one hand in the universe. It is God's hand. Whenever you have felt that your hand was empty, it has been because you have believed yourself something separate from God. Have you not felt, at times, great desire to give to others something that they needed or wanted, yet have not been able so to give. Have you not said many times within yourself, "Oh, if I only had money, how I would relieve anxiety and distress! If it were only in my power, how quickly would I give a lucrative position to this one needing work, freedom to that one wanting release from material bondage," and so forth? Have you not often said, "If I could only afford it, I would so gladly give my time and service to others with no thought of return"?

Whence, suppose you, comes this desire to give? Is it from the mortal of you? Nay, nay, it is the voice of the Giver of all good gifts crying out through you. It is God's desire to give through you. Cannot He afford to give whenever and wherever He will, and not be made poorer, but richer, thereby? Your hand is God's hand. My hand is God's hand. Our Father reaches out through these, His only hands, to give His gifts. We have nothing to do with the supply. Our part is to pass out the good freely and without ceasing. This we can do only by making a complete consecration (so far as our consciousness goes) of our hands, our entire being, to the service of God, the All-Good. When we have given anything to others we no longer consider it our own, but recognize it as belonging to them. So this conscious consecration of our hands to God helps us to recognize them as God's hands in which is (no longer "shall be") the fullness of all things.

When first the full recognition of there being but one hand was given to a certain woman, it was so real that for hours whenever she looked at her right hand she seemed unable to close it, so running over full of all good things did it seem. She said to herself: "Then if this be true, I have, in my hand, health to give the sick, joy to give the mourning, freedom to give those in bondage, money to give those needing it; it only needs that I keep the hand open for all good gifts to flow out." To all who came to her that day in need of anything she said mentally: "Here is just what you desire; take it and rejoice. All my gifts are in my hand to give; it is God's hand."

And the result of that day's work almost startled her, with such marvelous swiftness did the external manifestations of the heart's desire come to everyone to whom she gave the word. One aged man, who for five years had been in external bondage and exile in a foreign land, held there by the machinations of another, and in which case no external law had been of avail to free, was set into perfect liberty, with the most complete vindication of character and consequent public congratulations and rejoicings, by the word of liberty spoken for him through this woman that day. Recognizing her hand as God's hand, she only said, "Then in this hand are that man's freedom papers," and mentally extending to him her hand she said, "Here is your freedom. It is God's gift; wake up and take it; get up and go forth; you are free." Then she committed the whole matter to Him who invariably establishes the word spoken in faith, and He brought to pass the physical outpicturing of freedom.

"Thou openest thy hand, and satisfiest the desire of every living thing." Should you like to be able to do this? Then keep the hand open. Refuse to be hindered by fear of poverty, fear of want, fear that you will not be appreciated or justly dealt with. Go right on giving aid to all who need anything. "Only say the word" of giving. It is God's word spoken through your lips, and has He not said, "My word shall not return unto me void, but it shall accomplish that which I please"?

We cannot afford to withhold from giving our time, our intellect, our love, our money, to him who needs, for the law is that withholding makes poorer. "There is that scattereth, and increaseth yet more, and there is that withholdeth more than is meet, but it tendeth only to want," said Solomon.

The supply is inexhaustible. Its outflow can be limited only by demand. Nothing can hinder the hand that is consciously recognized as God's hand from being refilled, except, as was the case when the widow's oil was multiplied through Elisha, "there is not a vessel more." Let not the seeming emptiness of your hand at times stagger your faith for a moment. It is just as full when you do not see it as when you do. Keep right on recognizing it as God's right hand in which are all good gifts now; thus you will prove Him who said: "Prove me now herewith, saith

Jehovah of hosts, if I will not open you the windows of heaven, and pour you out a blessing, that there shall not be room enough to receive it."

God is surely calling us to "come up higher." To all those who are earnestly seeking Truth for Truth's sake, and not for the leaves and fishes, nor that they may be able to "give a sign" to those seeking signs. He is saying loudly: "Be not therefore anxious, saying, 'What shall we eat?' or, 'What shall we drink?' or, 'Wherewithal shall we be clothed?' For your heavenly Father knoweth that ye have need of all these things. But seek ye first his kingdom, and his righteousness; and all these things shall be added unto you." "Freely ye received, freely give." "Love your enemies, and do them good, and lend, never despairing: and your reward shall be great, and ye shall be sons of the Most High." God is forever giving, giving, giving, with no thought of return. Love always thinks of giving, never of receiving. God's giving is the spontaneous outflow of perfect love. The higher we rise in recognition and consequent manifestation of the Divine, the more surely we think always of the giving, not of what we shall receive.

We know now that money, houses, lands, and all material things can be made to come to us by our holding them in our thoughts as ours, but that is not the highest that God has in store for us. "Eye hath not seen, nor ear heard, neither have entered into the heart of man, the things which God hath prepared for them that love him." What? Self? No, but "that love him"—that love good more than self. Jesus said: "Every one that hath left houses, or lands, for my name's sake shall receive a hundredfold." They that have forsaken, they that have forsaken self, they that dare let their hands be forever open to their brothers, doing good and lending, hoping for nothing again, to them is the promise of a hundredfold even in this life.

God has called us to be stewards of His. He has chosen us as vessels to carry good to others, and it is only while carrying to others that we ourselves can be filled. The law is: "Give and it shall be given to you; good measure, pressed down, shaken together, running over." Give without thought of return.

"But," says one, "am I to give my time, my money, my best thoughts, to others, and not require of them something in return? It is not just." Give as God gives. He knows no mine and thine. He says: "All things that are mine are thine."

Look only to God for supply. If anything is returned to you through the one to whom you give, render thanks for it. If nothing visible is returned, give thanks just the same, knowing that no man can stand between you and the inexhaustible supply; that it is he that withholds who is impoverished thereby, not he from whom anything is withheld.

"Acquaint now thyself with him, and be at peace: thereby good shall come unto thee. If thou return to the Almighty, thou shalt be built up, if thou put away unrighteousness far from thy tents. And lay thou thy treasure in the dust and the gold of Ophir among the stones of the brooks; and the Almighty will be thy treasure."

When we have learned that God is our supply, and that from Him comes all our help, we shall no longer care whether "pay" is rendered for our services or not. We shall simply know that all things are ours now, and out of the fullness of love we shall give freely. God's hand is sure. Your hand is God's hand now, today. It is full now. Give out of it mentally to all who call on you, whatever they need. "Trust also in him, and he will bring it to pass".

God's Hands

1. What does the hand represent or symbolize?
2. Why does a person sometimes feel he is "empty-handed"?
3. Why do we say that man's hand represents the "hand of God"?
4. When do man's hands serve as the "hand of God"?
5. How did the woman cited in the text serve to bring freedom to a man?
6. Where does giving first take place?
7. Explain the phrase, "only say," and relate it to giving.
8. What is the relation between the "word" and the "hand"?
9. Of what is "giving" the natural outflow?
10. What blessings came to the one who serves as the "hand of God"?

If Thou Knewest

IT would seem almost childish and puerile, almost an insult to the intelligence of one's readers, to assert that the sunlight coming into a darkened room will annihilate the darkness. The merest child knows this, even if he does not understand the *modus operandi* of such fact. The sunlight does not have to make an effort to do this; it does not have to combat the darkness or wrestle or strain to overcome it; in fact, it does not change its course or its natural action in the least. It just goes on calmly radiating itself as usual. And yet the darkness is annihilated the instant it is touched by the light. Why? Because the darkness is not an entity having a reality of its own. It is nothing. It is simply the absence of a positive, real something. And when there is made a way for the something to rush in and fill to fullness the empty space, the nothing then is the nothing, the darkness annihilated, destroyed, healed; all there is left is the something, the light.

Where did the darkness go? It did not go anywhere because it was not; it had not existed. It was simply the lack of something, and when the lack was filled there was no longer any lack. So with all negation, with all that is not good, not light, not love, not health, not wholeness. They are each and every one the absence of the real and they are all annihilated or healed by letting in a something, a real substance that fills full the vacuum.

Remembering that the things that are seen are the temporal and the unreal, which pass away, while the things that are not seen are the eternal, the real, let us carry this thought of the "nothing" a little farther. Unhappiness is not a reality because it is not eternal; it belongs in the category of things that pass away. Envy, selfishness, jealousy, fear, and so forth are not real entities in our life. Each is a lack of love, its positive opposite. Lack of temporal goods, lack of health, lack of wisdom—these things do not belong to the kingdom of the real because they are all temporal things that will, as the philosopher Epictetus said, "Pass away." Nothing is real except the eternal, that which is based on the real substance—God—that which can never be changed or made less by any external circumstances whatever.

Does this not make a little clearer and more acceptable, a little less antagonistic to the mind of man, the oft-repeated statements, "There is no evil; sickness is not real; sin is not real," and so forth? I repeat, nothing is real that is not eternal and all conditions of apparent evil, of sickness, poverty, fear, and so forth, are not things, not entities in themselves, but they are simply an absence of the opposite good, just as darkness is the absence of light. In the deepest reality there is never an absence of the good anywhere, for that would mean absence of God there. God as life, wisdom, love, substance fills every space of the universe, or else He is not omnipresent. Who shall dare say He is not? Eventually our best healing of wrong conditions and human suffering is done when we recognize and affirm this great whole of Truth, the omnipresence of God, refusing absolutely to recognize anything else. The only "absence" that exists is in man's consciousness or lower senses. But in order to bring this matter to the human understanding piecemeal, to break the bread so that each shall have the portion which he is able with his present growth to take, let us take up a little detail.

Your friend is to all appearances very ill. God is life—all the life there is in the universe. Is your friend's illness an entity, a "real" thing (that is, an eternal thing)? No, it is rather like the darkened room, needing only the light to heal, an absence of perfect life in the body. Would not the incoming of newness of life—this perfect life—to all the diseased atoms heal and renew and make alive? Of course. Well, how are we to let in this fullness of life? We shall see later.

Take another example, for bodily illness is one of the least of the woes of blinded humanity with which we have to deal. A mother's precious son is going all wrong. He drinks, steals; he breaks his mother's heart with his unkindness and his dissipation. She weeps, rebukes, entreats, lectures, finally nags. What is all this that is killing the mother? It is nothing, nothing at all. It is not real because it is not eternal. It is the absence of love that is all. A perfect flood of love permeating and saturating that boy's being would heal all his diseases, both moral and physical, because he is simply manifesting a great selfishness that is absence of love—the darkened room again. How are we to get the remedy, fullness of love, let in and thus applied to the root of the disease? We shall see.

Poverty belongs among the no things, the nothings. It is not real, for only the eternal things are real, and poverty is temporal. It is an absence of substance and it is only permanently healed by an inflow of substance to fill the empty space. Sin is not real, for it is not eternal. It is failure to reach the mark. It is a blind, ignorant outreaching of the human for something not possessed, the sinner desiring and hoping thereby to gain happiness. This empty void, this awful outreaching that resulted in failure, is only satisfied and healed by the incoming flood of good that fills the lack, as the sunlight fills the darkness.

In overcoming undesirable conditions in our life there are two definite ways of arriving in our consciousness at the realization of the omnipotence of God—the great, comprehensive Truth, which heals all manner of diseases and which makes free, viz.: First, we persistently deny the reality of the seeming evil; second, we let in the substance of all good.

Everything undesirable passes away if we refuse absolutely to give it recognition by word, deed, or thought as a reality. This we can the more easily do when we remember that nothing is real except the eternal. A wiser one than we, said, "Give no place to the devil (evil)." It is not. It really has no existence whatever, any more than has the darkness that often causes us, children that we are, perfect spasms of fear and suffering. It has no more reality (remembering what is real) than the fiction of dreams. When one awakens from a particularly unpleasant dream, some moments of definite assertion to oneself that it was only a dream, not real, are required before the heart's normal action returns and the natural breathing is restored. Even with one's eyes wide open, the dream seems strangely real, but we all know that it was entirely a delusion of the senses, nothing else; no substance, no reality. So the physical and material troubles are not real, and they will disappear if we refuse absolutely to give them any life or reality by our word or thought. Let us rejoice in word; of thanksgiving that this is one of God's ways, simply that evils are not. This is our first step.

Now for the second step: Had a man any true conception of the gift of God to him, nothing in the created world would be able to withstand his power. We speak of a man's "gift" without realizing how truly we are speaking. We say he is gifted in this direction or that, as though he were in possession by nature of some remarkable ability inherited from parents, or created by peculiar environment. While many of us are ready to acknowledge in a general way that "Every good gift and every perfect gift is from above, and coming down from the Father of light," even we are not prepared for the reception of the marvelous truth of man's endowment from the Source. When a glimpse of it comes, it makes one almost breathless with wonder and astonishment.

"If thou knewest the gift of God." What is this inestimable gift? What, indeed, but that He has given the veritable Son of God to be forever within us. This is the marvelous way of creation and also of redemption from all human lack and suffering, Christ-in-you. "It was the good pleasure of the Father that in him (in this Christ, this Son of God) should . . . dwell . . . all the fullness of the Godhead," fullness of life, love, wisdom, substance yes, of the very substance of everything this human man can need or desire. "Christ in whom are all the treasures of wisdom and hidden knowledge, of his fullness we all received."

To have created man thus seemed wise to infinite wisdom, and the one object in this life should be with us as it must be in the mind of God, to make manifest this son of God. "Unto each one of us was the grace given (power, love, life, wisdom, substance) according to the measure of the gift of Christ." Not that God's giving is with partiality. Make no mistake here. The Creator of the universe is no respecter of persons. There are no favorites in His creation. All the "fullness of the Godhead" is embodied in His Son, this indwelling Christ. But this power, life, wisdom, this "all" that makes up the "fullness of the Godhead," is manifested only in proportion as we recognize this Christ as the Source of the good that we desire, look to Him for it, acknowledge Him as All, and affirm persistently in the face of all opposition that the Son of God is now made visible through us.

We are each of us small or great, gifted or otherwise; "according to the measure of the gift of Christ" we have received consciously. There must be an incoming of this divine Son of God to our conscious mind. The incoming will depend on our faithfulness in acknowledging the Source and affirming its manifestation. We cannot idly drift into it. We must speak the words of Truth before Truth will become manifest. John said, "To this end was the Son of God manifested, that he might destroy the works of the devil (evil)." Precisely so, just as the light is manifested to destroy the darkness by filling it full. Let us take and definitely use, day after day, this statement of Truth:

"The Son of God in me is now manifested, made visible in my body and all my affairs. He comes not to destroy, but to fill full."

If Thou Knewest

1. Give a definition of the word negation, and show how it is used in this lesson.
2. Where does the belief in the "absence of good" exist?
3. Explain the meaning of the words temporal and eternal.
4. How would you help a dear one who appears to be "going wrong" and expresses unkindness?
5. How would you "heal" the suffering of poverty?
6. Explain how the condition of evil is a "delusion of the senses."
7. What is a gift, and what is the greatest "gift" to man?
8. What is grace, and how is God's grace manifested?
9. What is meant by "the Godhead"?
10. Explain the meaning of the Scripture, "The Son of God was manifested, that he might destroy the works of the devil."

Trusting and Resting

HERE is a perfect passivity that is not indolence. It is a living stillness born of trust. Quiet tension is not trust. It is simply compressed anxiety.

Who is there among those who have learned the law of good and have tried to bring it into manifestation, who has not at times felt his physical being almost ready to snap asunder with the intensity of his "holding to the Truth." You believe in omnipresent life. You attempt to realize it for others. An obstinate case comes to you for help, a case in which the patient is always in a hurry for results, always wanting to know how much more time will be required, and so forth. His impatience and unbelief, together with your great desire to prove the law to him, stimulate you, after a few treatments, to greater efforts; and almost immediately you find yourself thinking frequently of him when not treating, and trying to throw more force into the treatment when he is present. Then, after giving a treatment, you find a sense of fullness in your head that is very uncomfortable; and very soon, what at first was a delight to you becomes a burden, and you almost wish the patient would go to someone else. You cannot help wondering why he improved so perceptibly with the first few treatments, and afterward, even with your increased zeal, seemed to stand still or get worse. Let me tell you why. When you first began to treat, you, so sure of the abundance of divine life, calmly and trustingly spoke the Truth to your patient. When he got in a hurry, you, beginning to take on responsibility that was God's, not yours, grew anxious and began to cast on him your compressed anxiety. You were no longer a channel for divine life, sweet, peaceful, harmonious, to flow through, but by your intensity and hurry, you completely shut off the divine influx and were able only to force on him, out of your anxious mortal mind, a few strained, compulsory thoughts that held him as in a vise, and exhausted you. Some healing and other demonstrations of power are brought to pass in this way, but it is always the stronger mortal thought controlling the weaker, and is always wearing to the one thus working. This plane is entirely one of mental suggestion, a mild form of hypnotism.

In the matter of God as our supply, or any other side of the divine law that we, from time to time, attempt to bring into manifestation, the moment we begin to be anxious our quiet becomes simply the airtight valve of tension or suppressed anxiety that shuts out the very thing we are trying to bring about, and so prevents its manifestation.

This way of holding with intensity to a thought, be it mental argument for healing or looking to God for material supply, recognizing that we ourselves have power by such firmness of thought to bring what we want into manifestation, is one way of obtaining results, but it is a hard way. We do thus give out what is within us, and it is helpful so far as it goes, but by some mental law this intensity of thought seems to cut off our consciousness from the Fountainhead, thus preventing inflow and renewal there from; hence the quick exhaustion and the burdened feeling.

We need to rise above this state of tension, to one of living trust. There is such a thing as an indolent shifting of our responsibility to an outside God, which means laziness and which never brings anything into manifestation. But there is also a state of trustful passivity, which we must enter into to do the highest work.

There are some things that we are to do ourselves, but there are others that God does not expect us to do. (When I speak of ourselves as something apart from God, I simply mean our conscious selves. We are always one with God, but we do not always realize it consciously. I speak of ourselves as the conscious part of us.) They are His part, and our greatest trouble lies in our trying to do God's part, just because we have not learned how to trust Him to do it. We are, with our conscious thought, to speak the words of life, of Truth, of abundant supply, and we are to act as though the words were true. But the "bringing it to pass" is the work of a power that is higher than we; a presence that we do not see with these mortal eyes, but which is omnipotent and will always rush to our rescue when we trust it.

From the smallest thing of our everyday life to the rolling away of the largest stone of difficulty from our path, this Presence will come in to deliver us. But its working depends on our trusting, and trusting means getting still inside.

In this effort of ours to bring into manifestation the good that we know belongs to every child of God, it is when we get beyond the point where we try to do it all ourselves and let God do His part that we get the desires of our heart.

After we have done our part faithfully, earnestly, we are told to "stand still, and see the salvation of Jehovah, which he will work for you. Jehovah will fight for you, and ye shall hold your peace. "See the conditions here imposed. This invisible Presence will remove from your path the big difficulties, which look to your mortal vision to be almost insurmountable, only on condition that you stand still. The Lord will fight for you if you hold your peace. But there is nowhere any such promise of deliverance for you while you preserve a state of flutter within. Either one—this state of internal unrest, or a forced external quiet, which simply means compressed anxiety—completely prevents this invisible omnipotent force from doing one thing for your deliverance. It must be peace, peace; possess your soul in peace, and let God work.

Marvelous have been the manifestations of this power in the writer's life when the "bringing to pass" has been left entirely to it. Ask not, then, when or how or why. This implies doubt. Only "rest in Jehovah, and wait patiently for him."

When, in the reign of Jehoshaphat, King of Judah, the Ammonites, Moabites, and others—a great multitude—came against the King in battle, he, in great fear, called the people together, and they sought counsel of the Lord, what to do saying: "We have no might against this great company that cometh against us; neither know we what to do; but our eyes are upon thee." Then the Spirit of the Lord came upon Jahaziel, and he said: "Hearken ye, all Judah . . . Thus saith Jehovah unto you, Fear not ye, neither be dismayed by reason of this great multitude; for the battle is not yours, but God's. Ye shall not need to fight in this *battle;* set yourselves, stand ye still, and see the salvation of Jehovah with you. O Judah tomorrow go out against them; for Jehovah is with you".

My friend, this battle you are trying to fight is not yours, but God's. You are trying to heal; you are trying to hold vigorously to the law of good in that very trouble at home which the world knows not of, but which at times nearly overwhelms you. Be still. Let go. The battle is God's, not yours, and because it is God's battle through you,

God desiring to manifest through you, victory was on your side before ever the battle began (in your consciousness, for that is the only place where there is any battle). Can you not calmly—aye, even with rejoicing claim the victory right now, because it is God's battle! You need no longer fight this battle, but "stand ye still," right where you are today, in the struggle to overcome material things, and "see the salvation of Jehovah with you."

Does some doubting Thomas say, "Yes, but I must have money today," or "I must have relief at once or this salvation will come too late to be of use; and besides I do not see how"? Stop right there, dear friend. You do not have to see how. That is not your business. Your business is to "stand still" and proclaim: "It is done."

God said to Jehoshaphat, "Tomorrow go out against them"; that is, they were to do calmly and in order the external things that were in the present moment to do, but at the same time they were to stand still or be in a state, mentally, of trustful passivity, and see God's saving power. Jehoshaphat did not say, "But, Lord, I do not see how"; or "Lord, I must have help right away or it will be too late, for already the enemy is on the road." We read, "They rose early in the morning . . . and as they went forth, Jehoshaphat stood and said, Hear me, O Judah believe in Jehovah your God; so shall ye be established." And then he appointed singers, who should go forth before the army, singing, "Give thanks unto Jehovah for his loving kindness endureth forever."

All this, and not yet any visible sign of the promised salvation of the Lord! Right into the very face of battle against an army mighty in number, singing, "Give thanks unto Jehovah."

Are you any nearer than this to the verge of the precipice, in this material condition that you are trying to overcome? What did Jehoshaphat do? Did he begin to think or pray hard and forcibly? Did he begin to send strong thoughts of defeat to the opposing army, and exhaust himself with his efforts to hold on to the thought until he should be delivered? Did he begin to doubt in his heart? Not at all. He simply remembered that the battle was God's and that he had nothing to do with the fighting, but everything to do with the trusting. Farther on we read:

"And when they began to sing and to praise, Jehovah set liars-in-wait against the children of Ammon, Moab, and Mount Seir that were come against Judah; and they were smitten."

It was only after they began to sing and to praise, that the Lord made the first visible move toward the manifestation of His promised salvation. It may be so with you. You may be at the very verge of apparent failure and the overthrow of your cherished principle. Your friends are already beginning to speak disparagingly to you of your foolish trust (the things of God are always foolishness with men), saying, "You must do something in this matter." Fear not. Just try to realize that the battle is God's through you; that because it is His battle, it has been victory from the start and can never be anything else. Begin to sing and praise Him for deliverance; and as surely as you do this, giving no thought to the when or the how, the salvation of the Lord will be made visible and the deliverance as real as it was in Jehoshaphat's case, even to the gathering of unexpected "spoils" following. For this narrative of Judah's king further says:

"And when Judah came to the watch-tower of the wilderness, they looked upon the multitude; and behold, they were dead bodies fallen to the earth, and there were none that escaped. And when Jehoshaphat and his people came to take the spoil of them, they found among them in abundance both riches and precious jewels, which they stripped off for themselves, more than they could carry away: and they were three days in taking the spoil, it was so much."

So God delivers when fully trusted—perfectly, fully, even beyond anything we have asked or thought; adding good that we have never dreamed of, as though to give double assurance of His favor and love to any who will trust Him. This is the "salvation of Jehovah" when we "stand still."

We must learn that the time of help's coming to us is not our part, but God's. We do know that in all the accounts in Scripture of those who realized God's special deliverance from their troubles—from Abraham's going forth to sacrifice his son, to the time when Jesus put out His hand to save the sinking and faithless Peter, and even after this in the experience of the apostles—this invisible power came to hand just at the right time always, never a moment too late.

The promise is, "God will help her, and that right early"; or, as the Hebrew reads, "at the turning of the morning," which means just the darkest moment before dawn. So if, in whatever matter you are trying to exercise trust in your Father, the way keeps growing darker and darker and apparently the help goes farther and farther away instead of coming into sight, you must grow more peaceful and still than ever and then you may know that the moment of deliverance is growing nearer for you with your every breath.

In Saint Mark's account of that early morning visit of the women to the tomb of Jesus, when, bent on an errand of loving service, they forgot entirely the immense stone weighing several tons lying across their path, until they were almost at their journey's end, and then one exclaimed in momentary dismay, "Who shall roll us away the stone from the door of the tomb? Then looking up, they see that the stone is rolled back: for it was exceeding great." Is not "exceeding great" full of meaning to us? The very greatness of the difficulty that made it impossible for the women to remove it was the more reason why it was done by this invisible Power.

"Man's extremity is God's opportunity." The more we are cut off from human help, the greater claim we can make on divine help. The more impossible a thing is to human or mortal power, the more at peace can we be when we look to Him for deliverance, for He has said: "*My* power is made perfect in weakness." And Paul, realizing that when he placed less confidence in the mortal he had more help from the Divine, said: "When I (the mortal) am weak, then I am strong."

Trusting means resting confidently. We are to rest confidently, saying: *"God is my strength; God is my power, God is my assured victory. I will trust in Him, and He will bring it to pass."*

"Commit thy way unto Jehovah; trust also in him, and he will bring it to pass."

"It is better to take refuge in Jehovah (in the invisible Presence) than to put confidence in princes."

"Thou wilt keep him in perfect peace, *whose* mind is stayed *on thee,* because he trusteth in thee."

Trusting and Resting

1. What is meant by the statement, "holding to the Truth"?
2. What is a "treatment"?
3. What is it that heals all infirmities?
4. What is "tension," and what is its effect on yourself and others?
5. Where does your responsibility end and God's commence?
6. What part does praise have in spiritual treatment?
7. What has "time" to do with the answers to prayer?
8. What is the "stone" that is so great that is rolled away?
9. What is the "Lord" that is to be trusted implicitly?
10. What is peace, and how is the consciousness of peace attained by the individual?

The Spoken Word

"WITHOUT him (the Word) was not anything made that hath been made."

"In the beginning God created the heavens and the earth."

How?

Listen: "The earth was waste and void; and darkness was upon the face of the deep. . . ."

"And God said, Let there be light; and there was light."

"And God said, Let there be a firmament and it was so."

"And God said, Let the waters under the heavens be gathered together unto one place, and let the dry land appear: and it was so."

"And God said, Let the earth put forth grass and it was so."

"And God said, Let us make man in our image, after our likeness and it was so."

God, infinite power, might have thought about all these things 'til doomsday. He might have wished during an indefinite time that they were formed and made visible. Nothing would ever have been created in visible form had there not been the spoken word put forth into the formless ether. It took the definite, positive "Let there be," to bring forth order out of chaos and to establish in visible results the thoughts and desires of even an infinite, omnipotent Creator.

To create is to bring into visibility; to form something where before there was nothing; to cause to exist or to take form that which before was without form and void. To exist (from *ex,* out from, and *sister,* to stand) is to stand out. Being always is; existence (from Latin, *existere,* to stand forth, emerge, appear) is that which stands forth as a visible entity.

God creates. Because man was created or brought into the visible universe in the image and likeness of God, he spiritually, has like powers with God: he has the power of creating, of bringing into visible form that which before did not exist. As God created by the spoken word, without which "was not anything made that hath been made," so man can create by his spoken word. In fact, there is no other way under heaven to bring into existence the visible conditions and the things that we want.

Today it is agreed by all scientists, (material as well as spiritual), that there is but one universal substance out of which all things are made. This substance is divine stuff that, though invisible and intangible, is lying all about us, as is the atmosphere. This divine substance is without form and void, as is also this same physical atmosphere. It is waiting, forever waiting, for man to form it as he wills, by his spoken word.

What is liquid air? It is compressed invisibility, is it not? It is invisible, formless substance pressed into form by a definite and continued process until it becomes visible and tangible. This God-stuff, divine substance, is likewise subject to the pressure of man's thought and word.

There are three realms in the universe: the spiritual, the mental or psychic, and the physical or material. These three, while in a way distinct, are so blended into one that it is difficult to know where one ends and another begins. All created things have Spirit, soul, and body. All things that we desire are now in being in the spiritual or invisible. But, as someone has said, thought and the spoken word stand between the invisible and the visible. By the action of these two—thought and the spoken word—is the invisible made visible.

When we desire anything—I use this word "anything" advisedly, for did not the Master in divine things say, "Whatsoever ye pray and ask for," "If ye shall ask anything"—we must take our thought entirely off the visible world and center it on God. We begin, as God began in creation, by speaking out into this formless substance all about us with faith and power, "Let there be so and so (whatever we want). Let it come forth into manifestation here and now. It does come forth by the power of my word. It is done; it is manifest." We continue this with vehemence a few moments and then let go of it. This should be repeated with firmness and regularity and definite persistence, at least in the morning and in the evening. Continue it, absolutely regardless of any evidence or want of evidence. Faith takes hold of the substance of the things hoped for and brings into evidence the things not seen.

The moment one takes cognizance of circumstances, that moment he lets go of faith. Our spoken word first hammers the thing desired into shape. Our continued spoken word brings this shaped substance forth and clothes it with a visible body. The first action brings that which is desired from the formless toward the external as far as the psychic; the continued action brings it forth still farther and clothes it with visible form or material body.

This was illustrated to the writer, a few years ago. A woman, Miss C____, had been for days vigorously "speaking the word" out into the great universe of substance, for something she much desired. She had no confidante and recognized no human help.

One day she wrote an ordinary business letter to a friend in the country. This friend, on receipt of the letter, immediately replied, saying: "What is this strange thing about this letter of yours? When I took it from the post office it had the appearance to me of being covered with so and so (the very thing which the writer had been shaping in the invisible by her spoken word). I opened the letter," she continued, "and for some minutes the opened letter took the form, to my sight, of a 'horn of plenty,' pouring out in unlimited quantity this same thing. Have I gone crazy, or what does it mean?"

Do you not see? The word spoken by Miss C____, alone in the silence of her own room, had shaped and brought forth toward the external, as far as the psychic realm, the thing desired. The vibrations of her thought had permeated, all unknown to her, everything that she had touched. The friend, having some psychic power developed, saw, plainly surrounding this letter, the shape that Miss C____ had created, though it was yet invisible to the natural eye. It is needless to say that the continued word very soon brought this shape forth another step into the visible world as a solid manifestation of exactly what Miss C____ desired.

In this process, there are two conditions that must be carefully observed. One is, do not talk with anyone about what you are doing. Talk scatters the precious divine substance; what we want to do is focus it. Needless talk diffuses and wastes one's power. One might as well pierce full of holes the boiler of a steam engine, letting the steam ooze at dozens of holes, and then expect to have enough power in the engine to draw the train. It is impossible both to diffuse and to focus at the same time.

The other important condition to observe is to continue with the spoken word. "Let us not be weary in well-doing: for in due season we shall reap, if we faint not."

The Spoken Word

1. Read Genesis 1 and John 1. To what phase of the creative process does each chapter refer?
2. To what do we refer when we write "word" with a capital "W"?
3. Name the days or steps in the creative process as given in Genesis 1 and 2, explaining the six days or periods of activity, culminating in the seventh day (step) or Sabbath. What follows these days or steps?
4. Why is it that man's prayers are often just wishes?
5. What distinguishes man as the highest manifestation of God?
6. Why do we say that divine substance is forever "waiting for man"?

7. When man prays, does God "withhold" from him what is not for his good?
8. How does man "make" his body and his world?
9. What place in creation has thought? Where does the spoken word act?
10. What part does faith play in the process of bringing forth good in our life? What other condition should be observed for perfect results?

Unadulterated Truth

THERE is a straight white line of absolute Truth upon which each one must walk if he would have demonstration. The slightest swerving in either direction from this line results in non-demonstration, no matter how earnest or intense one may be.

The line is this: *There is only God; all seeming else is a lie.*

Whosoever is suffering today from sickness, poverty, failure—any kind of trouble—is believing the lie.

We talk largely about Truth, and quote with ease and alacrity the words of the Master, "The truth shall make you free." Free from what? Free from sickness, sorrow, weakness, fear, poverty. We claim to know the Truth, but the question to be driven right home is, are we free from these undesirable things? And if not, why not?

Let us get right down to a good, hardpan, practical basis about this matter.

We talk much about the omnipresence of God. In fact, this is one of the basic statements upon which rests the so-called New Thought. "God is omnipresent, omnipotent, omniscient." When I was a child in spiritual things, I thought as a child and understood as a child. I believed that God was here, there, and everywhere, within hailing distance of every human being, no matter whether under the sea or on the mountain top, in prison or outside, in the sick chamber or at the wedding feast. In any and all places He was so near that in an instant He could be summoned to help. To me this was God's omnipresence. Then His omnipotence meant to me that while sickness and poverty, sorrow, the evil tongue of jealousy or slander, and so forth, had great power to make one suffer, God had greater power. I believed that if He were called on to help us, He surely would do it, but it would be after a fierce and prolonged combat between the two powers of good and evil, or of God and trouble.

I wonder if there are not others today whose real, innermost thoughts of God's omnipresence and omnipotence are much like this. Are you one of those who believe in God and—? God and—sickness? God and poverty?, God and something unpleasant in your life that you are daily trying to down by applying a sort of plaster of formal statements of Truth right over the sore place of your trouble, while at the same time you are giving in your own mind (if not also in your conversation) about equal power to the remedy and the disease? While you remain in this category, let me tell you that you will never escape from your bondage, whatever it may be.

Try for a moment to think what really is meant by omnipresent Spirit, remembering at the same time that what applies to your body, applies equally to all other forms of human affairs or conditions.

Each little atom of one's physical body, taken separately is completely filled, permeated by Spirit-life. This must be true because there could be no external form to the atom without first the *sub-stans*, that which stands under, or as the basis of all material things. The Spirit permeating each atom is now, always has been, and always will be absolutely perfect, because it is God, the only life in the universe. These atoms are held together each moment by the same Spirit. They work together because the Spirit pervading them is one Spirit and not several spirits. Spirit-life cannot change because if it did, there would be one place where, for a time, there would be lack of God, perfect life. One place for one instant without God would break up the entire law of omnipresence, which cannot be.

Jesus said, "The truth shall make you free." but He prefaced this statement by the word, "Ye shall know the truth." It is, then, knowledge of the Truth that sets free. We are free now but we do not know it. You may be the child of a king, but if you do not know it, you may live in poverty and squalor all your life. We are all, today, this very hour, free from all sickness, because God, who is perfect life, unchangeable and indestructible, abides within and completely fills every atom of our body. If God, divine substance, fills every part, every place and space as the atmosphere fills the room, there is certainly no absence of Spirit-life in any part. Then if today we are manifesting sickness, it is because we have believed the lie about ourselves and have reaped the results of the lie—that Is, apparent lack of health—in our consciousness.

All that is, is good, but lack of God In any part is not, that is, does not exist. Such a thing is a mortal impossibility.

Many earnest people are greatly puzzled right here. They are told that "there is no evil; all is good because all is God," and so forth. When they find themselves or others suffering apparent pain, sickness, lack of money, and so forth, they are staggered in faith, and begin to say: "Surely this is not good; lack of health is not good; sin is not good; poverty is not good. What is this?" For an answer they are often told, "Oh! Yes, this is good, for there is nothing but good (God) in the universe. This is unripe good, like the green apple."

Now the truth is that all which is not good (God) is nothing. It is the lie, and has only to be definitely characterized as such in order to disappear. What is the wild beast that sits on your chest with such overwhelming weight when you have a nightmare? Is it "unripe good"? Is it something that, after a few days or weeks or right thoughts, you can manipulate into good? Not at all. From beginning to end it is nothing, nothing but a vagary, a deception of the mortal brain and senses. Had it at any time any sort of reality whatever? Surely not. It is all a lie, which, at the time, seems so real that it requires almost superhuman efforts to throw it off, even after you realize that it is only a nightmare.

"There is one God, the Father, of whom are all things," said Paul. And again, "For of Him, and through him, and unto him, are all things."

If God, then, is the substance of all things visible and invisible, and is omnipresent, there is no such thing as lack of God or lack of substance in any place in this universe. Sickness would be lack of life in some part of the body. Impossible! Poverty would be lack of substance in the circumstances. Impossible. Foolishness, ignorance, insanity, would be lack of God, Divine Mind, omniscience in man. Impossible! These things cannot be.

Do you not see, then, how all these negatives are nothingness, not true, the lie? And how, instead of recognizing them as something to be overcome, we should put them at once and at all times into their real place of nothingness?

Let us go back to our straight, white line of absolute Truth: *There is only God.* All that is not God is nothing, that is, has no existence—is simply the nightmare. If we walk on this white line where we refuse to see or acknowledge anything but God, then all else disappears. In dealing with the everyday problems of life, we shall succeed in becoming free, just in proportion as we cease absolutely to parley with apparent evils as though they were entities. We cannot afford to spend a moment's time agreeing with their claim, for if we do, we ourselves shall be the overcome instead of the overcomers. We must rise to the highest, most sweeping statements of Truth that we know. Our great statement must be: *"There is only God."* Whatever is not God (good) is a lie. And this lie must be instantly and constantly crushed on the head as a viper the moment it appears in our mentality. Hit the hydra-headed monster (the lie) as soon as it appears, with the positive statement, "You are a lie. Get to where you belong. There is no truth in you. There is only God, and God is fullness of good, life, joy, peace, now and forever."

The absolute truth is there is no real lack anywhere, but a waiting abundance of every kind of good that man can possibly desire or conceive of. Stop believing the lie. Stop speaking it. Speak the Truth. It is the spoken Truth that makes manifest.

In the domain of Spirit there is neither time nor space. What is to be and already is must be spoken into visibility. Practice thinking and realizing omnipresence, that is, practice realizing that all good that you desire is here now, all-present; it is not apart from you and its coming to you does not require time. There is no time or space.

There is not God and—a body.

There is not God and—circumstance.

There is not God and—any sort of trouble.

There is only God, through and through and through all things, in our body, in our seemingly empty purses, in all our circumstances, just waiting as invisible Spirit substance, for us to recognize and acknowledge Him, and Him only, in order to become visible. All else is a lie.

God is. God is all.

God is manifest, because there is nothing else to manifest.

Unadulterated Truth

1. What is absolute Truth?
2. What is demonstration, and how is it made?
3. What is the primary cause of failure, poverty, sickness, death?
4. Explain each of the following terms: omnipresence, omnipotence, omniscience.
5. Explain "substance" and "life," and show how they are related to Spirit.
6. How may we be free from all undesirable conditions and circumstances?
7. What is meant by the statement, "There is no evil"?
8. When is anything "manifest"?
9. Why do we say that it is the spoken Truth that makes manifest?
10. Why is it necessary that we "realize" omnipresence?

Oneness With God

"Prayer that craves a particular commodity, anything less than all good, is vicious. Prayer is the contemplation of the facts of life from the highest point of view. It is the soliloquy of a beholding and jubilant soul. It is the Spirit of God pronouncing His works good. But prayer as a means to effect a private end is meanness and theft. It supposes dualism and not unity in nature and consciousness. As soon as the man is (consciously) at one with God, he will not beg."—Emerson

TRUE prayer, then, is just a continual recognition and thanksgiving that all is good, and that all good is ours now as much as it ever can be. Oh, when will our faith become strong and steadfast enough to take possession of our inheritance here? The Israelites entered not into the Promised Land because of their unbelief. Their inheritance was real and was awaiting them then and there, but it could not do them any good nor give any enjoyment until they took hold of it by faith, after which and as a result of which, would have come the reality. It is this taking by faith that brings anything into actuality and visibility. Why will this mortal mind of ours forever postpone the acceptance of all good as our rightful inheritance for this life? The heir of material wealth must accept his inheritance before he can possibly come into its possession or use. So long as he rejects it, he is as poor as though nothing had been provided for him. All things are ours now, fullness of love, of life, of wisdom, of power—aye, more than these, fullness of all good, which means abundance of all things, material as well as spiritual. "Every good gift and every perfect gift is from above, coming down from the Father of lights, with whom can be no variation, neither shadow that is cast by turning."

Thank God, some of His children are ceasing to look at the things of God from the objective standpoint, and are learning to contemplate the facts of life from the subjective, or higher side—even pronouncing all things good, as God does, until everything else but the thought of good drops out of mind, and only the good is manifest.

Oh, how marvelous are these little glimpses we are from time to time obtaining of things as God sees them! To what high points of privilege are we, His children, being lifted, in these latter days, so that it is possible for us to see things from the standpoint of pure intelligence, perfect wisdom! "Verily I say unto you, that many prophets and righteous men desired to see the things which ye see, and saw them not."

One instant's view of the facts of life from the subjective side (God's side) makes all our carnal aspirations and struggles, all our ambitions, all our boasted wisdom and pride sink into utter nothingness. We see instead "the wisdom of this world is foolishness with God." All other objects in life fade into insignificance beside the one of getting more and more into conscious oneness with the Father, where, at all times, we shall pray the true prayer of rejoicing and thanksgiving that all good is the only real thing in the universe. When we came into perfect recognition of unity instead of duality, then, indeed, shall we know prayer to be but the "soliloquy of a beholding and jubilant soul," and we shall cease forever to pray the prayer as a means to effect a private end, which is theft and meanness.

The nearer we approach to God, and the more we grow into the realization of our true relationship to Him, our Father, the more surely are all personalities, all divisions lost sight of; our oneness with all men becomes so vivid and real to us that a prayer for "private ends" becomes impossible to us. All desires of the little self are merged in the desire for universal good, because we recognize but One in the universe and ourselves as part of that One.

Now comes the question: How can we most quickly and most surely attain this conscious oneness with the Father, which will enable us to see things as He sees them—all good?

And instantly flashes over the wires of intuition, out from the stillness of the invisible, a voice saying "O return ye unto God." Return, turn back away from the mortal, away from people, from human ways; turn "within and look unto me, ye people, saith the Lord your God."

Seek the light from the interior, not from external sources. Why always seek to interpose human help between ourselves and God? Emerson says: "The relations of the soul to the divine spirit are so pure that it is profane to seek to interpose helps. Whenever a mind is simple and receives a divine wisdom, old things pass away—means, teachers, texts, temples fall."

"Let us not roam, let us stay home with the cause."

Constant reading, discussions, and interchange of opinions, are all external ways of reaching the Truth from the intellectual side. These are a way, but "I am the way, and the truth, and the life," spake the voice of the Father through the Nazarene. "The anointing which ye received of him abideth in you, and ye need not that anyone teach you." "The Spirit of truth shall guide you into all the truth and he shall declare unto you the things that are to come.

When will we cease running after Truth, and learn to "be still, and know that I am God"? In order that we may hear the inner voice and may receive the highest form of teaching, which alone can open the eyes of our spiritual understanding, the mortal self must cease its clamoring even for Truth, the human intellect must become absolutely still, forgetting to argue or discuss. The Father can lead into all Truth only when we listen to hear what He will say—not to what others will Say. We must learn to listen—not anxiously and with strained ears, but expectantly, patiently, trustingly. We must learn how to wait on God, in the attitude of "Speak Jehovah for thy servant heareth," if we would know Truth.

Jesus said, "Except ye turn, and become as little children (that is, teachable and trusting) ye shall in no wise enter into the kingdom of heaven," or the kingdom of understanding of Truth. And again He said, "I thank thee, O Father that thou didst hide these things from the wise and understanding (or intellectual), and didst reveal them unto babes."

We must put aside all preconceived opinions of Truth, either our own or any other person's, and with receptive mind opened toward the source of all light, say continually, "Lord, teach me." We must become as babes in human wisdom before we can enter into the deep things of God.

But believe me, the revelation that the Spirit of truth will make to you when you have withdrawn from all outside sources and learned to listen to the voice in your own soul, will be such as to make you know—no longer believe—your oneness with the Father and with all His children. They will be such as to fill you with great joy. "These things have I spoken unto you, that my joy may be in you, and that your joy may be made full."

The great God of the universe has chosen you and me through whom to manifest Himself. "Ye did not choose me, but I chose you."

Shall we forever limit this manifestation by making ourselves into a little, narrow mold of personality that will shape and size the Divine, or, worse still, shall we run here and there to borrow some measure our neighbor has made of himself, and hold it as our measure under the great rushing waters of infinite wisdom and love, thereby saying: "This full is all I want; it is all there is to be had, all that thou art"?

Away forever with such limitations.

> There's a wideness in God's mercy,
> Like the wideness of the sea:
> There's a kindness in His justice,
> Which is more than liberty.
> For the love of God is broader
> Than the measure of man's mind;
> And the heart of the Eternal
> Is most wonderfully kind.

Would you, then, know God, "whom to know aright is life eternal"? Go not abroad looking for the Divine. "Stay at home within thine own soul." Seek there earnestly, calmly, trustfully, the source of all good. Know at once and forever that only therein will you find Truth, and only thereby will you grow to be what you desire—self-centered, self-poised. Let go your little narrow thoughts of the Divine, cease to desire anything less than the fulfillment of God's will in you. His thoughts are higher than ours as the heavens are higher than the earth. Let nothing short of the perfect fulfillment of His thought in and through you satisfy you.

Do you comprehend this in its fullness—the desire of infinite love and pure intelligence being fulfilled (or filled full) in you and me?

Oh, how quickly and far recede the cankering cares of life, the frets and fumes, the misunderstandings and the being misunderstood! How sure we are when we have consciously—and by effort if need be—swept away all limitations of personal desire and are saying, "Here am I, infinite Father, Thou great Fountainhead of all good. I have no desire.

Thou art fulfilling thy highest thoughts in me, unhindered by my consciousness; Thou art now pouring Thyself through this organism into visibility; Thou art thinking Thy thoughts through this intellect; Thou art loving through this heart with Thine own tender Father-Mother love, which thinketh no evil, endureth all things, beareth all things, seeketh not its own; Thou art manifesting Thyself in Thine own way through this organism unto the visible world." I say, when we thus burst the bonds of personal desire and rise to a willingness that the Father's will be done through us every moment, how sure we are of the fatherly care that will clothe us with the beauty of the lilies and feed us as the birds of the air. Aye, with even a more lavish abundance of all good things than He gives to either of these, for "ye are of more value than many sparrows."

Do you fear to break loose from teachers, from human helps? Fear not. Trust to the great and mighty One that is in you and is limitless to manifest Himself as Truth to you and through you. There will be no failure, no mistake. Spend some time daily alone with the Creator of the universe. In no other way will you ever come into the realization that you desire. Learn to sever yourself from those around you. Practice this, and soon you can be as much alone with God in the street or in a crowded room, as you could be in the wilds of a desert. A little book called, *The Practice of the Presence of God*, by Brother Lawrence, tells how he, for years, kept himself consciously in the very glory of divine Presence, even while at the most humble daily tasks, by always keeping the thought. "I am in His presence." All things that were not divine in the man died out, and dropped away, not because he fought them or resisted the uprising of the natural man, but because he persistently practiced the Presence (or thought of the Presence) of God, and in that Presence all other things melted away like snow before a spring sun.

This is the only way of growth, of overcoming. "Have this mind in you, which was also in Christ Jesus." We do not have, by some supreme effort, to draw this Mind into us, but simply to let it come into us. Our part is to take the attitude consciously of receiving, remembering first to enter the "inner chamber" of our own soul, and to shut the door on all thought but that of divine Presence.

Each individual has his own salvation to work out—that is, his own true self to bring into visibility. This is not to be done by some intense superhuman effort, but by each one dealing directly with the Father.

So long as anyone clings to another, just so long will the manifestation of the real self, God, remain weak and limited. Wait only on God for the light you desire. He will tell you how to act, what to do. Trust your own inspiration; act on it, though all the world sit in judgment on it, for when any man puts aside selfish aims, and desires only to manifest the Highest, his life then becomes the perfect One manifesting through him.

When you learn to let God manifest Himself through you in His own way, it will not be like the manifestation through anyone else. You will think and speak and do without previous thought or plan. You will be as new and surprising to yourself as to anyone else. For it will not be you speaking, but the Spirit of your Father speaking in you.

Oh, what supreme tranquility we have when we are conscious that our thought is God's thought through us; our act, our word, God's act and word through us! We never stop to think of results; that is His care. We are quietly indifferent to criticism of lesser minds (mortal thought), for we know whom we have believed. We know that what we speak and do is right, though all the world be made wrong thereby. "What I must do is all that concerns me, not what the people think," says Emerson. Then God in you becomes a law to you, and you have no longer need of external laws. God becomes wisdom to you, ever revealing to you more and more of Himself, giving you new and clear visions of Truth, and indeed, "ye need not that anyone teach you." You have no longer use for external forms, which are but the limitations of Truth and not Truth itself. Then God shall be to you, and through you to others, not only wisdom and understanding, but love and life and the abundance of all things needful.

Then shall you have at all times something new to give to others, instead of looking to them to receive; for you will stand in the very storehouse of all good with the Master of the house, that through you He may pass out freely the bread and water of life to those who are still holding up their empty cups to some human hand to be filled—not yet having learned to enter into all the fullness of good for themselves.

Believe me, you who seek Truth, who seek life and health and satisfaction, it is nowhere to be found until you seek it directly from the Fountainhead who "giveth to all liberally and upbraideth not."

Begin at once to put aside all things that you have hitherto interposed between your own soul and the great cause of all things.

Cease now and forever to lean on anything less than the Eternal. Nothing less can give you peace.

Oneness With God

1. Where and how is true prayer exercised?
2. What mental faculty is of prime importance in the exercise of true prayer?
3. How can we say that good is the only reality in the universe?
4. Explain the meaning of the word fact and what it is to "contemplate the facts of life from the highest point of view."
5. What is meant by "conscious oneness with the Father", and how is this conscious oneness attained?
6. Name some of the results that come from conscious oneness with God.
7. What is meant by "God's will" in you?
8. How do you "Have this mind in you, which was also in Christ Jesus"?
9. Explain the distinction between "revelation" and "inspiration" as used in this lesson.
10. How do you seek directly from the "Fountainhead," and how does its supply come to you?

Minneapolis 1901

Florence Scovel Shinn

(1871-1940)

Teacher, Author & Illustrator

Florence Shinn graduated from the Art Academy, married Everett Shinn and moved to New York where he built her a small theater next to their studio at 112 Waverly Place. He created the Waverly Players and wrote her three plays in which she played the title role.

Prior to World War I, Florence worked as an illustrator of children's magazines and books. In 1912, her marriage failed, upon which Everett requested a divorce.

This led her to a more intense examination of her life, whereupon she turned to New Thought and soon became a New Thought teacher and wrote: *"The Game of Life and How to Play It"*. In 1925, having been unable to find a publisher for it, she published it herself. This was followed by *"Your Word is Your Wand"* in 1928. *"The Secret Door to Success"* was published shortly before her death on October 17, 1940. The *"Power of the Spoken Word"* is a student's compilation of her notes, which was published after her death in 1945.

Florence Scovel Shinn's ability to explain success principles and their application in an entertaining and easy-to-read style via sharing real-life stories has delighted readers around the world. Excerpts are from: *Your Word is Your Wand: A Sequel to The Game of Life and How to Play It.* (1)

Link & Acknowledgement
1.   newthoughtlibrary.comshinnFlorenceScovelbio_shinn.htm

Your Word is Your Wand
(1928)

Success
Prosperity
Happiness
Love
Forgiveness
Words of Wisdom
Faith
Loss
Debt
Guidance
Protection
The Divine Design
Health
Miscellaneous
Conclusion

Man's word is his wand filled with magic and power!

Jesus Christ emphasized the power of the word; "By thy words thou shalt be justified and by thy words thou shalt be condemned," and "death and life are in the power of the tongue."

So man has power to change an unhappy condition by waving over it the wand of his word.

In the place of sorrow appears joy, in the place of sickness appears health, and in the place of lack appears plenty.

For example: A woman came for a treatment for prosperity. She possessed just two dollars in the world.

I said: "We bless the two dollars and know that you have the magic purse of the Spirit; it can never be depleted; as money goes out, immediately money comes in, under grace in perfect ways.

I see it always crammed, jammed with money: Yellow bills, green bills, pink checks, blue checks, white checks, gold, silver and currency. I see it bulging with abundance!"

She replied: "I feel my bag heavy with money," and was so filled with faith that she gave me one of her dollars as a love offering. I did not dare refuse it and see lack for her, as it was important that I hold the picture of plenty.

Shortly afterwards she was made a gift of six thousand dollars. Fearless faith and the spoken word brought it to pass.

The affirmation of the magic purse is very powerful, as it brings a vivid picture to the mind. It is impossible not to see your purse or wallet filled with money when using the words, "crammed, jammed."

The imaging faculty is the creative faculty and it is important to choose words which bring a flash of the fulfillment of the demand.

Never force a picture by visualizing; let the Divine Idea flash into your conscious mind; then the student is working according to the Divine Design.

Jesus Christ said: "Ye shall know the Truth and the Truth shall make you free."

This means that man must know the Truth of every situation which confronts him.

There is no Truth in lack or limitation. He waves over it the wand of His Word and the wilderness rejoices and blossoms as the rose.

Fear, doubt, anxiety, anger, resentment pull down the cells of the body, shock the nervous system and are the causes of disease and disaster.

Happiness and health must be earned by absolute control of the emotional nature.

Power moves but is never moved. When man stands calm and serene, has a good appetite, feels contented and happy when appearances are against him, he has reached mastery. Then he has the power to "rebuke the winds and the waves," to control conditions.

His word is his wand and he transmutes apparent failure into success.

He knows his universal supply is endless and immediate and all his needs manifest instantly on the external.

For example, a woman at sea awoke in the morning hearing the fog-horns blowing. A dense fog had settled on the ocean with no apparent signs of clearing. She immediately spoke the word: "There are no fogs in Divine Mind, so let the fog be lifted! I give thanks for the sun!"

Soon the sun came out, for man has dominion over "the elements—over all created things."

Every man has power to lift the fog in his life. It may be a fog of lack of money, love, happiness or health.

Give thanks for the sun!

Success

There are certain words or pictures which impress the subconscious mind. For example: A man called asking me to speak the word for his right work. I gave him the statement: "Behold I have set before thee the open door of destiny and no man shall shut it!" It didn't seem to make much impression, so I was inspired to add: "And no man shall shut it for it is nailed back!"

The man was electrified and went out walking on air. Within a few weeks he was called to a distant city to fill a wonderful position which came about in a miraculous way.

I give another example of a woman who fearlessly followed a "hunch."

She was working for a small salary when she read my book, The Game of Life and How to Play It. The thought came in a flash, to start in business for herself and open a Tearoom and Candy Shop.

The idea staggered her at first, but it persisted, so she boldly went forth and procured a shop and assistants.

She "spoke the word for supply," for she did not have money to back her enterprise. It came in miraculous ways, and the shop opened! From the first day it was filled with people, and now it is "crammed jammed"; they stand in line and wait.

One day, being a holiday, her assistants became gloomy and said they could not expect to do much business. My student, however, replied that God was her supply and every day was a good day. In the afternoon an old friend came in to see the shop and bought a two pound box of candy. He gave her a check and when she looked at it she found it was for a hundred dollars. So it was indeed a good day! One hundred dollars for a box of candy!

She says every morning she enters the shop with wonder and gives thanks that she had the fearless faith that wins!

Affirmations

1. The decks are now cleared for Divine Action and my own comes to me under grace in a magical way.
2. I now let go of worn-out conditions and worn-out things. Divine order is established in my mind, body and affairs. "Behold, I make all things new."
3. My seeming impossible good now comes to pass, the unexpected now happens!
4. The "four winds of success" now blow to me my own. From North, South, East and West comes my endless good.
5. The Christ in me is risen, I now fulfill my destiny
6. Endless good now comes to me in endless ways.
7. I clap my cymbals and rejoice, for Jehovah goes before me making clear, easy and successful my way!
8. I give thanks for my whirlwind success. I sweep all before me for I work with the Spirit and follow the Divine Plan of my life.
9. My Spiritual Sporting blood is up! I am more than equal to this situation.
10. I am awake to my good, and gather in the harvest of endless opportunities.

11. I am harmonious, poised and magnetic. I now draw to myself my own. My power is God's power and is irresistible!

12. Divine Order is now established in my mind, body and affairs. I see clearly and act quickly and my greatest expectations come to pass in a miraculous way.

13. There is no competition on the spiritual plane. What is rightfully mine is given me under grace.

14. I have within me an undiscovered country, which is revealed to me now, in the name of Jesus Christ.

15. Behold! I have set before thee the open door of Destiny and no man shall shut it, for it is nailed back.

16. The tide of Destiny has turned and everything comes my way.

17. I banish the past and now live in the wonderful now, where happy surprises come to me each day.

18. There are no lost opportunities in Divine Mind, as one door shuts another door is opened.

19. I receive magical work in a magical way; I give magical service for magical pay.

20. The genius within me is now released. I now fulfill my destiny.

21. I make friends without hindrances and every obstacle becomes a stepping-stone. Every-thing in the Universe, visible and invisible, is working to bring to me my own.

22. I give thanks that the walls of Jericho fall down and all lack, limitation and failure are wiped out of my consciousness in the name of Jesus Christ.

23. I am now on the royal road of Success, Happiness and Abundance, all the traffic goes my way.

24. I will not weary of well-doing, for when I least expect it I shall reap.

25. Jehovah goes before me and the battle is won! All enemy thoughts are wiped out. I am victorious in the name of Jesus Christ.

26. There are no obstacles in Divine Mind, therefore, there is nothing to obstruct my good.

27. All obstacles now vanish from my pathway. Doors fly open, gates are lifted and I enter the Kingdom of fulfillment, under grace.

28. Rhythm, harmony and balance are now established in my mind, body and affairs.

29. New fields of Divine activity now open for me and these fields are white with harvest.

30. Man's will is powerless to interfere with God's will. God's will is now done in my mind, body and affairs.

31. God's plan for me is permanent and cannot be budged. I am true to my heavenly vision.

32. The Divine Plan of my life now takes shape in definite, concrete experiences leading to my heart's desire.

33. I now draw from the Universal Substance, with irresistible power and determination, that which is mine by Divine Right.

34. I do not resist this situation. I put it in the hands of Infinite Love and Wisdom. Let the Divine idea now come to pass.

35. My good now flows to me in a steady, unbroken, ever-increasing stream of success, happiness and abundance.

36. There are no lost opportunities in the Kingdom. As one door shuts another door opens.

37. There is nothing to fear for there is no power to hurt. I walk up to the lion on my pathway and find an angel in armor, and victory in the name of Jesus Christ.

38. I am in perfect harmony with the working of the law. I stand aside and let Infinite Intelligence make easy and successful my way.

39. The ground I am on is holy ground. The ground I am on is successful ground.

40. New fields of Divine Activity now open for me. Unexpected doors fly open, unexpected channels are free.

41. What God has done for others He can do for me and more!

42. I am as necessary to God as He is to me, for I am the channel to bring His plan to pass.

43. I do not limit God by seeing limitation in myself. With God and myself all things are possible.

44. Giving precedes receiving and my gifts to others precede God's gifts to me.

45. Every man is a golden link in the chain of my good.
46. My poise is built upon a rock; I see clearly and act quickly.
47. God cannot fail, so I cannot fail. "The warrior within me" has already won.
48. Thy Kingdom come in me, Thy will be done in me and my affairs.

Prosperity

Man comes into the world financed by God, with all that he desires or requires already on his pathway.

This supply is released through faith and the Spoken Word.

"If thou canst believe, all things are possible."

For example: A woman came to me one day to tell me of her experience in using an affirmation she had read in my book, The Game of Life and How to Play It.

She was without experience but desired a good position on the stage. She took the affirmation: "Infinite Spirit, open the way for my great abundance. I am an irresistible magnet for all that belongs to me by Divine Right."

She was given a very important part in a successful opera.

She said: "It was a miracle, due to the affirmation, which I repeated hundreds of times."

Affirmations

1. I now draw from the abundance of the spheres my immediate and endless supply. All Channels are free! All Doors are open!
2. I now release the gold-mine within me. I am linked with an endless golden stream of prosperity which comes to me under grace in perfect ways.
3. Goodness and mercy shall follow me all the days of my life and I shall dwell in the house of abundance forever.
4. My God is a God of plenty and I now receive all that I desire or require, and more.

5. All that is mine by Divine Right is now released and reaches me in great avalanches of abundance, under grace in miraculous ways.
6. My supply is endless, inexhaustible and immediate and comes to me under grace in perfect ways.
7. All channels are free and all doors fly open for my immediate and endless, Divinely Designed supply.
8. My ships come in over a calm sea, under grace in perfect ways.
9. I give thanks that the millions which are mine by Divine Right, now pour in and pile up under grace in perfect ways.
10. Unexpected doors fly open, unexpected channels are free, and endless avalanches of abundance are poured out upon me, under grace in perfect ways.
11. I spend money under direct inspiration wisely and fearlessly, knowing my supply is endless and immediate.
12. I am fearless in letting money go out, knowing God is my immediate and endless supply.

Happiness

In that wonderful moving picture, "The Thief of Bagdad," we were told in letters of light that happiness must be earned!

It is earned through perfect control of the emotional nature.

There can be no happiness where there is fear, apprehension or dread. With perfect faith in God comes a feeling of security and happiness.

When man knows that there is an invincible power that protects him and all that he loves, and brings to him every righteous desire of the heart, he relaxes all nervous tension and is happy and satisfied.

He is undisturbed by adverse appearances, knowing that Infinite Intelligence is protecting his interests and utilizing every situation to bring his good to pass.

"I will make a way in the wilderness, and rivers in a desert."

Uneasy lies the head that wears a frown. Anger, resentment, ill-will, jealousy and revenge rob man of his happiness and bring sickness, failure and poverty in their wake.

Resentment has ruined more homes than drink and killed more people than war.

For example: There was a woman who was healthy and happy and married to a man she loved.

The man died and left part of his estate to a relative. The woman was filled with resentment. She lost weight, was unable to do her work, developed gall-stones and became very ill.

A metaphysician called upon her one day. He said: "Woman, see what hate and resentment have done to you; they have caused hard stones to form in your body and only forgiveness and good-will can cure you."

The woman saw the Truth of the statement. She became harmonious and forgiving and regained her splendid health.

Affirmations

1. I am now deluged with the happiness that was planned for me in the Beginning. My barns are full, my cup flows over with joy.
2. My endless good now comes to me in endless ways.
3. I have a wonderful joy in a wonderful way, and my wonderful joy has come to stay.
4. Happy surprises come to me each day. "I look with wonder at that which is before me."
5. I walk boldly up to the lion on my pathway and find it is a friendly airedale.
6. I am harmonious, happy, radiant; detached from the tyranny of fear.
7. My happiness is built upon a rock. It is mine now and for all eternity.
8. My good now flows to me in a steady unbroken, ever-increasing stream of happiness.
9. My happiness is God's affair, therefore, no one can interfere.
10. As I am one with God I am now one with my heart's desire.
11. I give thanks for my permanent happiness, my permanent health, my permanent wealth, my permanent love.

12. I am harmonious, happy and Divinely magnetic, and now draw to me my ships over a calm sea.
13. God's ideas for me are perfect and permanent.
14. My heart's desire is a perfect idea in Divine Mind, incorruptible and indestructible, and now comes to pass, under grace in a magical way.

Love

With love usually comes terrific fear. Nearly every woman comes into the world with a mythical woman in the back of her mind who is to rob her of her love.

She has been called "the other woman." Of course it comes from woman's belief in duality. So long as she visualizes interference, it will come.

It is usually very difficult for a woman to see herself loved by the man she loves, so these affirmations are to impress the truth of the situation upon her subconscious mind, for in reality there is only oneness.

Affirmations

1. As I am one with God, the Undivided One, I am one with my undivided love and undivided happiness.
2. The light of the Christ within now wipes out all fear, doubt, anger and resentment. God's love pours through me, an irresistible magnetic current. I see only perfection and draw to me my own.
3. Divine Love, through me, now dissolves all seeming obstacles and makes clear, easy and successful my way.
4. I love everyone and everyone loves me. My apparent enemy becomes my friend, a golden link in the chain of my good.
5. I am at peace with myself and with the whole world. I love everyone and everyone loves me. The flood gates of my good now open.

Forgiveness
Affirmations

1. I forgive everyone and everyone forgives me. The gates swing open for my good.
2. I call on the law of forgiveness. I am free from mistakes and the consequences of mistakes. I am under grace and not under karmic law.
3. Though my mistakes be as scarlet, I shall be washed whiter than snow.
4. What didn't happen in the Kingdom never happened anywhere.

Words of Wisdom

"Faith without nerve is dead."
There is never a slip 'twixt the right cup and right lip.
Never look or you'd never leap.
God works in unexpected places, through unexpected people, at unexpected times, His wonders to perform.
Power moves but is never moved.
Loving your neighbor means not to limit your neighbor in word, thought or deed.
"Never argue with a hunch."
Christopher Columbus followed a hunch.
The Kingdom of Heaven is the realm of perfect ideas.
It is dark before the dawn but the dawn never fails. Trust in the dawn.
When in doubt play trumps, do the fearless thing.
It is the fearless thing that counts.
Never do today what intuition says to do tomorrow.
It's a great life if you don't reason.
Regard your neighbor as yourself.
Never hinder another's hunch.
Selfishness binds and blocks. Every loving and unselfish thought has in it the germ of success.

Be not weary of make-believing. When you least expect it you shall reap.
Faith is elastic. Stretch it to the end of your demonstration.
Before you call you are answered, for the supply precedes the demand.
What you do for others you are doing for yourself.
Every act committed while angry or resentful brings unhappy reaction.
Sorrow and disappointment follow in the wake of deceit and sub-
terfuge. The way of the transgressor is hard. "No good thing will be
withheld from him who walks uprightly.
There is no power in evil. It is nothing; therefore can only come to
nothing.
Fear and impatience demagnetize. Poise magnetizes.
Drown the reasoning mind with your affirmation. Jehoshaphat clapped
his cymbals so that he wouldn't hear himself think.
All bonding is an illusion of the race consciousness. There is always a
way out of every situation, under grace. Every man is free to do the will
of God.
Sure-ism is stronger than Optimism.
"Divine ideas never conflict."
It is dangerous to stop in the middle of a hunch. Infinite Spirit is never
too late.

Faith

Hope looks forward, Faith knows it has already received and acts
accordingly.

In my classes I often emphasize the importance of digging ditches
(or preparing for the thing asked for) which shows active faith and
brings the demonstration to pass.

A man in my class, whom I called "the life of the party," because
he always tried to find a question I couldn't answer, but he never succeeded, asked: "Why is it then, a lot of women who prepare Hope
Chests never get married?" I replied: "Because it is a Hope Chest and
not a Faith Chest."

The prospective bride also violates law in telling others about it.

Her friends come in and sit on the Hope Chest and either doubt or hope she'll never succeed.

"Pray to thy Father which is in secret, and thy Father which seeth in secret shall reward thee openly."

The student should never talk of a demonstration until it "has jelled," or comes to pass on the external.

So a Hope Chest should become a Faith Chest and be kept from the public eye, and the word spoken for the Divine Selection of a husband, under grace in a perfect way.

Those whom God hath joined together no thought can put asunder.

So a Hope Chest should become a Faith Chest and be kept from the public eye, and the word spoken for the Divine Selection of a husband, under grace in a perfect way.

Those whom God hath joined together no thought can put asunder.

Affirmations

1. Adverse appearances work for my good, for God utilizes every person and every situation to bring to me my heart's desire. "Hindrances are friendly" and obstacles spring boards! I now jump into my good!
2. As I am one with the Undivided One, I am one with my undivided good.
3. As the needle in the compass is true to the north, what is rightfully mine is true to me. I am the North!
4. I am now linked by an invisible, unbreakable magnetic cord with all that belongs to me by Divine Right!
5. Thy Kingdom is come; Thy will is done in me and my affairs.
6. Every plan my Father in heaven has not planned is dissolved and obliterated and the Divine Design of my life now comes to pass.
7. What God has given me never can be taken from me for His gifts are for all eternity.
8. My faith is built upon a rock and my heart's desire now comes to pass, under grace in miraculous way.

9. I see my good in a golden glow of glory. I see my fields shining white with the harvest.

10. God is my unfailing and immediate supply of all good.

11. I am poised and powerful, my greatest expectations are realized in a miraculous way.

12. I water my wilderness with faith and suddenly it blossoms as the rose.

13. Every plan my Father in heaven has not planned is dissolved and obliterated and the Divine Design of my life now comes to pass.

14. What God has given me never can be taken from me for His gifts are for all eternity.

15. My faith is built upon a rock and my heart's desire now comes to pass, under grace in miraculous way.

16. I see my good in a golden glow of glory. I see my fields shining white with the harvest.

17. God is my unfailing and immediate supply of all good.

18. I am poised and powerful, my greatest expectations are realized in a miraculous way.

19. I water my wilderness with faith and suddenly it blossoms as the rose.

20. I now exercise my fearless faith in three ways—by thinking, speaking and acting. I am unmoved by appearances, therefore appearances move.

21. I stand steadfast, immovable, giving thanks for my seeming impossible good to come to pass, for I know, with God, it is easy of accomplishment, and His time is now.

22. God's plans for me are built upon a rock. What was mine in the beginning is mine now and ever shall be mine.

23. I know there is nothing to defeat God; therefore, there is nothing to defeat me.

24. I wait patiently on the Lord, I trust in Him, I fret not myself because of evil doers (for every man is a golden link in the chain of my good) and He now gives to me the desires of my heart! (See 37th psalm.)

25. I have now the fearless faith of the Christ within. At my approach barriers vanish and obstacles disappear.

26. I am steadfast, immovable for the fields are already white with the harvest. My fearless faith in God now brings the Divine Design of my life to pass.

27. All fear is now banished in the name of Jesus Christ, for I know there is no power to hurt. God is the one and only power.

28. I am in perfect harmony with the working of the law, for I know that Infinite Intelligence knows nothing of obstacles, time or space. It knows only completion.

29. God works in unexpected and magical ways. His wonders to perform.

30. I now prepare for the fulfillment of my heart's desire. I show God I believe his promise will be kept.

31. I now dig my ditches deep with faith and understanding and my heart's desire comes to pass in a surprising way.

32. My ditches will be filled at the right time, bring all that I have asked for, and more!

33. I now "put to flight the army of the aliens" (negative thoughts). They feed on fear and starve on faith.

34. God's ideas cannot be moved; therefore, what is mine by Divine Right will always be with me.

35. I give thanks that I now receive the righteous desires of my heart. Mountains are removed, valleys exalted and every crooked place made straight. I am in the Kingdom of fulfillment.

36. I have perfect confidence in God and God has perfect confidence in me.

37. God's promises are built upon a rock. As I have asked I must receive.

38. "Let me never wander from my heart's desire."

39. I do not limit the Holy one of Israel, in word, thought or deed.

40. With God all things are easy and possible now.

41. I now stand aside and watch God work.

42. It interests me to see how quickly and easily He brings the desires of my heart to pass.

43. Before I called I was answered and I now gather in my harvest in a remarkable way. He who watches over my heart's desire, "Neither slumbers nor sleeps."

44. Seeming impossible doors now open; seeming impossible channels are free, in the name of Jesus Christ.
45. My good is a perfect and permanent idea in Divine Mind, and must manifest for there is nothing to prevent it.
46. I cast every burden on the Christ within and I go free!

Loss

If man loses anything it shows there is a belief of loss in his subconscious mind. As he erases this false belief, the article, or its equivalent will appear on the external.

For example: A woman lost a silver pencil in a theatre. She made every effort to find it but it was not returned.

She denied loss, taking the affirmation: "I deny loss, there is no loss in Divine Mind therefore I cannot lose that pencil. I will receive it or its equivalent."

Several weeks elapsed. One day she was with a friend who wore about her neck on a cord, a beautiful gold pencil, who turned to her and said: "Do you want this pencil? I paid fifty dollars for it at Tiffany's."

The woman was aghast, and replied (almost forgetting to thank her friend) "Oh! God aren't you wonderful! The silver pencil wasn't good enough for me!"

Man can only lose what doesn't belong to him by Divine Right, or isn't good enough for him.

Affirmations

1. There is no loss in Divine Mind; therefore, I cannot lose anything that is rightfully mine.
2. Infinite Intelligence is never too late! Infinite Intelligence knows the way of recovery.
3. There is no loss in Divine Mind; therefore, I cannot lose anything that is rightfully mine. It will be restored or I will receive its equivalent.

Debt

If a man is in debt or people owe him money, it shows that a belief of debt is in his subconscious mind.

This belief must be neutralized in order to change conditions.

For example: A woman came to me saying a man had owed her a thousand dollars for years which she could not compel him to pay.

I said: "You must work on yourself, not the man," and gave her this statement: "I deny debt, there is no debt in Divine Mind, no man owes me anything, and all is squared. I send that man love and forgiveness."

In a few weeks she received a letter from him saying he intended to send the money and in about a month came the thousand dollars.

If a student owes money, change the statement: "There is no debt in Divine Mind, therefore, I owe no man anything, and all is squared.

All of my obligations are now wiped out, under grace in a perfect way."

Affirmations

1. I deny debt, there is no debt in Divine Mind, therefore, I owe no man anything. All obligations are now wiped out under grace in a miraculous way.
2. I deny debt, there is no debt in Divine Mind, no man owes me anything, all is squared. I send forth love and forgiveness.

Guidance

Always on man's pathway is his message or his lead.

For example: A woman was much troubled over an unhappy situation. She thought to herself, "Will it ever clear up?"

Her maid was standing near and commenced to tell her of her experiences. The woman was too worried to be interested but listened patiently. The maid was saying: "I worked in a hotel once where there was a very amusing gardener; he always said such funny things. It had been raining for three days and I said to him: 'Do you think it will ever clear up?' And he replied, 'My God, doesn't it always clear up?'"

The woman was amazed! It was the answer to her thoughts. She said reverently, "Yes, with my God it always clears up!" Soon after, her problem did clear up in an unexpected way.

Affirmations

1. Infinite Spirit, give me wisdom to make the most of my opportunities. Never let me miss a trick.
2. I am always under direct inspiration. I know just what to do and give instant obedience to my intuitive leads.
3. My angel of destiny goes before me, keeping me in the Way.
4. All power is given unto me to be meek and lowly of heart. I am willing to come last, therefore, I come first.
5. I now place my personal will upon the altar. Your will, not my will; Your way not my way; Your time not my time—and in the twinkling of an eye it is done!
6. There are no mysteries in the Kingdom. Whatever I should know will now be revealed to me, under grace.
7. I am a perfect non-resistant instrument for God to work through, and His perfect plan for me now comes to pass in a magical way.

Protection
Affirmations

1. I am surrounded by the White Light of the Christ, through which nothing negative can penetrate.
2. I walk in the Light of the Christ and my fear giants dwindle into nothingness. There is nothing to oppose my good.

The Divine Design

There is a Divine Design for each man! Just as the perfect picture of the oak is in the acorn, the divine pattern of his life is in the super-conscious mind of man.

In the Divine Design there is no limitation, only health, wealth, love and perfect self-expression.

So on man's pathway there is always a Divine Selection. Each day he must live according to the Divine Plane or have unhappy reactions.

For example: A woman moved into a new apartment which she had almost furnished, when the thought came to her: "On that side of the room should stand a Chinese cabinet!"

Not long after, she was walking by an antique shop. She glanced in and there stood a magnificent Chinese cabinet about eight feet high, elaborately carved. She entered and asked the price. The salesman said it was worth a thousand dollars but the woman who owned it was willing to take less. The man added: "What will you offer for it?" The woman paused and the price "Two hundred dollars" came into her mind, so she answered: "Two hundred dollars." The man said he would let her know if the offer was satisfactory.

She did not want to cheat anyone or get anything which was not rightfully hers, so going home she said repeatedly: "If it's mine I can't lose it and if it isn't mine, I don't want it." It was a snowy day and she said she emphasized her words by kicking the snow from right to left, clearing a pathway to her apartment.

Several days elapsed when she was notified that the woman was willing to sell the cabinet for two hundred dollars.

There is a supply for every demand, from Chinese cabinets to millions of dollars.

"Before ye call I shall answer," but, unless it is the Divinely Selected cabinet or millions they would never bring happiness.

"Except the Lord build the house, they labor in vain that build it." (Psalm 127-1)

Health

When man is harmonious and happy he is healthy! All sickness comes from violation of Spiritual Law.

Jesus Christ said: "Be thou healed, your sins are forgiven."

Resentment, ill-will, hate, fear, etc., etc., tear down the cells of the body and poison the blood. (*See The Game of Life and How to Play It*, page 23.)

Accidents, old age and death itself, come from holding wrong mental pictures.

When man sees himself as God sees him, he will become a radiant being, timeless, birthless and deathless, for "God made man in His likeness and His image."

Affirmations

1. I deny fatigue, for there is nothing to tire me. I live in the Kingdom of eternal joy and absorbing interests. My body is "the body electric," timeless and tireless, birthless and deathless.
2. Time and space are obliterated!
3. I live in the wonderful now, birthless and deathless!
4. I am one; *The One!*
5. Thou in me art: Eternal joy. Eternal youth .Eternal wealth. Eternal health. Eternal love. Eternal life.
6. I am a Spiritual Being—my body is perfect, made in His likeness and image.
7. The Light now streams through every cell. I give thanks for my radiant health.

Miscellaneous

The thing you dislike or hate will surely come upon you, for when man hates, he makes a vivid picture in the subconscious mind and it objectifies.

The only way to erase these pictures is through non-resistance.

For example: A woman was interested in a man who told her repeatedly of his charming women cousins.

She was jealous and resentful and he passed out of her life.

Later on she met another man to whom she was much attracted. In the course of their conversation he mentioned some women cousins he was very fond of.

She resented it, then laughed, for here were her old friends "the cousins" back again.

This time she tried non-resistance. She blessed all the cousins in the Universe and sent them good-will, for she knew if she didn't, every man she met would be stocked up with women relations.

It was successful for she never heard cousins mentioned again.

This is the reason so many people have unhappy experiences repeated in their lives.

I knew a woman who bragged of her troubles. She would go about saying to people; "I know what trouble is!" and then wait for their words of sympathy.

Of course, the more she mentioned her troubles, the more she had, for by her words she "was condemned."

She should have used her words to neutralize her troubles instead of to multiply them.

For example, had she said repeatedly: "I cast every burden upon the Christ within and I go free," and not voiced her sorrows, they would have faded from her life, for "by your words you are justified."

"I will give to thee the land that thou seest."

Man is ever reaping on the external what he has sown in his thought world.

For example: A woman needed money and was walking along the street making the affirmation that God was her immediate supply.

She looked down and at her feet was a two dollar bill, which she picked up.

A man standing near (a watchman in a building), said to her: "Lady, did you pick up some money? I thought it was a piece of chewing-gum paper. A lot of people walked over it, but when you came it opened up like a leaf."

The others, thinking lack, had passed over it, but at her words of faith it unfurled.

So with the opportunities in life—one man sees, another passes by.

"Faith without works (or action) is dead."

The student in order to bring into manifestation the answer to his prayer must show *active faith*.

For example: A woman came to me asking me to speak the word for the renting of a room.

I gave her the statement: "I give perfect thanks that the room is now rented to the right and perfect man for the right price, giving perfect satisfaction."

Several weeks elapsed but the room had not been rented.

I asked: "Have you shown active faith? Have you followed every hunch in regard to the room?"

She replied: "I had a hunch to get a lamp for the room, but I decided I couldn't afford it."

I said: "You'll never rent the room until you get the lamp, for in buying the lamp you are *acting your faith*, impressing the subconscious mind with *certainty*."

I asked: "What is the price of the lamp?"

She answered: "Four dollars." I exclaimed: "Four dollars standing between you and the perfect man!"

She became so enthusiastic, she bought *two* lamps.

About a week elapsed and in walked the perfect man. He did not smoke and paid the rent in advance and fulfilled her ideal in every way.

Unless you become as a little child and dig your ditches you shall in no wise enter the Kingdom of manifestation.

"Without the vision my people perish." Unless man has some objective, some Promised Land to look forward to, he begins to perish.

We see it so often in small country towns, in the men who sit around a stove all winter, who "Ain't got no ambition."

Within each one is an undiscovered country, a gold mine.

I knew a man in a country town called "Magnolia Charlie," because he always found the first magnolia in the spring.

He was a shoemaker, but every afternoon left his work to go to the station to meet the four-fifteen train, from a distant city.

They were the only romances in his life, the first magnolia and the four-fifteen train.

He felt vaguely the call of the vision in the superconscious mind.

No doubt, the Divine Design for him included travel and perhaps he was to become a genius in the plant world.

Through the spoken word the Devine Design may be released and each one fulfill his destiny.

Affirmation: "I now see clearly the perfect plan of my life. Divine enthusiasm fires me and I now fulfill my Destiny."

The Spiritual attitude towards money is to know that God is Man's supply, and that he draws it from the abundance of the spheres, through his faith and spoken word.

When man realizes this he loses all greed for money, and is fearless in letting it go out.

With his magic purse of the Spirit, his supply is endless and immediate, and he knows also that giving precedes receiving.

For example: A woman came to me asking me to speak the word for five hundred dollars by the first of August. (It was then about the first of July.)

I knew her very well, and said: "The trouble with you is you don't give enough. You must open your channels of supply by giving."

She had accepted an invitation to visit a friend and did not want to go on account of the formality.

She said, "Please treat for me to be polite for three weeks, and I want to get away as soon as possible, and be sure to speak the word for the five hundred dollars."

She went to the friend's house, was unhappy and restless and tried continually to leave, but was always persuaded to stay longer.

She remembered my advice, however, and gave the people about her presents. Whenever possible she made a gift.

It was nearing the first of August and no signs of the five hundred dollars, and no way of escape from the visit.

The last day of July she said: "Oh God! maybe I haven't given enough!" So she tipped all the servants more than she had intended.

The first of August, her hostess said to her: "My dear, I want to make you a gift," and she handed her a check for five hundred dollars! God works in unexpected ways his wonders to perform.

Affirmations

1. God is incapable of separation or division: therefore, my good is incapable of separation or division. I am one with my undivided good. All that is mine by Divine Right is now released and reaches me in a perfect way under Grace.
2. God's work is finished now and must manifest.
3. I serve only faith and my unlimited substance is made manifest.
4. I am undisturbed by appearances. I trust in God—and He now brings to me the desires of my heart.
5. My good now overtakes me in a surprising way.
6. The Divine Plan of my life cannot be tampered with. It is incorruptible and indestructible. It awaits only my recognition.
7. There is no there—there is only here.
8. Reveal to me the way, let me see clearly the blessing which Thou hast given me.
9. Let Thy blessed will be done in me this day.
10. Hunches are my hounds of Heaven—they lead me in the perfect way.
11. All things I seek are now seeking me.
12. Divine Activity is now operation in my mind, body and affairs, whether I see it or not.
13. Since I am one with the Only Presence, I am one with my heart's desire.
14. I now have the single eye of the Spirit and see only completion.
15. I am a perfect idea in Divine Mind and I am always in my right place doing my right work at the right time for the right pay.
16. The Columbus in you will see you through.

17. I am an irresistible magnet for checks, bills and currency, for everything that belongs to me by Divine Right.
18. Thou in me art completion. As I have asked I must receive.
19. The law of God is the law of increase and I give thanks for increase under grace in perfect ways.
20. I dwell in a sea of abundance. I see clearly my inexhaustible supply. I see clearly what to do.
21. My "World of the Wondrous" now swings into manifestation and I enter my Promised Land under grace!
22. Great peace have I who loves thy law of nonresistance, and nothing shall offend me.
23. Thou in me art Inspiration, Revelation and Illumination.
24. Nothing is too good to be true.
25. Nothing is too wonderful to happen

Conclusion

Choose the affirmation which appeals to you the most and wave it over the situation which confronts you.

It is your magic wand, for your word is God in action.

"It shall not return void but shall accomplish that whereunto it is sent." (Isaiah 55-11) "But I say, have they not heard? Yes, verily, their sound went into all the earth and their words unto the end of the world." (Romans 10-8)

Creation

The impulse of all love is to create.
God was so full of love, in His embrace
He clasped the empty nothingness of space,
And lo! the solar system! High in state
The mighty sun sat, so supreme and great
With this same essence, one smile of its face
Brought myriad forms of life forth; race on race
From insects up to men.
Through love, not hate,
All that is grand in nature or in art
Sprang into being. He who would build sublime
And lasting works, to stand the test of time
Must inspiration draw from his full heart.
And he who loveth widely, well and much,
The secret holds of the true master touch.

Poems of Passion by Ella Wheeler Wilcox
Chicago : Belford, Clarke & Co, 1883.

Ursula Newell Gestefeld

(1845-1921)

Influential Early New Thought Teacher

Ursula Gestefeld was an insightful and brilliant individual who loved to argue about the nature of Divine Science. She began her journey to New Thought when she was loaned a copy of Mary Baker Eddy's *Science and Health*. (1) She began to apply its principles and, *"despite its contradictions and inconsistencies,"* gained an unprecedented state of health within 90 days. She felt that she had found: *"a truth that if applied to the problems of individual and social life would make all things new."*

Ursula Gestefeld, along with Emma Curtis Hopkins, were once trusted lieutenants in Mary Baker Eddy's Christian Science movement, but reacted against her authoritarian possessiveness and broke with her to become teachers of men and women who later founded movements of considerable extent and influence that have collectively been considered as New Thought groups.

Ursula Newell Gestefeld, a founder of the Illinois Woman's Press Association, also established the Science of Being, a New Thought religious system that gained her national prominence.

Born April 22, 1845 in Augusta, Maine, to an invalid mother, Gestefeld was a sickly child, and friends thought she would never live to maturity, but she did, married, and bore four children. By 1878, she and her husband, Theodore Gestefeld, moved to Chicago where he served as a reporter for The Chicago Tribune and as city editor of *The Statts-Zeitung*, a leading German newspaper.

She was already middle-aged before she heard of Christian Science, when a friend loaned her that copy of *Science and Health* by Mary Baker Eddy. Something of a radical by nature and training, she was out of sympathy with the traditional religious thought of the day, but in *Science and Health* she saw, "despite its contradictions and inconsistencies," "a truth that if applied to the problems of individual and social life would make all things new." Applying its principles to her own case she had in a period of three months, without the help of any practitioner, achieved a state of health beyond any previously enjoyed.

Her success led her to become not only a believer, but also a leader in the movement. When Mrs. Eddy appeared in Chicago and offered class instruction, she became a member and was taught by Mrs. Eddy in her class of May, 1884, held in Chicago. Mrs. Eddy early recognized in her a person of outstanding ability and welcomed her as an exponent of the new faith. Mrs. Gestefeld was a very able individual, and she gave herself unreservedly to the practice and teaching of Christian Science. A very effective teacher, she soon won a substantial following and established herself as a metaphysician. She practiced, wrote and taught mental healing in Chicago.

In her zeal to communicate her faith to others she turned to writing. In 1888, Gestefeld published a book under the title, *Ursula N.*

Gestefeld's Statement of Christian Science, and although she gave full credit to Mrs. Eddy as its founder, she got into trouble. Christian Science had already been stated by Mrs. Eddy in *Science and Health* and her other writings, and apparently she felt that was sufficient. She denounced Mrs. Gestefeld in the *Christian Science Journal* and practically cut her off from her movement.

She reacted vigorously to Mrs. Eddy's attack upon her and wrote a caustic pamphlet under the title *Jesuitism in Christian Science.* She was expelled from the association, but far from ending Mrs. Gestefeld's career as teacher and practitioner, this launched her on an independent career of healing and teaching. One of the most articulate of the early Eddy converts, she eventually became recognized as a leader in the metaphysical movement which came to be called New Thought.

A great deal of her work was done in Chicago where she established herself and regularly taught classes, maintained a center and a church, published books and wrote in magazines as a means of disseminating her ideas. To the system which she eventually evolved, she gave the name "Science of Being." She formed a club, the Exodus Club, a nonsectarian group which had for its purpose the imparting and receiving of instruction in the Science of Being. Out of the Exodus Club seems to have grown the church to which Mrs. Gestefeld gave the name, the Church of the New Thought. No member was required to make any profession of faith or to subscribe to anything which his or her reason rejected.

She trained women to become certified leaders, teachers, traveling proselytizers or pastors. In 1895, she contributed to The Woman's Bible, penned by Elizabeth Cady Stanton, a major figure in the Suffrage Movement at the turn of the century, (See Appendix C), and it summarized the Science of Being principles. She published two novels, several tracts and started the *Exodus,* a monthly magazine for the New Thought movement, serving as writer, editor and publisher. By 1902, she had at least 300 members, while more than 800 attended her weekly sermons.

Gestefeld is probably best known for her novel, *The Woman Who*

Dares, a protest against the hypocrisy of marriage. The work portrayed a male-dominated society that used all means—legal, political, economic and religious—to enforce women's sexual subservience to men.

By the turn of the century, Gestefeld had expanded her mental health theories to include material wealth. She was a frequent speaker in meta-physical movement congresses, served as member of the "Executive Committee of the Metaphysical League", and was present at the formation of the International New Thought Alliance in London in 1914. She continued to write and lecture throughout the 1910s. She died of toxemia in 1921 and is buried at Graceland Cemetery, Chicago.

Her other books, widely used by New Thought groups, were: *The Breath of Life: A Series of Self-treatments, Reincarnation or Immortality, The Builder and the Plan, A Chicago Bible Class,* and the only title by her currently in print, *How We Master Our Fate.* (2)

Links & Acknowledgements
1. divinelibrary.orggestefeldUrsulabio_gestefeld_02.htm
2. ursulagestefeld.wwwhubs.com

The Breath of Life

A Series of Self-Treatments
Published in 1897
Dedicated to all who can
"receive with meekness the engrafted word which is able to save your souls"
from suffering the common lot of humanity.

When There Is a Sense of Injury
When There Is a Lack of Confidence and Trust
When There Is Fear of Death
When There Is Difficulty in Letting Go of the Past
When There Is Dissatisfaction With Environment
When There Is A Need for Patience
When There Is Desire to Lose Fondness for Money

When There Is a Sense of Injury

I look upon a world filled with shapes of many kinds. I see in them no evil. They are good.

Though with my outsight I look upon them, with my insight I see through them; and I recognize their nature and office. I see souls, back of these shapes, who are being born into another world than that they look upon through the window of the physical body. I know that I do not live in time as they do, but that I live in the eternal, and that this eternal is now. For me there is no more time. To me all is good, for I see the divine purpose which is being carried out.

I see the God-man and his gradual appearing. I stand at the centre of being and all in existence arranges itself according to this purpose which is good only. There is no evil. I see above, below, and on either side. No one point is farther from this centre than another.

I am one with God and God is related to the whole circumference.

God is Good and Good is omnipotent. I have no enemies. I have only friends. Every soul is my brother, for every soul is from the same God and has the same destiny to fulfill.

No one can do me harm or work me evil. No soul really wishes to do me harm or work me evil. I am free from fear, for I know there is nothing to fear.

I have found the better way, the straight and narrow way; and with all my heart I desire to show this way and help others to walk therein. I see, feel, and know only love, and "perfect love casteth out fear."

I know that other souls will love me when I love them, I will serve me when I serve them, I will help me when I help them. Standing as one with God in my individual consciousness, I lay upon the altar of the outer life all fear, jealousy, and desire for revenge, all selfishness and personal ambition.

I offer these as a sacrifice to that Most high which is the over-ruling Good, the destroyer of all sense of evil. I know that the "fire from heaven" will consume this, my offering and that my purified sense of existence will make me a mediator for my brethren.

Love is my beginning and end, my centre and circumference, my substance and supply. I have found my God.

I live and move and have my being in God and nothing can disturb my peace.

When There Is a Lack of Confidence and Trust

"In thee 0! Lord! do I put my trust," for I know that in my real being dwells all power and might. As a pilgrim soul, I look to those eternal verities which are there.

I know that they are at my command. I know that God has given to my being all that God is and has. From this great and glorious store-house I can draw sufficient for my daily needs.

I know that thou wilt never fail nor forsake me. It is good that the mortal props fall away from me, one by one. Each is but a veil that hides thee from me. I am willing to be taken up. I am willing to be forsaken of all that is merely mortal, that I may be taken up.

"Thou art he who can do no evil."

Open thou mine eyes to behold thy glories. Though all that has seemed necessary forsake me, I know that thou art with me always. I can never fail because thou art at my right hand. I am free from all fear, for I feel thy presence. My confidence is perfect, I stand unshaken, though all around me seems tottering to a fall.

My business cannot fail, my home life cannot break, my loved ones cannot scatter and be lost to me; for I gather them all together to be taken up as I am taken up by thee. Thou wilt save to the uttermost all who trust in thee, and my trust is perfect, *my* confidence is secure.

When There Is Fear of Death

Whereas I was blind, now I see, and I know there is no death.

I see order where before was chaos. I see ascension into everlasting life where before was descent into death. I see birth, a becoming, not a ceasing to be. I see a Great Pulse which beats everywhere in nature and which is Life.

I see my own unity with this pulse and that it fills me more and more abundantly with inflowing, invigorating Life. I feel this inflow now. It thrills me into new perception. I am laid bare to myself. The veil of the temple is rent in twain. I stand before it awed and mystified no longer.

All graves give up their dead unto me. I have a right to demand this of them. No tomb can keep its secret from me. The tomb of death is the womb of life. I am, I was, I shall be, but I am being made—fashioned after the likeness of God. I must still come forth from my lesser self and go up higher. I must come forth from all selves less than the divine. I must ascend again and again, stopping for a season to see and know and going on toward divinity.

I must leave my garment "in their hands" while I press forward to my enduring habitation. As a naked soul I mount higher and higher leaving to the dust that which is of the dust. I go whence I came.

I walk through the valley of shadow; it cannot hold me to itself. I fear no evil in my journey, for there is no evil in it. I have put from me the sense of evil which gave birth to its kind. I see the eternal Good which overrules this continuous birth that mortal sense calls death. I feel the protection of this Good which never slumbers or sleeps.

I am not made sad at the prospect of leaving those who love me; for I see that we are all one in Christ; and that as the Christ consciousness awakens and comes forth from the tomb in which it has been slumbering, it will find and know its own. Those whom I love and who love me will never be separated from me because I leave my garment in their hands as I am born out of its world.

For love is not of that world. It is the fragrance of the soul that reveals its source. Though they see my garment silent and motionless, I shall be more alive than when I wore it. And they shall some time leave their own, dust mingling with dust even as soul blends with soul.

I have no fear. I see and I know. 0! death! where is thy sting? 0! grave! where is thy victory?

When There Is Difficulty In Letting Go of the Past

I am no more what I was. I am new-born. I am awake to my eternal being in which is all glory and all power. What I was when I was asleep is gone.

It belongs to the dead past in the recognition of my possible divinity I am resurrected from the dead.

I leave in the tomb all that belongs there. I carry nothing of it with me; I desire none of it. I see that no soul cometh to the Father except by the resurrection and the life. I am quickened from on high and I rise above the region of graves. I am not beholden of them, neither indeed can I be.

I am new, all things are new, my future is new.

Though my soul-journey is not finished, I know that my face is turned in the right direction and the land of graves is behind my back. Through the quickening spirit in me I shall conquer as I go, and find my home. I have no useless regrets. In my heart of hearts I am thankful for the measure of wisdom which is mine to-day, and which my past experiences have brought forth to me. They have borne some fruit; they will bear more. But in the strength of the Lord, by the help of His Christ, I shall gather this fruit with rejoicing and not sorrow. By it I am made strong. By it I prove my power of mastery over all unlikeness to God.

I am exercising this power now. By means of it I get farther and farther from the dead past. I am resurrected continually into more abundant life.

All is good. There is no evil. All that I have called evil has been good for me, for by it I have learned something. I have no sorrow, no regrets. I am filled with praise and rejoicing. I know that I am being weaned from my mortal sense self that I may show forth the divine likeness.

All that this sense calls affliction are but the growing-pains which are sure to be left behind. Nothing that anyone can say of me can hurt me or turn me aside.

I press forward steadily with no thought of blame for them who judge me according to the dead past. I know but one Judge and one Deliverer.

All malice, hatred, and enmity are left with that past. I bow only to love; I feel only love, for every human being. I begin to know God, for God is Love.

When There Is Dissatisfaction With Environment

Though to mortal sense I am hedged in, I know that I am but given what I need for my journey heavenward. I see that all external limitations are my opportunities to prove my real being. For them I rejoice and give thanks.

I praise thee, 0 God! I praise thee for all that shuts me in, for it is Love itself that compasses me round about. Even as the tiny bird is encircled by the protecting nest, so am I enfolded in that which guards me while I am finding my wings.

All thine is mine, and I am thine, and no harm can befall me for there is no evil. Though the pressure of environment lies heavy upon me, it is but my own pressure against the encircling wall; and I know that the wings Thou hast given me will bear me over and above it. I see them now, they are mine now, they are growing stronger and stronger for of Thee is their strength.

I am neither cast down nor dismayed, for as Thy child I am Lord of all.

Environment has no power to keep me from Thee.

Thou are drawing me from the protecting nest that I may prove my kinship with Thee. Here, within it, as the outward man held back by its embrace, in the within I am free to find and know Thee. This moment I am free to mount upward, though my flesh is held down by the things of sense.

None of the trammels of sense-consciousness can rob me of my heavenly wings. As the child seeks its mother's bosom, so fly I to Thee.

From this secure place I look down upon my fleshly environment and it lies before me as an open book which I read with the eyes Thou hast given me.

It is only the nest, only the nest. I thank Thee, Great God of the Universe, for every straw and twig, yea, even the tiny thorn in it.

All is good; for all is good *for* me, however with my mortal sense it has seemed *to* me. The nest is mine for a time, the time when I prove Thee.

But I am thine and Thou art mine, eternally.

When There Is a Need for Patience

I know that time is but my own perception and feeling, and that what seems to me a long time is only a moment in the great all. I know that with the Lord a thousand years is as one day. I know that my real being is the same during all this change in perception and feeling that I call time. I know that this real being of mine is working out its own manifestation, amid I can wait.

All is good, there is no evil anywhere.

I can see the end of time, for I was before it and I shall be after it.

I am only getting acquainted with my own nature and finding its Principle.

I welcome all I experience.

I am willing to let patience have its perfect work. I would be made perfect and entire in self-recognition and realization even as I am perfect and entire in being. I welcome the making. There is no pain or sorrow in it.

Disappointment is only a letting go to take a better hold. I am able to meet and master all that time brings me, for I am only proving my own possibilities. I need to prove these, to know that I know. I have patience with all limitation, for by it I prove the unlimited.

All that I encounter in time is friendly and I will make none of it an enemy.

Now, this moment, I am able to overcome all that seems hard and unpleasant, for I have dominion over all things as my birthright. "He that endureth to the end shall be saved" from the necessity for endurance.

I know that I, in my real being, am free from all that afflicts, and that I suffer only in my sense-consciousness. I have God-given power to rule this consciousness. I am ruling it with patience and steadfastness.

The way is short and the work is easy, for the Christ is my Helper and Comforter. The Son of God is with me, and he helps and strengthens the Son of Man. I am that I am, and nothing or experience in time can change my being.

I have taken His yoke upon me and the Christ works with and for me. I am housed in God all the while I look upon the mortal. I am able to wait for manifestation of the immortal, for I know that it is.

I am, and nothing can make me cease to be. Time and space are naught for me who am more than they. I speak and they obey. All is here and now.

The work that is proof is being done. I am.

When There Is Desire to Lose Fondness for Money

All that I am is from thee 0! God! All that I have which is worth keeping is of Thee also. I am filled with Thine abundance and my riches are inexhaustible.

I see that my worldly possessions pertain only to my sense-consciousness, and I withdraw my desire from them. When Thou callest me 0 God! Let me not be found with my money lest my soul say "Here am I." I desire Thee. I need Thee. Let me be found with Thee. From Thy bosom help me to say "Here am I." I am with Thee. My possessions cannot keep me from Thee for I give them up. They have no power to entice me and draw me away from my eternal home. My abiding place is not with them, but with Thee.

I know that this consciousness is the pearl of great price, and for it I give all I have on the sense-plane. No one can rob me; I cannot lose, for I give it all.

I know that every need of this plane will be met, and met the more abundantly as I possess Thy eternal riches. I love to give to others. I love to give to those who need, for I know that thus Thou givest to them through me. From Thy hand through my hand, they receive for their needs, and in my love for my fellow-men that Love which is Thee is manifested. I thank Thee and praise Thee for this opportunity that proves and tests me. I would hold back nothing that can come between myself and Thee. I will be a wise steward, a user of money, not a keeper. I will keep close to Thee instead.

Here, let me be found. In the light that shines from Thee I look upon the money and it has no value.

Used in Thy service it is transmuted into love. My love for it would keep it but base metal, and shut me out from Thee. My love and desire for Thee makes it pure gold, and me the dispenser of Thy blessings. From my abiding place in Thee I use Thy gold. I have no money.

I am Thy steward and I use Thy gold in Thy service. With it I do Thy will.

Ella Wheeler Wilcox

(With permission from the Wisconsin Historical Society)

(1850-1919)

New Thought Writer & Poetess

Ella Wheeler Wilcox, whilst perhaps not being one of America's greatest poets, was in her time one of the most popular, her verse appearing in innumerable magazines and periodicals as well as a number of books. She has probably been read by many more people than poets who have been considered her superiors. Whilst not all her poems are, of course, New Thought in outlook, in one of her books, *Poems of Power,* a dozen or more of her poems may be discerned typical of New Thought ideas and emphases.

However, it was probably as regular contributor to newspapers that Ella Wheeler Wilcox reached her widest public, for she wrote syndicated articles for the Hearst newspapers. Many of these were simply expositions of the central teachings of New Thought, though not definitely linked with that minority point of view. Thus New Thought ideas found an outlet to the public they could never have gotten through specifically New Thought channels. Many of these ideas commended themselves to the minds of readers which might well have been closed by denominational prejudices, had they come labeled as New Thought.

Ella was born November 5, 1850, in the village of Johnstown, Rock County, Wisconsin. Her parents were Marcus H. Wheeler, and Sarah Pratt Wheeler, with three older children they had followed, "Grandsir Pratt" from Vermont in 1849. In the spring of 1852 the Wheeler family settled in Dane County, Wisconsin in the town of Westport, where Ella grew up, in the home where she made her reputation as a writer of appealing poetry, until her marriage in 1884, when she went to Connecticut; from which state her Grandfather Wheeler had migrated to Vermont years before.

With a Great Grandfather Pratt seven years in the Revolutionary War, and his wife Elizabeth Currier of French blood; a Grandmother named Conner; a Mother, who, like most of her aunts and cousins, was addicted to the habit of composing verses, Ella had the inherited tendency as a regular family study of Shakespeare, Byron, Burns and modern poets went all year round. Her education was acquired in a district school, now named Ella Wheeler Wilcox School, except one short term at Wisconsin University, which was as she saw it a "waste of time."

Riding horseback, dancing, visiting girl friends, dreaming great dreams and being kind, was better than trying to master mathematics, of which she had a "holy horror." (1)

In the years between 1865 and 1875, a strong prohibition wave was sweeping over Wisconsin. Good Templar Lodges became numerous. Many of Ella Wheeler's earlier verses were in support of total abstinence and in opposition to booze, its makers, and its venders. Fifty-six of these were published in a volume entitled "Drops of Water." Her volume entitled "Shells" contained 119 poems—more than 175 poems and the author not 23 years old. It is doubtful if anyone knows the names of all her published poems. They were a great multitude and everyone found ardent admirers—and critics. (2)

Ella Wheeler Wilcox wrote verses which appealed to the public and never one verse strained or ungrammatical, as she states in her memoirs; her first check paid for a dress to wear to a wedding in March 1869. Her financial returns were not of importance until after 1880, though she was known and loved by thousands of readers. She wrote for the same reason that a bird sings. It was what she was made for. Her marriage in 1884 was a love match. The death of Mr. Wilcox overwhelmed her, until satisfied that she had received messages from him through her practice of Spiritualism. Then she resumed literary work, and other activities; including war work in France up to Armistice Day. (3)

Whilst Mrs. Wilcox was certainly New Thought in her general outlook, and in common with many who later became leaders of the New Thought movement, and attended classes by the "teacher of teachers," Emma Curtis Hopkins , she went much farther than many of the leaders of the movement in her espousal also of ideas which are regarded as occult. And some of the leaders were not always happy with what she wrote. She was strongly drawn to Spiritualism and gave much credit to Oriental—especially Indian thought, as the source of many of her ideas. She wrote not only poetry; but did a great deal of prose writing as well. A number of her essays specifically on New Thought themes appeared in a volume entitled *The Heart of New Thought,* which the publisher's preface described as a "Noteworthy interpretation of New Thought, the backbone of which philosophy is the Power of Right Thought. Mrs. Wilcox is ever the voice of the people: what she says is practical, what she thinks is clear, what she feels is plain." (1)

She died on October 30, 1919, at her home in Short Beach, Conn. A malignant growth in one breast caused her death at her home in Short Beach, Conn. (3)

"The art of being kind" was her religion, and she lived it every day of her life.

The world is better because Ella Wheeler Wilcox lived.

Links & Acknowledgements
1. ellawheelerwilcox.wwwhubs.com
2. library.wisc.eduetextwireaderWER0109.html
3. boards.ancestry.comtopics.obits251727mb.ashx?pnt=1

Poems

Beauty
Untitled
Attainment
Consciousness
God Rules Away
God's Majesty
Deathless
Devils
The Law
A Song of Faith

Beauty

The search for beauty is the search for God,
Who is All Beauty. He who seeks shall find;
And all along the paths my feet have trod,
I have sought hungrily with heart and mind
  And open eyes for beauty everywhere.
  Lo! I have found the world is very fair.
The search for beauty is the search for God.
  Beauty was first revealed to me by stars.
  Before I saw it in my mother's eyes,
Or, seeing, sensed its beauty, I was stirred
To awe and wonder by those orbs of light,
  All palpitant against empurpled skies.
They spoke a language to my childish heart
  Of mystery and splendor and of space,
  Friendly with gracious, unseen presences.
  Beauty was first revealed to me by stars.
Sunsets enlarged the meaning of the word.
  There was a window looking to the west:
  Beyond it, wide Wisconsin fields of grain,
And then a hill, where on white flocks of clouds
  Would gather in the afternoon to rest.
And when the sun went down behind that hill,
What scenes of glory spread before my sight—
  What beauty—beauty, absolute, supreme!
Sunsets enlarged the meaning of that word.
  Clover in blossom, red and honey-sweet,
  In summer billowed like a crimson sea
Across the meadow lands. One day, I stood
Breast-high amidst its waves, and heard the hum
  Of myriad bees that had gone mad like me
  With fragrance and with beauty. Over us,
  A loving sun smiled from a cloudless sky,

While a bold breeze kissed lightly as it passed
Clover in blossom, red and honey-sweet.
Autumn spoke loudly of the beautiful,
And in the gallery of Nature hung
Colossal pictures hard against the sky,
Set forests gorgeous with a hundred hues,
And with each morning some new wonder flung
Before the startled world—some daring shade,
Some strange, new scheme of color and of form.
Autumn spoke loudly of the beautiful.
Winter, though rude, is delicate in art—
More delicate than summer or than fall
(Even as rugged Man is more refined
In vital things than Woman). Winter's touch
On Nature seemed most beautiful of all—
That evanescent beauty of the frost
On window panes, of clean, fresh-fallen snow,
Of white, white sunlight on the ice-draped trees.
Winter, though rude, is delicate in art.
Morning! The word itself is beautiful,
And the young hours have many gifts to give
That feed the soul with beauty. He who keeps
His days for labor and his nights for sleep
Wakes conscious of the joy it is to live,
And brings from that mysterious Land of Dreams
A sense of beauty that illumines earth.
Morning! The word itself is beautiful.
The search for beauty is the search for God.

World Voices New York:
Hearst's International Library Company, 1916

ELLA WHEELER WILCOX

Untitled
(As You Go Through Life)

Don't look for the flaws as you go through life,
And even when you find them
It is wise and kind to be somewhat blind
And look for the virtue behind them.
For the cloudiest night has a hint of light
Somewhere in its shadows hiding.
And it's better by far to hunt for a star,
Than the spots on the sun abiding.
The current of life runs ever away
To the bosom of God's great ocean.
Don't set your force 'gainst the river's course
And think to alter its motion.
Don't waste a curse on the universe—
Remember it lived before you.
Don't butt at the storm with your puny form,
But bend and let it go o'er you.

The Constitution (Atlanta) 20 Jan., 1901: 10

Attainment

Use all your hidden forces. Do not miss
The purpose of this life, and do not wait
For circumstance to mould or change your fate.
In your own self lies Destiny. Let this
Vast truth cast out all fear, all prejudice,
All hesitation. Know that you are great,
Great with divinity. So dominate
Environment, and enter into bliss.
Love largely and hate nothing. Hold no aim
That does not chord with universal good.
Hear what the voices of the silence say,
All joys are yours if you put forth your claim.
Once let the spirit's laws be understood,
Material things must answer and obey.

The Papyrus 6, 3 April 1906, 32

Consciousness

God, what a glory, is this consciousness,
Of life on life, that comes to those who seek!
Nor would I, if I might, to others speak,
The fullness of that knowledge. It can bless,
Only the eager souls, that willing, press
Along the mountain passes, to the peak.
Not to the dull, the doubting, or the weak,
Will Truth explain, or Mystery confess.
Not to the curious or impatient soul
That in the start, demands the end be shown,
And at each step, stops waiting for a sign;
But to the tireless toiler toward the goal,
Shall the great miracles of God be known
And life revealed, immortal and divine.

Poems of Progress and New Thought Pastels
London: Gay & Hancock, 1911

God Rules Alway

Into the world's most high and holy places
Men carry selfishness, and graft and greed.
The air is rent with warring of the races;
Loud Dogmas drown a brother's cry of need.
The Fleet-of-Creeds, upon Time's ocean lurches;
And there is mutiny upon her decks;
And in the light of temples, and of churches,
Against life's shores drift wrecks and derelicts.
(God rules, God rules alway.)
Right in the shadow of the lofty steeple,
Which crowns some costly edifice of faith,
Behold the throngs of hungry, unhoused people;
The 'Bread Line,' flanked by charity and death.
See yonder Churchman, opulently doing
Unnumbered deeds, which gladden and resound,
The while his thrifty tenant is pursuing
The white slave trade on sacred, untaxed ground.
(God rules, God rules alway.)
For these are but the outward signs of fever;
Those flaunting signs, which through delirium burn;
And the clear-seeing eye of each Believer
Can note the coming crisis. It will turn,
For it has reached its summit. Convalescing,
The sick world shall arise to strength and peace,
And earth shall bloom, with each and every blessing
Life waits to give, when wars and conflicts cease.
(God rules, God rules alway.)
This is a mighty hour. No sounds of drumming,
No flying flags, no heralds do appear;
No Wise Men of the East proclaim His coming;
Yet He is coming—-nay, our Christ is here!
And man shall leave his fever dreams behind him;

Those dreams of avarice, and lust, and sin,
And seek his Lord; yea, he shall seek and find Him,
In his own soul, where He has always been.
(God rules, God rules alway.)
Man longs for God. Before the Christ we wot of,
With His brief mighty message, came to earth,
Before His life, or creed, or cross were thought of,
The love of love within man's breast had birth.
But blindly, through his carnal senses reaching,
He plucked dead fruit, and nothing has sufficed,
Nor can his soul find rest in any teaching,
Until he knows that he, himself, is Christ.
(God rules, God rules alway.)
Oh, when he knows this truth in all its splendour,
What majesty, what glory crowns his life:
And, one with God, his every thought is tender;
He cannot enter into war, or strife.
His love goes out to every race and nation;
His whole religion lies in being kind.
This is the creed that means the world's salvation;
The birth of Christ in every mortal mind.
(God rules, God rules alway.)

The Englishman and Other Poems, London:
Gay and Hancock, Ltd., 1912

God's Majesty

I look upon the budding tree;
I watch its leaves expand;
And through it all, O God, I see,
The marvel of Thy hand.
And all my soul in worship sings,
O praise the Lord, the King of Kings!
I look upon this mortal frame
So wonderfully made;
I note each perfect vein and nerve
And I am sore afraid;
I tremble, God, at thought of Thee
So awful in Thy Majesty.
I look upon the mighty sun,
Upon the humble flower;
In both, O great and heavenly One,
I read Thy wondrous power;
And in an ecstasy I raise
A song of thankfulness and praise.
I look upon the lightning's flash;
I see the rain drops fall;
I listen to the thunders crash,
And find Thee in it all;
In earth and sky, and sea and air,
Thou, O my God, art everywhere.

The Worlds and I, 1918, p. 30

Deathless

There lies in the center of each man's heart
A longing and love for the good and pure,
And if but an atom, or larger part,
I tell you this shall endure—endure
After the body has gone to decay—
Yea, after the world has passed away.
The longer I live and the more I see
Of the struggle of souls toward the heights above,
The stronger this truth comes home to me,
That the Universe rests on the shoulders of Love—
A love so limitless, deep, and broad,
That men have renamed it and called it God.
And nothing that ever was born or evolved,
Nothing created by light or force,
But deep in its system there lies dissolved
A shining drop from the great Love Source—
A shining drop that shall live for aye,
Tho' kingdoms may perish and stars may die.

Daughters of America. 5:2 February, 1891

Devils

God made man and manmade devils—
All of earth's evils
Are shaped and moulded by mortal thought
Carelessly fashioned or carefully wrought,
Life after life and time on time,
Thought-forms grow into creatures of crime,
Roaming about in the Regions of Mind,
Mischief to find.
Monstrous devils there are grown bold
Through ages untold;
Devils old
With sins repeated and unrepented,
Devils demented
By their own passions and lusts and greeds,
Or by steady diets of moss-grown creeds—
History tells how these devils would boil
Their differing brothers in kettles of oil:
And we know how the Maid of Orleans fared!
Still, if they dared,
Devils there are who would do it again,
Stalking among us as sanctified men.
Bleating aloud of their love for God,
Yet using the rod
Or the scourge on some brother whose faith seems too broad.
Imps of jealousy, envy and spite,
Grow into big devils, sometimes in a night,
Big, black, red-eyed devils of war,
Whom we all abhor.
There are feminine devils who must, I opine,
Have been mermaids or fishes, when seaward the swine
Ran over the cliffs and were drowned; but the Legion
Of devils was saved, for it found in that region
Mermaids and jelly-fish ready to give

All the comforts of home, and to help them to live.
Then into forms human
Each came as a woman:
Delilah, and Jezebel, Lilith and all
Females who stand but that others may fall:
And females who gossip and stir up strife,
And are thorns in the flesh of the neighbourhood life.
But the worst type of all, of the many that roam
Abroad in the land, is the devil at home.
A narrow-souled, mean little devil of self—
A petulant elf
Who smiles on the street, but at his (or her) board
Sits scowling or groaning or saying some word
That hurts those who hear it;
A mosquito-like spirit
That keeps up a buzzing and maddening hum,
And only is dumb
While sinking its sting into somebody's heart.
Oh this is the devil who plays a large part
In the world everywhere: yet full often his voice
(Or hers) in the churches is heard to rejoice
Over certain salvation for those who 'believe.'
Alas! You poor devils, you cannot deceive
The God of the Universe. You will be driven
Straight out of His heaven
Back into the sea by the Christ as of old:
And you will behold
Your thoughts and your deeds coming back on yourself,
You mean little petulant home-spoiling elf.
God made man and manmade devils;
But all earth's evils
Will wear themselves out as the cycles roll,
And nothing will live but the God in each soul.

Poems of Affection, London: Gay & Hancock, 1920

The Law

The tide of love swells in me with such force,
It sweeps away all hate and all distrust.
As eddying straws and particles of dust
Are lost by some swift river in its course.
So much I love my friends, my life, my art,
Each shadow flies; the light dispels the gloom
Love is so fair, I find I have no room
For anything less worthy in my heart.
Love is a germ which we can cultivate—
To grace and perfume sweeter than the rose,
Or leave neglected while our heart soil grows
Rank with that vile and poison thistle, hate.
Love is a joyous thrush, that one can teach
To sing sweet lute-like songs which all may hear.
Or we can silence him and tune the ear
To caw of crows, or to the vulture's screech.
Love is a feast; and if the guests divide
With all who pass, though thousands swell the van,
There shall be food and drink for every man;
The loaves and fishes will be multiplied.
Love is the guide. I look to heights above
So beautiful, so very far away;
Yet I shall tread their sunlit peaks some day,
Since close in mine I hold the hand of love.
Love is the law. But yield to its control
And thou shalt find all things work for the best,
And in the calm, still heaven of thy breast,
That God, Himself, sits talking with thy soul.

Yesterdays, London: Gay & Hancock, 1916

A Song of Faith

My glass of life with its brew of Being,
 I lift, with a toast, to the Universe.
Though black guns bellow and mad men curse
And a sick world hurries from bad to worse
I trust in the might of the One All Seeing—
 The One All Knowing, to set things right.
Though hate in the heart of the race may thunder,
 In rifle and cannon and bursting shell,
And the sea and the air their tales may tell,
Of the minds of mortals that seethe with hell,—
Yet in God's vast plan there can be no blunder—
 He is blazing the trail for the Super-man.
The creeds of ages may totter and tumble,
 And fall in ruins, but out of the dust,
And out of the wreckage of old things, must
 Rise better religion, and stronger trust,
And faith that knows, and knowing is humble.
 (Humility ever with knowledge goes.)
This speck in space on its orbit spinning,
 Swings safely along without aid from me,
A Mind that can order, an Eye that can see,
 Back of, and over it all must be—
And will be—and was from the first beginning,
 Not mine to question or doubt the Cause.
But mine to worship the Mighty Master
 And Maker of all things; mine to raise
 Ever an anthem of love and praise
In the light of the sun or in shadowed ways,
In the world's bright hour, or in world disaster,
 To see His glory and sing His power.
So my glass of life with its brew of Being
I lift, with a song of the One All Seeing—

Of the One All Knowing; though earth seems hurled
Out into chaos, I see it lying
In God's great palm—and my faith undying
Cries, "Lo! He is moulding a better world."

World Voices, New York : Hearst's International Library Company,
1916

Appendix A

Global New Thought
Association for Global New Thought
web site: www.agnt.org

The Association for Global New Thought's vision of planetary transformation is based on the conviction that there are universal spiritual truths which represent the emerging spiritual paradigm for the new millennium. The principles of universal spirituality are a statement of this paradigm and the essence of New Thought. They reflect the core teachings of the world's great spiritual traditions.

Vision

There is an inherent perfection and sacred worth in the universe, all of creation, and every individual. The community of all life is interconnected and interdependent. Consciousness is infinitely creative; we create our experience through our thoughts and feelings. Human consciousness is ever evolving into higher states of awareness.

Mission

We honor the diversity of cultures and faiths while aiming to articulate, practice, and embody universal spiritual principles. We encourage personal transformation and collective awakening. We practice the gift of active compassion and kindness through our service to all life. We foster a world that works for the highest good of all.

Core Values

Creativity, Community, Education, Integrity, Abundance, Spirituality, Unconditional Love, Compassion and Service.

Principles

God is the Creative Process in action: in everything, everywhere, always, all at once.

God is Love and Intelligence in relationship, expressing as the universe and all life.

God is Being each one of us.

Appendix B

New Thought Declaration of Principles

We affirm God as Mind, Infinite Being, Spirit, Ultimate Reality.

We affirm that God, the Good, is supreme, universal, and everlasting.

We affirm the unity of God and humanity, in that the divine nature dwells within and expresses through each of us, by means of our acceptance of it, as health, supply, wisdom, love, life, truth, power, beauty, and peace.

We affirm the power of prayer and the capacity of each person to have mystical experience with God, and to enjoy the grace of God.

We affirm the freedom of all persons as to beliefs, and we honor the diversity of humanity by being open and affirming of all persons, affirming the dignity of human beings as founded on the presence of God within them, and, therefore, the principle of democracy.

We affirm that we are all spiritual beings, dwelling in a spiritual universe that is governed by spiritual law, and that in alignment with spiritual law, we can heal, prosper, and harmonize.

We affirm that our mental states are carried forward into manifestation and become our experience in daily living.

We affirm the manifestation of the kingdom of heaven here and now.

We affirm expression of the highest spiritual principle in loving one another unconditionally, promoting the highest good for all, teaching and healing one another, ministering to one another, and living together in peace, in accordance with the teachings of Jesus and other enlightened teachers.

We affirm our evolving awareness of the nature of reality and our willingness to refine our beliefs accordingly.

(International New Thought Alliance Declaration of Principles) (http:newthoughtalliance.orgabout.htm)

Appendix C

The Woman's Bible
www.sacred-texts.comwmnwb

Elizabeth Cady Stanton 1898

Co-Leader of the Suffragette Movement
(with Susan B Anthony)

The Woman's Bible is a collection of essays and commentaries on the Bible compiled in 1895 by a committee chaired by Elizabeth Cady Stanton (1815-1902), one of the organizers of the Seneca Falls Convention (the first Woman's Rights Convention held in 1848), and a founder of the National Woman Suffrage Association. Elizabeth Cady Stanton worked closely and in partnership with Susan B. Anthony during the women's suffrage movement in the early 1900s.

Stanton's purpose was to initiate a critical study of biblical texts that are used to degrade and subject women in order to demonstrate that it is not divine will that humiliates women, but human desire for domination. In "denying divine inspiration for demoralizing ideas," Stanton's committee hoped to exemplify a reverence for a higher Christian "Spirit of all Good." (1)

Excerpt from:

THE WOMAN'S BIBLE
By Elizabeth Cady Stanton and the Revising Committee (1898)
THE BOOK OF GENESIS. CHAPTER I

The first step in the elevation of woman to her true position, as an equal factor in human progress, is the cultivation of the religious senti-ment in regard to her dignity and equality, the recognition by the rising generation of an ideal Heavenly Mother, to whom their prayers should be addressed, as well as to a Father.

If language has any meaning, we have in these texts a plain declara-tion of the existence of the feminine element in the Godhead, equal in power and glory with the masculine. The Heavenly Mother and Father! "God created man in his *own image, male and female.*" Thus Scripture, as well as science and philosophy, declares the eternity and equality of sex—the philosophical fact, without which there could have been no perpetuation of creation, no growth or development in the ani-mal, vegetable, or mineral kingdoms, no awakening nor progressing in the world of thought. The masculine and feminine elements, exactly equal and balancing each other, are as essential to the maintenance of the equilibrium of the universe as positive and negative electricity, the centripetal and centrifugal forces, the laws of attraction which bind together all we know of this planet whereon we dwell and of the system in which we revolve. (2)

The Woman's Bible
Appendix

The letters and comments are in answer to the questions:
- Have the teachings of the Bible advanced or retarded the emancipation of women?
- Have they dignified or degraded the Mothers of the Race?

Ursula Gestefeld's response:

Like the shield which was gold on one side and silver on the other, the Bible has two sides or aspects. As travelers approaching the shield from opposite directions quarreled over its nature because each saw only that side which he had approached, people have differed in their view of the Bible and its influence upon mankind because only one aspect has been visible to them.

Acceptance of the Bible literally tends to retard the development of both man and woman, and consequently the establishment of their highest and best relation to each other, a relation upon which depends their usefulness to the community. Both the law of Moses and the teachings of Paul, thus considered, belittle woman more than they exalt her. While words of praise and promises of future place and power are not altogether lacking, this is the impression left upon the mind of the reader who is not able to pass around to the other side and gain another view.

Exoterically considered, the Bible offers less of the ethical and the spiritual than of the physical possibilities of woman as the complement to man; but esoterically considered, it is found to exact the spiritual possibilities above the rest—above even the like possibilities of the man. The Bible has been, and will continue to be, a stumbling-block in the way of development of inherent resources, consequently of the truest civilization, in proportion to the strength of its exoteric aspect with the people. It will cease to be a stumbling block and become a powerful impetus in the desired direction instead, when its inner meaning becomes revelator, companion and friend.

In the literal rendering of the Bible, woman appears first and above all as man's subordinate; but this inner meaning shows her first and above all as the individual equal with him, and afterward his complement, or what she is able to be for him. Portrayed as the mother of the Saviour of the world, one woman is exalted above all women when only physical motherhood is seen; and the consequence has been that one woman has been worshiped and the sex has been crucified. This one woman has been lifted above her place; and all women have fallen correspondingly below it.

Not till "the light that lighteth every man that cometh into the world" shall pierce with its rays the darkness of the sensuous nature, will woman's spiritual motherhood for the race, be discerned as the way of its redemption from that darkness and its consequences. As that light is uncovered in individual souls the inner meaning of the Bible will appear, woman's nature as the individual and her true relativity to man be seen. Then the mistakes which have been ignorantly made will be rectified, because both sides of the shield will be seen. Men and women will clasp hands as comrades with a common destiny; religion and science will each reveal their destiny and prove that truth which the Bible even exoterically declares that "the woman is the glory of the man." Ursula N. Gestefeld. (2)

Links & Acknowledgements
1. http:www.hds.harvard.edulibraryexhibitsonlinebible12.html
2. http:www.sacred-texts.comwmnwb

Resources & Acknowledgments

Albanese, Catherine L, *A Republic of Mind and Spirit: A Cultural History American Metaphysical Religion,* Yale University Press, 2008

Anderson, C. Alan & Whitehouse, Deborah G., *New Thought: A Practical American Spirituality,* 2003, Authorhouse Publisher

Braden, Charles S., *Spirits In Rebellion,* Southern Methodist University Press, 1963

Gill, Gillian, *Mary Baker Eddy (Radcliffe Biography Series),* Da Capo Press, 1999

Harley, Gail M., *Emma Curtis Hopkins: Forgotten Founder of New Thought,* Syracuse Univ Pr (Sd); 2002

Hart, Hilary, *The Unknown She: Eight Faces of an Emerging Consciousness,* The Golden Sufi Center, 2003

Holmes, Ernest, *Science of Mind,* TarcherPutnam, 1998

Hopkins, Emma Curtis, *Scientific Mental Practices,* Later edition: 1974

The American Standard Version of the Holy Bible, 1901, Public Domain
http:ebible.orgasvoldindex.htm

James, William, *Varieties of Religious Experience,* Megalodon Entertainment LLC., 2008

Lewis, James R., *Perspectives on the New Age,* SUNY Press, 1992

Peale, Norman Vincent, *The Power of Positive Thinking,* Touchstone; First Fireside edition, 2003

Salzburg, Sharon, *Faith: Trusting Your Own Deepest* Experience Riverhead, 2002

Satter, Beryl, *Each Mind a Kingdom,* University of California Press; 2001

Stanton, Elizabeth Cady and the Revising Committee, *The Woman's Bible,* 1898

Wilcox, Ella Wheeler, *Poems of affection.* By London: Gay & Hancock, 1920.

Wilcox, Ella Wheeler, *Poems of experience.* London: Gay and Hancock, Ltd. 1910.

Wilcox, Ella Wheeler, *Poems of Progress and New Thought Pastels* London: Gay & Hancock, 1911.

Wilcox, Ella Wheeler, *The Englishman and Other Poems* by London: Gay and Hancock, Ltd., 1912.

Wilcox, Ella Wheeler, *World Voices* by New York: Hearst's International Library Company 1916.

Wilcox, Ella Wheeler, *The Worlds and I.* 1918, p. 30.

Wilcox, Ella Wheeler, *Yesterdays,* London: Gay & Hancock, 1916.

Links from the World Wide Web

websyte.comalan, Numerous New Thought resources are linked to this site.

newthought.infobeliefsbeliefs.htm

en.wikipedia.orgwikiNew_Thought

ezinearticles.com?The-History-of-New-Thought&id=2424533

new-thought-center.comthe-modern-history-of-new-thought

websyte.comalanintachrt.htm-New Thought History Chart

www.newthoughtlibrary.comhopkinsEmmaCurtisbio_Emma.htm

newthoughtlibrary.com

en.wikipedia.orgwikiMildred_Mann

annierixmilitz.wwwhubs.com

emmacurtishopkins.wwwhubs.com

Further Reading

Additional resources and writings related to
New Thought and the History of New Thought:

1. Anderson, C. Alan & Whitehouse, Deborah G., *New Thought: A Practical American Spirituality,* Crossroad Publishing Co, 1995
2. Atkinson, William Walker, *New Thought Its History and Principles,* Elizabeth Towne Co., 1915
3. *Become What You Believe, Mildred Mann.* Privately published c. 1955
4. Beebe, Tom, *Who's Who in New Thought,* CSA Press, 1977
5. Buck, *Cosmic Consciousness: a Study in the Evolution of the Human Mind,* Dutton & Co. 1901
6. *Change Your Mind—and Keep the Change.* Moab, UT: Real People Press 1987
7. Dresser, Horatio W., *History of the New Thought Movement,* Thomas Y Crowell Co., 1919
8. Dresser, Horatio W., *The Quimby Manuscripts,* Thomas Y. Crowell Co., 1921
9. Dresser, Horatio W., *The Spirit of the New Thought,* Crowell Co., 1917
10. Eddy, Mary Baker, *Science and Health with Key to the Scriptures,* First Edition 1875
11. Elder, Dorothy *From Metaphysical to Mystical,* Doriel Publishing Co., 1992
12. Emerson, Ralph Waldo, *Essays by Ralph Waldo Emerson,* Harper & Row, NY, 1926
13. Easwaren, Eknath, *The Bhagavad Gita,* Nigiri Press, 1985
14. Fox, Emmet *The Sermon on the Mount,* Harper & Brothers, 1934
15. *Healing Hypotheses: Horatio W. Dresser and the Philosophy of New Thought.* Garland Publishing, 1993
16. Holmes, Ernest, *New Thought Terms and Their Meanings: A Dictionary of the Terms and Phrases Commonly Used in Metaphysical and Psychological Study,* Dodd, Mead & Co., 1942

17. Hartman, William C., *Hartman's Who's Who in Occult, Psychic and Spiritual Realms,* Occult Press, 1977

18. *Heaven on Earth: Dispatches from America's Spiritual Frontier.* Crown Publishers, Inc., 1992

19. Hyre, K. M. & Goodman, Eli, *Price Guide to the Occult and Related Subjects,* Reference Guides, 1967

20. Ingalese, Richard, *The History and Power of Mind,* New Castle Pub., 1974

21. James, William *The Varieties of Religious Experience,* Longmans, Green & Co., 1902

22. Judah, J. Stullson *The History and Philosophy of the Metaphysical Movements in America,* Westminster Press, 1957

23. Larson, Martin A., *New Thought or A Modern Religious Approach,* Philosophical Library, (1985)

24. Michaels, Chris & Viljoen, Edward, *Practice the Presence: A Daily Journal,* Awakening Enterprises, 2009

25. *The Orient in American Transcendentalism: A Study of Everson, Thoreau, and Alcott.* Columbia University Press, 1932

26. *The Positive Thinkers: Religion as Pop Psychology from Mary Baker Eddy to Oral Roberts.* Pantheon Books, 1965

27. Quimby, Dr. P.P., *The Healing Wisdom of Frontal Lobe,* 1982

28. Stillson, Judah J. *The History and Philosophy of the Metaphysical Movements in America,* Westminster Press, 1967

29. Troward, Thomas, *The Edinburgh and Dore Lectures,* DeVorss, 1904

30. Underhill, Evelyn *Practical Mysticism,* Dutton & Co., 1915

31. Wilcox, Ella Wheeler, *The Heart of the New Thought,* Psychic Research Co., 1902

32. Wood, Henry, *The New Thought Simplified,* Lee & Shepard Co., 1903

Index